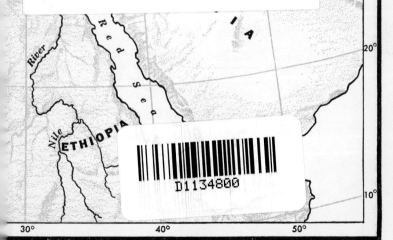

TO THE STUDENTS:

The fact that this volume is being used by the Christian Heritage College does not mean that the school necessarily endorses its contents from the standpoint of morals, philosophy, theology, or scientific hypotheses. The position of Christian Heritage College on these subjects is well known.

In order to standardize class work, it is sometimes necessary to use textbooks whose contents the school cannot wholly endorse. You understand, of course, that acceptable textbooks in certain academic fields are very difficult to secure.

CHRISTIAN HERITAGE COLLEGE
San Diego, California

"Things In Which It Is Impossible For God To Lie"

"In this manner God, when he purposed to demonstrate more abundantly to the heirs of the promise the unchangeableness of his counsel, stepped in with an oath, in order that, through two unchangeable things in which it is impossible for God to lie, we who have fled to the refuge may have strong encouragement to lay hold on the hope set before us."—Hebrews 6:17, 18.

PUBLISHERS
WATCHTOWER BIBLE AND TRACT SOCIETY
OF NEW YORK, INC.
INTERNATIONAL BIBLE STUDENTS ASSOCIATION
Brooklyn, New York, U.S.A.

Made in the United States of America

Dedicated

to the

"God of Truth"

and

Published for the Benefit of All Seekers of Life-giving Truth in All Nations

Symbols of Scripture translations quoted from or cited herein:

AS   – American Standard Version Bible, by the American Committee of Revision, of 1901

AT   – The Complete Bible: An American Translation, by J. M. P. Smith and E. J. Goodspeed, of 1939

AV   – Authorized or King James Version Bible, of 1611

Dy   – Roman Catholic English Translation of the Latin Vulgate made at Douay and Rheims, as of 1610

Kx   – The Holy Bible, translated by Monsignor R. A. Knox, as of 1949

Le   – The Twenty-four Books of the Holy Scriptures, by Rabbi Isaac Leeser, as of 1853

Mo   – A New Translation of the Bible, by Dr. James Moffatt, as of 1922

NEB – The New English Bible: New Testament, as of 1961

Ro   – The Emphasised Bible · A New Translation, by Joseph B. Rotherham, of 1897

RS   – The Holy Bible: Revised Standard Version, as of 1952

Torah – The Torah: The Five Books of Moses, by the Jewish Publication Society of America, as of 1962

Yg   – Young's Literal Translation of the Holy Bible, by Robert Young, as of 1862

Any Bible quotation or citation not followed by any specific abbreviation is made from the *New World Translation of the Holy Scriptures* (*NW*), the revised edition of 1961. Other translations of the Bible may be quoted or cited, but with the name of the translation not abbreviated.

DATING: In dating, the abbreviation B.C.E. stands for "Before Our Common Era," and C.E. stands for "Of Our Common Era," thus designating the number of the year before or after the year 1 C.E.

Made in the United States of America

6995

CONTENTS

CHAPTER 1

God Lives!
How We Know It

REGARDLESS of who he was, all of us will have to agree with the writer of nineteen centuries ago, when he said: "No man has seen God at any time."* And yet that man believed in God. Why did he do so, and how could he?

[2] So, then, God is invisible to man! What does that prove? The person who says he believes in only what he sees (or thinks he sees) takes the very invisibility of God to mean that God does not exist, does not live. For example, on August 6, 1961, because the Russian astronaut saw "no God or angels" during his seventeen orbits by a man-made rocket through outer space around our earth, he felt he had absolute proof that God did not exist.†

[3] However, the argument of this Russian atheist goes according to the same line of reasoning followed by the Roman idolaters of the first century of our Common Era. These Romans worshiped many gods and paid relative worship to these

---

* Written by John the son of Zebedee, of Bethsaida, Galilee, in John 1:18; also, 1 John 4:12.
† New York *Times*, as of May 7, 1962.

---

1. With what statement concerning God will all of us have to agree?
2. What do some persons take the invisibility of God to mean?
3. Such atheistic reasoning is similar to the thinking of what persons of the first century of our Common Era, and how?

mythical gods by means of idol images of various materials. When the followers of the so-called "sect of the Nazarenes" came along and worshiped the God of creation without the use of man-made idols or temples,* the Roman idolaters called them atheists, godless. Since those Roman idolaters could not see the God of this "sect of the Nazarenes," they could not believe that He really existed and that this "sect" had a living God.

⁴ The worship of the m y t h i c a l gods by the Romans has long since ceased and the beautifully carved statues of their gods and goddesses are mere relics in museums today; but the disciples of that despised "sect of the Nazarenes" continue their worship today.

⁵ Really, the Russian astronauts and those of other nations who have orbited through outer space have reason to give thanks that out there they saw "no God or angels." They should be

---

* See Acts of the Apostles, chapter twenty-four, verse five.

---

4. What has happened to the worship and the gods of the ancient Romans, but what of the worship carried on by the disciples of that so-called "sect of the Nazarenes"?
5, 6. (a) Why should the astronauts give thanks that they saw "no God or angels" in outer space? (b) Why is it unreasonable and unscientific to think that man could look at the Creator, and what did God say to a man who asked to see God's glory?

grateful that God remained invisible. Why so? Well, could they or their space ships have stood the experience? What do they think God is? Like a mere man, the way the mythical gods of an- 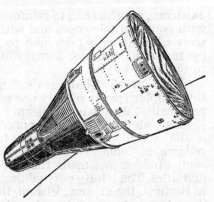 cient times were pictured in carved statues? Frail man cannot bear to look at a nuclear bomb explosion at close range without being blinded. Could man look at the Creator of the sun, which is a furnace of continuous nuclear explosions that send out streams of nuclear particles into outer space? Call to mind the man of the sixteenth century before our Common Era who made bold to ask to see God's glory. He did not know what he was asking for, because, by means of some intermediary, God said to this man on the mountaintop: "You are not able to see my face, because no man may see me and yet live."*

[6] This divine statement supplies us the scientific reason for it that no man on earth has seen God at any time. Man is not of the same stuff as God. He is too frail to survive contact directly with God, who is of boundless, immeasurable dynamic energy.

[7] To bring into his view many things long in

---

* See the second book of Moses entitled "Exodus," chapter thirty-three, verses eighteen through twenty-three. See also Exodus 20:18-22.

7. (a) To bring into his view many things that have long existed, what has man had to do? (b) So what must we conclude about man's ability to see with the naked eye?

existence, man has had to reinforce his weak vision with powerful telescopes and with electron microscopes linked with television to magnify objects by two million times. Many things are invisible to our naked eye.

⁸ "God lives!" That expression in the title of this chapter speaks of only one such individual or personality. Just who is meant? Even in the religious realms of twentieth-century mankind there is the worship of many gods. In discussing the religion of India, *The Encyclopedia Americana** said: "Indrea was made the ruler of 330,000,000 divinities. The trinity of Hinduism came into being in Brahma, the creator, Vishnu, the preserver, and Siva, the destroyer." An interesting viewpoint, as taken by Hindus regarding what they consider to be God, was explained on a Sunday in 1964 by a Hindu missionary and educator to a congregation of Unitarians in Brooklyn, New York. When explaining the difference between Hinduism and the religion of Christendom, the missionary went on to say:

> Christians believe that God created man and that man, therefore, is subject to God, but the Hindu believes that the soul of man always was and always will be and hence that man is coexistent with God. "Because of this," said he, "we regard God, not as father, but as friend."†

To Hindus, God was not before the human soul and the human soul is independent of God but always maintains a coexistence with God.‡

---

* *The Encyclopedia Americana,* Volume 14, page 196, edition of 1929.

† The New York *Times,* as of Monday, February 10, 1964.

‡ Similar to the Hindu thought regarding God is that set out in the book entitled "Science and Health,"

---

8. (a) When this book says "God lives!" to how many individuals does it refer? (b) Nevertheless, what makes it evident that even in this twentieth century many gods are worshiped?

[9] Let us turn again to *The Encyclopedia Americana,* this time for what it has to say on the subject of God. It says: "GOD, . . . in the Christian, Mohammedan, and Jewish sense, the Supreme Being, the First Cause, and in a general sense, as considered nowadays throughout the civilized world, a spiritual being, self-existent, eternal and absolutely free and all-powerful, distinct from the matter which he has created in many forms, and which he conserves and controls. There does not seem to have been a period of history where mankind was without belief in a supernatural author and governor of the universe. The most savage nations have some rudimentary ideas of a god or supreme being. Man is a religious as well as a rational animal. . . . It is rather maintained that the study of human history, or human nature especially on its moral and spiritual side, and of the world as far as science reveals it to us make for the existence of a God, demand such a postulate as the key of the universe, and render the belief in a personal God greatly more probable than any other thesis."*

[10] To what extent the above encyclopedic explanation of God is true, we shall yet see. Although that is the general sense in which the people of

by Mrs. Mary Baker Eddy, of 1917 edition, Boston, Massachusetts, on page 476 of Chapter 14:

"In divine Science, God and the real man are inseparable as divine Principle and idea. . . . God is the Principle of man, and man is the idea of God. Hence man is not mortal nor material. Mortals will disappear, and immortals, or the children of God, will appear as the only and eternal verities of man."

* *The Encyclopedia Americana,* Volume 12, 1956 edition, page 743.

9. In *The Encyclopedia Americana,* what is said about the identity of God and reasons for belief in a personal God?
10–12. (a) What differences and what similarities are there among the beliefs of the people of Christendom, the Mohammedans and the Jews concerning the personality of God? (b) Can all these conflicting beliefs be right? (c) Why is there the greatest need to learn the truth about God?

Christendom, the Mohammedans and the Jews understand God, these religionists certainly do differ from one another as to the personality of God and the purposes of God toward mankind.

[11] For instance, the main religions of Christendom believe that God is made up of three Persons, just the same as the Hindus believe in a trinity, whereas both the Mohammedans and the Jews believe that God is not a Trinity but One Person. However, the Mohammedans give no personal name to their God, whereas the Jews in their sacred writings give him a personal name repeated thousands of times over. The Mohammedans claim that God has no son,* but the Jews believe that God is their heavenly Father. Naturally, then, each of those religious systems worships God differently, and somewhere there must be error about God. Erroneous worship could never be acceptable to the one true God, just as a certain man said nineteen hundred years ago when discussing the difference between the Samaritan religion and the Jewish religion of that day: "God is a Spirit, and those worshiping him must worship with spirit and truth."†

[12] For this reason there exists the greatest need to learn the truth about God, in order to know who He is and what He is.

HOW TO KNOW THAT HE LIVES

[13] Since it is impossible to see the true God, we need to prove his living existence by some means other than that of actually seeing him with the naked human eye. It is a scientific fact that the existence, presence and activity of something invisible to the naked human eye can be proved by

---

* See the Koran, Sura XVII, 111; Sura XVIII, 1-4.
† See John 4:24.

---

13. By what means is it scientifically possible to prove the existence of something that is invisible to the naked human eye?

certain effects, results or consequences that we can observe with our senses of sight, smell, hearing, feeling and tasting.

[14] For example, the farthest out known planet of our solar system is the ninth one named after the ancient Roman god Pluto. It is invisible to the naked human eye and even beyond the range of small telescopes, so that even a 15-inch refractor telescope has a hard time bringing it to view. It was first discovered in the year 1930. However, the existence of Pluto was suspected back in 1905.

Why? Because of its influence that produced certain effects upon the planets Uranus and Saturn. It came to be called Planet X. By making scientific calculations according to those effects it was made possible to locate the position of this planet about 3,680,000,000 miles distant from our sun, so as finally to train a telescope of sufficient strength upon it and photograph it. Thus by an astronomer's prediction and by twenty-five years of research, this yellowish planet Pluto was proved to exist.

[15] In like manner the existence of a living God, the Great Creator, can be proved beyond doubt by the evidence that he gives of his being and of his activity. One argument in proof of this is an old one, but it is still good. A writer with solidly based

14. In what way was the planet Pluto proved to exist, though it was invisible to the naked human eye?
15. In what manner can the existence of God be proved beyond doubt?

faith in God used the argument for us nineteen hundred years ago. His argument was like this:

¹⁶ Take, for example, that famous Buddhist temple now in ruins in Angkor, Cambodia, known as the Angkor Wat; or, take the beautiful, magnificent tomb known as the Taj Mahal in Agra, India; or, take that Mohammedan

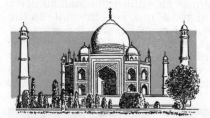

mosque known as the Dome of the Rock in the sacred area of the present-day walled city of Jerusalem. Nobody will deny that each of these buildings was constructed by some man. Such buildings did not come about by accident. Their structure calls for the use of intelligence and the ability to design, not the intelligence and ability of a fish, insect,

bird or beast, but those of an alive man with an active brain. What shall we say, then, of our visible universe, the heavens and the earth, which are of still more remarkable structure and of far more complicated design and permanence? Unavoidably all this called for the existence and activity of a personal intelligence with ability and a life-span boundlessly greater than those of intelligent man.

---

16. (a) What evident fact will everyone acknowledge concerning the construction of buildings such as Angkor Wat, the Taj Mahal and the Dome of the Rock? (b) So to what does the existence of the visible universe itself testify?

[17] Look at man himself! In what a wonderful, yes, fear-inspiring way he is constructed! He did not plan himself. The chances against his coming into existence, even in a small way at the start, by mere accident in the midst of chaos are endless.

[18] When we intelligently consider all things in the heavens and the earth with which we are acquainted, we can come to but one decision, one conclusion, that of the writer of nineteen centuries ago, in these words: "Of course, every house is constructed by someone, but he that constructed all things is God."* Today, after nineteen centuries since those words were written, all these constructed things continue to exist in that same structure and to function. This proves that the great Constructor must also live to this day as the Sustainer of all these constructed things that are so inferior to him, their Creator. Indeed, God lives!

[19] More than thirty-eight centuries ago a childless old man in the Middle East, not a Babylonian stargazer, was asked to look up into the night sky and count the stars, if he possibly could do so.† So many were the stars appearing to his naked eyes that he could not fix the number of them. He was told that the number of his offspring or "seed" would be like those stars, of a number not then known to any man. In recent years astronomers, equipped with their mighty telescopes, have been occupied with counting the number of the stars, the planets, the comets, the meteors, and the galaxies of stars. What impressions do they receive regarding need for God to exist, as

---

* See Hebrews, chapter three, verse four.
† See Genesis, chapter fifteen, verse five.

---

17. Did man design himself, or is there a reasonable chance that he came into existence by accident?
18. To what conclusion does an intelligent consideration of these facts lead us, and what does the continued existence of these constructed things prove?
19. If those who study the heavens take a narrow, materialistic view, what will they fail to learn?

they view the marvels of the heavens into which they are able to peer so deeply? Or, ought they to rule out the thought of God and take the narrow, shortsighted view of the philosophy of materialism? "Materialism," says *The Encyclopedia Americana,* is

the philosophical theory that everything which exists is ultimately material in nature, or that whatever is real can be derived and explained in accordance with the laws of material phenomena. This, of course, carries with it a denial of the reality of any finite or infinite spirit as an immaterial substance and a repudiation of all forms of idealism, which uses thought or intelligence as a principle of explanation. . . . Thorough-going materialism asserts that nothing exists but physical bodies and physical processes. What are called immaterial substances and processes it either declares to be unreal, or explains away as ultimately not different in nature from physical substances and processes. Moreover, for materialism of this consistent and uncompromising type, matter is dead and moves only by mechanical forces. It has no "psychic side," and the laws which it obeys are the expressions of a blind physical necessity. This extreme view . . . in various modified forms it still exists as a tendency to subordinate mental phenomena to physical processes.*

[20] Like all the rest of us today, the astronomers who count and name the stars need to be spoken

---

* See *The Encyclopedia Americana,* Volume 18 of the 1929 edition, page 425, under "Materialism."

20. In what way do all of us need to be spoken to concerning the things that we see in the heavens?

to just as a historical people of the eighth century before our Common Era were spoken to, in these words: "Raise your eyes high up and see. Who has created these things? It is the One who is bringing forth the army of them even by number, all of whom he calls even by name. Due to the abundance of dynamic energy, he also being vigorous in power, not one of them is missing."*

[21] Materialism cannot explain away the existence of all the heavenly bodies in all their abundance, their arrangement, their controlled movements, with the argument that matter always was and that it is simply "blind physical necessity" that causes them to move with such order and precision and without collision of one against the other. For motion of lifeless matter to exist, there must be a mover; and in this case it calls for an intelligent mover and lawgiver. Besides that, for matter to exist, there must be a creator of matter and a source of all its energy. If the materialist argues that matter has always existed (an argument that is disproved by exact science today), then the Creator of matter has always existed, being without beginning as well as without end. All matter is an effect, not a cause. Living matter derives its life from a living source, not from chemical accident.

[22] It takes mathematics of the highest sort to calculate the heavens and the laws of the universe. Did all the mathematical intelligence that is displayed in the heavenly bodies and their arrangements, movements and accommodations spring from sightless, lifeless, brainless matter because of a physical necessity that matter came to discern

---

* See Isaiah, chapter forty, verse twenty-six.

---

21. What facts concerning motion, matter and life show that the explanations of the materialist are not satisfying?
22. (a) What does the manifest application of mathematical principles in the universe prove to you? (b) Concerning a purely materialistic philosophy, what did scientist Robert A. Millikan say?

or appreciate? Sensible scientists and astronomers of our modern age do not think so. Even the avowed evolutionist Dr. Robert A. Millikan, an outstanding American scientist, was moved to make this admission: "A purely materialistic philosophy is to me the height of unintelligence. Wise men in all the ages have always seen enough to at least make them reverent."[*]

[23] In agreement with this statement is the comment made by the author of the well-known theory of relativity, Dr. Albert Einstein:

> It is enough for me to contemplate the mystery of conscious life perpetuating itself through all eternity; to reflect upon the marvelous structure of the universe, which we can dimly perceive, and to try humbly to comprehend even an infinitesimal part of the intelligence manifest in nature.

A HISTORICAL GOD

[24] However, it is not enough for us to reason out and believe that there must be a God who exists in some sort of vague, unclear or indefinite way. It does not satisfy the human heart and mind for us to be merely theists, persons who believe in the existence of gods or even of one God who is Creator of the universe but who has made no revelation of himself. It still leaves us weak in faith, uncertain as regards worship, if we are just deists, persons who believe in the existence of God as proved by our powers of reason and by the material universe, but which God has remained indifferent toward his creation and has given no supernatural revelation to mankind. For theists

---

[*] See the New York *Times*, as of April 30, 1948, under the heading "Materialism Hit by Dr. Millikan," when eighty years of age.

---

23. As testified by Dr. Albert Einstein, what is manifest in the marvelous structure of the universe?
24. Why will it not satisfy the heart and mind for one to be merely a theist, a deist or one who professes belief in God simply so others will not class him as an atheist?

and deists, and for persons who declare themselves
to be believers in God in order not to be classed as
Godless or atheists, God is a very remote Person,
a God who has no personal relationship to them or
whom they cannot get to know personally so as to
understand him and appreciate him and know what
he means to them. To them his moral and religious
laws remain unknown, his purpose in creating all
things stays in doubt, and his purpose for mankind's future lingers in the dark. Such belief in
God makes a person reverent but acts as no guide
in life.

[25] However, there is more to the existence and
activity of God than what the theists and deists
believe. God lives, and we can know it and we do
know it because he is a historical God. He is a
history-making God. From the very beginning he
has intervened in human affairs and, happily, he
is intervening in human affairs today. He has per-
ceptibly taken a hand in human affairs at definite
dates of history both before and during our Common Era and at specified places and locations. This
is no myth, fable, legend or religious fancy. It is
historically provable, with more proofs than many
of the commonly accepted events of history. We
know that God exists, not just as even dead, material stone may exist governed by the law of
inertia, but as a living Person, aware of what is
going on in all his creation. He is sensitive to what
is going on even on our tiny earth. He is livelily
reacting to what is going on or is needed and he
is intervening as this may be needed.

[26] We know that God has lived throughout the
course of man's history for these past six thousand years. We know that it has been He, because
he has said in advance what he would do and he

25. How can it be said that God is a maker of history, and in
what way does this affect our view of him as a Person?
26. How do we know that God has had a hand in the events of
human history?

has done it! Historic events have not been left to blind, accidental chance, and with no meaning or explanation. God has proved that nobody in heaven or on earth has been able to block what he has purposed to do and what he has said that he would do.

[27] It requires a real, living, all-powerful, intelligent God to do this; and such a living God has done it. The gods whom the nations worship by means of idols, images, statues of stone, wood, gold, silver or some other metal have been unable to do this. The one living and true God, the Creator of heaven and earth, has proved that he alone is God by doing it. He has not only created but also responsibly held this universe together throughout its billions of years of existence. He is not just a materialistic God occupied merely in creating visible, tangible material things. He is, above all, a moralistic God, a God who has divine qualities and the highest standard of righteousness and the perfect set of morals. Quite to be expected, then, there is a moral, religious issue tied in with human history. For that reason the living God, who is of the highest morality, has interested himself in human history.

[28] Man's history has not zigzagged its way across these thousands of years according to the political bickerings and bargains of kings, emperors and military generals, with no definite pattern and, as feared today, leading nowhere else but to a nuclear world war that will stop all further human history. From his supreme position the interested, living God of earth and heaven has been controlling the general course of human history toward the full realization of his divine purpose. This fact holds true also today in this nuclear, space age. By what

27. What kind of God has he proved to be, and why is it that he has interested himself in human history?
28. (a) Has the course of man's history been guided solely by the influence of powerful men, and what about our own day? (b) How can we know what God's purpose is, and what assures us that God has not lied?

this God said long ago with regard to the future he has put himself into modern historical events. He has determined his place in human affairs of our day. He has declared what he purposed to do in this momentous period and has had it put down in writing that is readable today. The evidences that are at hand today in ample abundance prove that God has not lied, has not broken his promise. He cannot lie.

²⁹ God lives—today, and informed persons on earth know it. Events that are immediately ahead of us and that will have an effect on all mankind will add further convincing proof that God lives, that he is keenly alive to mankind's best interests forever. Happy are all men and women who now seek to acquaint themselves with this one living and true God and who make a sincere effort to worship him in the right way, with spirit and truth.

---

29. Of what are informed persons convinced concerning God, and to what will the events immediately ahead of us add convincing proof?

CHAPTER 2

Which Sacred Book of Religion Is the Truth?

ACRED books of great age lie at the bottom of the principal religions practiced throughout the earth today. If you, our reader, are a Confucianist, you may have read the nine Chinese classical books, namely, the five *king* and the four *shu,* which set forth a system of morality. Or, if you have served as a saffron-robed Buddhist monk, you likely have read the Pali canon of Buddhism, with its three "pitaka" or "baskets," that is to say, the Sermon Basket, the Discipline Basket and the Doctrinal Basket.

² What if you, our reader, are a Hindu? On November 8, 1964, the building of the Community Church of New York City was turned into a Hindu temple as the congregation celebrated the Indian festival of light known as *Divan* and two worshipers did a choral reading from the ancient Hindu holy book Bhagavad Gita, "The Lord's Son."* You, as a Hindu, have probably read that

---

* The New York *Times,* as of Monday, November 9, 1964.

---

1. What sacred books are read by Confucianists and by Buddhists?
2. To what sacred writings do Hindus, Shintoists and Moslems look?

book, also the Vedas, the four Books of Knowledge, the Rig-Veda, the Yajur-Veda, the Sama-Veda and the Atharva-Veda,* besides the Brahmanas and the Upanishads. But if you are Japanese, you may have read the Kojiki ("Ancient Records"), containing the Shinto myths and legends as committed to writing in 712 C.E., or the Yengishiki ("Ceremonial Law"), as committed to writing in 927 C.E. If, however, you are a Moslem, you may be a devout reader of the Koran, the Mohammedan Bible of 114 suras, and you reverentially view it as the last word of God given to man through Mohammed the prophet of Allah, in the seventh century of our Common Era. The Koran, however, has never been made a part of the sacred Hebrew Scriptures, nor has it been made one piece with the Christian Bible.

³ Other sacred books of ancient times may come to the reader's mind. The users of the religious books named above consider them to be the truth and may even swear by them before giving testimony in court. How, though, can they all be the truth if they differ from one another, contradicting one another? Which one of them is the truth all the way through, without even an inside contradiction of itself? It does not do to take the position of some religionists who try to be very tolerant and who want to avoid religious discussion by saying to a person of a different religion, "Well, that is truth to you, and this is truth to me." A religious person certainly would not take that position when trading or doing business. He would insist that $1 + 1 + 1 = 3$, not 1, and that

---

* The Hindu Vedic Period is conservatively estimated to have begun about 1500 to 1000 before our Common Era.

3. (a) How are these various sacred books viewed by the ones who use them, but what questions is it fitting to ask? (b) What attitude concerning truth would we be unwise to adopt?

two and two makes four, not five, and not let himself be cheated.

⁴ Truth does not contradict itself or deny the facts. It does not go contrary to reality, nor is it one thing to one person and another thing, even a contradictory thing, to another person. The one truth applies to all persons, whether they recognize it or not. It does not change because of location or of time. The truth is provable by actual fact. The truth endures, persists, because it is genuine, actually existing, in harmony with reality. All this we have to recognize about religion also. A seeker of pure truth, absolute truth, will not take offense at the question, he will not consider the following question to be narrow-minded or intolerant: Among all the ancient sacred books of religion, which one is the truth? Which one is true to itself, not self-contradictory, and true by actual fact, right straight through?

⁵ In order for a religious book that is used in worship of God to be the truth, it must be from a truthful source. It must have a truthful author, who is acquainted with fact, reality, truth, and who is unafraid to tell the truth for the benefit of the lovers and seekers of the truth. Really, it should spring forth from the God of truth and should show God as he really is in his qualities, his position, his purposes and his works. When we examine the various basic books of religion, we find that, with the exception of the one sacred book of truth, they all have to do with demonism, encourage demonism, allow for it or lay the basis for it.

-----

4. (a) What should we recognize concerning truth? (b) Are these points applicable to religion also? (c) What question about sacred religious books will the seeker of pure truth not dismiss as intolerant?
5. (a) For a religious book to be the truth, what must be true as to its source? (b) Yet what does an examination of the various basic books of religion reveal?

⁶ The taint of demonism may be in the form of astrology, practice of magic, casting spells over victims, fortune-telling, consulting with spirit mediums in hope of getting in touch with dead persons, the worship or appeasing of dead ancestors, the imagining that all natural objects and even the universe itself have living souls in them or connected with them. The facts show that demons are liars and are malicious and have misled the vast bulk of mankind. So the very connection of any ancient religious books with demonism argues against their being from the one truthful source.

THE BOOK FREE FROM DEMONISM

⁷ The one book of truth must be free from all demonism. Such a book we find in the Sacred Scriptures known as the Holy Bible. The writing of this Book was begun in the sixteenth century before our Common Era, or in 1513 B.C.E., and was completed in the first century of our Common Era, about 98 C.E. It was begun in ancient Hebrew and was finished in the common Greek of nineteen centuries ago. It was written by men from southwest Asia, all of them being descendants of the patriarch Abraham the Hebrew, who was born in the twenty-first century before our Common Era. The one living and true God called this Abraham away from Ur of the Chaldeans near Babylon,

6. (a) In what forms may the taint of demonism be manifest in these books? (b) What does this argue as to their source?
7. (a) Which sacred writings are free from all demonism? (b) The writing of this Book covered what time period, and was done in what languages?

which was the birthplace of demonism in the form of astrology, magic, idolatry, deification of political heroes, and so forth.

[8] The Holy Bible is a collection of sixty-six books, all these being in harmony with themselves, from first to last. From its first book, now called Genesis, to its last book, now called Revelation, the Holy Bible is against demonism and exposes it as false and against the one true God. The first book reports that God said to a snake or serpent in a beautiful garden in southwest Asia: "Upon your belly you will go and dust is what you will eat all the days of your life. And I shall put enmity between you and the woman and between your seed and her seed. He will bruise you in the head and you will bruise him in the heel." God was there indirectly talking to a demon, and, of course, against him. (Genesis 3:14, 15) In the fifth book of the Bible this same God declared the following law against demonism, to forbid it among his worshipers:

[9] "When you are entered into the land that Jehovah your God is giving you, you must not learn to do according to the detestable things of those nations. There should not be found in you anyone who makes his son or his daughter pass through the fire, anyone who employs divination, a practicer of magic or anyone who looks for omens or a sorcerer, or one who binds others with a spell or anyone who consults a spirit medium or a professional foreteller of events or anyone who inquires of the dead. For everybody doing these things is something detestable to Jehovah, and on account of these detestable things Jehovah your God is driving them away from before you. You should prove yourself faultless with Jehovah your

hatre

---

8. (a) Are all the books that make up the Holy Bible harmonious? (b) In the first book of the Bible, what pronouncement by God against a demon is recorded?
9. Concerning what manifestations of demonism did God warn his worshipers, as recorded at Deuteronomy 18:9-14?

God. For these nations whom you are dispossessing used to listen to those practicing magic and to those who divine; but as for you, Jehovah your God has not given you anything like this." —Deuteronomy ("Second Law") 18:9-14.

[10] In the last book of the Bible here are some of the statements against demonism: "Thus with a swift pitch will Babylon the great city be hurled down, and she will never be found again. . . . for by your spiritistic practice all the nations were misled." (Revelation 18:21-23) "But as for the cowards and those without faith and those who are disgusting in their filth and murderers and fornicators and those practicing spiritism and idolaters and all the liars, their portion will be in the lake that burns with fire and sulphur. This means the second death." Also: "Outside are the dogs and those who practice spiritism and the fornicators and the murderers and the idolaters and everyone liking and carrying on a lie."—Revelation 21:8 and 22:15.

[11] Since all the Bible writers, from the prophet Moses the first of them to the Christian apostle John the last of those writers, were unitedly against demonism, they would seek no aid from the demons in any of their writings. The demons or unclean spirits were not permitted to give any testimony concerning God's purpose or his chosen servants. Nineteen centuries ago, when the anointed Prophet from Nazareth was carrying on his work in the Middle East, he refused to let demons share in his religious work. We read: "So he cured many that were ill with various sicknesses, and he expelled many demons, but he would not let the demons speak, because they knew him to be Christ." (Mark 1:34) "Even the unclean spirits,

---

10. In the Bible's last book, what statements against demonism are found?
11. (a) From what source did Bible writers never seek aid? (b) What did God's anointed Prophet from Nazareth refuse to let the demons do, and how does the Bible testify to this?

whenever they would behold him, would prostrate themselves before him and cry out, saying: 'You are the Son of God.' But many times he sternly charged them not to make him known." (Mark 3: 11, 12) "By laying his hands upon each one of them he would cure them. Demons also would come out of many, shouting and saying: 'You are the Son of God.' But, rebuking them, he would not permit them to speak, because they knew him to be the Christ." (Luke 4:40, 41) Christ's apostles imitated him in this respect.

[12] For example, we read this about Paul when preaching in Philippi, Greece: "As we were going

to the place of prayer, a certain servant girl with a spirit, a demon of divination, met us. She used to furnish her masters with much gain by practicing the art of prediction. This girl kept following Paul and us and crying out with the words: 'These men are slaves of the Most High God, who are publishing to you

the way of salvation.' This she kept doing for many days. Finally Paul got tired of it and turned and said to the spirit: 'I order you in the name of Jesus Christ to come out of her.' And it came out that very hour." —Acts 16:16-18.

[13] The spirit that had obsessed that slave girl was trying to put on an appearance here of serving the Most High God and was thus trying to give the idea that the predictions made by the girl up till then were inspired of God and were truthful,

12, 13. How did the Christian apostle Paul manifest an attitude like that of Christ toward the demons, and with what result?

reliable. The apostle Paul saw through this hypocrisy and deception and turned down all cooperation with a spirit demon. For doing this the masters of the slave girl caused Paul and his companion Silas to be put in prison; but God delivered them that night.—Acts 16:19-34.

[14] We can be sure, therefore, that no appeal was made to the demons in writing the sixty-six books of the Holy Bible. The fact is that the demons could never write or produce such a book as the Bible. For example, the experience of Joseph the great-grandson of the patriarch Abraham the Hebrew before Pharaoh the king of Egypt proved this. This is recorded in the first book of the Bible, in chapter forty-one. In the one night the God of Abraham and of Joseph sent two dreams to Pharaoh, while Joseph was yet unjustly in prison. To get the dreams interpreted, what did Pharaoh do?

[15] Genesis 41:8 tells us: "And it developed in the morning that his spirit became agitated. So he sent and called all the magic-practicing priests of Egypt and all her wise men, and Pharaoh went on to relate his dreams to them. But there was no interpreter of them for Pharaoh." The demons had not inspired those meaningful dreams of Pha-

14, 15. In what way did the experience of Joseph before Pharaoh in Egypt prove that the Bible was not written with the help of demons?

raoh nor could they help those Egyptian magicians and wise men to interpret the dreams. Finally Pharaoh was obliged to summon Joseph from prison to interpret the dreams. Before doing so, Joseph said to Pharaoh: "I need not be considered! God will announce welfare to Pharaoh. . . . The dream of Pharaoh is but one. What the true God is doing he has told to Pharaoh." (Genesis 41:16, 25) Pharaoh's dreams, Joseph's interpretation of them, and the accurate fulfillment of the dreams upon the land of Egypt are written down in the first book of the Bible, all without the help or participation of the demons and their magicians, of course.

[16] Another case showing the inability of the demons to produce such a book of truth as the Bible is that of Daniel, another descendant of the patriarch Abraham, before Nebuchadnezzar the king of Babylon. God sent the king a dream of a great image, of four sections of metals, that a stone cut out of a mountain without human hands crushed to powder. The king forgot the dream by morning, but demanded that the dream be both recalled and then explained. The account of the matter says: "So the king said to call the magic-practicing priests and the conjurers and the sorcerers and the Chaldeans to tell the king his dreams." (Daniel 2:1, 2) The practicers of demonism proved unable to do so.

[17] Then the prophet Daniel, whom the king called Belteshazzar, asked to see the king and he both recalled the king's dream and told its remarkable meaning. When proceeding to do this, Daniel said: "The secret that the king himself is asking, the wise men, the conjurers, the magic-practicing priests and the astrologers themselves are unable to show to the king. However, there exists a God in the heavens who is a Revealer of secrets, and

16, 17. How did the events associated with Nebuchadnezzar's dream about a great image again demonstrate the inability of the demons to produce such a book of truth as the Bible?

he has made known to King Nebuchadnezzar what is to occur in the final part of the days." The inability of the demon gods of Babylon was thus made painfully apparent.—Daniel 2:27-45.

[18] On a later occasion King Nebuchadnezzar had another dream from the God of heaven. In telling what followed, the king said: "At that time the magic-practicing priests, the conjurers, the Chaldeans and the astrologers

were entering; and I was saying before them what the dream was, but its interpretation they were not making known to me." Thus again the demons disappointed their earthly servants. The prophet Daniel as the servant of the Most High God proved able to tell the meaning of the dream. Just as he interpreted the dream, so it happened with the king. Like the preceding dream of King Nebuchadnezzar, this second dream and Daniel's explanation of it and how it was fulfilled upon the king are recorded in the Bible, free of all help from the demons. (Daniel 4:1-37) The Holy Bible owes nothing to the demons, but everything to God, and for that reason it is the one book of truth.

[19] In Ephesus, a city of Asia Minor, the Christian apostle Paul taught for some months and also performed miraculous cures: "And the wicked spirits came out" of demon-possessed people. What resulted? Paul's companion Luke writes to tell us:

18. (a) On a later occasion, how did the demons again disappoint their earthly servants, but what reliable information did the Most High God convey to the prophet Daniel? (b) Where is this recorded?
19. What occurrences in Ephesus make it clear that the Holy Bible borrowed nothing from books of magic inspired by demons?

"And many of those who had become believers would come and confess and report their practices openly. Indeed, quite a number of those who practiced magical arts brought their books together and burned them up before everybody. And they calculated together the prices of them and found them worth fifty thousand pieces of silver. Thus in a mighty way the word of Jehovah kept growing and prevailing." (Acts 19:11-20) This makes it clear that the Holy Bible has borrowed nothing from books of magic inspired by demons.

[20] The Bible does not mix God's word with that of the demons. It plainly says to worshipers of the living and true God: "The things which the nations sacrifice they sacrifice to demons, and not to God; and I do not want you to become sharers with the demons. You cannot be drinking the cup of Jehovah and the cup of demons; you cannot be partaking of 'the table of Jehovah' and the table of demons." (1 Corinthians 10:20, 21) Instead of sharing with the demons, it is necessary for worshipers of the living and true God to fight against the demons. To the worshipers of God at Ephesus the apostle Paul wrote: "Put on the complete suit of armor from God that you may be able to stand firm against the machinations of the Devil; because we have a fight, not against blood and flesh, but against the governments, against the authorities, against the world rulers of this darkness, against the wicked spirit forces in the heavenly places." In this warfare, God's worshipers need "the sword of the spirit, that is, God's word." —Ephesians 6:11-17.

[21] As never before in human history, we today need to war against those "wicked spirit forces in the heavenly places," the demons. We are living

20. Does the Bible mix God's word with that of demons, and how do the Scriptures make this clear?
21. To what warning written nineteen centuries ago should we pay particular attention in our day?

nineteen centuries later from when Paul wrote thus against the demons, and by now at least we should be living in a later period against which he warned, saying: "The inspired utterance says definitely that in later periods of time some will fall away from the faith, paying attention to misleading inspired utterances and teachings of demons, by the hypocrisy of men who speak lies, marked in their conscience as with a branding iron; forbidding to marry, commanding to abstain from foods which God created to be partaken of with thanksgiving by those who have faith and accurately know the truth."—1 Timothy 4:1-3.

[22] Since Paul wrote, many persons who claim to worship the one living and true God have fallen away to religions, ancient and more recent, that are soaked or tainted with demonism, "the misleading inspired utterances and teachings of demons." In our search to find out which sacred book of religion is the truth we need to avoid all such expressions of demonism, in order not to be misled. In its hostility to demonism the Holy Bible avoids and rejects all such misleading inspired utterances and teachings of demons. This guarantees that the Bible is the truth, God's Word. If we follow it faithfully we shall not be misled, to our destruction.

FORETELLER OF THINGS TO COME

[23] Another way by which the Holy Bible can be proved to be the one sacred book of divine truth is by proving that what it has foretold has come true. The Bible is distinguished from all other venerated books of religion in that it is prophetic. *As a whole* it is a Book of prophecy, since it both records prophecies and reports the fulfillment of

22. To what have many persons fallen away, and why will the Bible aid us to avoid being misled?
23. What else distinguishes the Bible from all other venerated books of religion?

those prophecies that had time to be fulfilled before the Bible was finished nineteen hundred years ago.

[24] In its very first book, Genesis, the Bible sets out prophecies that are fundamental and of the greatest importance to the happiness and welfare of mankind; and in its sixty-sixth and last book, Revelation, it presents a whole prophecy. The opening words of Revelation bear witness to that fact, saying: "A revelation by Jesus Christ, which God gave him, to show his slaves the things that must shortly take place. And he sent forth his angel and presented it in signs through him to his slave John, who bore witness to the word God gave and to the witness Jesus Christ gave, even to all the things he saw."—Revelation 1:1, 2.

[25] If it is true that God gave this last great prophecy of the Holy Bible through Jesus Christ, it is also true that this same God gave us the first prophecy written down in the Holy Bible, in its first book, Genesis. Read again those words in Genesis 3:15, addressed really to the demon that was invisibly behind the victimized serpent that died about six thousand years ago: "I shall put enmity between you and the woman and between your seed and her seed. He will bruise you in the head and you will bruise him in the heel." Who spoke those words? It was Jehovah God. His words were a prophecy, the first prophecy recorded in the Bible, a prophecy from which the Bible never gets away. As to the final fulfillment of that prophecy, there is a complete connection between that first prophecy in the first book of the Bible and the revelation of its fulfillment in the last book of the Bible, as follows:

24. (a) In Genesis what kind of prophecies are set out? (b) Who is identified as the originator of the prophetic information recorded in the last book of the Bible?
25. (a) What is the first prophecy in the Holy Bible, and who spoke it? (b) Is there any further mention of this prophecy in the Bible?

²⁶ "And I saw an angel coming down out of heaven with the key of the abyss and a great chain in his hand. And he seized the dragon, the original serpent, who is the Devil and Satan, and bound him for a thousand years. And he hurled him into the abyss and shut it and sealed it over him, that he might not mislead the nations any more until the thousand years were ended. After these things he must be let loose for a little while."—Revelation 20:1-3.

²⁷ After seeing that in a miraculous prophetic vision, the apostle John was carried forward in time for a thousand years, to when that great Demon, "the dragon, the original serpent, who is the Devil and Satan," is let out of the abyss and fails in his new try at misleading all mankind on earth and is then wiped out of all existence anywhere, as if plunged into fire mixed with sulphur. (Revelation 20:7-10) He has not yet been bound and imprisoned in an abyss for a thousand years. For the past six thousand years he has been on the loose and is still misleading the vast majority of mankind today. When the apostle John wrote the Revelation, it was at the close of the first century of our Common Era.

²⁸ So what the apostle John saw in vision, in signs, were "the things that must shortly take place." All the evidences are that the Demon, Satan the Devil, must yet be bound and put away in an abyss for the foretold thousand years. By measuring on this basis we can see that the Holy Bible foretells the future history of mankind for at least a thousand years in advance of our day.

²⁹ The original prophecy of God concerning the bruising of the Serpent's head is a 'thing in which

26, 27. (a) In Revelation 20: 1-3, 7-10, what is said as to the fulfillment of that prophecy in Genesis? (b) Have these things yet taken place?
28. So how far beyond our day does the Bible foretell the history of mankind?
29. Is that prophecy about the bruising of the Serpent's head reliable?

it is impossible for God to lie' and in which he will never be proved a liar.

[30] None but the true, ever-living God could produce a book of prophecy that comes true in all its prophecies. As to prophecy, the Holy Bible is outstanding and is unequaled by any other religious book in the history of man, past or present.

[31] Counting from the first occurrences in Numbers 11:25-27 the verb "to prophesy" is found 143 times in the Sacred Scriptures, Hebrew and Greek. The words "prophet(s)" and "prophetess" occur 471 times, counting from Genesis 20:7, where God called the Hebrew patriarch Abraham a "prophet." The word "prophetic" occurs twice, and the word "prophecy" or "prophecies" occurs 22 times, the word "prophesying" once. Besides this, the Hebrew word for "seer" is used 11 times, as, for instance, in connection with the prophet Samuel. (1 Samuel 9:9, 11, 18, 19) The seven Hebrew words and the two Greek words that are translated "vision(s)" occur 84 (71 + 13) times. The Hebrew word for "visionary" is used 22 times.

[32] Besides this, there is the Hebrew word for "burden" or "weighty message" or "pronouncement," which is used 29 times from Proverbs 30:1 on to Malachi 1:1 in the sense of a solemn prophecy or a prophecy of doom. Thus, in the case of Malachi, who is the last of the Twelve Minor (Lesser) Prophets, his prophecy, written in Hebrew, is called "a pronouncement" (*massá*). This location of Malachi's prophecy in the Hebrew Scriptures corresponds with the fact that the book listed last in the whole Bible of sixty-six books is the prophecy called Revelation, written in Greek. From this it is seen that the whole Bible, from start to finish, is abundantly marked by references

---

30. What must be true as to authorship of such a book of true prophecy, and is there more than one such religious book? 31, 32. What expressions mark the Bible, from start to finish, as a book of prophecy?

to prophecy, without fear that any of its prophecies would fail and prove to be a lie, a falsehood.

[33] According to what is said in the letter of Jude (the second-last book of the Bible), verses fourteen and fifteen, the man Enoch of 3404-3039 before our Common Era was the first human prophet faithful to God. The last one of the entire Bible was the Christian prophet, the apostle John, who received the Revelation.

[34] According to the Bible, there were pre-Christian prophets, the last of whom was John the Baptist, the son of Zechariah the priest, and there were Christian prophets, the first of whom was Jesus Christ. He was the greatest of all the prophets reported in the Bible. (Acts 3: 19-25; Ephesians 2:19, 20; 4:11-16) One thing is certain about all these faithful prophets of the living God: they were not under the influence of demons nor inspired by the demons. King David said concerning his prophecies: "The

spirit of Jehovah it was that spoke by me, and his word was upon my tongue." (2 Samuel 23:1, 2) "The holy spirit spoke beforehand by David's mouth." (Acts 1:16) The Christian apostle Peter points to the nondemonic, godly source of the Bible prophecies by saying: "No prophecy of Scripture springs from any private interpretation. For prophecy was at no time brought by man's will, but men spoke from God as they were borne along by holy spirit."—2 Peter 1:20, 21.

[35] In the last book of the Bible God's angel spoke of an essential idea in genuine prophecy when he said to the apostle John: "All I am is a fellow slave of you and of your brothers who have the work of witnessing to Jesus. Worship God; for the bearing witness to Jesus is what inspires prophesying." —Revelation 19:10.

[36] Thus the holy writings of the complete Bible were written under no demonic inspiration, but under the inspiration of the spirit of God, who does not lie and who cannot lie. The last two books of the inspired Hebrew Scriptures to be written were those of Jerusalem's Governor Nehemiah and the prophet Malachi, about the year 443 B.C.E. When Jesus Christ, about whom the Hebrew Scriptures prophesy, was born, it was the autumn of the year 2 B.C.E. Between his birth and the last Hebrew prophet there was a gap of 441 years.

[37] This gap allowed over four centuries of time to pass by for the Hebrew Scriptures concerning the promised Messiah, Jesus, to begin to come true. That they would come true was made sure by the fact that so many of the earlier Bible prophecies had already been fulfilled and the fulfillment of those prophecies was reported in the Hebrew Scriptures. But after the passage of these four centuries since the finishing of the writing of the

---

35. What did God's angel tell the apostle John as to genuine prophecy?
36, 37. (a) Why can we feel confident as to the truthfulness of the Bible? (b) How many years elapsed between the writing of the last books of the inspired Hebrew Scriptures and the birth of Jesus Christ, but what made sure the fulfillment of the prophecies about the Messiah?

Hebrew Scriptures the time was approaching for the prophecies concerning the coming of the promised Messiah, Jesus, to go into fulfillment. Certainly, then, the God of those Hebrew Scriptures would see to it that the fulfillment of such prophecies should also be put on record. Where?

[38] In inspired Scriptures written in the common Greek of the time, which was the international language of the first century of our Common Era. It would be reasonable to expect that in those inspired Greek Scriptures the writers would call attention to the fulfillment of the ancient Hebrew Scriptures. In fact, that was one purpose for writing those inspired Greek Scriptures, to prove the fulfillment of ancient Hebrew prophecies. Thus God the One who inspired the prophecies would prove true, and his promised Messiah and his chosen people would be plainly identified to us.

[39] In the inspired Greek Scriptures the life account of the Messiah as written by the apostle Matthew is generally put first. Well, now, in the very first chapter of Matthew's account the fulfillment of Hebrew prophecy in the year 2 B.C.E. is remarked upon, in these words: "All this actually came about for that to be fulfilled which was spoken by Jehovah through his prophet, saying: 'Look! The virgin will become pregnant and will give birth to a son, and they will call his name 'Immanuel,' which means, when translated, 'With Us Is God.' "—Matthew 1:22, 23; Isaiah 7:14.

[40] In the second chapter of Matthew three fulfillments of prophecy are noted, in these words: (1) "He stayed there until the decease of Herod, for that to be fulfilled which was spoken by Je-

---

38. Where is the record of the fulfillment of those Hebrew prophecies, and what does it prove about the One who inspired those prophecies?
39. In the very first chapter of Matthew's account of the life of the Messiah, what prophecy fulfillment is remarked upon?
40. What three fulfillments of prophecy are noted in the second chapter of Matthew?

hovah through his prophet, saying: 'Out of Egypt I called my son.' " (2) "Then that was fulfilled which was spoken through Jeremiah the prophet, saying: 'A voice was heard in Ramah, weeping and much wailing; . . .' " (3) "He withdrew into the territory of Galilee, and came and dwelt in a city named Nazareth, that there might be fulfilled what was spoken through the prophets: 'He will be called a Nazarene.' "—Matthew 2:15, 17, 18, 22, 23; Hosea 11:1; Jeremiah 31:15; Isaiah 11:1.*

[41] Thereafter throughout the rest of the Greek Scriptures the records of the fulfillments of inspired Hebrew Scriptures are introduced with such expressions as "That there might be fulfilled what was spoken," or similar expressions. For instance: "But all this has taken place for the scriptures of the prophets to be fulfilled." (Matthew 26:56) "Nevertheless, it is in order that the Scriptures may be fulfilled." (Mark 14:49) "These are my words which I spoke to you while I was yet with you, that all the things written in the law of Moses and in the Prophets and Psalms about me must be fulfilled." (Luke 24:44) "But it is that the word written in their Law may be fulfilled, 'They hated me without cause.' " (John 15:25) "But in this way God has fulfilled the things he announced beforehand through the mouth of all the prophets, that his Christ would suffer." (Acts 3:18) "The good news about the promise made to the forefathers, that God has entirely fulfilled it to us their children in that he resurrected Jesus; even as it is written in the second psalm."—Acts 13:32, 33.

---

* The Hebrew word *netser*, meaning "branch," in Isaiah 11:1 is possibly the root of the name Nazareth, possibly meaning "Branch-town."

41, 42. (a) Throughout the rest of the Greek Scriptures, what expressions are used to introduce records of fulfillment of the Hebrew Scriptures? (b) How many times do such expressions occur in the inspired Greek Scriptures?

[42] Such expressions about the fulfillment of ancient Hebrew prophecies occur twenty-seven times in the inspired Greek Scriptures.

[43] In Matthew 2:5, 6 we read: "They said to him: 'In Bethlehem of Judea; for this is how it has been written through the prophet, "And you, O Bethlehem of the land of Judah, . . . out of you will come forth a governing one, who will shepherd my people." ' " In scores of places the coming true of prophecy is called to our attention by the expression "It is written," or, "Just as it is written," or something similar, to emphasize that God's authentic prophecies were written down in the *Hebrew* Scriptures. Such expressions concerning the fulfillment of the written Hebrew prophecies occur ninety or more times in the Greek Scriptures.

[44] Jesus Christ himself was a prophet who called attention to the way in which God's law applied and to the way in which the Hebrew prophecies were fulfilled, by repeatedly using the expression "It is written," or a like expression. Why did Jesus Christ thus continually refer back to the written Word of God? It was because, as he said in his prayer to God for his followers, "I have given your word to them, . . . Sanctify them by means of the truth; your word is truth." (John 17:14-17) There Jesus Christ called the inspired Hebrew Scriptures, from which he continually quoted, the "truth." Moreover, what he preached and taught his disciples was also the word from God and was likewise the "truth." So when his disciples wrote down what Jesus said, that written record in Greek was the "truth." Such a thing can be said for no

43. What other expressions are used to identify the fulfillment of written Hebrew prophecies, and how many times do these expressions occur in the Greek Scriptures?
44. (a) Why did Jesus Christ continually refer to the written Word of God? (b) How can it be said that the written record made by his disciples was the "truth"? (c) So which sacred book of religion contains the "truth"?

other religious book on earth. The Holy Bible alone contains such "truth."

[45] The Hebrew Scriptures tell of the fulfillment of many of the prophecies that came true before Jesus was born in the year 2 B.C.E. Referring to the divine prophecy in 1 Samuel 2:21-36 and 3:10-14, the account in 1 Kings 2:27 reports: "So Solomon drove out Abiathar from serving as a priest of Jehovah, to fulfill Jehovah's word that he had spoken against the house of Eli in Shiloh."

[46] Referring to Jeremiah's prophecies concerning the desolation of Jerusalem and the land of Judah for seventy years, the account in 2 Chronicles 36:20-23 says: "He carried off those remaining from the sword captive to Babylon, and they

came to be servants to him and his sons until the royalty of Persia began to reign; to fulfill Jehovah's word by the mouth of Jeremiah, until the land had paid off its sabbaths. All the days of lying desolated it kept sabbath, to fulfill seventy years. And in the first year of Cyrus the king of

45, 46. What record of the fulfillment of prophecy do we find in the Hebrew Scriptures themselves at (a) 1 Kings 2: 27? (b) 2 Chronicles 36: 20-23?

Persia, that Jehovah's word by the mouth of Jeremiah might be accomplished, Jehovah roused the spirit of Cyrus the king of Persia, so that he caused a cry to pass through all his kingdom, and also in writing, saying: 'This is what Cyrus the king of Persia has said.' " In this way the inspired Hebrew Scriptures contain within themselves their own evidence of their truthfulness, besides the testimony from the later Greek Scriptures.

[47] However, not all the prophecies were reported in the Greek Scriptures as fulfilled. There are many Hebrew prophecies that have had fulfillment since the writing of the Christian Greek Scriptures, and many of these prophecies are having fulfillment in our own modern day. Furthermore, the Christian Greek Scriptures themselves contain prophecies that have undergone fulfillment since being written, and many of these have been undergoing fulfillment since the year 1914, in which World War I broke out.

[48] What does all this evidence concerning the fulfillment of divine prophecy serve to prove? This, that all the other Bible prophecies that are yet due to be fulfilled will certainly come true. Such prophecies, having still a future fulfillment, are just as reliable for us as were those prophecies already come true. The Bible's prophetic value and truthfulness are thus strengthened.

[49] It is just as the Christian apostle Peter wrote concerning the experience that he and James and John had in the mountain in the Middle East, when Jesus Christ was gloriously transfigured before

---

47. (a) Had all the Hebrew prophecies been fulfilled at the time of writing of the Christian Greek Scriptures? (b) Particularly since what year have many prophecies in the Christian Greek Scriptures been undergoing fulfillment?
48. What is proved by all this evidence concerning the fulfillment of divine prophecy?
49, 50. (a) How has the fulfillment of Bible prophecy affected us in the same way that the transfiguration of Jesus affected those of Jesus' apostles who were with him on that occasion? (b) So, of all the sacred books of religion in existence, which one must we conclude is the "truth"?

their eyes and God's words from heaven were
heard: "Yes, these words we heard borne from
heaven while we were with him in the holy mountain. Consequently we have the prophetic word
made more sure; and you are doing well in paying
attention to it as to a lamp shining in a dark place,
until day dawns and a daystar rises, in your
hearts. For you know this first, that no prophecy
of Scripture springs from any private interpretation. For prophecy was at no time brought by
man's will, but men spoke from God as they were
borne along by holy spirit."—2 Peter 1:16-21.

⁵⁰ In like manner, by the steady fulfillment of
its hundreds of prophecies, we have the Holy Bible
"made more sure" as being God's Word, the truth.
Out of all the sacred books of religion in existence,
the Holy Bible is the one Book that is the "truth."

IN GOD'S OWN NAME

⁵¹ God's prophecies in the Holy Bible are "things
in which it is impossible for God to lie." He gave
those prophecies in his own name, over his own
signature, as it were. In harmony with that fact
the Holy Bible is the only ancient book of religion
that revealed God's personal name to us. In the
second chapter of its first book God's name is
revealed to us; and for 6,961 times that name is
written in the thirty-nine books of the Hebrew
Scriptures, it being spelled with the four Hebrew
letters יהוה (Yod, He, Waw, He, to correspond with
our YHWH). Since the twelfth century of our
Common Era Europeans have pronounced the
name as "Jehovah." But today there are many
scholars who think its correct pronunciation is
"Yahweh." For the honor of his name, Jehovah
God must keep his word and fulfill his prophecies
that he might prove himself to be true, reliable,

---

51. (a) What is the personal name of God, and where is this
revealed to us? (b) How is God's name associated with the fulfillment of Bible prophecy?

faithful to his word, and not a liar. He has already brought honor to his name by fulfilling so many prophecies. He will yet completely vindicate his name, "that people may know that you, whose name is Jehovah, you alone are the Most High over all the earth."—Psalm 83:18, *NW; AV; AS; Yg.* P. 686

C 662

⁵² By proving that he is the one God of true prophecy, the God who is almighty and able to make his prophecies come true, Jehovah distinguishes himself from all the false gods of the false religions. In the Holy Bible he challenges all the gods of the worldly nations to prove that they are gods of true prophecy. Let such gods seek the help of the demons to prove their own godship. Let those false gods produce their witnesses, their priests, their clergymen, their monks, their nuns, their preachers, and let these would-be witnesses prove from all other sacred books of religion that their gods are gods of true prophecy and hence are true gods, worthy of being worshiped as gods.

⁵³ As regards himself, Jehovah has produced eyewitnesses of his deeds in actual history down to this day. Today his witnesses can recognize and identify his works and doings by the fulfillment of his written prophecies. They can point to his written Word, the Holy Bible, and locate the prophecy that fits the fulfillment and can say: "It is the truth!" To his faithful worshipers who bear witness for him he says in the words of his prophet Isaiah (according to the American Standard Version Bible): "Ye are my witnesses, saith Jehovah, . . . I have declared, and I have saved, and I have showed; and there was no strange god among you: therefore ye are my witnesses, saith Jehovah, and I am God. Yea, since the day was I am he; and there is none that can deliver out of my hand: I

52. How does reliable prophecy distinguish Jehovah as the true God?
53. (a) Does Jehovah have witnesses who testify to his deeds? YES (b) How can they identify his works in the events of our day?

will work, and who can hinder it?"—Isaiah 43: 10-13.

[54] For this reason the written Word of God, the Holy Bible, stands forth as a challenge against all the other ancient sacred books of religion. None of these latter books can stand up against the Bible as the Book of true prophecy and hence as the infallible Word of the one living and true God. As the one Book that is the truth, the Holy Bible does not contradict itself or contradict the true facts, the realities, the works of creation, the authentic history of man, nor even the proved scientific facts of our day. The Bible pursues one theme throughout all its pages from beginning to end. It holds forth as its dominant teaching the promised kingdom of God as exercised through his promised Messiah, the Anointed One, for blessing all the families of the earth.

[55] Prove to yourself that the Holy Bible is the one Book of the truth. Read it, study it, follow it, and receive the greatest blessing in your life.

---

54. (a) How does the Bible prove itself superior to all the other sacred books of religion? (b) What is its dominant teaching? 55. How should we use the Bible, and with what benefit to ourselves?

CHAPTER 3

The True-Life Story
as Told by the Holy Bible

THE HOLY BIBLE opens up its true-life story by stating the most fundamental scientific truth: "In the beginning God created the heavens and the earth."

² In creating the earth God's purpose was to have it peopled with a race of perfect men and women, gifted with his own divine qualities of love, wisdom, justice and power and having in subjection the fish of the sea, the flying creatures of the heavens and every other living creature moving on the ground. In six periods of time or creative "days" he prepared the conditions on and about the earth for the appearance of man and woman at the end of the sixth creative "day."

³ First he caused light to shine toward this earth in preparation. Then he produced an expanse of atmosphere above the water that covered all the globe by elevating above and around the earth a blanket of waters in such quantity as to be able to deluge the earth for forty days in succession at God's due time. This produced a

PROOF FOR THE ABOVE CAN BE FOUND IN GENESIS CHAPTERS 1 AND 7.

1. With a statement of what fundamental truth does the Bible's true-life story open?
2. What was God's purpose in creating the earth?
3-5. During six creative "days" or periods of time, what did God do by way of preparing the earth for habitation by man?

45

hothouse condition about our planet. He next caused dry land to appear above the surface of the seas upon the globe, thereafter clothing the earth with abundant vegetation and fruitful trees.

[4] Then God cleared up the atmosphere about the earth enough to let the light from the sun, moon and stars (already in existence) filter through the water blanket and reach the surface of the ground, so that day and night followed each other on the earth.

[5] Next "day" he made the waters on the earth swarm with moving forms of life and made flying creatures to wing their way through the atmosphere. On "day" six he created animals to move about on the dry land and, as a glorious crown to his earthly creation, he made, first, man as

GENESIS CHAPTER 1 IS THE BASIS FOR INFORMATION GIVEN HERE.

an earthly "son of God," and, then, woman, to be his wife and the mother of his children. At the close of the sixth creative "day" God saw that everything that he had made was "very good," and not sinful.

⁶ Thus with satisfaction God the Creator could enter into a seventh "day," to enjoy a sabbath by desisting from his earthly creative work. For this reason he blessed this seventh "day," that it might realize all his purpose to have this earth filled with his earthly children in full-grown human perfection, completely righteous, healthy and happy. In concluding the "history of the heavens and the earth" God the Creator tells his human creatures his name. It is Jehovah (יהוה).

⁷ "Jehovah God planted a garden in Eden, toward the east, and there he put the man whom he had formed." Adam, the man came to be called. That he might live healthily and happily in this earthly Paradise forever, his heavenly Father warned him not to eat from a certain kind of tree, "the tree of the knowledge of good and bad," upon which a prohibition was placed. If man sinned by breaking this prohibition, man, who was a "living soul," would die and return to the ground from which he had been taken.

THE FACTS SET OUT ABOVE ARE TAKEN FROM GENESIS 1, 2, LUKE 3.

6. (a) What was the seventh "day" to be for God, and on this "day" what was to be realized as respects the earth? (b) Where does God reveal his name, and what is it?
7. Who was the first man, and under what conditions could he have lived forever in his paradise home?

DEATH ENTERS THE WORLD OF MANKIND

⁸ Unseen to the man Adam and his wife Eve, an angelic son of God in the heavens had rebelled against Jehovah God, thus making himself Satan ("Resister"). He proceeded to make himself also a Devil ("Slanderer") by becoming a "liar and the father of the lie." Using a serpent in Eden to

lie to Eve against Jehovah God, Satan deceived Eve to sin by eating the forbidden fruit. Then she induced her husband Adam to sin by his also eating the forbidden fruit. At the sound of God's voice from the unseen heavens they tried to hide themselves. God held a court of judgment there at Eden. In sentencing Satan the Devil as a resister, slanderer, liar and manslayer, God used the serpent as a symbol of the great Deceiver, and said: "I shall put enmity between you and the woman and between your seed and her seed. He will bruise you in the head and you will bruise him in the heel."

⁹ In these words of the Bible's first prophecy Jehovah God revealed his newly formed purpose to produce a "seed" or offspring from the "woman"

SEE GENESIS 3 AND JOHN 8 FOR CONFIRMATION OF THIS ACCOUNT.

8-10. (a) Who is Satan the Devil, and how did he lead mankind into sin and death? (b) When sentencing Satan, how did God point to a future relief from the harm that that wicked one had done?

of his choice, which "seed" would destroy the great Serpent and all the Serpent's offspring and then undo all the harm that he had done to mankind and take away all the slander and reproach that he had brought upon God's name. Who that "seed" of God's "woman" would be, God let remain a sacred secret or mystery for more than the next four thousand years. But little by little during those thousands of years God gave hints of through which family head or patriarch, through which nation, through which tribe, through which family, through which "woman," this mysterious "seed" would at last come for mankind's salvation.

[10] To bring about the death of sinful Adam and Eve, God drove them out of the garden of Eden and away from its "tree of life," into the unsubdued earth, now put under a curse on Adam's account.

[11] Like one "who originated with the wicked one," their first son Cain killed their God-fearing second son Abel, the first one of "so *Hebrew* great a cloud of wit-*12-1* nesses" for God. Another son born to Adam after Abel's death was called Seth, and he became the one through whom the human line of de-

BASED ON THE RECORD AT GENESIS 3, 4, 1 JOHN 3 AND HEBREWS 11, 12.

11-13. (a) Through which son of Adam does the Bible trace the human line of descent of the Seed of God's "woman"? (b) How did Abel, Enoch and Noah show themselves to be different from others of mankind?

scent of the Seed of God's "woman" is traced in the Holy Bible.* The sixth generation, when counted from Seth, produced Enoch, a man who kept "walking with the true God" and whom God made his prophet to foretell the coming of Jehovah God as Judge "to execute judgment against . . . all the ungodly."

^{12} Enoch's great-grandson was Noah, another man who "walked with the true God." Meantime mankind in general had become very wicked. Even angelic sons of God fell in love with beautiful daughters of men and took on flesh to marry and live with them and to produce heroic Nephilim. Earth became filled with violence.

Gen 6
1 -

^{13} God instructed Noah to build an ark and to take inside all his family and specimens of animal and bird life to preserve them through the coming global flood. On the day of the flood Noah and his wife and their three sons, Japheth, Shem and Ham, and their three wives, took refuge in the ark. Then for forty days in a row the blanket of water that God had miraculously kept in suspension since the second creative "day" poured down, destroying

---

* From here on, the reader might find it a complementary help to consult the genealogical chart following most of this chapter, on pages 112, 113.

THIS ACCOUNT IS DRAWN FROM GENESIS 5-7, JUDE AND 2 PETER 3.

that "world of ungodly people" outside the ark. The next
year, in the same lunar month
of the year, God told Noah and
his family to leave the ark.
They resumed life on a dry
earth by first rendering wor-
ship with animal sacrifices to
God. God now let them add the flesh of animals to
their diet but forbade them to eat or drink the
blood of these. God commanded Noah and his sons
to make their descendants swarm in the earth. But
through which of the three sons would come the
Seed of God's woman?

AFTER THE GLOBAL FLOOD

[14] Noah became a farmer. Because of disrespect-
ful, shameless misconduct committed against him,
he cursed his grandson Canaan, son of Ham, and
pronounced a superior blessing upon Shem, thus
indicating the one in whose line of descent the
promised Seed would come. However, the line of
Ham pretended to produce the Seed, through
another son of Ham named Cush. Cush became
father to Nimrod, the "mighty hunter in opposition to Jehovah." Nimrod was the first human to
set himself up as king. This he did at Babel, or
Babylon. When Jehovah God saw the unfaithful
people building the city together with a tower
of false religion, he broke up their project by
confusing the one human language of that time.
So the city came to be called Babel or Babylon,
which means "Confusion."

GENESIS 8-11 AND 2 PETER 2 PROVIDE THE BASIS FOR THE ABOVE.

14, 15. (a) Which son of Noah was the one in whose line of
descent the promised Seed would come? (b) What kind of rep-
utation did Nimrod make for himself, and so how did false
religion spread into all parts of the world? *OVER*

[15] The frustrated build- ers scattered to other lo- cations according to lan- guage groups but car- ried along with them

their false Babylonish religion. Thus an empire of false Bab- ylonish religion was founded that became worldwide, which religious empire the last book of the Bible calls Babylon the Great. Nimrod also founded Nineveh, which later became the capital of the political em- pire of Assyria. Nimrod did not prove to be the promised Seed.

[16] The tenth generation, counted from Shem, brought forth the faithful man Abram, in the land of Ur of the Chaldeans, to the southeast of Babylon. Shem was still alive, at 525 years of age, when his descendant Abram left his homeland and family relationship at God's call and entered the Promised Land, the land of Canaan, to clinch God's promise to him: "I shall make a great na- tion out of you and I shall bless you and I will make your name great; and prove yourself a blessing. And I will bless those who bless you, and him that calls down evil upon you I shall curse, and all the families of the ground will certainly bless themselves by means of you." God changed his name to Abraham, meaning "Father of a Mul-

GENESIS 10-12, 17, REVELATION 17 ARE SOURCES FOR THIS ACCOUNT.

16, 17. What promise did God make to faithful Abram, and how did God test his faith in connection with his son Isaac?

titude," and revived the reproductive powers of him and of his wife Sarah and gave them a son, Isaac. Years later, when God tested Abraham's

faith in the resurrection of the dead and asked him to offer up Isaac as a human sacrifice, Abraham proceeded to obey.

[17] God spared Isaac and gave Abraham the promise: "I shall surely multiply your seed like the stars of the heavens and like the grains of sand that are on the seashore; and your seed will take possession of the gate of his enemies. And by means of your seed all nations of the earth will certainly bless themselves." So the Seed of God's "woman" was to come in Abraham's line through Isaac.

[18] God renewed the promise of the Seed to Isaac and then to one of his twin sons, not Esau the older, but Jacob the younger. Later, although not aware of it, the aged, nearly blind Isaac pronounced the vital blessing upon Jacob, as heir

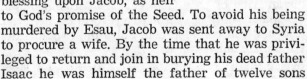

to God's promise of the Seed. To avoid his being murdered by Esau, Jacob was sent away to Syria to procure a wife. By the time that he was privileged to return and join in burying his dead father Isaac he was himself the father of twelve sons

GENESIS 17, 18, 21, 22, 25-31, 35 CONTAINS ADDITIONAL DETAILS.

18. After Abraham, to whom was the promise of the Seed renewed?

and some daughters. At the time of his return he was given the surname Israel by Jehovah God.

[19] God sent prophetic dreams to Jacob's eleventh son, Joseph. In jealousy, older brothers sold Joseph to traders, who sold him into slavery in Egypt. Through faithfulness to God despite hardship and temptation, Joseph rose to be a ruler in Egypt, second to Pharaoh. During the seven-year-long famine, which Joseph had predicted, his brothers came down to Egypt for food and were reconciled to him. Joseph then arranged for his father Jacob and all his family to move down to Egypt to live. Seventeen years later, on his deathbed, Jacob spoke a prophecy over each of his twelve sons and blessed them in farewell. Through which son would the line leading to the promised Seed of God's "woman" run? Jacob revealed this when he prophesied over his fourth son, Judah, saying: "The scepter will not turn aside from Judah, neither the commander's staff from between his feet, until Shiloh comes; and to him the obedience of the people will belong." So the Seed would be a Judean.

[20] Then the twelve sons and their families were called "the twelve tribes of Israel." After the death of Joseph as prime minister of Pharaoh, sentiment in Egypt turned against the twelve tribes of Israel, who were living in the province of Goshen. During this time there lived in the not distant land of Uz a God-fearing man named Job, descendant of Shem through a certain Uz. Jehovah God had full confidence in Job's unbreakable devotion to Him.

CONSULT GENESIS 30, 32, 37, 39-47, 49, 50, EXODUS 1 AND JOB 1.

19. How did the descendants of Jacob come to be in Egypt, and through which son of Jacob was it revealed that the Seed would come?
20, 21. Who was Job, how did he prove his faithfulness to Jehovah God and prove Satan to be a Slanderer?

[21] In angelic meetings in heaven Satan the Devil challenged God to let him put Job's religious soundness to the test, Satan being sure that he could make Job turn and curse God to his face. Given permission, Satan brought terrible afflictions upon Job, short of actually taking away his life. Down to the grand climax of the test Job remained true to Jehovah God, blessing God and proving Satan to be a great Slanderer, a Devil. In reward God restored the health of Job, made him twice as wealthy as he was before and blessed him with ten children, the same number that

Satan had killed. After his triumph over Satan, Job lived a hundred and forty years. The Bible mentions him even more than 1,500 years later.

[22] Sixty-four years after Joseph died Moses was born in Egypt, in the Israelite tribe of Levi. He was saved from death in the Nile River and was adopted by Pharaoh's daughter as her son. When forty years old, Moses made a move to free his people from slavery in Egypt but was obliged to flee from the country. Forty years later Moses, as a shepherd, led his sheep to Mount Sinai in Arabia. There, by His angel, God spoke to Moses from a burning bush. He ordered Moses to return

READ JOB 1-42, JAMES 5, EXODUS 2, 3 FOR ADDITIONAL DETAILS.

22. How was Moses used by Jehovah to free the Israelites from slavery in Egypt?

to Egypt to lead his people out, and to do so in the name of Jehovah. Moses did so. He demanded that Pharaoh let the enslaved tribes of Israel go free, to worship their God Jehovah. Pharaoh defied Jehovah and refused. Through Moses Jehovah sent terrible plagues on all Egypt. Before the tenth and last one Jehovah through Moses told the tribes of Israel to hold the Passover meal in their homes behind doorways splashed with blood of the passover lamb. For doing this all their firstborn ones were passed over, but all the firstborn of man and beast of the Egyptians died. Now, at the urging of Pharaoh, Moses led the Israelites, together with a "vast mixed company" of other people, out, bound for the Promised Land.

²³ Almighty God parted the waters of the Red Sea to let his lib-

erated people pass through, but drowned Pharaoh's military forces who came in pursuit. At Mount Sinai in Arabia the tribes of Israel halted. Through Moses as his prophet and mediator, Jehovah God brought the tribes into a covenant or binding contract with him and gave them the Ten Commandments and hundreds

SEE ALSO THE RECORD FOUND AT EXODUS 3-15, 19-24, 31-34.

23. What did Almighty God do on behalf of Israel at the Red Sea and at Mount Sinai?

of other related laws. He commanded the Israelites to build him a sacred tabernacle, a tent for worship in connection with which the priests would offer sacrifices for the nation. Jehovah chose Aaron the Levite, Moses' older brother, to be his high priest and Aaron's sons to be under-priests. The other qualified male members of the tribe of Levi were to be their assistants at the tabernacle as official Levites. The first day of the

DATES *ANNO MUNDI* (A.M.), COUNTED FROM MAN'S CREATION

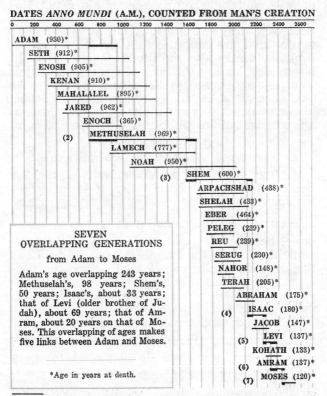

SEVEN OVERLAPPING GENERATIONS

from Adam to Moses

Adam's age overlapping 243 years; Methuselah's, 98 years; Shem's, 50 years; Isaac's, about 33 years; that of Levi (older brother of Judah), about 69 years; that of Amram, about 20 years on that of Moses. This overlapping of ages makes five links between Adam and Moses.

*Age in years at death.

SEE EXODUS 25-40, 6, GENESIS 5, 11, 25, 35, 47 AND DEUTERONOMY 34.

year after their coming out of Egypt the tabernacle was set up and Moses ordained the priests. After that they began officiating as Jehovah's priests.

²⁴ Under God's guidance the nation moved toward the southern border of the Promised Land. Because of fearfulness and a lack of faith in God, he sentenced the nation to wander in the wilderness for forty years until the rebellious, faithless older Israelites died off. Because of a rash act, Moses was not allowed to enter the Promised Land. Before he died at the end of the forty years, he wrote what are now the first five books of the Bible, evidently also the life account of Job. He began what became the Book of Psalms, he writing what is now Psalm 90, likely also Psalm 91. At God's command he ordained as Israel's new leader his faithful minister and military general, Joshua, a descendant of Joseph, through his son Ephraim.

INTO THE LAND
"FLOWING WITH MILK AND HONEY"

²⁵ After Moses died on Mount Nebo east of the Dead Sea, Joshua led the tribes of Israel across the Jordan River, God clearing the way by cutting off the river's waters from the north for the time needed to cross. Thus again the whole nation of Israel became witnesses of Jehovah as the true, almighty God. In the Promised Land, Jericho was the first Canaanite city to fall before the conquering Israelites, miraculously. Then followed six years of subduing the inhabitants of the land, under the generalship of Joshua.

²⁶ God had sentenced the Canaanites, the descendants of Canaan the cursed son of Ham, to

EX. 40; NUM. 10-14, 20, 27; DEUT. 31, 32, 34; JOSH. 1-12; GEN. 9.

24. Why was it not until forty years later that they entered the Promised Land, and what writing did Moses do during this time?
25, 26. In what ways did Jehovah help Israel to take over the Promised Land, and for what reasons?

extermination. So, to make good his covenant with Abraham to give this land to Abraham's seed or offspring, "Jehovah himself was fighting for Israel," making even the sun and the moon to stand still during one battle. After that the conquered portions of the land were divided by lot among the twelve tribes, in fulfillment of Jacob's deathbed prophecy. The priests and the Levites were given no allotment of land but were given forty-eight cities scattered throughout the land.

[27] The Israelites had no visible human king. Jehovah God was their invisible, heavenly King. So from Joshua onward there followed a period of 356 years during which God raised up judges to govern his people and to deliver them from their oppressive foes. These fifteen judges included Samson, the physically strongest man that ever lived on earth. Toward the end of that period of the judges there lived in the city of Bethlehem, in the territory of the tribe of Judah, a man named Boaz, a descendant of Judah upon whom dying Jacob had pronounced the Kingdom blessing. In the old age of Boaz a non-Israelitess, Ruth the

M o a b i t e s s, married a relative of Boaz. She forsook the worship of the Moabite god Chemosh and became a convert to the worship of Israel's god, Jehovah. W h e n h e r mother-in-law,

GEN. 12, 49; JOSH. 10, 13-21; JUDG. 1-21; RUTH 1-4; 1 SAM. 4, 7.

27, 28. Who governed the Israelites from the days of Joshua onward, and in time how did they come to have human kings?

Naomi, now a widow, returned to Judah, widowed Ruth came along and got married to Boaz according to God's law on levirate or brother-in-law marriage. She bore to Boaz of Bethlehem a son named Obed, who became the grandfather of David.

²⁸ The prophet Samuel the Levite was the last of that line of fifteen judges. When he grew old the Israelites asked him to set up a visible human king over their nation, thus rejecting Jehovah as their King. Jehovah instructed Samuel to anoint Saul the son of Kish of the tribe of Benjamin to be king. *first*

²⁹ With King Saul there began a period of 510 years of kings reigning in Jehovah's name over the Israelites. Early in his reign Saul proved disobedient to Jehovah. Hence Jehovah through Samuel told Saul that the kingdom would be taken away from his family and be given to a man agreeable to God's own heart. In due time God sent Samuel to Bethlehem to anoint the young shepherd boy David to become the future king over all Israel. After David, armed with a slingshot, killed the Philistine giant Goliath in single combat, King Saul made David an army commander. On becoming suspicious that David was the one whom God had chosen to take over the kingdom from Saul's family, he forced David to flee for his life and kept pursuing him to destroy him. In this he failed. Finally, after reigning forty years, he died. His son Ish-bosheth succeeded him.

³⁰ However, after King Saul's death the tribe of Judah made David their king as the "anointed of Jehovah." For seven and a half years he reigned in the Judean city of Hebron. Then after the assassination of Ish-bosheth the other eleven tribes asked

RUTH 1-4; 1 SAM. 3, 7, 8-13, 15-31; 1 CHRON. 10-12; 2 SAM. 1-5.

29, 30. Why did King Saul lose Jehovah's favor, and how did the kingly scepter finally come into possession of the tribe of Judah, as had been foretold? *over*

David to reign over them. At last the kingly scepter and commander's staff came into possession of Judah, as the dying Jacob had predicted. Shortly after David became king over the united nation, he captured the city of Jerusalem and made it the national capital. There, near his palace on Mount Zion, he pitched a special tent and had the Aaronic priests bring into it the holy ark of the covenant, which had got separated from the sacred tabernacle when at the city of Shiloh. Thus in a symbolic way Jehovah began to reign on Mount Zion in Jerusalem, whereas David, as God's visible representative, sat on "Jehovah's throne."

[14] [31] Not satisfied that Jehovah's ark of the covenant should dwell under tent curtains, David made known to the prophet Nathan his thought of building a glorious temple for Jehovah's worship and for housing His ark. But Jehovah told Nathan to inform King David that he, a man of war, was not to build the temple. Building of the temple would be left to a son of his. Moreover, because of David's heart devotion to him, Jehovah would build for David a royal house, in that the kingdom over God's people would remain in David's family line forever: "Your house and your kingdom will certainly be steadfast to time indefinite before you; your very throne will become one firmly established to time indefinite." This covenant of God with David for an everlasting kingdom made it certain that the Shiloh foretold by the dying Jacob would come in David's line, and, hence, too, the Seed of God's "woman" would come in David's line.

[32] Although a man of war, David was a musician and poet, and he wrote many psalms, seventy-five of which (including Psalms 2 and 95) are found

GEN. 49; 2 SAM. 5-7; 1 CHRON. 11, 13-17; 1 SAM. 4; 1 CHRON. 29.

31, 32. (a) What did God's covenant with David for an everlasting kingdom make certain? (b) In what Bible book are writings of David found? *over*

among the 150 psalms of the Bible Book of Psalms, with possibly Psalm 72 being also ascribable to David.

[33] However, primarily through which one of David's sons would the line of descent run leading directly to the Shiloh, the permanent heir of the everlasting Davidic kingdom, the Seed of God's "woman" for bruising Satan the Serpent in the head? According to the names on record, David finally had twenty sons. Would that one be David's successor on "Jehovah's throne" and the builder of Jehovah's temple at Jerusalem? During David's forty years of reigning he brought into subjection all the enemies throughout the land that God had promised to give the offspring of Abraham. Shortly before dying, David abdicated his throne in favor of his wise son Sol-

1 CHRON. 3, 11, 14, 18-20; 2 CHRON. 11; 2 SAM. 5, 8-12; 1 KI. 1, 2.

33, 34. What important building work did David's son and successor to the throne do, and which Bible books was he inspired by God to write?

omon and had him anointed as king over all twelve tribes of Israel.

[34] In the fourth year of his reign, or in the four hundred and eightieth year of Israel's deliverance from the land of Egypt, King Solomon began building Jehovah's temple on Mount Moriah, north of Mount Zion. He finished it in seven years and six months. Jehovah's ark of the covenant was brought into its Most Holy, and God sanctified the temple and put his name Jehovah upon it. The wisdom of Solomon and the happiness of his subjects became known worldwide. Under inspiration of God's spirit he wrote the Bible books of Ecclesiastes and the Song of Solomon and most of Proverbs.

[35] In the course of his forty years of reigning Solomon married hundreds of wives and concubines, a thousand all together, many of these being foreigners, non-Israelitesses. In his old age these foreign women turned Solomon to the worship of their false gods. In displeasure God told Solomon that he would rip ten tribes of Israel away from Solomon's successors and leave to these only the tribe of Benjamin besides his own tribe of Judah. So troubles set in for Solomon. His rule became oppressive, like a heavy yoke.

[36] Solomon's royal successor, his son Rehoboam, turned down the demand of the people to lighten the burden upon them. At this, ten tribes of Israel broke away and made Jeroboam of the tribe of Ephraim their king, just as Jehovah's prophet Ahijah the Shilonite had foretold. This new ten-tribe kingdom of Israel lasted for 257 years, waging war against the kingdom of Judah for much of the time, as Judah had stayed loyal to David's royal house. Fearing what might happen

BASED ON RECORDS FOUND AT 1 KINGS 1-12 AND 2 CHRONICLES 1-12.

35, 36. What events led to division of the nation, and finally to destruction for the ten-tribe kingdom?

if the ten rebellious tribes kept going up to the temple in Jerusalem in the kingdom of Judah to worship Jehovah as God, King Jeroboam set up the worship of golden calves at the cities in his own territory, Dan and Bethel. This portended sure destruction for the ten-tribe kingdom of Israel in time to come.

[37] Nineteen kings followed Jeroboam upon the royal throne, and all of them fell victim to the sin that he had introduced into Israel. The eighth king from Jeroboam, namely, Ahab, married Jezebel, a foreign Baal worshiper, and introduced Baal worship into Israel at his capital city Samaria. God raised up his prophet Elijah to reprove King Ahab, and to begin the destruction of the priests and prophets of Baal in Israel. During the famine of three and a half years that he predicted and for which he prayed, Elijah performed the first miracle of its kind on this earth, that of raising a person from the dead, the son of a widowed woman outside Israel, in whose home he was in hiding. In a test with 450 prophets of Baal on Mount Carmel, he called down fire from heaven to consume the sacrifice on Jehovah's altar, after which he slew the Baal prophets and prayed for rain to end the long drought. God used Elijah to foretell the violent deaths of King Ahab and Queen Jezebel and to appoint Elisha as his successor.

[38] Elijah performed a miracle by striking the Jordan River with his official garment to make the waters part for him and his appointed successor Elisha to cross. As the two walked on, Elijah was separated and carried skyward by a whirlwind in company with a fiery chariot and horses, and Elisha became his active successor.

FOR FURTHER DETAILS SEE 1 KINGS 12-22 AND 2 KINGS 1-10, 13-17.

37-39. By what means was Baal worship introduced into Israel, but how was it demonstrated that Jehovah was using the prophets Elijah and Elisha as his servants?

[39] According to the words of Jehovah's prophet Malachi, Elijah was a prophetic picture of a future prophet commissioned to turn people back to Jehovah God "before the coming of the great and fear-inspiring day of Jehovah." His successor Elisha acted as prophet down into the days of Jehoash, Israel's thirteenth king. He performed twice as many miracles as Elijah, that is, sixteen, including the second resurrection of Bible record, the restoring to life of the son of a Shunammite woman. During his prophetic ministry he witnessed King Jehu's total destruction of Baal worshipers out of Israel. Elisha died a natural death.

[40] After him, Jehovah's prophet Jonah was thrown from a ship during a storm in the Mediterranean Sea and was swallowed by a great fish. After spending parts of three days inside the fish he was discharged on dry land. In obedience to Jehovah he now went to Nineveh, the capital of Assyria, to preach its destruction in forty days. The Ninevites repented at the preaching of this foreigner, and Jehovah spared the Ninevites as a lesson of mercy to Jonah. More than two hundred years after Jonah, Jehovah sent his prophet Nahum to declare and write his prophecy on the coming certain destruction of Nineveh, signifying the downfall of the Assyrian Empire. More than a hundred years before Assyria was overthrown as a world power, its king Sargon II captured and destroyed Samaria, capital city of the ten-tribe kingdom of Israel. He carried into exile the surviving Israelites and repopulated the land with foreigners. This fulfilled prophecies by Hosea and Amos.

MAL. 4; 2 KI. 2-10, 13, 17; JON. 1-4; NAH. 1-3; HOS. 8-11; AMOS 5-7.

40. (a) Which of his prophets did Jehovah cause to preach and write concerning Nineveh, the capital of Assyria? (b) Before Assyria was overthrown, what did it do to the ten-tribe kingdom of Israel, in fulfillment of prophecy?

KINGDOM COVENANT WITH DAVID
CONTINUES IN FORCE

[41] As for the kingdom of Judah, the royal line of David continued on "Jehovah's throne," in Jerusalem. But was this royal line through Solomon the direct one in which the Seed of God's "woman" would come in fulfillment of Jehovah's prophecy in the garden of Eden? No! Among David's twenty sons was one named Nathan, not the prophet Nathan. Over five hundred years later the prophet Zechariah spoke of the "family of the house of Nathan" in connection with David's house. Nathan's son was Mattatha; and it was through Nathan's line by Mattatha that the promised Seed, Shiloh, came directly, in the forty-second generation when counted from Nathan. The twenty-first and twenty-second generations merged with the royal line of Solomon, in the cases of Shealtiel and Governor Zerubbabel. It then parted company, till at last Joseph, a descendant in Solomon's line, became a son-in-law to Nathan's line and thus became foster father to the promised Seed in the flesh.

[42] Nineteen kings followed King Solomon on "Jehovah's throne" in Jerusalem. In the days of Solomon's great-grandson, King Asa, Jehovah God answered the king's prayer and defeated King Zerah the Ethiopian, who came against King Asa with a million soldiers and three hundred chariots. Some time later God raised up the prophet Joel to foretell the time when Jehovah would pour out his spirit "on every sort of flesh" and that those receiving the spirit would prophesy and only those calling upon the name of Jehovah would be saved.

2 SAM. 5; ZECH. 12; LUKE 3; MATT. 1; 2 CHRON. 14; JOEL 2.

41. Through which of the sons of King David did the promised Seed come?
42, 43. What are some of the outstanding things that Jehovah caused his prophets Joel, Amos, Isaiah and Micah to foretell during the time of the kingdom of Judah?

In the days of King Uzziah God raised up his prophets Amos, Hosea and Isaiah.

[43] Amos was used to prophesy that the time would come when Jehovah would take out of the non-Jewish nations a people for his name, "all the nations upon whom my name has been called." As a sign to bad King Ahaz, the prophet Isaiah foretold that a "maiden," evidently meaning a virgin girl, would give birth to a son and would call his name Immanuel, meaning "With Us Is God." Isaiah also foretold the fall of Babylon as a world power and even foretold the very name of Babylon's conqueror, Cyrus, by whom Jehovah's people would be released from exile in Babylon and would rebuild Jehovah's temple and Jerusalem and cultivate again the desolated land of Judah. Isaiah also foretold the earthly sufferings of the promised Seed of God's "woman" when being bruised at the heel by the great Serpent. A contemporary prophet, Micah, foretold the very city in which the Seed of God's "woman" would be born in the flesh, namely, in David's city of Bethlehem in the territory of Judah.

[44] Hezekiah succeeded bad King Ahaz on the throne of Jerusalem. Hezekiah saw the ten-tribe kingdom of Israel with its capital at Samaria fall to the king of Assyria because of Israel's worship of the golden calves and general wickedness. Years later, Sennacherib king of Assyria invaded the land of Judah and threatened Jerusalem, boastfully defying Jehovah God. Jehovah answered and told King Hezekiah by his prophet Isaiah that King Sennacherib would fail and would have to return to his own land, there to fall at the hand of assassins. That night Jehovah's angel put to death 185,000 of Sennacherib's troops and thus

AMOS 9; ISA. 7, 13, 21, 44, 45, 47, 50, 53; MIC. 5; 2 KI. 18, 19.

44. Although Samaria fell to the king of Assyria, why was Sennacherib unable to capture Jerusalem?

ISAIAH 7-14 & 53-3-8

MARK-9-12 =

sent him scurrying home. Hezekiah now became sick unto death, the alarming thing about it being that he had no heir to his throne. The prophet Isaiah recorded the prayer that Hezekiah prayed to God for mercy. God informed him through Isaiah that Jehovah would add fifteen years to his life. After his recovery he had a son. Consequently, when his son Manasseh came to the throne, he was but twelve years old. At that time Elmadan was the one carrying forward Nathan's line.

[45] Manasseh reigned fifty-five years. He turned to idolatry and caused unjust bloodshed, filling Jerusalem with blood "from end to end." For this, Jehovah God determined to destroy Jerusalem, thus overthrowing the kingdom. Even Manasseh's reform at the end of his reign did not change Jehovah's purpose. Neither did the righteous reign of his godly grandson Josiah do so. The prophet Zephaniah cried Woe! to the city, and warned of the coming "great day of Jehovah" and told how one might be "concealed in the day of Jehovah's anger." In the thirteenth year of King Josiah's reign, or forty years before Jerusalem was destroyed, Jehovah God raised up a young prophet, Jeremiah. He mourned greatly over the death of good King Josiah at the age of thirty-nine years, when trying to prevent Pharaoh-Nechoh of Egypt from passing through Israelite territory toward Assyria. Swift decline now befell Judah.

[46] The Jews made Jehoahaz, the second living son of King Josiah, to be his successor. However, Pharaoh-Nechoh of Egypt interfered and took him captive to Egypt and made his older brother Eliakim the king and changed his name to Jehoiakim.

2 KI. 20-24; 2 CHRON. 32-36; ISA. 38; LUKE 3; ZEPH. 1-3; JER. 1.

45. (a) For what reason did Jehovah later determine to destroy Jerusalem? (b) In what capacity did Zephaniah and Jeremiah serve Jehovah in the years that followed?
46, 47. As a result of what events did the kings of Judah become vassals to Babylon, and who were among those taken captive to Babylon a few years later?

Three years later Nebuchadnezzar became king of Babylonia and defeated the Egyptians in battle. Then, as foretold in Habakkuk's magnificent prophecy, the Babylonians moved against Jerusalem. There, in the eighth year of King Jehoiakim's reign, Nebuchadnezzar made him a vassal to Babylon.

⁴⁷ Three years later King Jehoiakim rebelled _6678.c._ against Babylon in favor of Egypt. So Nebuchadnezzar proceeded to come against Jerusalem. Meantime, in the eleventh year of his reign, Jehoiakim died and his eighteen-year-old son Jehoiachin was made king, to reign only three months. He went out of the besieged city of Jerusalem and surrendered to the Babylonians. Nebuchadnezzar then took him and some thousands of other Jews captive to Babylon, including two young men who became the prophets Daniel and Ezekiel, and also a Benjaminite named Kish, who became the great-grandfather of Mordecai and Esther. Nebuchadnezzar also took Jehoiachin's uncle, Josiah's fourth son named Mattaniah, and made him king of Jerusalem and changed his name to Zedekiah. He too ruled as a vassal of Babylon.

⁴⁸ The prophet Jeremiah was left in Judah and continued to prophesy. He foretold the coming destruction of Jerusalem and the complete desolation of the land of Judah and Jerusalem, without man or domestic beast, for seventy years in a row. In contrast with that, Jeremiah also foretold the downfall of imperial Babylon at the hands of its enemies and then the release of captive Jews to return to Zion, to Jerusalem, to repeople the land and to restore the worship of Jehovah at a rebuilt temple. Jeremiah was also inspired to foretell that Jehovah God would make a new covenant

JER. 6, 29-31, 46; HAB. 1; 2 KI. 24; DAN. 1; EZEK. 1; ESTHER 2.

48. What events involving Jerusalem and Babylon did Jeremiah, a prophet in Judah, foretell?

with his people, but not according to the Law covenant that he had made with the twelve tribes of Israel through the prophet Moses. Jeremiah advised the Jews to be subject to Babylon.

⁴⁹ Meantime, in the fifth year of his exile in Babylon, Ezekiel began to prophesy in Babylon to the Jewish captives there. By inspiration Jehovah God kept Ezekiel informed of what was happening at Jerusalem, that thus Ezekiel could inform the Jewish captives in Babylon, even informing them of the very day when the final siege of Jerusalem began. After Jerusalem's fall was reported to him, Ezekiel began to prophesy of the restoration of the desolated land of Judah and the return of the Jewish captives from Babylon. He also foretold in grand detail the building of a new temple for Jehovah's worship, near a city called Jehovah-shammah ["Jehovah Himself Is There"]. For more than sixty times in his written prophecies Ezekiel reports Jehovah as declaring that the various nations and peoples will certainly know that He is Jehovah.

⁵⁰ At Jerusalem, contrary to the advice of the prophet Jeremiah, King Zedekiah rebelled, in the ninth year of his reign, against Nebuchadnezzar in favor of Egypt. So at Babylon Ezekiel directed this prophecy against the rebellious King Zedekiah: "Remove the turban, and lift off the crown. . . . A ruin, a ruin, a ruin I shall make it. As for this also, it will certainly become no one's until he comes who has the legal right, and I must give it to him." He thus referred to the coming of the rightful Permanent Heir of King David's throne. But now Nebuchadnezzar again came from Babylon and laid siege to Jerusalem. For a time the

JER. 27, 31, 38, 52; EZEK. 1, 21, 24, 33, 36, 37, 39-48; 2 KI. 24, 25.

49, 50. Who was serving as Jehovah's prophet to the captive Jews in Babylon at this time, and what did he prophesy about restoration and the coming Permanent Heir of King David's throne?

siege was lifted, to permit Nebuchadnezzar to put down the threat from the armies of Pharaoh of Egypt. The prophet Jeremiah was then arrested, but, just as he had warned, the Babylonians came back and renewed the siege.

⁵¹ After eighteen months of siege Jerusalem was breached by the Babylonians in the eleventh year of its King Zedekiah. The fleeing king was captured, and the prophet Jeremiah was released from prison by the Babylonian general. The following month the city of Jerusalem and its temple built by Solomon were destroyed. King Zedekiah's sons were executed. He himself was blinded and was taken away to prison in Babylon. His nephew Jehoiachin was already at Babylon and was becoming father to sons in captivity, to carry forward Solomon's royal line. Most of the Jews surviving the fall and destruction of Jerusalem were carried into exile into Babylon. Among the captive Jews there during the next seventy years was one named Neri, who had descended from King David through his son Nathan. This family line now became interrelated with Solomon's family through Shealtiel and his son Zerubbabel.

⁵² As for the prophet Jeremiah, the Babylonian general released him to go to Mizpah to live with the Jewish governor Gedaliah and the poor Jews still left in the land. Jeremiah's grief at the destruction of Jerusalem was expressed in his book entitled Lamentations. Sadly, in the seventh lunar month of the year, Gedaliah was murdered, and against the advice of the prophet Jeremiah the people took him and fled down to Egypt for fear of reprisals from Babylon. Thus the land of Judah and Jerusalem began lying completely desolate, to keep a sabbath of noncultivation for seventy years.

2 KI. 25; 2 CHRON. 36; JER. 37, 39-43, 52; 1 CHRON. 3; LUKE 3.

51, 52. What series of events led to the destruction of Jerusalem and the complete desolation of the land of Judah?

About this time the prophet Obadiah finished his book, telling the enemies of Jehovah's people not to gloat over the calamity upon the Jews and warning them of coming vengeance from Jehovah God.

[53] In Babylon the prophet Ezekiel continued prophesying until sixteen years after Jerusalem's destruction. But God raised up another prophet in Babylon, namely, Daniel, in the second year after Nebuchadnezzar destroyed Jerusalem and thus became the dominant king of the earth. Daniel interpreted the prophetic dream of King Nebuchadnezzar, and showed that the period of Gentile (non-Jewish) domination of the earth would run for seven prophetic times, or for 2,520 years, from the destruction of Jerusalem and desolation of the land of Judah. After that God's kingdom would be established and would crush all earthly political governments and would stand forever, without successor.

[54] Daniel was used to foretell the succession of the world powers from Babylon onward, how Babylon would fall before the Medes and Persians, and how the Medo-Persian World Power would fall before the Greeks. The Grecian World Power would, in turn, give way to another world power, not identified by name but described with some detail. On the night that Babylon fell to the

Medes and Persians, which night worldly history *in* establishes as occurring in the year 539 before our *history* Common Era, Daniel interpreted to Belshazzar, Nebuchadnezzar's grandson, the miraculous handwriting that had appeared on the wall of Belshazzar's banquet hall. That night Belshazzar was killed by the conquerors, and for a time Darius the Mede ruled as king of Babylon.

[55] During the rule of Darius the Mede, Daniel prayed to Jehovah God because the seventy years of desolation of Judah and Jerusalem were then near their end. At that time Jehovah revealed to Daniel that Messiah the princely Leader was coming and would appear on earth sixty-nine weeks of years (or, 483 years) after the imperial order was issued and put into effect for rebuilding the broken-down walls of the rebuilt Jerusalem. In the middle of the seventieth week of years (or, three and a half years after his appearance) the Messiah or Appointed One would be cut off sacrificially. Yet God's covenant, made long ago with their forefather Abraham, would continue to have special application to the Jewish nation until the end of the seventieth week of years, or at the end of the 490-year period. So now the people of Jehovah God would have a means of measuring exactly when the Messiah, the Shiloh, the Seed of God's "woman," would appear on earth.

[56] Daniel also foretold the "time of the end" upon the non-Jewish nations after certain histor-

BASED ON THE RECORD IN DANIEL 5, 9, 11, 12 AND GENESIS 3, 12, 49.

53. For how long would this Gentile domination of the earth continue before the establishment of God's kingdom, according to Jehovah's prophet Daniel in Babylon?

54. What succession of world powers was foretold by Daniel, and when did Babylon fall to the Medes and Persians?

55. Toward the end of the seventy-year period of desolation of Jerusalem, what did Jehovah reveal concerning the coming of Messiah?

56, 57. When were the Jews released from Babylon, but what caused the completion of rebuilding of the temple to be delayed for many years?

ical events that God's angel revealed to Daniel. When the Jews were released from Babylon by the decree of King Cyrus, in 537 B.C.E. (according to our history), in the seventieth and last year of Jerusalem's desolation, aged Daniel did not go with the remnant of faithful Jews back to their homeland, to rebuild the temple of Jehovah. He died, evidently, during the imperial rule of King Cyrus the Persian. Zerubbabel, who was born in Babylon, led the remnant back as their appointed governor.

[57] In accordance with Cyrus' decree, the rebuilding of the temple was promptly begun. But the enemies roundabout interfered and at last blocked the work by appeal to the imperial Persian government. Fifteen years after the start of the temple work Jehovah God raised up his prophet Haggai and then his prophet Zechariah to encourage the work. When the enemies again appealed to the Persian government against the Jews, the Jews explained matters to the emperor, Darius. He had an investigation of records made, uncovered the true facts, and lifted the ban on the temple building. Four years five months and some days later the temple was completed by Governor Zerubbabel and High Priest Joshua and was dedicated.

[58] Emperor Darius was succeeded by Ahasuerus, of whom secular history speaks as Xerxes I. To replace his disobedient wife Vashti, the emperor married Esther (Hadassah) the cousin of Mordecai the Jew, who was in the emperor's service. However, Haman the Agagite was made premier. In his effort to destroy Mordecai the Jew, Haman maneuvered King Ahasuerus into signing a decree for all the Jews to be slaughtered throughout all the imperial provinces, including Judah and Jerusalem. Under the counsel of her cousin Mordecai,

SEE EZRA 1-6; 1 CHRON. 3; HAG. 1, 2; ZECH. 1, 4; ESTHER 1-4.

58, 59. During the reign of King Ahasuerus of Persia, how was a plot against the life of the Jews thwarted?

Queen Esther risked her life to gain a special audience with her imperial husband. At a special meal, to which she invited both King Ahasuerus and his prime minister to be present, she revealed herself to be a Jewess and exposed Haman as being the one who schemed for the destruction of her people. In anger King Ahasuerus ordered Haman to be hanged on the same gallows that he had built for hanging Mordecai. He then made Mordecai his prime minister.

[59] Queen Esther again risked her life to appeal to the king to permit a decree allowing the threatened Jews to defend themselves on the day assigned for their slaughter, the thirteenth of Adar. Thus, on that day, the Jews everywhere defended themselves and slaughtered all those seeking to slaughter them. Even Haman's ten sons were hanged. At the im-

FOR FURTHER DETAILS OF THESE EVENTS READ ESTHER CHAPTERS 5-9.

perial capital the Jews continued slaughtering their enemies for a second day. In celebration of this the annual feast day of Purim was started among the Jews. Mordecai continued to use his high office for the benefit of the Jews.

[60] Xerxes was succeeded by Artaxerxes as emperor of Persia. In the seventh year of his reign he sent the Jewish priest named Ezra, who was also a copyist of the Holy Scriptures, to Jerusalem with special contributions for the temple. Without military protection Ezra and a body of Jewish exiles, including Levites, and Nethinim, made it safely to Jerusalem. On learning that the restored Jews had undertaken mixed marriages with the non-Jewish peoples roundabout, Ezra purified the nation by having these mixed marriages dissolved on a set occasion.

[61] In the twentieth year of King Artaxerxes' reign the news came to his butler, Nehemiah the Jew, that the walls of Jerusalem were in very bad condition. When Artaxerxes learned that this caused grief to his butler, he granted the request for Nehemiah to go to Jerusalem to rebuild the city walls. Soon after arrival there Nehemiah arranged for the rebuilding of the walls. The enemies, including Geshem the Arabian, tried to frighten the Jews off from their defense work, but Nehemiah armed the builders against surprise attack, and the work went on. In fifty-two days the walls were completed, on the twenty-fifth day of the lunar month of Elul (August-September) in the twentieth year of King Artaxerxes, or in the year 455 B.C.E. according to worldly history. After that there was a joyful inauguration of the city

BASED ON RECORD AT ESTHER 9, 10, EZRA 7-10 AND NEHEMIAH 1-6, 12.

60. Who was Ezra, and how did he advance the interests of Jehovah's worship?
61. How was the rebuilding of Jerusalem's walls accomplished, and why was that a time of prophetic importance?

walls with a special celebration. It was at this accomplishment in the year 455 B.C.E. that the seventy weeks of years as foretold by the prophet Daniel began to count, thus marking the year 29 of our Common Era as the year for the promised Messiah to appear on earth.

walls
70 wks.

⁶² The priest Ezra, the expert copyist of God's law, was associated with Governor Nehemiah in his work, particularly in teaching the restored Jews the written Word of God. Governor Nehemiah ruled justly and corrected bad conditions in the land, especially seeing to it that Jehovah's worship at the rebuilt temple was faithfully kept up. After an absence of some time Nehemiah returned to Jerusalem and found it necessary to purify the temple and also undo the mixed marriages into which Jews had entered.

⁶³ About this time a prophet with a special message concerning the temple of Jehovah appeared. He foretold that Jehovah God would send ahead of himself a messenger. This one would prepare the way before Jehovah in advance of Jehovah's sudden coming to the temple accompanied by his "messenger of the covenant." For the sake of the pure worship of the one living and true God, Jehovah would purify the temple priests and the Levites. He would also bear witness from the temple against the wrongdoers in the nation of Judah and Jerusalem, that they might offer up acceptable sacrifices as their forefathers had done long ago. The prophet, Malachi by name, also foretold the coming of the fiery day of Jehovah for the destruction of the wicked. But with that day in view, he would send to his people the one whom he calls

SEE DANIEL 9, NEHEMIAH 8-10, 12, 13 AND MALACHI 3, 4 FOR DETAILS.

62, 63. (a) How did Governor Nehemiah demonstrate his interest in the temple at Jerusalem? (b) What did the prophet Malachi say about future action to be taken in connection with the temple, and so to what did he cause the people to look forward?

"Elijah the prophet" to bring God's straying people back to him So the prophet Malachi finished his work apparently in the fifth century before our Common Era, leaving Jehovah's chosen people looking ahead to the coming of this important forerunner and reformer.

[64] After Malachi's work the "seven times" of Gentile domination of the world of mankind continued to run as Jerusalem, the one-time seat of God's typical kingdom on earth, continued in subjection to the Gentile world powers. The seventy weeks of years also continued counting. In the eighteenth week, or in 331 B.C.E., the "mighty king" foretold by the prophet Daniel, namely, Alexander the Great, the Macedonian, overthrew the Persian Empire, to set up the Grecian or Macedonian Empire as the new world power. Eight years later he died at Babylon on the Euphrates River; and now, as Daniel's prophecies had foretold, his empire became broken up into four Hellenic kingdoms. In time this situation gave way to the next world power, the Roman, just as Daniel had foreseen.

[65] It was in the fifty-seventh week of years, or in 63 B.C.E., that Jerusalem became subject to the Roman Empire. In time the Roman Senate appointed an Edomite named Herod, the son of Antipater, to be king of Jerusalem, and in 37 B.C.E. he established himself there as king. In the year 30 B.C.E. Egypt became a Roman province and by that event at the latest Rome became the new world power, with Octavius as ruler. In the sixty-second week of years, or in 27 B.C.E., the Roman Senate decreed Octavius to be Augustus. It was

BASED PRINCIPALLY ON MALACHI 4, DANIEL 4, 7-9, 11 AND MATTHEW 2.

64, 65. What two additional Gentile powers exercised control over Jerusalem during the remaining years until the events related in the second part of the Bible began to take place?

during his reign, which lasted till August 19 of the year 14 of our Common Era, that the events of the second part of the Holy Bible, written in common Greek of that time, began to take place.

PART II

[66] In the sixty-fifth week of years of the seventy weeks foretold by the angel Gabriel to the prophet Daniel, during the reign of Augustus Caesar of Rome, there occurred the long-awaited birth. But in whose family? In that of Herod the Great, then king of Jerusalem? No; for he was an Edomite, a descendant of Esau the twin brother of Jacob. Although he was king of Jerusalem and was a descendant of the patriarch Abraham, he was not of the house of David with whom Jehovah God had made a covenant for an everlasting kingdom. Under God's protection two registered lines of descent from King David were still being kept up, one through David's royal son Solomon and the other through David's son Nathan. In the line through Solomon, Jacob had a son named Joseph, born in Bethlehem. But in the line through Nathan, Heli had a daughter named Mary, born in Bethlehem. Mary became betrothed to Joseph, while he was working as a carpenter in Nazareth. Mary was living there also.

DANIEL 9; 2 SAMUEL 7; 1 CHRONICLES 17; MATTHEW 1; LUKE 1-3.

66. Among whose descendants did a long-awaited birth occur during the reign of Augustus Caesar of Rome?

[67] According to the prophecy of Malachi of centuries previous there was to be a forerunner of Jehovah's "messenger of the covenant," a forerunner who would correspond with Elijah the prophet. In view of this, God sent his angel Gabriel to the temple of Jerusalem to inform the priest Zechariah that, despite the age of him and his wife Elizabeth, he would have a son, whom he was to call John. Moreover, Gabriel said: "Many of the sons of Israel will he turn back to Jehovah their God. Also, he will go before him with Elijah's spirit and power." In the sixth month of Zechariah's wife's pregnancy God sent his angel Gabriel to Nazareth to tell her kinswoman Mary that she was God's choice for bearing David's Permanent Heir to the everlasting kingdom. She was to call his name Jesus.

[68] This Jesus "will be called Son of the Most High; and Jehovah God will give him the throne of David his father, and he will rule as king over the house of Jacob forever, and there will be no end of his kingdom." Mary would conceive this son, not by intercourse with Joseph her betrothed, but God's spirit would make her

CONSULT MALACHI 4, LUKE 1 FOR CONFIRMATION OF THIS ACCOUNT.

67-71. (a) Why did God send an angel to announce the birth of a son to the priest Zechariah? (b) How did Jesus come to be born of Mary as the Permanent Heir of David's throne?

pregnant; "for that reason also what is born will be called holy, God's Son."

⁶⁹ Mary agreed to all this, and the angel Gabriel disappeared. Then there happened what the apostle Paul reveals to us: God's principal Son in heaven, God's "only-begotten Son," emptied himself of his heavenly form and glory, that God, his heavenly Father, might miraculously transfer his life to the womb of Mary the Jewish virgin, and have a human birth and come to be "in the likeness of men." Thus God's Son came down from heaven. Isaiah's prophecy of Immanuel's birth from a young woman began fulfilling.

⁷⁰ When Joseph discovered that Mary his betrothed was pregnant, he thought of divorcing her secretly. But God's angel appeared to him in a dream to disclose to him that what was begotten in Mary was by holy spirit. So, obeying the angel, Joseph married Mary.

⁷¹ In due time John was born to priest Zechariah and Elizabeth, and his father pronounced a prophecy over him, that he would "be called a prophet of the Most High."

⁷² In those days the Roman emperor issued a decree for the people to get registered at their native places. To comply with this decree, Joseph took the pregnant Mary and went down to Bethlehem. There one night Mary gave birth to Jesus and laid him in an animal's food manger, as all lodging rooms were full. That was thirty years before the Messiah the Leader was due to appear according to Daniel's prophecy of seventy weeks, hence in the year 2 B.C.E. That same night God's angel announced Jesus' birth to shepherds watching over the flocks out in the fields by night, after

LUKE 1, 2; PHILIPPIANS 2; ISAIAH 7; MATTHEW 1; DANIEL 9.

72, 73. (a) How did Jesus come to be born in Bethlehem, and what angelic announcement was made concerning his birth? (b) What human ancestry did he have?

which an army of angels appeared and said: "Glory in the heights above to God, and upon earth peace among men of good will." The shepherds followed directions and visited the newborn babe Jesus.

[73] So, through Mary, God's Son was born in David's line through Nathan. On the eighth day Jesus was circumcised as a member of the nation of Israel. On the fortieth day Joseph and Mary presented him as a firstborn in the temple at Jerusalem, and Joseph, who was of David's house through Solomon, adopted Jesus as his son, reinforcing Jesus' lineage in the royal house of David.

[74] Less than two years later, some astrologers in the east saw what appeared to be a star. They took it to announce the birth of the promised "king of the Jews." The "star" guided them to Jerusalem. King Herod of Jerusalem interviewed them. At his inquiry the Jewish priests and scribes told him that the Messiah or Christ was to be born in Bethlehem according to Micah's prophecy. So King Herod sent the astrologers there to locate the child and report back to him. First *now* the "star"

READ THE BIBLE RECORD AT LUKE 2, 3, MATTHEW 1, 2 AND MICAH 5.

74. Less than two years later, how was Jesus' life endangered, and how did it come about that he grew up in Nazareth?

led them to the house in Bethlehem and there they presented gifts to Jesus. God's angel warned them in a dream not to report back to Herod. Then God's angel appeared in a dream to Joseph and told him to take Jesus and Mary and flee, not to India, but down into Egypt. King Herod, disappointed by the astrologers, sent executioners to Bethlehem to slaughter all boys there "from two years of age and under." After King Herod the Great died, God's angel told Joseph to take his family back to the land of Israel. For safety's sake he did not return to Bethlehem in Judah but went back to Nazareth in Galilee.

75 When Jesus was twelve years old, Joseph and Mary took him

1-8-67

THIS INFORMATION IS DRAWN FROM THE BIBLE AT MATTHEW 2, LUKE 2.

75. When Jesus was twelve years old, where did Joseph and Mary find him after they had all attended the passover celebration in Jerusalem?

down from Nazareth to attend the passover celebration in Jerusalem. After the celebration they
found him in the temple discussing God's Word
with teachers there. To Joseph and Mary he said:
"Did you not know that I must be in the house of
my Father?" He returned with them to Nazareth
and became a carpenter like Joseph.

[76] At Rome Tiberius Caesar succeeded Augustus
on August 19 of 14 C.E. "In the fifteenth year of
the reign of Tiberius Caesar," or in spring of
29 C.E., God sent John the son of priest Zechariah,
to baptize Jews in symbol of their repentance and
to await the coming of "the Lamb of God that
takes away the sin of the world."

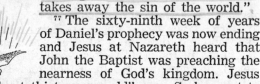

[77] The sixty-ninth week of years
of Daniel's prophecy was now ending
and Jesus at Nazareth heard that
John the Baptist was preaching the
nearness of God's kingdom. Jesus
"was about thirty years old" now. So he went to
John the Baptist at the Jordan River and had John
baptize him in water. As the baptized Jesus came
up out of the water the heavens appeared to open,
a dove descended toward him in symbol of the

descending of God's
spirit upon him, and
a voice came from
heaven, saying:
"This is my Son, the
beloved, whom I
have approved."
Thus "God anointed
him with holy spir-
it and power," and
Isaiah's prophecy
concerning the

MATT. 3; MARK 1, 6; LUKE 2, 3; JOHN 1; ACTS 10; DAN. 9; ISA. 61.

76. In what year did John begin to baptize, and his work was
in preparation for what?
77. When was Jesus baptized, and who did he prove to be?

anointing of God's greatest Prophet and Preacher began to be fulfilled. Thus Jesus became the Messiah, the Christ or Anointed One; and the sixty-ninth week of Daniel's prophecy ended, there in 29 C.E. The Promised Seed of God's "woman" had come to earth.

[78] By God's spirit Jesus Christ was now impelled to go into the wilderness to fast for forty days and to be put to a threefold test by Satan the Devil. He resisted the Devil's temptations, and then returned to John the Baptist at the Jordan River. John pointed him out as the "Lamb of God," and Jesus was approached by future disciples, first by Andrew and John the son of Zebedee, later by Peter. One day Jesus and his mother and disciples of his attended a wedding celebration. To meet an emergency Jesus here performed his first miracle, turning over a hundred gallons of water into the best of wine. The following spring he and disciples went up to Jerusalem for the passover festival. He now used his spiritual authority to cleanse the temple of commercial operations there being carried on.

[79] Under Jesus' direction his disciples began to baptize repentant Jews with John's baptism. Thereafter John the Baptist's public work ceased, when John condemned the incestuous marriage of the district ruler Herod Antipas with his half-brother Philip's wife.

[80] When Jesus heard of John's imprisonment, he retired to the Province of Galilee and began

ISA. 61; DAN. 9; MATT. 4, 14; MARK 1, 6; LUKE 3, 4; JOHN 1-3.

78. (a) Who endeavored to tempt Jesus, but without success? (b) What was Jesus' first miracle, and the following spring what did he do about commercial operations in the temple at Jerusalem?

79, 80. (a) After John the Baptist's public work ceased, what did Jesus begin to preach, and what prophecy of Isaiah did he apply to himself? (b) What kind of miracles did he perform?

preaching: "Repent, for the kingdom of the heavens has drawn near." Making a visit to his hometown of Nazareth, he attended the sabbath meeting in the synagogue and read to the audience Isaiah's prophecy concerning the anointing of Jehovah's Prophet and Preacher with holy spirit, and he declared this prophecy to be now fulfilled in him. There in Galilee his miracles of healing began, even leprosy, demon possession and paralysis being cured. He also called disciples away from their secular work to follow him continually.

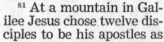

[81] At a mountain in Galilee Jesus chose twelve disciples to be his apostles as special witnesses of him. After that he gave his famous Sermon on the Mountain. His miracles now reached a climax in even raising the dead. Messengers from the imprisoned John the Baptist reached him, and, after sending the messengers back with answers to John's questions, he declared that John the Baptist was the messenger sent ahead to prepare the way, as foretold by the prophet Malachi, and that John was also the Elijah who Malachi said would come before the fiery day of Jehovah God.

MATTHEW 4-9, 11; MARK 1-3; LUKE 4-7; JOHN 4; MALACHI 3, 4.

81. (a) After choosing his twelve apostles, what famous sermon did Jesus give? (b) Whom did he declare John the Baptist to be?

[82] Jesus went from city to city and from village to village, preaching and teaching and using many illustrations or parables. To extend the campaign of preaching the nearness of God's kingdom, Jesus sent out his twelve apostles, two by two, to preach and heal.

[83] However, now came along the birthday of Herod Antipas the district ruler and, like a pagan, he celebrated with feasting and dancing. Here he was tricked into having the imprisoned John the Baptist beheaded in order to give his head to the captivating dancer, the daughter of his scheming wife Herodias. But Jesus became reunited with his twelve apostles, and kept up his preaching and doing powerful works. After he fed a crowd of 5,000 men, besides women and children, from but five barley loaves and two small fishes, the satisfied people wanted to make him king of the Jews; but Jesus left them, in refusal. It was after this that he walked on the waters of the Sea of Galilee to reach his disciples who were caught in rough weather. On an earlier occasion, when crossing the Sea of Galilee in a boat, he rebuked the winds and the raging waves and produced a sudden calm.

[84] In the course of the year 32 C.E. he came into the region of Caesarea Philippi. There he questioned his apostles as to his own identity, and Simon Peter acknowledged him to be "the Christ, the Son of the living God." Jesus then declared that he would build a congregation on a symbolic rock, and the gates of Ha'des would not overpower this congregation. He would also give to the apos-

MATTHEW 8-11, 13, 14, 16; MARK 4, 6, 8; LUKE 8, 9; JOHN 6.

82. Where did Jesus carry on his preaching and teaching, and how was the scope of the work extended?
83. (a) Did the execution of John the Baptist cause Jesus to quiet down in his preaching? (b) What further powerful works did he perform?
84. (a) On being questioned by Jesus, what did Simon Peter acknowledge concerning the identity of Jesus? (b) What did Jesus say about the building of a congregation, and what would he entrust to Peter?

tle Peter the keys, not to the gates of Ha'des, but to the kingdom of the heavens. Jesus then began to advise them of his own coming violent death and his resurrection on the third day.

[85] About a week later he took the disciples Peter, James and John up into a high mountain. Before their eyes he was gloriously transfigured, and there was a vision of the prophets Moses and Elijah talking with him. God's voice came from heaven, saying: "This is my Son, the beloved, whom I have approved; listen to him." When they were descending the mountain, Jesus told them to tell this vision to nobody till after his resurrection from the dead.

[86] Jesus continued teaching and performing miracles. After the Jewish festival of tabernacles in early autumn of the year he spread out the preaching campaign still more by sending out seventy other disciples, by twos, as evangelizers to preach the nearness of God's kingdom. The time was now approaching the middle of the seventieth week of years of Daniel's prophecy. Now Jesus' dear

friend Lazarus,
brother of Mary

MATTHEW 16, 17; MARK 9; LUKE 9, 10; JOHN 11; DANIEL 9.

85. About a week after this, what did three of Jesus' disciples see and hear when with Jesus in a mountain?
86. (a) In what way did Jesus spread out the preaching campaign later that year? (b) Lazarus had been buried how long when Jesus resurrected him?

and Martha of Bethany, fell sick and died and was entombed. He was already four days in the tomb when Jesus and his apostles arrived. He had the stone rolled away from the opening, and called, and Lazarus rose and came out. Now the enemy religious leaders wanted to kill, not only Jesus, but also the resurrected Lazarus.

[87] Before the passover season of 33 C.E. arrived, Jesus now went on a preaching tour through the regions of Samaria, Galilee and Perea. From Perea he crossed the Jordan River westward and proceeded toward Jerusalem. On the ninth day of the lunar month of Nisan he set out from nearby Bethany and made a triumphal ride into Jeru-

salem, in fulfillment of Zechariah's prophecy. On his way he stopped to view Jerusalem and foretell its terrible destruction. The next day he again cleansed the temple of commercial business.

[88] The chief priests and religious scribes now schemed to get Jesus and kill him. On Nisan 11 he publicly denounced the hypocritical scribes and Pharisees. While on a tour through the temple he foretold its destruction. Afterward, while he was

MATTHEW 19-24; MARK 10-13; LUKE 17-21; JOHN 11, 12; ZECHARIAH 9.

87. (a) Before the passover of 33 C.E., through what regions did Jesus make a preaching tour? (b) When making a triumphal ride into Jerusalem, what did Jesus foretell? (c) On the next day, what action did he again take in the temple?
88. Following a tour of the temple, what did Jesus tell his disciples as to the concluding of the present system of things?

on the Mount of Olives overlooking Jerusalem, four of his apostles asked him privately about some sign of the concluding of the present system of things. He foretold international war, famine, pestilence, earthquakes, lawlessness, persecution of his followers, an earth-wide preaching of the good news of God's kingdom, and a judgment period of his own followers, a separation of people of the nations like sheep and goats, and a time of trouble such as mankind had never known previously, bringing a complete end to this system of things.

[89] The religious leaders were planning Jesus' death. At this convenient time the apostle Judas turned traitor and arranged to betray Jesus to them for thirty pieces of silver. The passover night came, Nisan 14, with Jesus and his twelve apostles gathered in an upper room in Jerusalem. Jesus conducted the celebration and then dismissed Judas, who went out. With the eleven remaining

apostles Jesus then instituted a new supper, the Lord's supper, with unleavened bread to picture his sacrificed body and

READ MATTHEW 24-26, MARK 13, 14, LUKE 21, 22 AND JOHN 13.

89. (a) Who was it that schemed together to have Jesus put to death? (b) After the passover celebration, what new thing did Jesus institute with his faithful apostles, and what hope did he set before them?

with red wine to picture his shed blood. His blood, symbolized by the wine, would put into force God's new covenant as foretold by the prophet Jeremiah. Jesus also told the apostles that he would make a covenant with them for a place with him in God's heavenly kingdom, a kingdom covenant. He also promised to send to them holy spirit from heaven. After a final prayer with them Jesus led them out to the garden of Gethsemane.

[90] In Gethsemane Jesus went a short distance beyond his disciples and kneeled and prayed three times to his heavenly Father, asking that God's will take place. The traitor Judas Iscariot now arrived at the garden, leading an armed band. They seized Jesus and led him away, whereas his apostles fled. At the city house of Annas, a chief priest, Jesus was questioned. Then Annas sent Jesus to his son-in-law, the high priest Caiaphas. False witnesses were brought forward, and Jesus was accused of blasphemy and condemned to 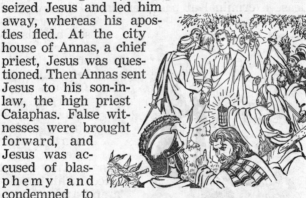 die. Meantime, outside, the apostle Peter denied Jesus three times, just as Jesus had foretold earlier when Peter was boasting. Later Judas in remorse threw down the money before the religious leaders and went and hanged himself.

[91] At dawn the Sánhedrin, the Supreme Court of Jerusalem, met, consulted together and then

MATT. 26, 27; MARK 14, 15; LUKE 22; JOHN 13-18; JER. 31; ACTS 1.

90-92. Where was Jesus arrested, and what kind of treatment was he given when brought before various religious and political officials?

had Jesus handed over to the Roman Governor Pontius Pilate. To him they accused Jesus of sedition.

⁹² Pilate's examination of Jesus showed him to be innocent and that his accusers had handed him over because of envy at his marvelous ministry. Even when the visiting Herod Antipas from Galilee was allowed to examine Jesus, he found no cause for the death penalty in Jesus. Back again before Pontius Pilate, Jesus declared that his kingdom was no part of this world and that he had come into the world to "bear witness to the truth." Pilate asked: "What is truth?" Authorized to release a criminal at passover time, Pilate wanted to release Jesus, but his accusers cried out for the robber Barabbas. Jesus was scourged and abused. Displaying him, Pilate said: "See! Your King!" The crowd cried for his impalement and yelled: "We have no king but Caesar." That settled matters!

⁹³ In due order the impalement of Jesus at Calvary or Skull Place followed. A condemned evildoer was impaled on either side of him. Turning sympathetic, one evildoer asked Jesus to remember him when, in resurrection, he came into his

THIS IS BASED ON MATTHEW 27, MARK 15, LUKE 23 AND JOHN 18, 19.

93, 94. With whom was Jesus impaled, and where was he buried?

kingdom. Jesus answered: "Truly I tell you today, You will be with me in Paradise."

94 Toward midafternoon Jesus died of a broken heart. A secret disciple, Joseph of Arimathea, got Pilate's permission to bury Jesus' body in a newly hewn tomb in a nearby garden. Next day, Nisan 15, the enemy religious leaders got Pilate's authorization to seal the stone closing the tomb and to station a soldier guard there, to prevent theft of the body. That was the weekly sabbath.

95 Early in the morning of Nisan 16, the third day of Jesus' death and burial, Almighty God raised his Son Jesus Christ from the dead, unseen to human eyes. There was an earthquake, and the guards saw a glorious angel descend and roll away the stone, to reveal an empty tomb. When the guards hurried away and reported the facts to the religious leaders, these bribed them to say that Jesus' disciples had stolen his body away by night.

96 In the course of that day the resurrected Jesus materialized hu-

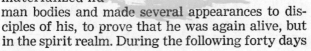

man bodies and made several appearances to disciples of his, to prove that he was again alive, but in the spirit realm. During the following forty days

CONSULT MATTHEW 27, 28, MARK 15, 16, LUKE 23, 24 AND JOHN 19, 20.

95, 96. (a) On the third day of Jesus' death, what action did God take on his behalf, and how did Jesus' disciples come to know this? (b) Before leaving them and ascending to heaven, what did Jesus tell his disciples that they should be?

he made appearances, on one occasion to as many as some five hundred Christian brothers. On the fortieth day he appeared and led his disciples to the top of the Mount of Olives. After telling them that they would receive holy spirit and would be witnesses of him to the most distant parts of the earth, he ascended heavenward and disappeared from their sight.

SPIRITUAL CONGREGATION ESTABLISHED

[97] As instructed, the disciples stayed in Jerusalem, and Matthias was chosen by lot to take the place of unfaithful Judas Iscariot.

[98] On Pentecost, or the fiftieth day from Jesus' resurrection, the promised holy spirit was poured out upon the 120 disciples in an upper room in Jerusalem, and they all began speaking with tongues that were foreign to them. Thousands of Pentecostal celebrators gathered to observe this spectacle. As the one to be given the keys of the

kingdom of the heavens, the apostle Peter addressed them and told them that what they saw and heard was a fulfillment of Joel's prophecy about the pouring out of God's spirit on all sorts of flesh in the later times. The Jesus whom the religious leaders had had killed on pass-

SEE 1 CORINTHIANS 15, LUKE 24, ACTS 1, 2, MATTHEW 16 AND JOEL 2.

97-99. (a) In Jerusalem, what occurred on Pentecost, as had been promised by Jesus? (b) To the fulfillment of what prophecies did the apostle Peter point on this occasion, and how did his listeners respond?

over day, God had raised from the dead, in fulfillment of David's psalm (16), and he was now
pouring out the spirit from heaven. David had also
foretold Jesus' exaltation to God's right hand in
heaven, in another psalm (110). Jesus, the Son or
descendant of David, had now become David's
Lord, for now God had "made him both Lord and
Christ."

[99] Many listeners repented at what they heard
and got baptized in water in the name of Jesus and
continued associating with the apostles of Jesus
Christ. About three thousand from among the
Jews and proselytes were added to the congregation that day, and they received holy spirit after
water baptism.

[100] On a later day the apostles Peter and John
cured a lame man at the "Beautiful" Gate of the
temple. To the crowd that gathered, Peter declared
that the miracle had been performed in Jesus'
name, and that Jesus was the Prophet long ago
foretold by the prophet Moses. God had raised
from the dead this Prophet like Moses and had
sent him to bless the people by turning them from
their sins.

[101] Many listeners believed, and the number of
believers became about five thousand. However,
for preaching the resurrection of Jesus the apostles
Peter and John were put in jail by the temple
authorities. The next day, after a trial, they were
released. The work of preaching and teaching and
the performance of miracles kept on. At this the
jealous religious leaders of Jerusalem seized all
the apostles and jailed them. But that night God's
angel released them and told them to go back to

THIS IS BASED ON THE BIBLE RECORD AT ACTS 2-5, DEUTERONOMY 18.

100, 101. (a) On a later day, what increase took place in the
number of believers? (b) What opposition did they now encoun-
ter, but how did God's angel take action on their behalf, and
what were the apostles determined to do?

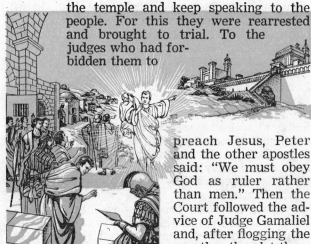

the temple and keep speaking to the people. For this they were rearrested and brought to trial. To the judges who had forbidden them to preach Jesus, Peter and the other apostles said: "We must obey God as ruler rather than men." Then the Court followed the advice of Judge Gamaliel and, after flogging the apostles, they let them go. But the apostles continued preaching daily at the temple and from house to house.

[102] In order to see to it that the Greek-speaking Jews were given the same "daily distribution" as the Hebrew-speaking Jews of the congregation in Jerusalem, the apostles had seven capable men appointed as assistants to them. Of those seven, Stephen got into lively discussion with the opposers. By force they took him before the Sánhedrin for trial. Here Stephen defended himself against the false testimony leveled against him. He pointed out that those judges were resisters of God's holy spirit and had become the murderers of "the righteous One." At the climax Stephen described the vision that he was having of the resurrected Jesus standing at God's right hand in the heavens. This was too much for the judges. So they stoned Ste-

READ THE DETAILED ACCOUNT AT ACTS 5-7 IN YOUR BIBLE.

102. Relate the events that led to Stephen's being stoned to death.

phen to death outside Jerusalem.

[103] Standing by approvingly as a witness to Stephen's stoning was a Pharisee named Saul of the city of Tarsus in Asia Minor. When great persecution now went ahead against the congregation, Saul took a leading part in it. Those who were scattered from Jerusalem went everywhere preaching the good news of God's Word. Stephen's fellow worker, Philip, went down to the city of Samaria and there brought about many conversions, followed by water baptism in Jesus' name. Peter and John were sent down to impart holy spirit to the baptized ones. Then God's angel directed Philip to a meeting with an Ethiopian eunuch on his way home from Jerusalem. Philip preached to him in his chariot. On driving alongside a body of water, the Ethiopian had Philip baptize him and then went on his way rejoicing.

[104] While Saul of Tarsus was on his way to Damascus of Syria to extend his persecutions there, he was encountered by the resurrected Jesus in a blinding vision. In answer to

ACTS 7-9 IS THE BASIS FOR THE INFORMATION SET OUT ABOVE.

103, 104. (a) How did the scattering of the disciples as a result of persecution affect the preaching of the good news? (b) What part did Saul of Tarsus have in this persecution, but how did he become a believer in Jesus?

his inquiry Saul was told: "I am Jesus, whom you are persecuting." For three days Saul continued blind in Damascus. Then a disciple named Ananias was sent to open Saul's eyes and encourage him to get baptized. He did so and became "filled with holy spirit." He joined the congregation there and began preaching Jesus, "that this One is the Son of God." Because unbelieving Jews plotted to kill him and kept watching the city gates, Paul had to escape by being lowered in a basket through an opening in the wall. He went back to Jerusalem, but because of attempts upon his life there he returned to Tarsus, his home city in Asia Minor.

[105] Meantime the apostle Peter traveled about preaching and performing cures, even raising the dead disciple Tabitha or Dorcas to life. While stopping at Joppa, he had a vision one noon, the purpose of which vision was summed up in these words to him: "You stop calling defiled the things God has cleansed." Peter was now told to go with three men just arriving from Caesarea. The Italian centurion Cornelius had yesterday had a vision in which an angel told him to send for Peter. So Peter, the one entrusted with the "keys of the kingdom of the heavens," went along to Caesarea and entered a Gentile home. There he preached to the uncircumcised Gentile Cornelius and those whom he had gathered into his house. These believed Peter's message, and, while he yet spoke, God's holy spirit fell upon these first uncircumcised Gentile believers and they began talking with foreign tongues. Then Peter "commanded them to be baptized in the name of Jesus Christ." At this event the seventieth week of years, as foretold by the prophet Daniel, concerning the

FOR FURTHER DETAILS READ ACTS 9, 10, MATTHEW 16 AND DANIEL 9.

105. (a) Explain how the first uncircumcised Gentiles came to be believers. (b) Of what time period did this mark the end?

special favor of the Abrahamic covenant to exclusively the circumcised Jews, ended. This was in the autumn of 36 C.E.

[106] Thereafter the message was preached to Gentiles and Jews alike. Then Barnabas, a Levite believer, went to Tarsus and brought Saul to Antioch of Syria. There they taught for a whole year. Here in Antioch of Syria the disciples of Jesus Christ were first called "Christians." About that time the apostle James was killed at Jerusalem, and King Herod Agrippa I threw the apostle Peter in prison to have him killed after the Jewish passover. However, God's angel delivered Peter from prison. Peter advised the brothers of God's answer to their prayers and went into hiding.

[107] Under instructions by means of holy spirit, the congregation at Antioch sent out Saul and Barnabas on a missionary tour. They went first to Cyprus and then up into Asia Minor into the Roman Province of Galatia. Many uncircumcised Gentiles as well as Jews believed. After exciting experiences, including a stoning of Saul, they returned to Antioch and made report. There a dispute arose over whether the Gentile converts

FOR A MORE DETAILED ACCOUNT SEE ACTS 11-14 AND GENESIS 12.

106. How did Saul come to be with the disciples in Antioch, and what did they come to be called first in this place?
107, 108. (a) Into what territory did Saul and Barnabas make a missionary tour? (b) Back in Antioch, what dispute arose over circumcision, and how was it settled?

should be circumcised in the flesh like the Jews. Saul, who had now come to be called Paul, and Barnabas and others were sent up to Jerusalem to have the matter settled there by the governing body. A young Gentile convert, Titus, accompanied Paul to Jerusalem. At this session of the apostles and other older men of the Jerusalem congregation Peter told of the conversion of the uncircumcised Cornelius, and Paul and Barnabas told of their experiences with Gentile converts.

[108] After that the disciple James, apparently the half brother of Jesus Christ, called this the fulfillment of the prophecy of Amos, that Jehovah God would take out of the non-Jewish nations a "people for his name." James then made known his own decision. The governing body acted and drew up a letter, saying that Gentile believers did not need circumcision but should keep from Gentile idolatry, Gentile eating and drinking of blood and sexual immorality.

[109] Paul and Barnabas took this letter to Antioch to read to the congregation. In a discussion with the apostles Peter (Cephas) and John and the disciple James, it had been agreed that Paul and Barnabas should go preaching to the uncircumcised Gentile nations, whereas they (Peter, John and James) should specialize on the circumcised Jews. Paul and Barnabas now thought of going back over the territory of their first missionary tour, but a disagreement between them caused a separation. Barnabas went with his cousin Mark to Cyprus, but Paul selected Silas (Silvanus) and proceeded through Syria and into Asia Minor. At Lystra he arranged for the young man Timothy, half-Jew, half-Greek, to accompany them in the missionary work. One night at Troas on the Ae-

FOR THIS PAGE AND THE NEXT, SEE ACTS 15-17, GALATIANS 2, AMOS 9.

109. On a further missionary tour, who came to be Paul's new traveling companions, and how did his experiences get recorded for us?

gean Sea, Paul had a vision of a European man, a Macedonian, beseeching him: "Step over into Macedonia and help us." Paul decided that to do this was God's will. It was at this point that Luke, a medical doctor, joined the missionary group and began to write Paul's experiences as contained in the Bible book, the Acts of the Apostles.

[110] By ship the missionary party reached the shores of Europe. At Philippi, the chief Macedonian city, Lydia and her household believed and got baptized and a congregation was established. Paul's casting a demon out of a girl employed professionally as a predictor of events led to the throwing of Paul and Silas into prison. At midnight an earthquake freed them, and the prison keeper asked how to be saved. He and his household believed and got baptized. Later the city magistrates came and brought them out from prison, because Paul and Silas were Roman citizens. After bidding the congregation good-bye, Paul and his party moved on to Thessalonica.

[111] Here a congregation was established. But the jealous Jews caused a riot in demonstration against Paul. The brothers sent him and Silas out to Beroea. Despite the interest here, the Jews in pursuit obliged Paul to leave here, and the brothers brought him to Athens, to

110-112. (a) How was their preaching received by the people in cities from Philippi down to Corinth? (b) What letters did Paul write while he was in Corinth, and why?

await the arrival of Silas and Timothy. Paul's speaking, not only in the Jewish synagogue, but also in the marketplace, resulted in his being brought before the high Athenian court atop Mars' Hill or the Areopagus. His powerful witness to God the Creator and to Jesus and his resurrection from the dead gained his dismissal, but one court judge, Dionysius, and others believed.

[112] Moving south to Corinth, Paul took up lodging with the Jewish couple Aquila and Priscilla, working part time as a tentmaker. While here, Paul wrote and sent his first letter to the Thessalonians, to comfort and build them up spiritually. He followed this up by a second letter, warning the Thessalonians, to stabilize them regarding Christ's second coming and the day of Jehovah, and warning them of the coming apostasy or falling away from the Christian faith. After teaching in Corinth for a year and a half and establishing a congregation, Paul was brought into court by the unbelieving Jews, but the case was thrown out of court.

[113] After some days Paul sailed east for Caesarea, making a stop at Ephesus in the Province of Asia and preaching there. From Caesarea he paid a visit to the congregation at Jerusalem and then returned to Antioch of Syria. Possibly from here Paul wrote his letter to the Galatian Christians, warning them against renouncing Christ by getting circumcised and thereby indebting themselves to keep the whole law of the prophet Moses, like natural circumcised Jews.

READ ACTS 17, 18, 1 THESS. 1-5, 2 THESS. 1-3, GAL. 1-6.

113. Possibly after his return to Antioch, what warning did Paul write to the Galatian Christians?

[114] On his third missionary tour Paul came back to Ephesus. He rebaptized twelve men who had been baptized with only the baptism of John the Baptist and imparted to them the gift of the holy spirit, so that they spoke with foreign tongues and prophesied.

[115] In Ephesus Paul worked for years, teaching and performing miracles. At last the makers of shrines to the goddess Artemis (Diana) gave vent to their resentment and stirred up a riot against Paul. The mob, crying out, "Great is Artemis of the Ephesians!" rushed to the theater, forcibly taking traveling companions of Paul along. In the theater the city recorder finally calmed them down and dismissed the irregular assembly. Paul decided to travel on to Macedonia, but it was from Ephesus that Paul wrote his first letter to the Corinthian Christians, to discourage the forming of sects among them and to answer their many vital questions. He also sent Titus there to help the Corinthians.

[116] Receiving word from Corinth through Titus, Paul in Macedonia wrote his second letter to the Corinthians, exposing their "superfine apostles" and defending his own genuine apostleship. Before returning East from Greece, Paul wrote his magnificent letter concerning Christian faith to the congregation of believers at Rome, telling them he wanted to stop and see them on his way to Spain.

[117] On his way eastward to Jerusalem, Paul preached in Troas and raised the accidentally killed Eutychus to life. He also stopped at Miletus and here had a farewell meeting with the congre-

---

ACTS 19, 20; 1 CORINTHIANS 1-16; 2 CORINTHIANS 1-13; ROMANS 1-16.

114-116. (a) Where did Paul spend much of the time on his third missionary tour, and with what results? (b) On what beneficial matters did he write to the Christians in Corinth and in Rome?
117, 118. (a) On his return to Jerusalem, how did Paul come to be imprisoned? (b) What were his experiences before the Jewish Sanhedrin and before the Roman governor Felix?

gation overseers of Ephesus, expecting to see them no more, and so reminding them of how he had taught them for three years "publicly and from house to house." After putting in port at Caesarea, Paul went up to Jerusalem. While he was in the temple to fulfill a vow, certain Jews recognized him and stirred up a mobbing. Roman soldiers from the nearby fortress rescued Paul. On his way up the stairs to the soldiers' quarters Paul gained permission to speak to the Jews from there in Hebrew. He explained how he had been converted to Christianity; but when he told them of his commission to preach to the Gentiles, the prejudiced Jews began rioting again.

[118] To prevent the Roman soldier from whipping him, Paul identified himself as a Roman citizen. Next day Paul was brought out to appear before the Jewish Sánhedrin of Jerusalem. Paul's identifying himself as a Pharisee and a believer in the resurrection split the Sánhedrin. To save Paul from being pulled to pieces by the contending sectarians, the soldiers grabbed him and took him back to their quarters. In the face of a plot of fanatical Jews to kill Paul, the military commander sent him under heavy guard down to Caesarea. Some days later the Jewish religious leaders came down to plead against Paul before the Roman governor, Felix. Before him Paul proved that he was innocent of stirring up a riot at Jerusalem but was a peaceable believer in the resurrection.

[119] Paul was kept in custody in Caesarea for two years, till Festus became successor to Governor Felix. At Jerusalem the Jewish religious leaders filed charges with Festus against Paul. Back at

READ ALSO THE DETAILED ACCOUNT IN THE BIBLE AT ACTS 20-25.

119. How long was Paul kept in custody in Caesarea, and, finally, to whom did he appeal his case?

THE TRUE-LIFE STORY AS TOLD BY THE HOLY BIBLE 105

Caesarea, Festus had Paul brought in to hear charges made by the Jews from Jerusalem. Paul again affirmed his innocence of any wrongdoing deserving of death, and concluded: "I appeal to Caesar!" Said Festus: "To Caesar you shall go."

[120] On a visit of King Herod Agrippa and his wife Bernice to Governor Festus at Caesarea, Festus arranged for the king to hear Paul. Then Paul related his religious background and told how he miraculously saw the resurrected Christ and was converted. Festus interrupted to say that Paul was going mad because of great learning. Paul denied and then addressed himself to King Agrippa, asking: "Do you, King Agrippa, believe the Prophets? I know you believe." Agrippa answered: "In a short time you would persuade me to become a Christian." Paul wished that he and others would do so. Afterward in discussion Festus and Agrippa agreed that Paul was innocent but, as he had appealed to Caesar, he had to see Caesar.

[121] During Paul's years of detention here at Caesarea, it appears, Luke the medical doctor wrote his life account of Jesus Christ, as addressed to Theophilus. When Paul was now put aboard ship for the voyage to Rome, Doctor Luke went along. While they were en route the Jewish fast day of atonement passed by, in the early fall of the year. Bad weather set in. So in the port of Fair Havens, Crete, Paul recommended that the ship pass the winter there. However, enticed by a soft south wind, the ship sailed on, only to run into a tempestuous wind. On the third day of the tempest they had to jettison the tackling of the

PROOF FOR THE ABOVE CAN BE FOUND AT ACTS 25-27 AND LUKE 1.

120. In what way did Paul make good use of the hearing he had before King Agrippa?
121-124. (a) What was Luke doing during the time of Paul's imprisonment? (b) Relate what happened while they were en route to Rome.

boat. Then for days they were tempest-tossed without benefit of sun or stars. During this time an angel of God appeared to Paul by night to say: "Have no fear, Paul. You must stand before Caesar, and, look! God has freely given you all those sailing with you." So Paul encouraged them all to eat something, for they were to suffer shipwreck on an island.

[122] On the fourteenth night the sailors took soundings and found they were being driven landward. The ship's anchors were cast off, and Paul told the sailors to stay aboard and not try to escape by a skiff; otherwise they would be lost. Then Paul led them all in taking food against the ordeal ahead. At daybreak the ship ran aground despite lightening the ship, and it began to be broken to pieces. In order to save Paul, the army officer would not let the soldiers kill the prisoners aboard. Then by swimming or by aid of floatable things all 276 passengers made it to land safely.

[123] It proved to be the island of Malta, south of Italy. The islanders showed these stranded people great kindness. Paul survived a snakebite and also healed the father of Publius, a principal man of Malta, after which many people came to Paul to be cured.

[124] Three months later the shipwreck survivors were able to sail away for Italy. In due time they landed at Puteoli (the modern Pozzuoli). Here the Christian congregation entertained Paul for seven days. The brothers in Rome heard of Paul's coming and came to the Market Place of Appius and Three Taverns to greet him. On seeing them Paul thanked God and was encouraged as he now entered Rome as a prisoner. There he was permitted to stay in a house of his own with soldiers to guard him.

THIS NARRATIVE IS DRAWN FROM THE BIBLE ACCOUNT AT ACTS 27, 28.

[125] Three days after arrival Paul was visited by principal Jews of Rome, because, said they, "as regards this sect it is known to us that everywhere it is spoken against." So a meeting was arranged for later, and then Paul gave the gathering a witness concerning God's kingdom and concerning Jesus. At this the Jews disagreed among themselves; only some believed. Hence Paul commented that the message of salvation had to go to the uncircumcised Gentiles: "They will certainly listen to it." Thus, for at least two years before coming to trial before Caesar, Paul witnessed to those visiting his lodging place, boldly preaching and teaching God's kingdom and the Lord Jesus Christ. All of Caesar's praetorian guard heard about him; of course, others did too. Even some of Caesar's own household be-  came believers, and the Roman congregation was greatly strengthened and emboldened by Paul's presence.

[126] Here at Rome Doctor Luke, Paul's companion, was able to write Theophilus and send him the complete account of the Acts of the Apostles. Also, while under house arrest and in bonds, Paul wrote

READ ALSO ACTS 28 AND PHILIPPIANS 1, 4 IN THE BIBLE.

125, 126. (a) To what good use did Paul put his time during the two years under guard in Rome before he came to trial? (b) What writing did Luke and Mark also do in Rome during this period?

letters, of which there still are copies, to the Ephesians, to the Philippians and to the Colossians; and he sent a runaway slave, Onesimus, now converted, back with a letter to his master Philemon. The inside evidence in the letter to the Hebrews is very strong that this too was written by Paul from Rome. John Mark, the cousin of Paul's former missionary partner Barnabas, visited Paul in Rome, and evidently while here Mark wrote his life account introduced with the words "The beginning of the good news about Jesus Christ." Later Mark rejoined the apostle Peter, in Babylon on the Euphrates River in Mesopotamia.

[127] God's angel had told Paul: "You must stand before Caesar." Those unbreakable words had to come true. The evidence from future developments is that Caesar (Nero) pronounced Paul innocent and let him go. Paul renewed his missionary activity, in association with Timothy and Titus, who were appointed to be regional overseers. After having left them at posts of duty, Paul wrote his first letter to Timothy and a similar letter of organizational instructions to Titus, both letters probably from Macedonia.

[128] In the meantime Jesus' half brother, the disciple James at Jerusalem, wrote his inspired letter "to the twelve tribes that are scattered about." As for the apostle Peter, he visited the ancient but declining city of Babylon on the Euphrates River, John Mark being with him there. From Babylon Peter wrote his first letter to the Christian "temporary residents scattered about in [the Asia Minor provinces of] Pontus, Galatia, Cappadocia, Asia, and Bithynia." Later, probably while still in ancient Babylon, Peter wrote his second letter, to

PHILEM.; COL. 4; MARK 1; 1 PET. 1, 5; ACTS 27; 1 TIM. 1; JAS. 1.

127. What apparently happened when Paul was brought to trial before Caesar, and so what activity did he renew afterward?
128. In the meantime, what were the disciple James and the apostle Peter doing?

possessors of the same Christian faith. In it Peter writes of "our beloved brother Paul" and classes Paul's writings with "the rest of the Scriptures."

[129] When next we hear from the apostle Paul he is evidently in prison in Rome, due to make his final defense before Caesar, this time apparently as a criminal offender against the Roman Empire. Doctor Luke alone is attending upon him. From here Paul writes his second letter to Timothy, saying in its conclusion: "The due time for my releasing is imminent. I have fought the fine fight, I have run the course to the finish, I have observed the faith." Whether before this he had extended his missionary work into Spain, Paul does not say. But probably about this time, in the Near East in Palestine, the disciple Jude, the younger brother of James the half brother of Jesus Christ, wrote his letter "to the called ones who are loved in relationship with God the Father and preserved for Jesus Christ." It is somewhat similar to Peter's last letter.

[130] However, now the prophetic words of Jesus Christ, spoken back in the year 33 C.E., concerning the terrible destruction of Jerusalem and its temple were nearing fulfillment. At this time his words applied to his disciples in Jerusalem and the province of Judea, to flee out of the entire province after they see Jerusalem for a time surrounded by enemy armies, that they might take refuge in the mountains on the other side of the Jordan River and there continue their Christian ministry. Jesus' inspired words came true in 70 C.E., when, according to worldly history, the Roman armies under General Titus destroyed

INFORMATION IS FROM 2 PETER 3, 2 TIMOTHY 1-4, JUDE AND LUKE 21.

129. (a) How did Paul apparently come to be imprisoned in Rome a second time, and what did he write to his fellow worker Timothy at this time? (b) Back in Palestine, to whom did the disciple Jude address a letter about this time?
130. In fulfillment of Jesus' words, what happened to Jerusalem in the year 70 C.E., and of what did this give assurance?

Herod's temple and the rebellious city of Jerusalem, from which the Christians had obediently fled to other provinces. In the year 73 C.E. the last Jewish stronghold in the Province of Judea, the fortress of Masada on the west side of the Dead Sea, fell to the Roman conquerors. This fulfillment of Jesus' words gave strong assurance that the rest of Jesus' prophecy concerning the many-featured "sign" that would mark the "conclusion of the system of things" would unfailingly come true.

[131] Ever since the last days of the apostle Paul, Rome had become an enemy and persecutor of the apostles of Jesus Christ and the rest of his disciples. Thus in process of time, likely toward the end of the first century C.E., the aged apostle John found himself a prisoner on Rome's penal island of Patmos in the Aegean Sea, "for speaking about God and bearing witness to Jesus." Here John was favored with the "revelation by Jesus Christ, which God gave him, to show his slaves the things that must shortly take place."

[132] The things that John saw in miraculous vision he was told to write down, sending an account thereof to the Christian congregations in Ephesus, Smyrna, Pergamum, Thyatira, Sardis, Philadelphia and Laodicea. That John would be freed from his exile on the isle of Patmos seems to be indicated by the words said to John after he had eaten the little opened scroll at an angel's hand: "You must prophesy again with regard to peoples and nations and tongues and many kings."

[133] Apparently after this, the apostle John wrote his life account of the Lord Jesus Christ, that the readers thereof "may believe that Jesus is the

MATTHEW 24, 25; MARK 13; LUKE 21; REVELATION 1-22; JOHN 1-21.

131. Toward the end of the first century C.E., why was the aged apostle John confined on the penal island of Patmos, and with what was he favored while there?
132, 133. To whom did John write the things he there saw in vision, and what further writing did he do apparently after his release?

Christ the Son of God, and that, because of believing, you may have life by means of his name." In the closing lines John speaks of himself as a witness and says: "We know that the witness he gives is true." In this same closing period of John's life he wrote three letters, the second being directed to "the chosen lady," and the third to "Gaius, the beloved." John hoped to see Gaius shortly.

[134] Thus, by the "revelation by Jesus Christ" that was given to John on the isle of Patmos, the words of the resurrected Jesus concerning John as uttered back in the spring of 33 C.E. virtually came true: "If it is my will for him to remain until I come, of what concern is that?" By those words, however, Jesus did not mean that John would not die the same as the rest of the Christian believers. In the final revelation to John a vision was given of the glorified congregation of 144,000 faithful disciples of Jesus Christ, standing in Kingdom power with Jesus Christ on the heavenly Mount Zion. There was also seen a "great crowd" of earthly worshipers of God, these being without known number and being taken from "all nations and tribes and peoples and tongues." The heavenly Lamb, Jesus Christ, becomes their shepherd and "will guide them to fountains of waters of life."

[135] In the revelation John was also given a vision of the birth in heaven of God's Messianic kingdom, over which fact the Gentile nations on earth became angry, "wrathful." For this reason God's own wrath comes upon them. At that time, by means of war, Satan the Devil and his demons are cast out of heaven and then carry on a war with the remaining ones of the seed of God's "woman."

JOHN 20, 21; 1 JOHN 1-5; 2 JOHN; 3 JOHN; REV. 1, 7, 11, 12, 14.

134. In the revelation given to John, where did he see the congregation of 144,000 faithful disciples of Jesus, and what "great crowd" was he also shown?
135. A vision of what birth was also seen by John, followed by what events on earth?

THE EARTHLY LINE OF DESCENT OF THE SON

(The Ones Directly in the Line of Descent

ADAM

Cain   Abel   **SETH**   "sons and daughters"

ENOSH   "sons and daughters"

KENAN   "sons and daughters"

MAHALALEL   "sons and daughters"

JARED   "sons and daughters"

ENOCH (Prophet)   "sons and daughters"

METHUSELAH   "sons and daughters"

LAMECH (Prophet)   "sons and daughters"

NOAH   "sons and daughters"

Japheth   **SHEM**   Ham (father of Canaan and of Cush, the father of Nimrod, King)

ARPACHSHAD (CAINAN)   Elam   Asshur   Lud   Aram   Uz   Hul   Gether   Mash

SHELAH   "sons and daughters"

EBER   "sons and daughters"

PELEG   Joktan   "sons and daughters"

REU   "sons and daughters"

SERUG   "sons and daughters"

NAHOR   "sons and daughters"

TERAH   "sons and daughters"

Nahor   Haran   **ABRAM (ABRAHAM)**   Sarai (Sarah), daughter

Ishmael   **ISAAC**   Zimran   Jokshan   Medan   Midian   Ishbak   Shuah

Esau   **JACOB (ISRAEL)**

Reuben   Levi   **JUDAH**   Dan   Naphtali   Asher   Zebulun   Benjamin
Simeon   Gad   Issachar   Joseph   Dinah, daughter

Er   Shelah   **PEREZ**   Zerah   Manasseh
Onan   Ephraim

HEZRON   Hamul

Jerahmeel   **RAM**   Chelubai

AMMINADAB

NAHSHON

(SALMON) SALMA   Elimelech(?)   So-and-So(?)

BOAZ

OBED

JESSE

(1) Nebaioth, (2) Kedar,
(3) Adbeel, (4) Mibsam,
(5) Mishma, (6) Dumah,
(7) Massa, (8) Hadad,
(9) Tema, (10) Jetur,
(11) Naphish, (12) Kedemah;
and a daughter Mahalath,
who married Esau

Eliab   Abinadab   Shimea   Nethanel   Raddai   Ozem   (?)   **DAVID (King)**   (Zeruiah, Abigail, daughter) daughter

Amnon   Shobab   **NATHAN**   Solomon   Elishua   Jerimoth
Chileab   Shammua   (Shimea)   (King)   (Elishama)   Eliphelet
(Daniel)   Ibhar   Eliphelet   Eliada
Absalom   (Shimea)   **MATTATHA**   Nogah   Elishama
Ithream   Rehoboam   Nepheg   Japhia
Adonijah   Shephatiah   **MENNA**   (King)   Tamar, daughter

MELEA

1,000 B.C.

MARY   JOSEPH

OF GOD AS THE SEED OF GOD'S "WOMAN"
Being Indicated by Bold Capital Letters)

MARY   *JOSEPH*

ELIAKIM	Abijah (King)	27 other sons	60 daughters
JONAM	Asa (King)		
JOSEPH	Jehoshaphat (King)		
JUDAS	Jehoram (King)	6 other sons	
SYMEON	Ahaziah (King)	42 older brothers	Jehoshabeath, daughter
LEVI	Jehoash (King)		
MATTHAT	Amaziah (King)	other sons	daughters
JORIM	Uzziah (Azariah, King)		
ELIEZER	Jotham (King)		
JESUS	Ahaz (King)	*Joshua in Hebrew*	
ER	Hezekiah (King)	sons (sacrificed to Baal)	
ELMADAM	Manasseh (King)		
COSAM	Amon (King)	sons (sacrificed to idols)	
ADDI	Josiah (King)		
MELCHI	Johanan Eliakim (Jehoiakim, King)	Jehoahaz (Shallum, King)	Mattaniah (Zedekiah, King)
NERI	Jechoniah (Jehoiachin, King)		

SHEALTIEL	**SHEALTIEL**	Malchiram	Shenazzar	Hoshama
ZERUBBABEL	**ZERUBBABEL** (Governor)	Pedaiah	Jekamiah	Nedabiah
	Hananiah (1 Chronicles 3: 19, 21)			

RHESA	
JOANAN	
JODA	Abiud
JOSECH	Eliakim
SEMEIN	
MATTATHIAS	
MAATH	
NAGGAI	
ESLI	Azor
NAHUM	
AMOS	
MATTATHIAS	Zadok
JOSEPH	Achim
JANNAI	Eliud
MELCHI	Eleazar
LEVI	Matthan
MATTHAT	Jacob
HELI	
MARY (virgin)	Joseph (foster father of Jesus)

> The Only Complete
> Genealogy in All
> Human History —
>
> The Last Genealogy
> Recorded in the
> Holy Scriptures
>
> See Luke 3: 23-38.

JESUS, "Son of God"	James	Joseph	Simon	Judas	daughters

[136] As in the prophet Daniel's vision that used wild beasts as symbols of the political world powers, John sees Satan's worldwide system of political rule under the symbol of a wild beast with seven heads and ten diademed horns. A two-member political system is pictured as a two-horned, one-headed beast that urges the worship of the seven-headed beast. It finally brings about the making of an image of the many-membered system of political rule pictured by the seven-headed beast. God's wrath is against these beastly political systems and the idolatrous "image of the wild beast." So God does not bless them but plagues them terribly.

[137] While God's plagues are being poured out upon them, John sees all the Gentile nations, their kings and their armies, marching to the "war of the great day of God the Almighty" at Har–Magedon, under the influence of the Dragon, Satan the Devil, and his demons. Then John sees God's judgment upon Babylon the Great, the world empire of false Babylonish religion. She commits reli-

gious fornication with earth's political rulers, to the oppression of the peoples. She rides a beast of scarlet color like the seven-headed, ten-horned

SEE THE BIBLE RECORD AT REVELATION 13, 15-17 AND DANIEL 7, 8.

136. With what symbols did John see political systems represented, and who expresses wrath against them?
137, 138. (a) To what end does Babylon the Great come, as seen by John, and so what does God tell his people to do? (b) What follows for the political systems of earth and their supporters? (c) How are the Devil and his demons dealt with?

wild beast. Finally all this political combination turns against religious Babylon the Great and destroys her. After that the political combination wars against the kingdom of the heavenly Lamb of God, the "Lord of lords and King of kings."

[138] In view of the coming destruction of Babylon the Great, God urgently tells his people to get out of her, and then gives a vision of her sudden, swift destruction. At her destruction all heavenly creatures will cry Hallelujah, meaning "Praise Jah, you people." The "war of the great day of God the Almighty" follows at Har–Magedon, and his King of kings destroys the whole political combination on earth, killing off all the political rulers, their military armies and all their supporters and servants. Immediately following that the Dragon, Satan the Devil, and his demons are seized, chained and imprisoned in an abyss for a thousand years.

[139] The "first resurrection" is seen, namely, that of those faithful disciples who will reign with Christ in heaven for those thousand years, also serving as judges and as "priests of God and of the Christ." The resurrection of the "rest of the dead" takes place on earth, from Ha'des and the sea, and they have their judgment before God's throne. At the end of the thousand years Satan and his demons are let loose from the abyss and are permitted to test out mankind. Those on earth who then side in with Satan and revolt against God's kingdom, the "heavenly Jerusalem," do not get their names written in the "book of life" and are destroyed in the "lake of fire," a symbol of "the second death." This leaves the earth occupied by only those enrolled in the "book of life." Satan

CONFIRMATION OF THIS IS FOUND AT REVELATION 17-20 AND LUKE 8.

139. (a) Who are seen resurrected from the dead? (b) What test comes upon mankind at the end of the thousand years, and then what will happen to Satan and all who join him in revolt against God's kingdom?

and his demons are then also destroyed forever, in "second death."

[140] When Satan and his demons were chained and hurled into the abyss after the battle of Har-Magedon a thousand years previous to their destruction, a "new heaven and a new earth" came into existence. The marriage time came for the symbolic Bride of Christ, namely, the congregation of his 144,000 faithful disciples who become his heavenly joint heirs. The Bride, "the Lamb's wife," is pictured as a glorious city, named New Jerusalem, coming down out of heaven to bless mankind. God then wipes out the tears of sorrow from the people's eyes, and even the death inherited by all mankind from the sinful Adam "will be no more."

[141] The New Jerusalem is made to shine by the glory of God the Almighty and his Lamb Jesus Christ. By means of the light from the New Jerusalem the nations here on earth will walk. Through New Jerusalem God's provision for life everlasting on earth will flow to mankind, like a "river of water of life, clear as crystal, flowing out from the throne of God and of the Lamb." As it were, life-sustaining fruit trees line both banks of the symbolic river.

[142] The Permanent Heir of ancient King David says to John: "I, Jesus, sent my angel to bear witness to you people of these things for the congregations. I am the root and the offspring of David, and the bright morning star." Thus the genealogy of the Seed of God's "woman" through the royal house of David reaches its goal.

REVELATION 20-22 AND MATTHEW 25 ARE THE BASIS FOR THIS RECORD.

140, 141. (a) A thousand years before this, after Satan and his demons were abyssed, what happy event took place in heaven? (b) What is the New Jerusalem, and what blessings does God bestow upon mankind by means of it?
142. As the revelation draws to a conclusion, how is attention again drawn to the Seed of God's "woman" through the royal house of David?

[143] The "words of the prophecy" of this Revelation to John are not to be sealed up, "for the appointed time is near." Harmoniously with this fact the apostle John makes this observation: "And the spirit and the bride keep on saying: 'Come!' And let anyone hearing say: 'Come!' And let anyone thirsting come; let anyone that wishes take life's water free." To preserve the pureness and correctness of the "prophecy of this scroll," no addition is to be made to it nor anything taken away from it, under penalty of plagues and destruction. Jehovah's great Witness, Jesus Christ, finally says to John: "Yes; I am coming quickly." John replies: "Amen! Come, Lord Jesus." Then the last book of the Bible closes with the words: "May the undeserved kindness of the Lord Jesus Christ be with the holy ones."

REVELATION 22 IS THE INSPIRED RECORD ON WHICH THIS IS BASED.

---

143. With what assurance and prayerful request does this last book of the Bible close?

CHAPTER 4

When "All the Sons of God Began Shouting in Applause"

HERE was once a time when there was no earth nor any sun, moon and stars to shine upon it. There was then no material universe, of which our small earth is a part, in boundless space. And yet life existed somewhere. Where? In the realm that is invisible to us who are made of earthly material, a realm that we cannot feel or touch. It is a realm that is higher than our human, materialistic realm. For that reason the Holy Bible calls it "heaven" or "the heavens." Life in the heavenly realm is also of a higher order than that of man here on earth.

² It is in the heavens invisible to us that God the Creator lives. In the one hundred and fifteenth psalm it is written: "As regards the heavens, to Jehovah the heavens belong, but the earth he has given to the sons of men." (Psalm 115:16) In psalm eleven, verse four says: "Jehovah—in the heavens is his throne. His own eyes behold, his own beaming eyes examine the sons of men."

1. Before there was a material universe, where did life exist?
2. Where does God the Creator live, as explained by psalms in the Bible?

118

[3] To show how lowly our earthly home is in comparison with God's heavenly realm, it is written, in Isaiah 66:1: "This is what Jehovah has said: 'The heavens are my throne, and the earth is my footstool.' " He is the Creator of our material universe, more and more of which our astronomers with their tremendous telescopes are able to see. So He existed and enjoyed life before our material universe began. As the Holy Bible says at its very start: "In the beginning God created the heavens and the earth."—Genesis 1:1.

[4] God is the source of all life outside of himself. Psalm 36:9 admits this fact, saying to God: "With you is the source of life." The prophet Moses recognized that the living God had no beginning, even as he will have no end, when he wrote: "O Jehovah, you yourself have proved to be a real dwelling for us during generation after generation. Before the mountains themselves were born, or you proceeded to bring forth as with labor pains the earth and the productive land, even from time indefinite to time indefinite you are God."—Psalm 90:1, 2.

[5] Not only did our material universe as a creation have a start, but creation in the invisible realm of heaven also had a beginning. The everliving God was before even such heavenly creation, and at that time he was all alone. The time came when God decided to create. He began by creating living things. What did he create first? His own Word tells us. To us he says: " 'The thoughts of you people are not my thoughts, nor are my ways your ways,' is the utterance of Jehovah. 'For as the heavens are higher than the earth, so my ways are higher than your ways, and my thoughts than your thoughts.' " (Isaiah 55:8, 9) So God did not follow any unrealistic idea

---

3. How did the material universe come into existence?
4. Did God have a beginning?
5. (a) Were the first things created by God living or were they lifeless? (b) What form of creature life did God make first?

like that of "evolutionists" and start with the lowest and most simple form of life, of earthly material. Instead, he started with the highest form of creature life, a heavenly one. He made it the best living creation in all existence.

⁶ Just as with a human father and his firstborn son, "that one is the beginning of his generative power," so it was with the great Creator and his first heavenly creation. It was the "beginning of his generative power." (Deuteronomy 21:17) Or, as the patriarch Jacob said of his firstborn son Reuben: "You are my first-born, my vigor and the beginning of my generative power, the excellence of dignity and the excellence of strength." (Genesis 49:3) So the "right of the first-born's position" belonged to God's first heavenly creature. This first creation of God came to be called "his only-begotten Son."—John 3:16.

⁷ Here a Moslem will recognize that there is a difference between the Koran and the Holy Bible, and he will have to choose which book he will accept as true in this regard. The Koran, in its Sura XVII, verse 111, says: "Say: 'Praise be to God, who begets no son, and has no partner in (His) dominion: nor (needs) He any to protect Him from humiliation: yea, magnify Him for His greatness and glory.'" And in Sura CXII, verses 1-4, it says: "Say: He is God, the One and Only, God, the Eternal, Absolute; He begetteth not, nor is He begotten; and there is none like unto Him."*

⁸ However, it was the prophet Jesus Christ, who, six hundred years before the Koran, said: "God

---

* Quoted from "The Holy Koran—Text, Translation and Commentary," by Abdullah Yusuf Ali, the edition of 1946 in two volumes.

6. How was the first heavenly creation like a firstborn son, and what kind of Son is he called at John 3:16?
7, 8. (a) Does the Moslem Koran agree that God has begotten a Son? (b) How long before the Koran did the prophet Jesus Christ declare that God has an "only-begotten Son," and what hope did he associate with the exercising of faith in that one?

loved the world so much that he gave his only-begotten Son, in order that everyone exercising faith in him might not be destroyed but have everlasting life. For God sent forth his Son into the world, not for him to judge the world, but for the world to be saved through him. He that exercises faith in him is not to be judged. He that does not exercise faith has been judged already, because he has not exercised faith in the name of the only-begotten Son of God." (John 3:16-18) Hence for six centuries before the Koran was written, true worshipers of the one, living and true God were exercising faith in the "only-begotten Son of God," to gain salvation. Did they believe wrong?

[9] This "only-begotten Son of God" took the "first-born's position" in all of God's creation, and rightfully so. As the "beginning of [God's] generative power" he would excel all future creation in dignity, strength and wisdom. He was the embodiment of God's wisdom, and because of this the words of Proverbs 8:22-31, where Wisdom is portrayed as speaking to us as learners, are generally applied to the "only-begotten Son of God," as follows:

[10] "Jehovah himself produced me as the beginning of his way, the earliest of his achievements of long ago. From time indefinite I was installed, from the start, from times earlier than the earth. When there were no watery deeps I was brought forth as with labor pains, when there were no springs heavily charged with water. Before the mountains themselves had been settled down, ahead of the hills, I was brought forth as with labor pains, when as yet he had not made the earth and the open spaces and the first part of the dust masses of the productive land. When he prepared the heavens I was there; when he decreed a hori-

---

9, 10. To whom are the words of Proverbs 8:22-31 generally applied, and why?

zon upon the face of the watery deep, when he made firm the cloud masses above, when he caused the fountains of the watery deep to be strong, when he set for the sea his decree that the waters themselves should not pass beyond his order, when he decreed the foundations of the earth, then I came to be beside him as a master worker, and I came to be the one he was specially fond of day by day, I being glad before him all the time, being glad at the productive land of his earth, and the things I was fond of were with the sons of men."

[11] Notice that here wisdom personified is spoken of, not as the beginner or originator, but as the "beginning" of God's way. Wisdom personified is also the "earliest" of God's achievements. According to this language the "only-begotten Son of God" was the "beginning" of God's way and there was no achievement by God earlier than this "only-begotten Son." This language is like what is said in Revelation 3:14. In fact, Proverbs 8:22 is quoted from in Revelation 3:14, where the glorified Son of God in heaven says regarding himself: "These are the things that the Amen says, the faithful and true witness, the beginning of the creation by God." According to his own words he was the "beginning" (not, beginner) of God's creation, so that God's creating of creatures began with this Son.

[12] For this reason God, whose personal name is Jehovah, stands out as the One Creator and all other things are what he created. In harmony with this truth, Revelation 4:9-11 reports the creatures in the invisible heavens as saying to God: "You are worthy, Jehovah, even our God, to receive the glory and the honor and the power, because you

---

11. (a) How does the scripture just quoted from Proverbs, chapter 8, show whether the one speaking was the originator of God's creation or was himself created? (b) In Revelation what application is made of Proverbs 8: 22?
12. So what exclusive position does Jehovah God occupy in relation to all other things?

created all things, and because of your will they existed and were created."

IS SOMETHING BEGOTTEN A CREATION?

[13] However, there are many students of the Holy Bible who have difficulty in understanding the "only-begotten Son of God" to be also a creation. They say that he was begotten by God but was not created and that he was the beginner or origin of the creation of God rather than the "beginning of the creation of God." (Revelation 3:14, *AV; AS; RS*) Well, then, was there some female person in heaven by whom Jehovah God *begot* his only-begotten Son? If there were, then that female person would have to be before the only-begotten Son of God. But the Holy Bible does not teach such a thing. Rather, the only-begotten Son was the original and first direct creation by God without any intermediary such as a wife or female person. Also, because of begetting, we are not to imagine that God has a womb like a female person. God is not female.

[14] What does the word "beget" mean in the original Hebrew and common Greek? Look it up in the dictionary. It says that "beget" means "to procreate or generate (used chiefly of the male parent); to cause; produce as an effect." (*The American College Dictionary*, 1948 edition) The word "only-begotten" (*monogenés*, Greek) means *"the only member of a kin or kind:* hence, generally, *only, single; unique."* And the Greek word (*gennáo*) translated as "beget" means, according to the Greek-English Lexicon, "mostly of the father, *beget;* of the mother, *bring forth, bear;* in

13. (a) What do many students have difficulty in understanding about the "only-begotten Son of God"? (b) Why would it be wrong to conclude that God begot his only-begotten Son by some female person in heaven?
14. Define (a) "beget," also (b) "only-begotten."

the Middle Voice, *produce from oneself, create; produce, grow;* metaphorically, *engender, produce; call into existence."*

[15] The inspired Hebrew Scriptures speak of giving birth to things that are not even persons or animals. For example, Proverbs 27:1 warns us: "Do not make your boast about the next day, for you do not know what a day *will give birth to."* Also, Isaiah 55:10 says: "The pouring rain descends, and the snow, from the heavens and does not return to that place, unless it actually saturates the earth and *makes it produce* and sprout." Isaiah 59:4 says: "There has been a conceiving of trouble, and a *bringing* of what is hurtful *to birth."* Job 38:28 says: "Does there exist a father for the rain, or who *gave birth to* the dewdrops?" Also, in the first book of the Holy Bible, or in Genesis 2:4, the prophet Moses writes: "These are the generations† of the heavens and of the earth when they were created, on the day that the LORD God made earth and heaven." (I. Leeser's translation) Who generated those heavens and that earth? The LORD God. Shall we, then, call God the *Father* of the heavens and the earth, because he is the generator of them?

[16] We do not usually do so, because the heavens and the earth are impersonal. Rather, in harmony with the further words of Genesis 2:4, we call him the Creator of the heavens and the earth. So here the things generated are his creations. Just be-

---

* Column 1, page 344, of Volume 1, of *A Greek-English Lexicon,* compiled by H. G. Liddell and Robert Scott, revised, reprinted 1948.

† The Hebrew word for "generations" is derived from the verb *yalád,* which means "to bear, bring forth"; in passive voice, "to be brought forth; to be born."

15, 16. (a) How do the inspired Hebrew Scriptures use "give birth to" and related expressions? (b) "Giving birth to" actually can mean what?

cause the heavens and the earth are called "generations," we cannot say that they are not creations. In harmony with his language in Genesis 2:4 the prophet Moses says, in Psalm 90:1, 2: "Lord! a dwelling-place hast thou become to us from generation to generation: before the mountains *were born* or thou hadst brought forth [marginal reading: 'Or, "given birth to" '] the earth and the world, even from age unto age thou wast God."* Just because the Lord God gave birth to the mountains and to the earth and the world, we cannot say that these earthly things are not his creations. So here, with reference to God's work, "giving birth to" has the meaning of "creating."

[17] In like manner the "only-begotten Son of God" can speak of himself as being the "beginning of the creation of God." God his heavenly Father begot him in the sense that God produced him from himself without any intermediary and thus created him. As one who is begotten or generated or who is created, the "only-begotten Son" had a beginning to his life and existence. Because he was created like God or in resemblance of God, rather than created as some lifeless creation, he was called the Son of God and so God was his Father or Begetter. He was not then brought forth or created as a human, earthly creature, but was created as a spirit creature, becoming a spirit person like his heavenly Father. On earth the Prophet Jesus Christ said: "God is a Spirit [or, God is spirit], and those worshiping him must worship with spirit and truth." (John 4:24) The "only-begotten Son of God" was like God his heavenly Father in being spirit and thus being superhuman.

---

* Quoted from *The Emphasised Bible,* by Jos. B. Rotherham, edition of 1902. See also the *New World Translation of the Holy Scriptures.*

---

17. In what sense did God *beget* his "only-begotten Son," and why was it appropriate that he be called the *Son* of God?

OTHER SONS OF GOD IN HEAVEN

[18] Are Jehovah God and the "only-begotten Son of God" the only inhabitants of the invisible, spiritual heavens? No! The Holy Bible speaks of numberless other living, intelligent inhabitants of the heavens. For example, the prophet Daniel tells of a supernatural vision in the sixth century B.C.E. and says: "I kept on beholding until there were thrones placed and the Ancient of Days sat down. . . . There were a thousand thousands that kept ministering to him, and ten thousand times ten thousand that kept standing right before him." (Daniel 7:9, 10) Over six centuries later the apostle John had a supernatural vision of God's throne and of God's Son who was offered like a lamb in sacrifice; and John describes it in this way: "I saw, and I heard a voice of many angels around the throne and the living creatures and the older persons, and the number of them was myriads of myriads and thousands of thousands, saying with a loud voice: 'The Lamb that was slaughtered is worthy.'" (Revelation 5:11, 12) How did all those millions of heavenly angels come into existence? The Holy Bible explains.

[19] Recall how Proverbs 8:30 quoted Wisdom personified as saying: "I came to be beside him as a master worker." So the wise "only-begotten Son" of God became a master worker beside the great Creator Jehovah God. His heavenly Father did not leave him idle but used him in the producing of all other things living and lifeless. Concerning this "master worker," who was at the side of God the Creator, the words of John 1:1-3 have this to say, according to *An American Translation:* "In the beginning the Word existed. The Word was with God, and the Word was divine. It was he that was with God in the beginning. Everything came into

18. How does the Bible make clear that there are other inhabitants of the invisible, spiritual heavens?
19. How did all those heavenly angels come into existence?

existence through him, and apart from him nothing came to be."*

20 The apostle Paul calls attention to this heavenly "master worker" who was used by God the Creator, in his letter to the Colossians, chapter one, verses fifteen through seventeen, which read: "He is the image of the invisible God, the first-born of all creation; for in him all things were created, in heaven and on earth, visible and invisible, whether thrones or dominions or principalities or authorities—all things were created through him and for him. He is before all things, and in him all things hold together."—Revised Standard Version of the Bible, of 1952.

21 This "master worker" was and is the "image of the invisible God," and so he imitated God his Father in His work. As the "only-begotten Son of God" he was the "first-born of all creation," so that all other created things followed him and were created by God "through him and for him," since he, as God's "first-born," was the Heir of all things. Because all these other creations were brought into existence "through him," this "first-born" Son of God remained in a unique position, forasmuch as he remained the only Son who was created or begotten directly by God the Creator. Thus he remained "only-begotten," the only direct creation of Jehovah God.

22 That is how these millions of angels of God came into existence. Even though they were created *through* the "only-begotten Son," they were still called "sons of God," because their life

---

* Quoted from *The Complete Bible—An American Translation*, by J. M. Powis Smith and Edgar J. Goodspeed, twelfth impression of 1948. For further discussion of John 1:1-3, see chapter 12, pages 261 (¶13)-269 (¶34).

20, 21. What do we learn about this heavenly "master worker" at Colossians 1: 15-17?
22. Why are the angels fittingly called "sons of God," and what should we keep in mind as to their makeup?

came from Jehovah God, with whom is the fountain or source of life. (Psalm 36:9) Thus the "only-begotten Son" of God was their older heavenly, spiritual brother. These perfect angelic creatures were spiritual in their makeup; they were spirit creatures. They were not human creatures who had died on earth and who had been transformed after death into heavenly spirit creatures. None of these angels of heaven were formerly human creatures here on earth. The spiritual makeup of the heavenly angels and the material, earthly makeup of the human creatures are two separate and distinct things. They cannot be mixed. Heavenly angels were before men, not men on earth before angels in heaven.

23 Because of their superior makeup as heavenly, spiritual creatures, those angels are superior to mankind. In the letter to the Hebrews, chapter two, verses six and seven, we read: "What is man that you keep him in mind, or the son of man that you take care of him? You made him a little lower than angels."

24 This is a quotation from the eighth psalm, verses four and five, which, according to the meaning of the Hebrew word used, calls the heavenly angels "godlike ones," saying: "What is mortal man that you keep him in mind, and the son of earthly man that you take care of him? You also proceeded to make him a little less than godlike ones." The higher form of life that angels enjoy is also pointed up in this reminder in 2 Peter 2:10-12, which speaks about men "who go on after flesh with the desire to defile it and who look down on lordship" and which then goes on to say:

25 "Daring, self-willed, they do not tremble at glorious ones but speak abusively, whereas angels, although they are greater in strength and power, do not bring against them an accusation in abusive

terms, not doing so out of respect for Jehovah. But these men, like unreasoning animals born naturally to be caught and destroyed, will ... suffer destruction."

²⁶ A man cannot dematerialize himself and put himself in the spiritual realm. However, the Holy Bible shows that God has given to angels power to materialize and appear in human bodies as men; and after they have appeared to men and carried out their angelic appointment from God, they have dematerialized and thus disappeared from human sight and returned to the spiritual realm.

For example, when the wicked cities of Sodom and Gomorrah were to be destroyed by fire and sulphur from the skies, two materialized angels first brought Abraham's nephew Lot and his family out of Sodom for safety and then disappeared by dematerializing. (Genesis 19:1-22) Also, when Mary the daughter of Heli was to become the mother of the promised "seed" of Abraham in spite of her being a virgin, the "angel Gabriel was sent forth from God" and materialized and thus appeared to Mary and notified her and got her consent. "At that the angel departed from her," by dematerializing.—Luke 1:26-38.

26. On what occasions have angels materialized in human bodies, and did they continue to live as fleshly creatures?

WHY ANGELS SHOUTED IN APPLAUSE

²⁷ When the promised "seed" of Abraham was born to Mary at Bethlehem that night of 2 B.C.E., it was a joyful occasion for the heavenly angels. A leading angel materialized and appeared in glory to shepherds keeping watch over their flocks out in the field by night and said to them: "Look! I am declaring to you good news of a great joy that all the people will have." Then, by materializing in order that the shepherds might see them, there appeared "a multitude of the heavenly host, praising God and saying: 'Glory in the heights above to God, and upon earth peace among men of good will.'" After that the angels "departed from them into heaven." (Luke 2:8-15) However, there was a much earlier occasion when the heavenly angels rejoiced, shouting in applause to God over a different event. When was that?

²⁸ Jehovah God himself remembered that earlier occasion and spoke of it to a man in the seventeenth century B.C.E., named Job, in the land of Uz in the Middle East. Despite a terrible sickness Job gained the victory in a long controversy with his critics and silenced them. But he needed to be reminded of how unimportant he was and how unnecessary he was for God's creation on the earth on which Job lived. Hence the account in Job 38:1-12 says:

²⁹ "And Jehovah proceeded to answer Job out of the windstorm and say: 'Who is this that is obscuring counsel by words without knowledge? Gird up your loins, please, like an able-bodied man, and let me question you, and you inform me. Where did you happen to be when I founded the earth? Tell me, if you do know understanding.

---

27. In connection with what grand event did materialized angels join in rejoicing in the year 2 B.C.E.?
28, 29. When was the occasion of which Jehovah told Job when "all the sons of God began shouting in applause"?

Who set its measurements, in case you know, or who stretched out upon it the measuring line? Into what have its socket pedestals been sunk down, or who laid its cornerstone, when the morning stars joyfully cried out together, and all the sons of God began shouting in applause? And who barricaded the sea with doors, which began to go forth as when it burst out from the womb; when I put the cloud as its garment and thick gloom as its swaddling band, and I proceeded to break up my regulation upon it and to set a bar and doors, and I went on to say, "This far you may come, and no farther; and here your proud waves are limited"? Was it from your days onward that you commanded the morning? Did you cause the dawn to know its place?' "

[30] Job had to acknowledge that he was not even in existence at the creation of the earth. But on that occasion "sons of God" were present or observing the marvelous things of creation that are described in the first chapter of the Holy Bible. Since these "sons of God" were alive and active before the creation of man on the earth, they must have been the invisible heavenly angels. They included God's "master worker," the "only-begotten Son of God," because "through him" God created the heavens and the earth. That those "sons of God" were in the heavens with God is proved in Job, chapters one and two, where we read: "Now it came to be the day when the sons of the true God entered to take their station before Jehovah, and even Satan proceeded to enter right among them. Then Jehovah said to Satan: 'Where do you

---

30. (a) Who must those "sons of God" have been who were present to observe and applaud God's works of creation? (b) Where were those "sons of God," as shown by Job, chapters one and two?

come from?' At that Satan answered Jehovah and said: 'From roving about in the earth and from walking about in it.' "—Job 1:6, 7; 2:1, 2.

³¹ Jehovah thus called the heavenly, invisible, spirit angels his sons, "the sons of God." They were not men and women who had been taken from earth to heaven and changed into spirit angels to populate the heavens. Neither were these angels spirit creatures who were to be sent to earth to become men and women in order to people the earth, thus to humble them or lower them. They were God's creations prior to man, higher than man, and of a superior quality above man. As to this difference between angels and men, Psalm 104: 1-4 says: "O Jehovah my God, you have proved very great. . . . The One . . . making the clouds his chariot, walking upon the wings of the wind, making his angels spirits." Hebrews 1:7 says: "Also, with reference to the angels he says: 'And he makes his angels spirits.' " That is why they are invisible to man. According to Bible history, they have served God's purposes toward man, and man is greatly indebted to these holy angels.

---

31. (a) Had those angels ever been humans on earth or were they to become humans to populate the earth? (b) Why are we humans interested in the holy angels?

[32] However, when we look at the world situation here on earth today, six thousand years from man's creation, we might ask ourselves, Was it in vain that at earth's creation "all the sons of God began shouting in applause"? Did they rejoice and applaud too soon, without thought of possible failure of God's purpose for the earth? Not at all! Thousands of years after that, when the conditions among men on earth were already quite bad, God said through his prophet Isaiah: "This is what Jehovah has said, the Creator of the heavens, He the true God, the Former of the earth and the Maker of it, He the One who firmly established it, who did not create it simply for nothing."—Isaiah 45:18.

[33] Consequently the heavenly angelic "sons of God" will yet have still greater reason for "shouting in applause" to Jehovah God. That will be when his unfailing purpose toward our earth is gloriously realized and all the families of the earth are partakers of God's eternal blessing in a Paradise earth.—Genesis 12:3.

32, 33. (a) In view of the present world condition, would we be justified in concluding that those heavenly sons of God applauded too soon and that God's purpose for the earth faces possible failure? (b) What will give those angels yet greater reason to shout in applause?

CHAPTER 5

Your "Soul" Is You

YOUR SOUL—is it really you? Does the Holy Bible say that it is you? In Psalm 121:7 the true worshiper of God is given this comforting promise: "Jehovah himself will guard you against all calamity. He will guard your soul." That expression "your soul" is used again in Proverbs 2:10, 11, which reads: "When wisdom enters into your heart and knowledge itself becomes pleasant to your very soul, thinking ability itself will keep guard over you." The mother of the prophet Samuel used the same expression when she presented her son to the high priest Eli and said: "By the life of your soul, my lord, I am the woman that was standing with you in this place to pray to Jehovah." (1 Samuel 1:26) To his chosen people Jehovah God said through the prophet Isaiah: "Listen intently to me, and eat what is good, and let YOUR soul find its exquisite delight in fatness itself. Incline YOUR ear and come to me. Listen, and YOUR soul will keep alive." (Isaiah 55:2, 3) What is being spoken to as "your soul"?

² Besides the expression "your soul," the Holy Bible contains the expressions "my soul," "her soul," "his soul," "our soul," and "their soul."

---

1. In what settings is the expression "your soul" used in the scriptures quoted in this paragraph?
2. Where can we get a reliable explanation of what the soul is, and against what will this information protect us?

134

Just what is meant by all those expressions, particularly by that word "soul," which is modified by all those personal pronouns? We, of course, want the Bible's answer to the question, or what the Bible indicates to be the answer, because the inspired Bible is the truth of God the Creator. "Your saying is very much refined, . . . and your law is truth." (Psalm 119:140-142) "Your word is truth." (John 17:17) By getting the answer of God's Word we shall be protected from the confusing philosophy of this world.

[3] Of course, the original Bible writers did not call it "soul." The Hebrew writers, all the way from the prophet Moses to the prophet Zechariah, called it "néphesh" (נפש), and this word occurs 750 times in the inspired Hebrew Scriptures. When those Hebrew Scriptures were translated into common Greek in the last three centuries before our Common Era, thus producing what is called the Greek Septuagint Version, the translators used the Greek word *psykhé* (ψυχή) for the Hebrew word *néphesh*. When the Christian Greek Scriptures were written in the first century of our Common Era, the inspired writers continued to use the word *psykhé;* and this word occurs 102 times in the Christian Greek Scriptures. The Holy Bible, therefore, has much to say about what is called "soul," speaking of it, all together, 852 times.

[4] To those who do not know what the soul really is, it may be a surprise to learn that the first book of the Bible, in its account of creation, tells us that there were souls (*néphesh*) on earth before man was created. On the fifth day of God's work of earthly creation, according to Genesis 1:20-22, "God went on to say: 'Let the waters swarm forth a swarm of living souls [*néphesh*] and let flying

3. (a) What word was used by the inspired Hebrew writers to designate the soul? What word was used in Greek? (b) In all, how many times does the Bible speak of the soul?
4, 5. What souls were on the earth before man was created?

creatures fly over the earth upon the face of the expanse of the heavens.' And God proceeded to create the great sea monsters and every living soul [néphesh] that moves about, which the waters swarmed forth according to their kinds, and every winged flying creature according to its kind. And God got to see that it was good. With that God blessed them, saying: 'Be fruitful and become many and fill the waters in the sea basins, and let the flying creatures become many in the earth.' "

⁵ In the first part of the sixth day of his creation, according to Genesis 1:24, 25, "God went on to say: 'Let the earth put forth living souls [néphesh] according to their kinds, domestic animal and moving animal and wild beast of the earth according to its kind.' And it came to be so. And God proceeded to make the wild beast of the earth according to its kind and the domestic animal according to its kind and every moving animal of the ground according to its kind. And God got to see that it was good."

⁶ All through the remainder of the Bible, God continues to refer to these great sea monsters and other creatures gliding through the waters, and to the flying creatures that fly over the earth, and to wild beasts and domestic animals and the other animals moving over the earth as "souls." For instance, to his ancient chosen people God's law said: "And everything in the seas and the streams that has no fins and scales, out of every swarming creature of the waters and out of every living soul that is in the waters, they are a loathsome thing for you." "This is the law about the beast and the flying creature and every living soul that moves about in the waters and concerning every soul that

6-8. Give examples from other parts of the Bible to show that, right to the last book, it is consistent in referring to these creatures as souls.

swarms upon the earth." (Leviticus 11:10, 46)
Telling of the vision that he saw of the waters
that issued from God's temple and that flowed
eastward and down to the Dead Sea or Sea of Salt,
the prophet Ezekiel writes:

[7] "Every living soul that swarms, in every place
to which the double-size torrent comes, will get
life. And it must occur that there will be very
many fish, because there is where this water will
certainly come, and the sea water will be healed,
and everything will be alive where the torrent
comes."—Ezekiel 47:9.

[8] In the very last book of the Bible we read:
"A third of the creatures that are in the sea which
have souls died. . . . And the second [angel] poured
out his bowl into the sea. And it became blood as
of a dead man, and every living soul [*psykhé*]
died, yes, the things in the sea."—Revelation 8:9;
16:3.

[9] These animal souls that God created on the
fifth creative day and in the first part of the sixth
creative day were not souls that had already
existed and that had transmigrated from somewhere else, that is to say, had not migrated from
human persons that had died. At that time there
were no human creatures on the earth from which
souls could transmigrate, because God had not yet
created the first man and woman. When the fish,
the flying creatures, the wild beast and the swarming and creeping insects died, their souls did not
transmigrate to new bodies that were brought into
existence. God's Word says that those animal souls
died, ceased to exist, because those lower animals
were souls in themselves. The Bible speaks of them
as souls; and certainly God knows what he says
in the Bible.

9. (a) Why is it certain that these animal souls had not transmigrated from humans that had died? (b) What happened
to these souls when the animals died?

CREATION OF THE HUMAN SOUL

[10] The Bible speaks of the time when those thousands of forms of lower creature life on earth had no man to dominate over them. Genesis 2:5, 6 tells of that time, saying: "There was no man to cultivate the ground. But a mist would go up from the earth and it watered the entire surface of the ground." In the latter part of the sixth creative day God proceeded to make his highest earthly creature, man. Evidently speaking to his "master worker," his "only-begotten Son," God said: "Let us make* man in our image, according to our likeness, and let them have in subjection the fish of the sea and the flying creatures of the heavens and the domestic animals and all the earth and every moving animal that is moving upon the earth." Then, by means of his "master worker" who was at his side,

---

* Because God the Creator is speaking to someone aside from himself, he says, not, 'Let us create,' but, "Let us make"; thus using the Hebrew word 'asáh instead of the word bará.

10. To whom did God speak when he said, "Let us make man in our image"?

"God proceeded to create the man in his image, in God's image he created him; male and female he created them."—Genesis 1:26, 27.

[11] Please, pay close attention to that language. It does not say that God created man in the image of a wild beast or of a domestic animal or of a fish. It says that God created man separate and distinct from fish, birds and land animals and made man "in God's image." Such a thing was not said in the case of those lower forms of creature life. Millions of people today may worship fish, birds, insects, wild beasts and domestic animals as gods, but that does not mean that God's image is like those lower creatures that have thousands of different sorts of bodies. "At no time has anyone beheld God." (1 John 4:12) And so nobody on earth knows the form or shape of God's body, and we cannot liken the body of any creature here on earth to God's glorious, heavenly, spiritual body.

[12] Because man would be created "in God's image," he could be called a "son of God," as Luke 3:38 calls him. His body is adapted to life on earth, not life in the invisible heavens. Nevertheless, man is "in God's image" in that he is created with moral qualities like those of God, namely, love and justice, and he has powers and wisdom above those of animals, so that he can appreciate the things that God enjoys and appreciates, such as natural beauty and the fine arts of music, writing, reading, speaking, reasoning, the science of numbers, and such processes of the mind of which the lower animal creatures are not capable. For such reasons man was able to have in subjection the lower forms of creature life in the skies, the earth and the sea.

[13] In order to create man, did God take a "soul," a *néphesh* or a *psykhé* that was flitting around in

11, 12. In what sense is man "in God's image"?
13. How does the Creator describe his creating of the first man?

the invisible heavens like a butterfly,* and imprison it in a human body? Did God take a heavenly angel, one of the heavenly "sons of God," and put him on a lower plane of life by transforming him into a man on earth? No; but let us read what the Creator's own written Word says about it, in Genesis 2:7: "And Jehovah God proceeded to form the man out of dust from the ground and to blow into his nostrils the breath [neshamáh, Hebrew] of life, and the man came to be a living soul [néphesh]." Thus the first human soul came into existence.

[14] What was the "living soul" that there came into existence? It was not the "breath of life" that Jehovah God blew into the nostrils of the human body that He had formed from the dust of the ground. The "living soul" was the man himself. The Christian apostle Paul emphasizes that fact when he writes, in 1 Corinthians 15:45: "The first man Adam became a living soul [psykhé]." Adam, our first human father, was a "living soul." He did not have some shadowy, invisible, weightless, unfeelable thing inside him that could escape from his body when he died and that could go on existing as a "living soul" in a spiritual realm that was just as invisible as the human soul is thought to be. No; not according to the creation account of God's Word. This first human "living soul" was visible to eyes on earth, to the eyes of the lower animal creatures. This "living soul" was feelable, sensible to the touch of those lower animal creatures, for they also were "souls" and this human "living soul" was made from the same earth that

---

* In ancient Greek the word psykhé (ψυχή) means, not only "soul," but also "butterfly" or "moth."

14. (a) Exactly what was that "living soul," and how does the Bible itself make that clear? (b) Was that first human "living soul" visible to the eyes of earthly creatures? Was it feelable?

they were. In fact, man was told to eat the produce of the earth to keep himself alive.

[15] As 1 Corinthians 15:47-49 goes on to say: "The first man is out of the earth and made of dust; . . . As the one made of dust is, so those made of dust are also; . . . we have borne the image of the one made of dust." For this reason you also who bear the image of the first human "living soul" are yourself a "soul."

[16] In the light of the Bible's teaching, it is plain that much confusion has existed in people's minds regarding what the human soul is. This fact was called attention to at the time that a new translation of the first five books of the Bible was published, under the title "The Torah - The Five Books of Moses" and with a Preface dated September 28, 1962. In an interview with a New York *Times* reporter in Philadelphia, Pennsylvania, the editor in chief Dr. Harry M. Orlinsky discussed the new translation and said that the word "soul" had virtually been eliminated. He said: "The Hebrew word in question here is 'nefesh.' . . . The Bible does not say we have a soul. 'Nefesh' is the person himself, his need for food, the very blood in his veins, his body." (New York *Times,* as of October 12, 1962) Accordingly, this new translation of the Hebrew Torah ("Law") translates Genesis 2:7 to read: "The LORD God formed man from the dust of the earth, and He blew into his nostrils the breath of life, and man became a living being."

[17] Other modern Bible translations (the Revised Standard Version, An American Translation, Dr. James Moffatt's translation, and so forth) say "living being" instead of "living soul" in Genesis 2:7. All this goes to show that the "living soul" is

---

15. What are all of us who bear the image of the first human soul?

16, 17. (a) What did the editor in chief of a new translation of the first five books of the Bible say as to the meaning of "soul"? (b) So what expression does that translation, as well as some others, use instead of "living soul"?

not something implanted invisibly inside the human body but is the human person himself. Consequently, when God's Word uses the expression "your soul," it means you yourself, your very being, your life as a human soul.

[18] So, according to *An American Translation*, when Hannah presented her son Samuel to the high priest Eli, she said: "O sir! as surely as you [not, your soul] live, sir, I am the woman," and so forth. (1 Samuel 1:26; also Moffatt's; *Revised Standard Version*) And Proverbs 2:10 says: "Knowledge becomes a pleasure to you [not, to your soul]." (*AT; Mo; Kx*) And Isaiah 55:3 says: "Incline your ear, and come to me; listen, that you [not, your soul] may live." (*AT; Mo*) And Psalm 121:7 says: "The LORD will guard your life [not, your soul]." (*AT; Mo; RS*)* The reader can look up other scriptures in the Hebrew Scriptures and see how modern translators render the word *néphesh*.

[19] If the reader will look up a modern Hebrew-English Lexicon, for example, *Lexicon on the Old Testament Books,* by L. Koehler and W. Baumgartner, he will find that:

[20] "My *néphesh*" means "I" (Genesis 27:4, 25; Isaiah 1:14); "your [singular] *néphesh*" means "thou" or "you" (Genesis 27:19, 31; Isaiah 43:4; 51:23); "his *néphesh*" means "he, himself" (Numbers 30:2; Isaiah 53:10); "her *néphesh*" means "she, herself" (Numbers 30:5-12); "our *néphesh*" means "we, ourself" (Psalm 124:7); "your [plural] *néphesh*" means "you" (Leviticus 26:15); "their *néphesh*" means "they, themselves" (Isaiah 46:2; 47:14); "every *néphesh*" means "every man"

---

* See the quotation of the same Bible verses on page 134, paragraph 1, and then make comparisons with the above quotations.

18. How do some of these modern translations, by their rendering, show the meaning of the expression "your soul"?
19, 20. When used along with various modifying words, what does *néphesh* mean, as illustrated in a Hebrew-English Lexicon?

(Exodus 12:16); "every *néphesh* which" means "whosoever" (Leviticus 7:27; 17:15; 23:29); "the *néphesh* which" means "who, the man who" (Leviticus 7:20, 27; Numbers 15:30). Also, *néphesh* means "life" (282 times); *"néphesh* of the man" means "the life of man" (Genesis 9:5); and "upon (or, for) your *néphesh"* means "your life is at stake" (Genesis 19:17). And as to *néphesh* in Genesis 9:4, 5; Leviticus 17:11, it says: "the soul (strictly distinct from the Greek notion of soul) the seat of which is in the blood." Regarding *néphesh* in Genesis 1:20 it says: "the breathing substance, making man and animals living beings."*

[21] How, then, did the human soul come into existence? By God's creating the human body from the dust of the ground and combining with it "the breath of life." This means that the human soul is maintained by breathing the needed air through the nostrils. It does not mean that the human creature, man, is maintained alive by having inside himself an invisible, spiritual, intelligent something called "soul" that can separate from the body at death and that can continue its intelligent, conscious existence in an invisible, spiritual realm, either with angels or with demons.

IS OUR SOUL DEATHLESS, IMPERISHABLE?

[22] The reasonable question now comes up, If the human soul is brought into existence by God's combining the human body made from all the elements of the earth with the "breath of life," what happens when that breath of life is separated

---

* See Volume 2 of the above-named Lexicon, of the 1953 edition, page 627, under the heading *Nephesh* (נפש).

21. How did the human soul come into existence, and how is it kept alive?
22. What happens to the soul when the breath of life is separated from the human body?

from the human body? The Creator's written Word answers that question also. It says that the human soul dies, ceases to exist. Where does it say so?

[23] In Leviticus 23:30 God says: "As for any soul that will do any sort of work on this very day, I must destroy that soul from among his people." In Numbers 23:10 the prophet Balaam, under inspiration of God's spirit, says: "Let my soul die the death of the upright ones." In Numbers 31:19 God says to Israelite soldiers: "Everyone who has killed a soul and everyone who has touched someone slain, you should purify yourselves." Concerning the conquerors of the Promised Land we read: "They devoted every soul that was in it to destruction." (Joshua 10:35, also 37, 39) When pulling down the temple of Dagon upon the Philistine worshipers, Judge Samson said: "Let my soul die with the Philistines." (Judges 16:30) Concerning the prophet Elijah, when in flight from the persecutor Queen Jezebel, we read: "He began to ask that his soul might die and to say: 'It is enough! Now, O Jehovah, take my soul away, for I am no better than my forefathers.' "—1 Kings 19:4.

[24] According to those Bible statements and over sixty others that could be quoted from the Hebrew Scriptures, the human soul must not be deathless or deathproof. It must be mortal. Further to that effect, God the Creator says against the false prophetesses: "Will you profane me toward my people . . . in order to put to death the souls that ought not to die and in order to preserve alive the souls that ought not to live by your lie to my people, the hearers of a lie?" (Ezekiel 13:19) To the sinful people God said: "As the soul of the father so likewise the soul of the son—to me they belong.

23, 24. (a) How do the Hebrew Scriptures make it plain that the human soul dies? (b) Is there any support at all in the inspired Hebrew Scriptures for belief in immortality of animal souls or human souls?

The soul that is sinning—it itself will die." (Ezekiel 18:4, also 20) In harmony with that basic truth, there is not one verse in all the thirty-nine books of the inspired Hebrew Scriptures that says that the animal soul or the human soul (*néphesh*) is immortal, deathless, indestructible, imperishable.

25 The twenty-seven books of the inspired Christian Greek Scriptures are perfectly in agreement with the Hebrew Scriptures that the human soul is mortal, able to be wiped out of existence.

26 In order to support the pagan Babylonian teaching and the pagan Greek teaching that the human soul is immortal and does not die with the death of the human body, some clergymen of Christendom quote the words: "Fear not them which kill the body, but are not able to kill the soul." They stop short of quoting all of Jesus' words, for the verse (Matthew 10:28, *AV*) goes on to say: "But rather fear him which is able to destroy both soul [*psykhé*] and body in hell [*Gehenna*]." So it is not impossible for Almighty God to destroy the human soul, put it out of existence.

27 Some hours before he was put to death by his enemies, Jesus Christ said to his apostles: "My soul [*psykhé*] is deeply grieved, even to death." (Matthew 26:38) Referring to Jesus Christ as the promised Prophet from Jehovah God, the apostle Peter said: "Any soul that does not listen to that Prophet will be completely destroyed from among the people." (Acts 3:23) Jesus' half brother, the disciple James, said: "He who turns a sinner back from the error of his way will save his soul from death."—James 5:20.

28 The Greek word for "immortality," *athanasia,*

25-27. (a) Are the inspired Christian Greek Scriptures in agreement that the human soul is mortal? (b) What scriptures make this clear?
28. (a) How many times does the Greek word for immortality occur in the Christian Greek Scriptures, and is it ever applied to human souls on earth? (b) In his first letter to Timothy, whom did the apostle Paul mention as having immortality?

occurs only three times in the Christian Greek Scriptures, but the word is never applied to human souls on earth. Back in the first century the apostle Paul wrote to Timothy about the "manifestation of our Lord Jesus Christ" and said: "This manifestation the happy and only Potentate will show in its own appointed times, he the King of those who rule as kings and Lord of those who rule as lords, the one alone having immortality, who dwells in unapproachable light, whom not one of men has seen or can see."—1 Timothy 6:14-16.

[29] The faithful followers of Jesus Christ gain immortality with him in the heavens by way of the resurrection of the dead, about which the apostle Paul says this to his fellow disciples: "We shall be changed. For this which is corruptible must put on incorruption, and this which is mortal must put on immortality. But when this which is corruptible puts on incorruption and this which is mortal puts on immortality, then the saying will take place that is written: 'Death is swallowed up forever.' " (1 Corinthians 15:52-54) Immortality and incorruption are things that the human soul does not possess. They have to be gained by suffering a sacrificial death with Jesus Christ and sharing in his resurrection.

[30] God will reward these faithful seekers for heavenly incorruptibility, according to what we read in Romans 2:6, 7: "He will render to each one according to his works: everlasting life to those who are seeking glory and honor and incorruptibleness by endurance in work that is good." Such a heavenly reward was made possible by the resurrection of Jesus Christ, as the apostle Peter points out to his fellow disciples, saying: "Blessed be the God and Father of our Lord Jesus Christ,

29. Who from this earth gain immortality, and how?
30, 31. Who is the One who gives the reward of heavenly incorruptibility, and has it always been available to men?

for according to his great mercy he gave us a new birth to a living hope through the resurrection of Jesus Christ from the dead, to an incorruptible and undefiled and unfading inheritance. It is reserved in the heavens for you." (1 Peter 1:3, 4) Before the resurrection of Jesus Christ the possibility of gaining the prize of such heavenly incorruptibility and immortality did not exist. Paul gives God the credit for this, saying:

[31] "He saved us and called us with a holy calling, not by reason of our works, but by reason of his own purpose and undeserved kindness. This was given us in connection with Christ Jesus before times long lasting, but now it has been made clearly evident through the manifestation of our Savior, Christ Jesus, who has abolished death but has shed light upon life and incorruption through the good news."—2 Timothy 1:9, 10.

NOT DYING HOPELESS LIKE ANIMALS

[32] Since the human soul does not have immortality and incorruption but dies with the body, some religionist might ask in indignation, Does this mean that we humans die like animals? Nothing could answer that question better than God's own inspired Word. In Ecclesiastes 3:19-21 it says: "There is an eventuality as respects the sons of mankind and an eventuality as respects the beast, and they have the same eventuality. As the one dies, so the other dies; and they all have but one spirit, so that there is no superiority of the man over the beast, for everything is vanity. All are going to one place. They have all come to be from the dust, and they are all returning to the dust. Who is there knowing the spirit of the sons of mankind, whether it is ascending upward; and the spirit of the beast, whether it is descending downward to the earth?"

32. What does God's Word say about the death of the sons of mankind in comparison with the death of beasts?

[33] Those were not the words of a materialist or of an atheist. The inspired writer of those words closes the book of Ecclesiastes saying: "Fear the true God and keep his commandments. For this is the whole obligation of man. For the true God himself will bring every sort of work into the judgment in relation to every hidden thing, as to whether it is good or bad." (Ecclesiastes 12:13, 14) In that same closing chapter the same writer advises young persons to remember and serve God during their youth, because old age brings its bodily difficulties, and shortly death stops all human activities: "Then the dust returns to the earth just as it happened to be and the spirit itself returns to the true God who gave it."—Ecclesiastes 12:1-7.

[34] In the above verses quoted from the book of Ecclesiastes the Hebrew word for "spirit" is, not *néphesh* (meaning "soul"), but *rúahh*. The Holy Bible makes a difference between "soul" and "spirit." In Hebrews 4:12 we read: "The word of God is alive and exerts power and is sharper than any two-edged sword and pierces even to the dividing of soul [*psykhé*] and spirit [*pneúma*]." The human soul is the individual himself, the living human creature, visible and touchable. The spirit is something invisible and yet active, an active force like the wind. In man's case it is the invisible active force that moves the visible, earthly human soul.

[35] Such spirit or active force from God moves also the lower earthly creatures, the lower animal souls. One spirit or unseen active force operates in both man and lower animals. At death the bodies of lower animal souls and of human souls go back to the dust of the ground. In these re-

---

33. How does the closing chapter of the book of Ecclesiastes describe what happens at death?
34. Is the "spirit" the same as the "soul"?
35. In what respects are man and animals alike, but in what way is man's position more favorable?

spects man and the animals in subjection to him are alike. However, God has provided a future for man.

[36] At death the human soul does not return to God, for it was never with God. The human soul is the man himself, and man was never in heaven with God. Where man returns at death is to the dust from which his body was made; his nostrils stop breathing the "breath [neshamáh] of life." Ecclesiastes 12:7 says that it is the "spirit" that returns to God who gave it. The Hebrew word rúahh used in this verse is never translated "soul."* Not the soul, but the spirit or active force returns to God, who is the great Source of the spirit, the Source of all life.—Psalm 36:9.

[37] In Ecclesiastes 8:8, wise King Solomon wrote: "There is no man having power over the spirit to retain the spirit; neither is there any power of control in the day of death." In the day of death the dying person cannot retain the spirit or force of life and keep it from returning to God the Giver and Source, so as to live longer. Even physicians cannot help him. Dying humans cannot control the day of death or prevent it from ever reaching them. They cannot be discharged from the war that the enemy Death wages against all mankind without exception. Sinful man cannot get some other sinful man to substitute for him in death and thus enjoy a furlough from Death. Even Pharaohs of Egypt and Emperors of Rome who claimed to be gods could forge no weapon to beat off death and gain victory over it. They could not

---

* In the popular King James (Authorized) Version Bible the Hebrew word rúahh is translated as "air, anger, blast, breath, cool, courage, mind, quarters, side, spirit, spiritual, tempest, vain, whirlwind, wind, windy," but never as "soul."

---

36. What is it that returns to God when one dies?
37. Does man have the power to prevent death by holding back the spirit from returning to God?

hold back the spirit from returning to the great Life-giver and leaving them lifeless.

[38] Psalm 104 is addressed to Jehovah and shows our dependence on Him, saying: "You open your hand—they get satisfied with good things. If you conceal your face, they get disturbed. If you take away their spirit [rúahh], they expire, and back to their dust they go. If you send forth your spirit, they are created; and you make the face of the ground new. The glory of Jehovah will prove to be to time indefinite."—Psalm 104:28-31.

[39] So, then, under present circumstances you as a mortal human soul are facing death. Your only hope for a future after that depends, not on any imagined immortality of your soul, but on God's provisions to "create" you anew, for your "soul" is you!

38, 39. As pointed out in Psalm 104, upon what does our hope for a future after death depend?

CHAPTER 6

How the Demons Came into Existence

THE inspired prophets of the Holy Bible did not laugh at such a thing as the existence of demons or devils. They were very familiar with the evidence that demons existed, and they condemned the practice of demonism and warned all worshipers of the living and true God against it. The prophet Moses gave a farewell speech to his people before his death and said concerning their unfaithful forefathers: "They went sacrificing to demons [evil spirits], not to God, gods whom they had not known, new ones who recently came in, with whom your forefathers were not acquainted." (Deuteronomy 32:17, *NW; Le*) Because the conquerors of the Promised Land did not kill off the demon-worshiping occupants of the land, Psalm 106:34-38 tells us what happened:

² "They did not annihilate the peoples, as Jehovah had said to them. And they went mingling with the nations and took up learning their works. And they kept serving their idols, and these came to be a snare to them. And they would sacrifice their sons and their daughters to demons [evil spirits]. So they kept spilling innocent blood, the

---

1, 2. (a) Does the Bible teach such a thing as the existence of demons or devils? (b) To whom do the Scriptures show that persons unfaithful to Jehovah God offered sacrifice?

blood of their sons and their daughters, whom they sacrificed to the idols of Canaan; and the land came to be polluted with bloodshed."—*NW; Le.*

³ Centuries afterward the Christian apostle Paul wrote to the fellow believers in Corinth, a Grecian city where demonism was then being practiced: "What, then, am I to say? That what is sacrificed to an idol is anything, or that an idol is anything? No; but I say that the things which the nations sacrifice they sacrifice to demons, and not to God; and I do not want you to become sharers with the demons. You cannot be drinking the cup of Jehovah and the cup of demons; you cannot be partaking of 'the table of Jehovah' and the table of demons."—1 Corinthians 10:19-21.

⁴ The practice of demonism cannot be denied. Human history records the practice of it by the nations. There was some basis for it. The questions are therefore not baseless and are not posed merely for philosophical discussion, but are realistic: When did the demons come into existence? How did they come into existence?

⁵ One thing is certain and is no lie: Jehovah God did not create the demons. It being impossible for him to lie, he would not create liars. He would not create intelligent creatures with whom he could not associate. He would not create spirit creatures in opposition to him and whom he would cast out of his heavenly organization. When the greatest of Jehovah's prophets, Jesus Christ, was on earth nineteen centuries ago, he cast out more than a legion of demons. By whose power? Jesus answered when he said to those who criticized his expelling of the demons from people: "If it is by means of God's finger I expel the demons, the kingdom of

---

3. The Christian apostle Paul points out that the people of the nations are in reality sacrificing to whom?
4. What two questions concerning the demons are posed for serious consideration, and why?
5, 6. Did Jehovah God create the demons, and why do you so answer?

God has really overtaken you." (Luke 11:20) Those demons who oppose God's kingdom are sinful and imperfect. God, for his part, directs his activity toward what is righteous and perfect. To free God of any accusation of creating imperfect things, Moses said:

⁶ "I shall declare the name of Jehovah. Do you attribute greatness to our God! The Rock, perfect is his activity, for all his ways are justice. A God of faithfulness, with whom there is no injustice; righteous and upright is he. They have acted ruinously on their own part; they are not his children, the defect is their own. A generation crooked and twisted!"—Deuteronomy 32:3-5.

⁷ So, too, the ruinous acting on the part of the demons is of their own accord; their defectiveness is of their own making. They have taken themselves out of the family of God's children. But how did this occur, and when? Why have the demons come to be associated so closely with mankind, continually besieging mankind? To learn the true Bible answers, we have to go back to the beginning of man's history. Logically we go back to the first book of the Holy Bible.

⁸ In the latter part of the sixth creative day, the same day on which the land animals were created, the Creator of heaven and earth made the first man. He was perfect; he was righteous. That is why he could be called "the son of God," as the physician Luke calls him when tracing the lineage of Jesus Christ back to the first man Adam. (Luke 3:38) That is why, also, God his Creator could have association with him; and to this end God equipped Adam with the powers of speech and gifted him with a language immediately that

---

7. To the Bible's record of what period of time do we turn for reliable answers to our questions concerning the origin and activities of the demons?
8. Of what quality was God's work in creating the first man, and so what does the physician Luke say that that man was?

Adam "came to be a living soul." (Genesis 2:7) What now?

⁹ The first man was created in the "garden of Eden" in what is now southwest Asia, in the neighborhood of the Tigris and Euphrates Rivers. The name Eden means "Pleasure," evidently to indicate that the region was one pleasant for man. The creation account says: "Jehovah God planted a garden in Eden, toward the east, and there he put the man whom he had formed. Thus Jehovah God made to grow out of the ground every tree desirable to one's sight and good for food and also the tree of life in the middle of the garden and the tree of the knowledge of good and bad." What was the man to do in this garden, and what was he not to do? God told him, and the man was able to understand God's speech. "And Jehovah God proceeded to take the man and settle him in the garden of Eden to cultivate it and to take care of it. And Jehovah God also laid this command upon the man: 'From every tree of the garden you may eat to satisfaction. But as for the tree of the knowledge of good and bad you must not eat from it, for in the day you eat from it you will positively die.'" (Genesis 2:8, 9, 15-17) God did not desire his son to die.

¹⁰ God made Adam acquainted with the animals and flying creatures in the garden of

---

9. In what surroundings did God place the first man, and what command did he give him?
10. (a) What was to be Adam's position in relation to all the animals? (b) Did Adam find any of his own kind among the animals?

Eden, for Adam was to have all of them in subjection, as he was created above their kinds. So God "began bringing them to the man to see what he would call each one; and whatever the man would call it, each living soul [*néphesh*], that was its name." But after Adam met and named them all, yet "for man there was found no helper as a complement of him." (Genesis 2:19, 20) Man was superior in kind; he was alone in his kind on earth. He found no one else like him in the garden of Eden. Of course, Adam could have no association higher and more delightful than association with his Creator, his heavenly Father.

[11] God, though, was not satisfied to have one human son on earth; he was not satisfied to have his earthly family consist of just one son, one man. He purposed to have the entire earth filled with his human sons or children. In view of this, God saw the need for Adam to have a wife, with whom he could have a companionship higher than that with the lower animals. At the same time his wife could become a mother to his children, born in perfection, and at last all the earth would be filled with them. God himself said: "It is not good for the man to continue by himself. I am going to make a helper for him, as a complement of him." —Genesis 2:18.

[12] Some time still remained on God's sixth creative day for him to work at another earthly creation, a helper for Adam. "Hence Jehovah God had a deep sleep fall upon the man and, while he was sleeping, he took one of his ribs and then closed up the flesh over its place. And Jehovah God proceeded to build the rib that he had taken from the man into a woman and to bring her to the man. Then the man said: 'This is at last bone of

---

11. Why did God provide Adam with a wife?
12. How did the first woman come into existence?

my bones and flesh of my flesh. This one will be called Woman, because from man this one was taken.' " (Genesis 2:21-23) Thus God married the man and woman.

¹³ God gave them a marriage-day talk and blessed their union. Regarding this, Genesis 1: 27-30 says: "God proceeded to create the man in his image, in God's image he created him; male and female he created them. Further, God blessed them and God said to them: 'Be fruitful and become many and fill the earth and subdue it, and have in subjection the fish of the sea and the flying creatures of the heavens and every living creature that is moving upon the earth.' And God went on to say: 'Here I have given to you all vegetation bearing seed which is on the surface of the whole earth and every tree on which there is the fruit of a tree bearing seed. To you let it serve as food. And to every wild beast of the earth and to every flying creature of the heavens and to everything moving upon the earth in which there is life as a soul [*néphesh*] I have given all green vegetation for food.' " On this wedding day God did not go into details about all the trees, bringing up the subject of death for eating the forbidden fruit of the tree of the knowledge of good and bad. Later Adam told his wife about this.

---

13. What did God tell this first human couple on their wedding day, and what information did Adam pass on to his wife later?

THE FIRST DEMON APPEARS—IN EDEN

¹⁴ At this time Adam the first man was not the only son of God in existence. There were countless other "sons of God" in existence at that time, but these were invisible to Adam and Eve and were in the invisible heavens, the realm of spirit persons. They were the "sons of God" whom Jehovah later mentioned to the faithful man Job and who "began shouting in applause" when God laid, as it were, the cornerstone of the earth at its creation. (Job 38:7) Doubtless they shouted for joy also when God created the first human inhabitants of this earth, the finest things on earth. These heavenly "sons of God" were no doubt keenly interested in their earthly brother and sister, and said Amen to God's blessing.

¹⁵ For Adam and Eve there was no temptation to loose moral conduct or sexual uncleanness. Genesis 2:25 plainly tells us that "both of them continued to be naked, the man and his wife, and yet they did not become ashamed." They were pure in heart. And yet, strangely, temptation invaded that garden in Eden. From what direction did it come and how? In Genesis 3:1-5 God's Word says:

¹⁶ "Now the serpent proved to be the most cautious of all the wild beasts of the field that Jehovah God had made. So it began to say to the woman: 'Is it really so that God said you must not eat from every tree of the garden?' At this the woman said to the serpent: 'Of the fruit of the trees of the garden we may eat. But as for eating of the fruit of the tree that is in the middle of the garden, God has said, "You must not eat from it, no, you must not touch it that you do not die."' At this

14. Were there other "sons of God" in existence at this time? 15, 16. As explained in the Bible, how did temptation invade the garden of Eden?

the serpent said to the woman: 'You positively will not die. For God knows that in the very day of your eating from it your eyes are bound to be opened and you are bound to be like God, knowing good and bad.' "

[17] Here encouragement was presented to the woman to do what God had said not to do, in other words, to sin, to miss the mark of perfect obedience to God. What the serpent said to Eve, did it think up and say of its own accord? Impossible! We know that no serpent has the brains of a man to understand God's command to Adam before his wife was created and married to him. A serpent does not have the speech organs of a man to be able of itself to converse with man in man's own language—no more so than a female ass can talk to man in man's language. And yet, long after the days of Adam, a female ass actually did talk to the prophet Balaam to warn him that danger was standing in the prophet's path. (Numbers 22:22-33) As the Christian apostle Peter said, fifteen centuries later, "a voiceless beast of burden, making utterance with the voice of a man, hindered the prophet's mad course." (2 Peter 2:15, 16)

17. (a) What was the woman actually being encouraged by the serpent to do? (b) Did the literal serpent speak to Eve of its own accord?

That miracle occurred from Almighty God. If, now, an ass could be made to talk man's language, a serpent could be made to do so.

[18] Who, then, caused the serpent to talk to Eve? It was not God, because he does not lie or contradict himself, whereas what the serpent said was the opposite of what God said, and it said that God was lying for selfish reasons. It must have been some superhuman invisible intelligent creature that made the serpent talk. It must have been one of those "sons of God" who had shouted in applause at God's creation of the earth. This angelic son had now turned traitor to his own heavenly Father. Not only did he himself rebel against God his Father but he also began teaching others to rebel against God. He thus made himself a resister or adversary of God, and the Hebrew word for "resister" or "adversary" is *satán*, which Hebrew word is sometimes translated as "Satan." (Numbers 22:22, 32; 1 Samuel 29:4; Job 1:6-9) In this way, by rebelling and making himself a resister or adversary of Jehovah God, this son of God made himself Satan. Because of developing a greed for power over mankind, this rebellious son of God actually took steps to turn mankind away from obedience to God and to line mankind up on his side as rebels against Jehovah God.

[19] There was nothing impure, immoral or wicked on the earth to tempt this perfect son of God to sin. However, an opportunity did offer itself for this spirit son of God to enlarge his power over earthly children of God at the expense of their heavenly Father. Such enlargement of personal power could be gained only at the expense of the great Sovereign of the heavens and the earth.

18. (a) Who was it that caused the serpent to talk to Eve, and why do you give that answer? (b) So when and how did Satan come into existence?
19, 20. How was it possible for this perfect spirit son of God to be enticed into a course of rebellion against his heavenly Father?

[20] This son of God did not dismiss such a thought when once it had presented itself to him. Instead, he let himself go to thinking about the desirability of such a thing. Here he let himself be tempted and he could never say that God tempted him. It is just as James 1:13-15 states: "When under trial, let no one say: 'I am being tried by God.' No; for with evil things God cannot be tried nor does he himself try anyone. But each one is tried by being drawn out and enticed by his own desire. Then the desire, when it has become fertile, gives birth to sin; in turn, sin, when it has been accomplished, brings forth death." So this perfect heavenly son of God let himself be enticed by his own newly aroused desire and committed the sin of rebellion against his heavenly Father.

[21] Thus this spirit son of God became a self-made Satan or Adversary of the Sovereign of heaven and earth. Himself invisible to the woman Eve, he used the visible serpent in the garden of Eden. The Christian apostle Paul does not call all this a myth but says: "The serpent seduced Eve by its cunning." (2 Corinthians 11:3) By use of the serpent the power-greedy son of God presented a deception to Eve to tempt her into disobeying God's known law. He presented himself to Eve as an enlightener of her mind.

[22] It was as the apostle Paul goes on to say: "Satan himself keeps transforming himself into an angel of light." (2 Corinthians 11:14) The spirit son of God, now Satan, used a lie to deceive Eve. He called God a liar but he made himself a liar. He lied in saying that for her and her husband Adam to eat the forbidden fruit of the tree of the knowledge of good and bad would result, not in their death, but in their becoming "like God," with the

---

21. How does the Christian apostle Paul view this account concerning events in Eden?
22. Though posing as an enlightener of Eve, to what did Satan resort in order to mislead her?

ability to determine for themselves what is good and what is bad.

[23] This is the first lie on record, and the speaker of it made himself therefore the father or originator of lying. Who that father of lying is was made known by no one else than the faithful Son of God, Jesus Christ, when he said to those who desired to slay him: "You are from your father the Devil, and you wish to do the desires of your father. That one was a manslayer when he began, and he did not stand fast in the truth, because truth is not in him. When he speaks the lie, he speaks according to his own disposition, because he is a liar and the father of the lie." (John 8:44) So it was the first devil that became the "father of the lie."

[24] The name "Devil" is drawn from the Greek word *diábolos* and means "false accuser, misrepresenter, slanderer." (1 Timothy 3:11; Titus 2:3) By this lie against God the rebellious son of God made himself a devil or false accuser, misrepresenter or slanderer of God. In this way he became the one whom the Holy Bible calls Satan the Devil. —Revelation 12:9; 20:2.

[25] The fact that a heavenly, spirit son of God became Satan the Devil is no bad reflection upon the perfection of God's work. Satan the Devil was not of God's making, but he was what he as the enticed son of God made himself. Almighty God could read his heart, but his try at tempting the woman Eve by deception brought his iniquity or unrighteousness out into the open. He departed from the way of perfection. It could be said to him

23. Whom does Jesus Christ identify as the speaker of that first lie?
24. What does the name "Devil" mean, and why does it apply to that rebellious son of God?
25. Why is the fact that a spirit son of God became Satan the Devil no bad reflection on God's work?

then, just as it was long afterward said to the king of the city of Tyre: "You were faultless in your ways from the day of your being created until unrighteousness was found in you."—Ezekiel 28:15.

[26] Because he used the earthly serpent in starting off his work of seducing and deceiving mankind, Satan the Devil came to be symbolized by the serpent. Indeed, the last book of the Bible calls him "that old serpent," or, "the original serpent." (Revelation 12:9; 20:2, *AV; NW*) Hence, when God brought his rebellious son to account and pronounced a condemnatory judgment upon him, God used the serpent as a symbol of Satan the Devil. Only on the surface appearance of things did God speak to the serpent, for God knew that the literal serpent in Eden could not understand what he said and it would not live long, only a serpent's normal life at most.

[27] This is how the situation is to be understood when we read Genesis 3:14, 15: "And Jehovah God proceeded to say to the serpent: 'Because you have done this thing, you are the cursed one out of all the domestic animals and out of all the wild beasts of the field. Upon your belly you will go and dust is what you will eat all the days of your life. And I shall put enmity between you and the woman and between your seed and her seed. He will bruise you in the head and you will bruise him in the heel.' "

[28] As the Bible history proves, that literal serpent in Eden did not live long enough to see the promised "seed" of the woman born on earth and then to be bruised in the head by that "seed." However, the symbolic serpent, "the original serpent," Satan the Devil, did live long enough to bruise the Seed of the woman "in the heel," and

26, 27. Who came to be symbolized by the serpent, and so to whom are God's words recorded in Genesis 3:14, 15 addressed?
28. By God's words to the serpent, what notice was served on Satan the Devil?

he continues living on till now. God's words to apparently the literal serpent in Eden served notice on Satan the Devil that he was not to be 'bruised in the head' right at once. Rather, the execution of the sentence upon him would take place later at some time not definitely known to him. During the time that his life would be spared, he would be on the lookout for the promised Seed.

WHY EXECUTION WAS PUT LATER

[29] Why did not God destroy Satan the Devil immediately at the time that he pronounced sentence upon him there at Eden about six thousand years ago? Almighty God could have done so. Satan the Devil is not immortal, indestructible. However, in the great controversy or disagreement of thought that had now arisen the point to be settled was not the question of power or who is most powerful. It was the question of sovereignty in heaven and earth. Who will rule all heaven and earth with the willing submission of all living persons in heaven and earth? Satan the Devil had started the first rebellion in all creation, and so now how far could he go with it? How far could he go with this rebellion in inducing other sons of God to join him? Would he and any other creatures who would join him be able to take away the universal sovereignty from the only living and true God, Jehovah? To settle this dispute by providing the full answer, it would take time.

[30] God indicated that others would join Satan the Devil in rebellion if time were allowed for it, because God said to the serpent: "I shall put enmity between you and the woman and between your seed and her seed." It would take time for

---

29. Why did not God destroy Satan the Devil as soon as he pronounced sentence upon him, instead of allowing him to remain these thousands of years?
30. (a) If time were allowed for it, what would Satan produce? (b) How would God's sovereignty be vindicated?

God to allow the "woman" to produce her "seed." It would take time for the "original serpent" Satan the Devil to produce his seed, and God did not deny the possibility that Satan the Devil would produce a "seed," an offspring of fellow rebels against the universal sovereignty of Jehovah. But not all of God's sons would go over onto the side of the "original serpent." Jehovah God, also, would have a loyal seed, and in the final outcome this "seed" would bruise the "original serpent" in the head, killing him. This would vindicate the unshakableness of God's sovereignty over heaven and earth.

[31] By letting Satan the Devil proceed with his rebellion the state of affairs would arise like in the case of the demon-worshiping Pharaoh of Egypt in the days of the prophet Moses. Back there, why did Jehovah God permit the defiant Pharaoh to survive six devastating plagues or blows against the land of Egypt? The purpose of it God stated to Pharaoh through Moses before the seventh plague struck Egypt: "By now I could have thrust my hand out that I might strike you and your people with pestilence and that you might be effaced from the earth. But, in fact, for this cause I have kept you in existence, for the sake of showing you my power and in order to have my name declared in all the earth." (Exodus 9:15, 16) In his appointed time Jehovah God will show his almighty power over the great rebel, Satan the Devil, by means of the Seed that would stay loyal to the rightful Universal Sovereign, Jehovah God.

[32] Referring to that loyal Seed, who would be bruised, as it were, "in the heel," Hebrews 2:14,

31. How would the situation involving Satan be like that in the case of the demon-worshiping Egyptian Pharaoh in the days of Moses?
32. At Hebrews 2:14, 15, what do we learn about the Seed that would stay loyal to Jehovah God?

15 says: "Since the 'young children' are sharers of blood and flesh, he also similarly partook of the same things, that through his death [being bruised in the heel] he might bring to nothing the one having the means to cause death, that is, the Devil; and that he might emancipate all those who for fear of death were subject to slavery all through their lives."

[33] Although sentence was pronounced upon the "original serpent" at Eden, he, that is, Satan the Devil, was not barred by Jehovah God from the holy heavens or from further contact with the still faithful "sons of God" up there. Over two thousand years later, when the twelve tribes of Israel were sojourning down in Egypt, Satan the Devil was still having access to the realm of the holy angels. So we read in the book of Job, a relative of the patriarch Abraham. When it tells about how Job's faithfulness to Jehovah God came to be tested at the hands of Satan, the opening chapter of the book says: "Now it came to be the day when the sons of the true God entered to take their station before Jehovah, and even Satan proceeded to enter right among them. Then Jehovah said to Satan: 'Where do you come from?' At that Satan answered Jehovah and said: 'From roving about in the earth and from walking about in it.' " After the interview and an agreement as to the testing of Job's integrity, the account says: "Satan went out away from the person of Jehovah." —Job 1:6, 7, 12; see also 2:1-7.

[34] Toward the end of the first century of our Common Era it was revealed to the Christian apostle John that Satan the Devil would not be cast out of the holy heavens until after the birth

---

33. Did Satan the Devil continue to have access to heaven after sentence was pronounced at Eden, and how do we know?
34. When was the Devil to be cast out of the holy heavens?

of the promised kingdom of God. In the miraculous revelation given to John, he first describes the birth of God's kingdom as like the birth of a child from a heavenly woman. Then he writes: "War broke out in heaven: Michael and his angels battled with the dragon, and the dragon and its angels battled but it did not prevail, neither was a place found for them any longer in heaven. So down the great dragon was hurled, the original serpent, the one called Devil and Satan, who is misleading the entire inhabited earth; he was hurled down to the earth, and his angels were hurled down with him. And I heard a loud voice in heaven say: 'Now have come to pass the salvation and the power and the kingdom of our God and the authority of his Christ, because the accuser of our brothers has been hurled down, who accuses them day and night before our God!' " (Revelation 12:1-10) That was to happen after the days of the apostle John.

[35] Satan the Devil is thus said to have his own angels, these being with him even up in heaven. These must be his heavenly "seed." How did he produce them? Evidently from among the "sons of God" in the heavens. At least some of these were induced to come over onto Satan's side in the days of the prophet Noah, before he built the ark for his family to survive the earth-wide flood. How this came about we read in Genesis 6:1-4, in these words:

[36] "Now it came about that when men started to grow in numbers on the surface of the ground and daughters were born to them, then the sons of the true God began to notice the daughters of men, that they were good-looking; and they went taking wives for themselves, namely, all whom they chose. After that Jehovah said: 'My spirit

35, 36. How were some of the angels induced to join Satan in the days of Noah, as explained at Genesis 6:1-4?

shall not act toward man indefinitely in that he is also flesh. Accordingly his days shall amount to a hundred and twenty years.'
The Nephilim proved to be in the earth in those days, and also after that, when the sons of the true God continued to have relations with the daughters of men and they bore sons to them, they were the mighty ones who were of old, the men of fame."

[37] To marry the daughters of men, those heavenly sons of God materialized human bodies, clothing themselves with fleshly bodies like those of men on earth. Regardless of what their duties were up in heaven, they remained in the flesh with their good-looking wives and made them fruitful. Their sons were called Nephilim, "Fellers," and were "mighty ones," who made a name for themselves.

[38] When the Flood came, those disobedient sons of God could not get into Noah's ark, and so, to escape from the floodwaters, they dematerialized, dissolved their assumed human bodies, and re-

---

37. How was it possible for these heavenly sons of God to marry women on earth, and what were their offspring called?
38, 39. When the Flood came, what happened to those disobedient sons of God, as explained in the Bible?

turned to the spirit realm. They were not admitted back to the heavenly family of God's perfect, sinless sons. They were degraded to a very low state that the Bible calls "Tartarus." Of this we read:

[39] "God did not hold back from punishing the angels that sinned, but, by throwing them into Tartarus, delivered them to pits of dense darkness to be reserved for judgment; and he did not hold back from punishing an ancient world, but kept Noah, a preacher of righteousness, safe with seven

others when he brought a deluge upon a world of ungodly people." (2 Peter 2:4, 5) "And the angels that did not keep their original position but forsook their own proper dwelling place he has reserved with eternal bonds under dense darkness for the judgment of the great day."—Jude 6.

[40] For this reason the apostle Peter speaks of them as the "spirits in prison, who had once been disobedient when the patience of God was waiting in Noah's days, while the ark was being constructed, in which a few people, that is, eight souls [psykhé], were carried safely through the water." —1 Peter 3:19, 20.

40. So what expression does the apostle Peter use to describe them?

[41] In view of this form of imprisonment those disobedient spirit "sons of the true God" cannot materialize anymore and live like husbands with women. But they still keep as close as they can to mankind, especially to women, whom they prevail upon to serve as spirit mediums, fortune-tellers, clairvoyants, and so forth. They are no longer counted among the sons of God, because they have made demons of themselves. They have become the angels of the great symbolic dragon, Satan the Devil, the first demon. As the leader in demon activities, he has become their prince or ruler. The Bible speaks of him as "the ruler of the demons." As such, he was given the name Beelzebub. (Matthew 9:34; 12:24; Luke 11:15) In the Tartarean darkness of God's disfavor they are held reserved for the "judgment of the great day." To prove ourselves the friends of God and gain everlasting life, we must resist the demons and avoid all forms of demonism.—1 Timothy 4:1; Revelation 9:20; Ephesians 6:11-18.

41. (a) From what are those disobedient angels now restrained, but in what activities do they still engage? (b) To gain God's approval and everlasting life, what must we avoid?

CHAPTER 7

How Death and Imperfection Invaded Mankind

OD created man and made provision for him to live forever in a Paradise on earth. Death among mankind did not have to be! God would want perfect man to keep living, even more so than he wanted sinful, imperfect humans to live, to whom he said by his prophet Ezekiel: "'Throw off from yourselves all your transgressions in which you have transgressed and make for yourselves a new heart and a new spirit, for why should you die, O house of Israel? For I do not take any delight in the death of someone dying,' is the utterance of the Lord Jehovah. 'So cause a turning back and keep living, O you people.'" (Ezekiel 18:31, 32) The first man on earth, Adam, was not created out of harmony with Jehovah God but was a perfect human "son of God." Much less, then, would God his Creator want him to die. God made him to live.

² The opportunity of living forever in the Paradise of pleasure on earth was set before the first

1. (a) Was it God's purpose from the beginning for man to die? (b) Concerning this, what did God say even to sinful humans through his prophet Ezekiel?
2. What grand opportunity was set before man, and to that end what provisions were made?

man and, in him, before all mankind. God made the first man perfect, with a body that was working perfectly in all its parts and members. To the end that the perfect man in God's image and likeness might live forever in his Paradise home, God made provision of all food needed to keep the man's body in perfect working condition and repairing itself continually.

[3] This happy fact was very plain from what God told his perfect human son in Eden: "From every tree of the garden you may eat to satisfaction. But as for the tree of the knowledge of good and bad you must not eat from it, for in the day you eat from it you will positively die." (Genesis 2:16, 17) What, then, if the perfect man never ate from the forbidden fruit tree as long as God did not give him permission to do so? Naturally, the perfect man would live on forever in the earthly Paradise. Man's freedom from death depended, therefore, not only on his eating the necessary food from the trees from which he was allowed to eat, but on obeying God.

[4] God gave the man Adam a perfect wife, built up from material that God took from the man's perfect body so that thus she was bone of his bones and flesh of his flesh. They were one flesh, just as Jesus Christ later said to some questioners: "Did you not read that he who created them from the beginning made them male and female and said, 'For this reason a man will leave his father and his mother and will stick to his wife, and the two will be one flesh'? So that they are no longer two, but one flesh." (Matthew 19:4-6) In this way the first man's wife was created perfect and did not need to die. By being a real helper to her husband and by eating of the fruit from the trees allowed

---

3. On what did man's freedom from death depend, as shown in Genesis 2: 16, 17?
4. Was Adam's wife also perfect, and did she too have the prospect of living eternally?

and by obeying God perfectly, she would never come under condemnation. She would never die but live eternally with her husband and with her family.

⁵ God's purpose in creating this earth was to people it with persons higher than the fishes, the sea monsters, the birds and flying creatures, the wild beasts and the domestic animals. This divine purpose was given unmistakable expression when God provided a wife for the lone man Adam and then blessed the newly married couple and explained to them their privilege of producing children, saying: "Be fruitful and become many and fill the earth and subdue it." With regard to the fishes and great sea monsters and other moving things in the waters, God had said: "Be fruitful and become many and fill the waters in the sea basins, and let the flying creatures become many in the earth." (Genesis 1:22) And now finally God gave a like command to his highest creatures here on earth. They were to "fill the earth" with many perfect offspring.

⁶ The earth was to stay filled with their perfect, righteous descendants, their children, their grandchildren and their great-grandchildren. These descendants were not meant to die off and make room on earth for others to occupy. The earth was not meant to be a proving ground for mankind before they would be transferred to another place, presumably to heaven. The earth was not meant to be a breeding ground to provide inhabitants for heaven. Adam and Eve were not told to become many and fill the heavens. They were told to "fill the earth and subdue it." God did not need their help to fill heaven with people. He assigned to Adam and Eve and, through them, to their off-

5. What was God's purpose in creating this earth, and how was this made known to the first human couple?
6. Did God say anything about the earth as being a proving ground for mankind before they would be transferred to heaven?

spring the privilege of filling the earth to stay filled with human creatures living in perfect harmony with God.

[7] Modern-day scientists tell us that, despite the billions of stars and galaxies throughout the visible heavens, the most impressive thing about outer space is its emptiness. That being so, then it would take a long time for Adam and Eve and their offspring to populate the boundless heavens, that is to say, if it was God's purpose for them to do so. But it was not. Psalm 115:16 here bears repeating, for it says: "As regards the heavens, to Jehovah the heavens belong, but the earth he has given to the sons of men." So man has no responsibility for outer space.

[8] By remaining sinless and perfect, Adam and Eve were to bring perfect children into earthly life, under no condemnation or disability. They would bring up these perfect children in the perfect way of God, so that these, in turn, would bring forth perfect children into the earthly Paradise, these likewise being under no divine condemnation against their living for all time. Thus the reproducing of perfect children in righteousness and godliness would continue on till the whole earth was filled with them, to the same extent that the fishes fill the waters of the sea, with complete comfort and sufficient roominess for all. Then, with none of the offspring of Adam and Eve dying off, the earth would keep filled forever, Paradise at that time being not confined to just Eden but being extended all around the subdued earth. This would bring to final reality the purpose of earth's Creator, "who did not create it simply for nothing, who formed it even to be inhabited."—Isaiah 45:18.

7. In Psalm 115:16, what does it plainly identify as the place that God has given to man for his habitation?
8. What life prospects were the offspring of Adam meant to have, and so how would God's purpose for the earth finally have been realized?

⁹ Had God's command to our first parents been carried out faithfully, death of mankind would never have occurred. Of course, the lower forms of creature life would have continued dying after reproducing their kinds, just as they had done on earth on the fifth and sixth creative days before the creation of Adam and Eve. Those lower "living souls" were not designed to live forever as individual creatures, but their kinds were meant to continue reproducing forever, in subjection to mankind. However, humankind were constructed with the ability to live forever on earth in complete willing subjection to the will of their Creator, dependent upon his everlasting provisions for them in their earthly Paradise.

¹⁰ Had this divine purpose thus been carried out without interference or obstruction, there would have been no need for any emergency arrangement to get over the interference or obstruction, in order that God's purpose for the earth might not fail. There would have been no emergency arrangement that called for a human sacrifice and that made a marvelous provision for 144,000 members of mankind to be redeemed from the earth and exalted to immortal life in the heavens with Jesus Christ and Jehovah God. Yet, in its human perfection in the earthly Paradise, mankind would never have felt that it was missing anything, missing a higher life, and would never have wanted more. Nor would it become presumptuous and ask or demand more from God. Everlasting life in perfection, peace and happiness is a privilege, an undeserved kindness, for creatures on any plane or level of existence. So all perfect, intelligent creatures on the Paradise earth would have continued

9. (a) Were the lower animals designed to live forever? (b) How would it have been possible for humankind to live forever? 10. How did the provision for some from among mankind to be exalted to life in heaven come about, and would mankind have been discontented without that provision?

contented and would unceasingly give thanks to their heavenly Father and God.

THE ENEMY INVADES

[11] In the garden in Eden, Adam's wife Eve was not afraid of a snake. So, when a surprise greeted her and a snake began talking to her, she did not run away. She interestedly stayed to listen. The snake or serpent, in an innocently sounding way, asked her about God's law. She told the serpent that her everlasting life in Paradise depended upon her perfect obedience to God's law.

[12] With open contempt for God's law, the serpent told Eve she could enjoy eternal life in the earthly Paradise without being bound by God's law. In fact, as the serpent argued, she and her husband could enjoy a freer, independent life in a more enlightened way through the very act of disobeying God's law, defying him and taking to herself God's powers to determine what was good and what was bad. "For," said the serpent, "God knows that in the very day of your eating from it your eyes are bound to be opened and you [Adam and Eve] are bound to be like God, knowing good and bad." (Genesis 3:4, 5) The serpent seemed to want to help Eve and her husband, and so she began viewing it as a benefactor, not a liar.

[13] It was really Satan the Devil, appearing as an "angel of light," who was talking to Eve. But she did not realize this. What she now began wanting to do was to become "like God, knowing good and bad," and to help her husband Adam to become like God also. How Eve let herself be "thoroughly deceived" and how she broke God's law and also

---

11. With what apparently innocent inquiry did the serpent in Eden approach Eve, and what did she reply?
12, 13. (a) Though the serpent showed open contempt for God's law, why did Eve begin to view it as a benefactor and so let herself be "thoroughly deceived"? (b) How did her husband become involved in this transgression of God's law?

induced her husband to transgress God's law is told in a simple way in Genesis 3:6: "The woman saw that the tree's fruit was good for food and that it was something to be longed for to the eyes, yes, the tree was desirable to look upon. So she began taking of its fruit and eating it. Afterward she gave some also to her husband when with her and he began eating it."—1 Timothy 2:14.

[14] The serpent's voice was heard no more, but in due time God's voice was heard. He asked Adam: "From the tree from which I commanded you not to eat have you eaten?" Adam answered: "The woman whom you gave to be with me, she gave me fruit from the tree and so I ate it." Then Eve explained: "The serpent—it deceived me and so I ate." (Genesis 3:11-13) Disobedience to God's law had now invaded the earth. Sin had broken out among mankind. It deserved its penalty.

[15] In pronouncing condemnatory judgment upon Eve, God said: "I shall greatly increase the pain of your pregnancy; in birth pangs you will bring forth children, and your craving will be for your husband, and he will dominate you." Her husband had listened to her instead of to God, and so God said to Adam: "Because you listened to your wife's voice and took to eating from the tree concerning which I gave you this command, 'You must not eat from it,' cursed is the ground on your account. In pain you will eat its produce all the days of your life. And thorns and thistles it will grow for you, and you must eat the vegetation of the field. In the sweat of your face you will eat bread until you return to the ground, for out of it you were taken. For dust you are and to dust you will return."
—Genesis 3:16-19.

---

14. When questioned by God about the matter, how did both Adam and Eve endeavor to shift the blame, but would their sin go unpunished?
15. What was the judgment passed upon Eve and upon Adam?

¹⁶ With those words God pronounced the sentence of death upon Adam and, because she was one flesh with him and also guilty of transgression, upon Eve. Where, in those words of God, is there any sentencing of Adam and Eve to eternal torture in everlasting fire and sulphur after they died? There is none. God had not threatened Adam with eternal torment by fire, brimstone and immortal worms after death, but God had said to Adam: "As for the tree of the knowledge of good and bad you must not eat from it, for in the day you eat from it you will positively die."—Genesis 2:17.

¹⁷ God, who does not lie, must stick to the stated penalty for sin, and not punish man with more than what God had said. Adam knew what death would mean for him. He had no fear of what demonistic religions today describe as "everlasting torment in hell-fire and brimstone at the hands of red devils." Justly Jehovah God the Judge did not sentence Adam with more than God's stated law had threatened. God sentenced Adam to death. For Adam this meant going back to the ground, from which he had been taken to become a "living soul." (Genesis 2:7) This did not mean returning to heaven, for neither he nor his wife Eve had ever been in heaven. They had never been in a "hell burning with fire and brimstone," and so they could not "return" there. However, Adam could return or go back to lifeless dust. This is what he now expected.

¹⁸ Adam and Eve immediately began dying. They did not die on that same day of twenty-four hours. If Eve were to "bring forth children" in birth pangs, she would need to have at least nine months of time of pregnancy after conception. When sentencing Adam, God mentioned to him "all the days

<hr>

16, 17. Why is it evident that Adam and Eve did not go to "everlasting torment in hell-fire" or to heaven?
18, 19. (a) Did Adam and his wife die "in the day" that they sinned, and how so? (b) Has any man ever lived more than a thousand years?

of your life," and for Adam to eat bread in the sweat of his face he would have to live some days. Evidently when God spoke to him about dying in the day of his eating the forbidden fruit, God was speaking from the standpoint of one of His ways of measuring time as described by the apostle Peter: "One day is with Jehovah as a thousand years and a thousand years as one day." (2 Peter 3:8) God's Word allows therefore for the six days of his earthly creative activity to be each more than twenty-four hours long. On such a basis the sinner Adam could not live longer than a thousand years. And he did not do so.

[19] Concerning Adam, Genesis 5:4, 5 says: "He became father to sons and daughters. So all the days of Adam that he lived amounted to nine hundred and thirty years and he died." Whether Adam's wife Eve outlived him is not stated, but she did not live longer than a thousand years. God's sentence on her husband prevented that. Today, about six thousand years from Adam's creation, such an age is unheard of. But we must remember that Adam fell from human perfection with its possibility of living forever. For that reason he would be long in deteriorating till finally his now ailing body would not function anymore, causing his death. But earthly conditions before the flood of Noah's day may also have contributed to such a long life. The man who is reported to have lived the longest was Methuselah, but he was the eighth generation when counting from Adam the once-perfect man. Still he died *under* a thousand years of age, when nine hundred and sixtynine years old, in the very year in which the Flood broke.—Genesis 5:27.

[20] When Adam died, in the year 3096 B.C.E., he really died; that is, he ceased to be, he passed out of all existence anywhere. He had not been

20. When Adam died, did he have any prospect of future life?

created in sin so that he was helpless against sin. He was a willful sinner, and so he did not even have a hope of resurrection. Hence he could not become God's first prophet still alive in heaven. Genesis 2:7 plainly states that God created Adam to be a "living soul [*néphesh*]." And in Ezekiel 18:4 the same God says: "The soul that is sinning —it itself will die." So the "living soul" Adam died. There was no immortal human soul to escape from his dead body and to live on after Adam died.

²¹ Adam was sentenced to "eat the vegetation of the field," among "thorns and thistles," not to eat the fruit of the trees of the garden of Eden. Hence God drove him and his wife out of the garden of Eden to die. This was, as God said, "in order that he may not put his hand out and actually take fruit also of the tree of life and eat and live forever." (Genesis 3:22, 23, edition of 1953) "Live forever"—where? Why, right here on earth where that tree of life was growing. To prevent Adam from getting back into the Paradise garden and getting to the tree the eating of which guaranteed one's living forever, God did something more. Genesis 3:24 says: "He drove the man out and posted at the east of the garden of Eden the cherubs and the flaming blade of a sword that was turning itself continually to guard the way to the tree of life."

21. Why were Adam and his wife driven out of the garden of Eden, and how were they prevented from returning?

[22] It was after Adam and Eve began dying as sinners outside the garden of Eden that they began to have children, just as the next verse (Genesis 4:1) goes on to say: "Now Adam had intercourse with Eve his wife and she became pregnant. In time she gave birth." They could not produce children in human perfection, for they did not have it themselves anymore. They could not produce righteous children, because they themselves were sinners under sentence of death. For this reason a later descendant of Adam and Eve said: "Man, born of woman, is short-lived and glutted with agitation. Like a blossom he has come forth and is cut off, and he runs away like the shadow and does not keep existing. Yes, upon this one you have opened your eye, and me you bring into judgment with you. Who can produce someone clean out of someone unclean? There is not one." —Job 14:1-4.

[23] Is it any wonder, then, that all of us who have been begotten by a sinful human father as well as been "born of woman" are unclean from birth, unclean in God's sight? Is it strange that we have been born sinful? It is with us just as King David of Jerusalem said in his confession of sin to God: "Look! With error I was brought forth with birth pains, and in sin my mother conceived me." (Psalm 51:5) From conception onward we are sinful, imperfect, unclean to God, and are rightly therefore under God's condemnation of death. So we are born dying. This condemned condition, this dying condition of ours, we inherited from Adam. No man born of a human father and mother, not even the Hindu prince Siddhartha who came to be called Gautama the Buddha, was able to escape it or has been able to do so. Even to the nation over

22. When did Adam and Eve begin to have children, and in what condition were they born?
23. How do the Scriptures show whether newborn children have inherited sin and are therefore under a condemnation of death?

which King David had ruled, God said: "Your own father, the first one, has sinned, and your own spokesmen have transgressed against me."—Isaiah 43:27.

²⁴ King David's people tried to gain everlasting life on earth by keeping the Law given to their nation by God through the prophet Moses. But they were unable to keep it perfectly and gain merit for themselves that would earn everlasting life for them. Why so? Explaining it, the Christian apostle Paul, who himself was once under that Law of Moses, said: "Through one man sin entered into the world and death through sin, and thus death spread to all men because they had all sinned—. For until the Law sin was in the world." (Romans 5:12, 13) And the inability of Moses' own people to keep the Ten Commandments and the other related ordinances and statutes of God's Law proved that sin could not be wiped out by one's gaining merit for oneself in this way; but that sin was continuing among all the world of mankind, whether one was under the Law of Moses or not. The Christian apostle Paul goes on to say: "The wages sin pays is death." (Romans 6: 23) So death has continued to rule as king over all mankind down to our very day.

²⁵ The death that all of us inherited from our first human father Adam is sometimes fittingly called "the Adamic death." The Holy Bible has much to say about this Adamic death, from the first of its books down to its last book. The first book, Genesis, in its third and fourth chapters, tells us how death invaded the world of mankind, thus posing for us the hard question: "What able-bodied man is there alive who will not see death? Can he provide escape for his soul [*néphesh*] from

24. Why was it not possible for those living under God's law given through Moses to wipe out sin by obedience to that Law, and so what has continued to rule as king over mankind? 25. Is it possible for anyone to be delivered from the death that all of us have inherited from Adam?

the hand of Sheol?" (Psalm 89:48) Of course, no man inheriting Adamic death can do this of himself. Nevertheless, Almighty God can deliver persons from Adamic death and from Sheol to which it leads. What is more, God has promised to do so. One day the invader Death will have to beat a retreat, robbed of all its spoils by the power of Almighty God as exercised through the promised "seed" of the woman, who must shortly bruise the "original serpent" in the head.—Genesis 3:15.

[26] The conditions that will prevail on earth when God brings this about are described in the last book of the Bible. Revelation 21:3, 4 says prophetically: "Look! The tent of God is with mankind, and he will reside with them, and they will be his peoples. And God himself will be with them. And he will wipe out every tear from their eyes, and death will be no more, neither will mourning nor outcry nor pain be any more. The former things have passed away."

26. What conditions will prevail on earth when God brings about this deliverance for mankind?

of the Christian congregation, James the son of
Joseph, wrote about Abraham's faith,
works and declarations that justified him as having
Abraham put faith in Jehovah, and it was counted
to him as righteousness, and he came to be called
'Jehovah's friend.' . . . You see that a man is to
be proved righteous by works, and not by faith
alone."—James 2:23, 24.

CHAPTER 8

The True Seed of
"Abraham My Friend"

NUMBER of peoples today claim to be
descended from the ancient patriarch
Abraham in a fleshly way. When we count from
Shem, who survived the great flood with his father
Noah, Abraham was the tenth in the line of descent and was born in 2018 B.C.E., one hundred
and fifty years before Shem died. Why is it that
these peoples are so eager to trace their family
line of descent from Abraham, either by his first
son Ishmael, or by his second son Isaac, or by his
grandson Esau? It is because God himself declared
Abraham to be "his friend" and promised to use
Abraham's seed or offspring in a way that would
result in blessing for all the families and nations
of the earth. Consequently it would be an honor
and privilege to be that particular seed of the
man who was God's friend, God's lover. This would
make that particular people of importance to all
mankind.—Genesis 11:10 to 12:7.

[2] What brought Abraham this friendship with
God? It was Abraham's works of faith, his acts
showing belief in the one living and true Almighty
God. One of Abraham's natural descendants, a

1. Why are certain peoples today eager to be identified as the
fleshly descendants of Abraham?
2. How did Abraham become "Jehovah's friend"?

183

man of the Middle East named James the son of Joseph of Nazareth, wrote about Abraham's faith and said: "The scripture was fulfilled which says: 'Abraham put faith in Jehovah, and it was counted to him as righteousness,' and he came to be called 'Jehovah's friend.'" (James 2:23) Before speaking about Abraham's faith, another of his descendants wrote and showed why Abraham pleased God, saying: "Without faith it is impossible to please him well, for he that approaches God must believe that he is and that he becomes the rewarder of those earnestly seeking him." (Hebrews 11:6) Abraham's faith laid the basis for his becoming God's friend.

[3] When Abraham came prominently to view in Bible history he was living in Ur of the Chaldeans, a city about 150 miles southeast of Babylon where demonism was openly practiced. Being a descendant of Shem, he was in the right line of descent, for Noah had pronounced a blessing upon Shem, saying: "Blessed be Jehovah, Shem's God, and let Canaan become a slave to him. Let God grant ample space to Japheth, and let him reside in the tents of Shem." (Genesis 9:26, 27) This blessing was a broad indication that the promised Seed of the woman, who was to bruise the Serpent in the head, was to come in Shem's line of descent. Abraham was in that line of descent.

[4] Where Shem was at that time we do not know; but when he was 525 years old, in 1943 B.C.E., Shem's God revealed himself to Abraham in Ur of the Chaldeans. Solemn testimony in the highest religious court of ancient Jerusalem confirms that historical fact, in these words of Stephen, a descendant of Abraham: "Brothers and fathers,

3. Of whom was Abraham a descendant, and why is this significant?
4, 5. (a) Why did Abraham move out, first, from Ur of the Chaldeans and later from Haran? (b) What blessing was promised if Abraham showed faith by obeying this call from God, and who would benefit from it?

hear. The God of glory appeared to our forefather Abraham while he was in Mesopotamia, before he took up residence in Haran, and he said to him, 'Go out from your land and from your relatives and come on into the land I shall show you.' Then he went out from the land of the Chaldeans and took up residence in Haran. And from there, after his father died, God caused him to change his residence to this land in which you now dwell." (Acts 7:2-4) This call put a great test upon Abraham's faith in Shem's God. However, a blessing was promised if Abraham would obey. The prophet Moses brings this to our attention in his account of the matter, saying:

[5] "Jehovah proceeded to say to Abram: 'Go your way out of your country and from your relatives and from the house of your father to the country that I shall show you; and I shall make a great nation out of you and I shall bless you and I will make your name great; and prove yourself a blessing. And I will bless those who bless you, and him that calls down evil upon you I shall curse, and all the families of the ground will certainly bless themselves by means of you.' "—Genesis 12:1-3.

[6] Of all the nations that have descended from Abraham, which one was to be and has proved to be that "great nation"? This all depended on God's choice, and not just on fleshly line of descent. When childless Abraham (or, at first, Abram by name) got into the land that God showed him, he at once extended his worship of God there in that new land where the demon god Baal was worshiped by the Canaanites. At a place near Shechem, God appeared to Abraham and said: "To your seed I am going to give this land." Apparently that seed was to become Abraham's "great

6. What would determine which nation would be that "great nation" of which God spoke to Abraham?

nation" through whom blessing would go to all the families of the ground.—Genesis 12:6-8.

⁷ Abraham's nephew named Lot came with him into the Promised Land. Later they had to separate. But when invaders from outside Canaanland captured Lot, Abraham went in pursuit and recovered Lot. On his way back from this victory over the invading kings, Abraham was met by

Melchizedek, who was king of the city of Salem and was also "priest of the Most High God." Melchizedek gave the credit for Abraham's victory to God. Very plainly, then, Abraham had God's blessing. So Melchizedek blessed Abraham and said: "Blessed be Abram of the Most High God, Producer of heaven and earth; and blessed be the Most High God, who has delivered your oppressors into your hand!" In honor to God and in gratitude to him, Abraham gave a tenth part of all the spoils of victory to God's priest Melchizedek. Things that the invaders had taken in plunder from the people of Sodom, Abraham restored to them. Instead of enriching himself by plunder, Abraham looked to God to make him rich, that thus God's blessing upon him might be more manifest.—Genesis 14:18-23.

---

7. After Abraham rescued his nephew Lot, what king-priest came out to meet him, and how did he make clear that it was God who was blessing Abraham?

[8] Being advanced in years, Abraham was troubled about not having an heir to his estate. One night God had him go outside his tent and look up to the stars to see if he could count them. Then God said: "So your seed will become." Abraham put faith in that promise, and God counted Abraham's faith in Him as righteousness, this making it possible for him and God to be friends.—Genesis 15:5, 6.

[9] Abraham also wanted to know when he would take possession of the Promised Land. So God went through the formal ceremony of making a covenant with him concerning the land. In that connection God again took up the prophetic role and said to Abraham: "You may know for sure that your seed will become an alien resident in a land not theirs, and they will have to serve them, and these will certainly afflict them for four hundred years. But the nation that they will serve I am judging, and after that they will go out with many goods. As for you, you will go to your forefathers in peace; you will be buried at a good old age. But in the fourth generation they will return here, because the error of the Amorites has not yet come to completion."—Genesis 15:13-16.

[10] The question now arose, Which people that would descend from Abraham would have this experience, the people descending from him through his son Ishmael, or the people descending from him through his son Isaac, or the people descending from him through his grandson Esau, the twin brother of Jacob? The particular people that would have this experience would be marked as being the chosen "seed" of Abraham and as being the desig-

---

8. (a) At a time when Abraham was troubled about not having an heir, what promise did God make? (b) What resulted from Abraham's faith in that divine promise?
9. How did God reassure Abraham about taking possession of the Promised Land, but what did he say would happen first?
10. Why are we interested in knowing which people would undergo this experience foretold to Abraham?

nated heirs of the land that was promised to their forefather Abraham.

[11] Abraham's true wife Sarah continued barren, and so she had her Egyptian slave girl Hagar have relations with her husband Abraham. In due time Hagar bore Ishmael to Abraham, who was now eighty-six years old. Abraham loved Ishmael very much, but God did not accept Ishmael to be Abraham's heir with a title to the promised privileges. In the course of time Ishmael became father to twelve chieftains; but the people who descended from these chieftains did not go through the experience that God predicted when he made his formal covenant with Abraham for possession of the Promised Land.—Genesis 25:13-16.

[12] Hence when Abraham was ninety-nine years old, Jehovah God made an appearance to him and spoke of a seed of Abraham different from Ishmael the son of the slave girl Hagar. God said to Abraham: "Your name will not be called Abram [Father of Exaltation] any more, and your name must become Abraham [Father of a Multitude], because a father of a crowd of nations I will make you. And I will make you very, very fruitful and will make you become nations, and kings will come out of you." This was to be through his true wife Sarah, concerning whom God now added this promise: "As for Sarai your wife, you must not call her name Sarai [Contentious], because Sarah [Princess; mother of kings] is her name. And I will bless her and also give you a son from her; and I will bless her and she shall become nations; kings [not just chieftains] of peoples will come from her."—Genesis 17:3-6, 15-17; 25:12-19.

[13] Thus the lone son of Sarah the free woman was to be the seed through whom would come

11, 12. Did Abraham's son Ishmael prove to be the heir to the promises made by God to his father, and how do we know?
13, 14. So through which of Abraham's sons was the promised seed to come, and what was remarkable about his birth?

Abraham's promised seed as numberless as the stars of heaven. God said that his name was to be called Isaac, meaning "Laughter."—Genesis 17:19.

¹⁴ According to the covenant that God established at this time Abraham got circumcised and then had his son Ishmael circumcised. It was as a circumcised man that Abraham became father to Isaac by his true wife Sarah, miraculously so, because both Abraham and Sarah were then past the natural age of procreating children, she being ninety years old and he being a hundred.—Genesis 21:1-7.

¹⁵ Years later, when a feast was held to celebrate the weaning of Isaac, his mother Sarah saw teen-age Ishmael "poking fun" or playing with him in a mocking way. Fearing for her son Isaac's future, Sarah asked Abraham to send the slave girl Hagar and her son away. This request displeased Abraham, but God said: "Listen to her voice, because it is by means of Isaac that what will be called your seed will be. And as for the son of the slave girl, I shall also constitute him a nation, because he is your offspring." So Abraham had to show faith in God and obey. He was comforted in that Ishmael his half-Egyptian son would become a "nation" able to claim descent from Abraham, but what would be called the "seed of Abraham" would be through Isaac, the son of the free woman Sarah. Next morning Abraham sent Hagar the Egyptian and Ishmael her son away, she being free to go where she wanted.—Genesis 21:8-14.

¹⁶ God protected Ishmael's life for Abraham's sake. He grew up and preferred to dwell in the wilderness as an archer. His mother married him into her own Egyptian nation. (Genesis 21:15-21; 16:1, 11-16) As for Isaac, years later, when Isaac

---

15. How did Ishmael come to be separated from the household of his father, but what promise was made concerning him?
16, 17. Why did God command that Isaac be offered as a human sacrifice, and how did Abraham meet this test?

became forty years old, his father Abraham took a wife for him from his Shemite relatives, the granddaughter of his brother Nahor. (Genesis 24: 1-67; 25:19, 20) However, years before Isaac's marriage God spared his life from being sacrificed. For prophetic purposes God commanded Abraham to offer up his heir Isaac as a human sacrifice upon one of the mountains in the land of Moriah, near the city of Salem where King Melchizedek was priest of the Most High God. By faith Abraham met this test, just as we read in Hebrews 11:17-19:

[17] "By faith Abraham, when he was tested, as good as offered up Isaac, and the man that had gladly received the promises attempted to offer up his only-begotten son, although it had been said to him: 'What will be called "your seed" will be through Isaac.' But he reckoned that God was able to raise him up even from the dead; and from there he did receive him also in an illustrative way."

[18] When Abraham was about to kill Isaac, already bound upon the altar on the mountain of Moriah, God's angel stopped him from going farther. Abraham's attention was drawn to a ram caught in a thicket nearby, and  this animal he offered up instead. He called the place Jehovah-jireh, meaning "Jehovah Will See to It," or, "Jehovah Will Provide." Then God's an-

---

18. (a) Did Abraham actually put his son Isaac to death on the altar? (b) What further significant promise did Jehovah make at this time?

gel called to Abraham and said: " 'By myself I do swear,' is the utterance of Jehovah, 'that by reason of the fact that you have done this thing and you have not withheld your son, your only one, I shall surely bless you and I shall surely multiply your seed like the stars of the heavens and like the grains of sand that are on the seashore; and your seed will take possession of the gate of his enemies. And by means of your seed all nations of the earth will certainly bless themselves due to the fact that you have listened to my voice.' "—Genesis 22:1-18.

[19] What God there swore to do, swearing by himself because he could swear by no one greater, no person afterward on earth could change, not even if he was a later prophet. God's word and his oath were "two unchangeable things in which it is impossible for God to lie." (Hebrews 6:13-18) It is therefore unchangeably the will of God that "all nations of the earth" (including those nations descended from Ishmael and Esau) must "bless themselves" by means of Abraham's seed through his son Isaac. It does us no good to become nationalistic and to show prejudice against what proves to be the true seed of Abraham for blessing all mankind. Does natural descent determine who this "seed" is? We shall see.

[20] What was foreshadowed by that prophetic drama that Abraham and Isaac enacted on Mount Moriah over thirty-eight centuries ago? The prophet Jesus of Nazareth explained. One night in Jerusalem he said to a man who considered him to be a teacher from God: "God loved the world so much that he gave his only-begotten Son, in order that everyone exercising faith in him might not be destroyed but have everlasting life." (John 3:1-16) So God's prophet said!

---

19. What did God's word and his oath on this occasion constitute, and so what is unchangeably his will for all nations?
20. What was foreshadowed by Abraham's offering up of Isaac?

THE COURSE LEADING UP TO THE TRUE SEED

²¹ Fifteen years before Abraham died, his son Isaac had twin sons born to him. The first one brought forth was named Esau. The one next brought forth was named Jacob. Did God decree that these two sons should become one nation of but two tribes, the one tribe of it being headed by Esau the firstborn and the other tribe of it being headed by Jacob? No! Even before their birth God told their mother Rebekah: "Two nations are in your belly, and two national groups will be separated from your inward parts; and the one national group will be stronger than the other national group, and the older will serve the younger." (Genesis 25:21-26) God did not lie in this prophecy, for history shows that Esau's descendants did serve in subjection to the descendants of the younger twin Jacob. Why was this? Because Jacob became the heir of the promise or covenant that God had made first with Abraham and then had renewed with Isaac. After Jacob left home he had a dream of a ladder between heaven and earth. "There was Jehovah stationed above it, and he proceeded to say:

²² " 'I am Jehovah the God of Abraham your father and the God of Isaac. The land upon which you are lying, to you I am going to give it and to your seed. And your seed will certainly become like the dust particles of the earth, and you will certainly spread abroad to the west and to the east and to the north and to the south, and by means of you and by means of your seed all the families of the ground will certainly bless themselves.' "—Genesis 28:13-15.

21, 22. (a) Before the birth of Isaac's two sons, what did God foretell concerning them? (b) Which of these two sons became heir of the covenant that God had made with Abraham, and what did God say to him?

²³ Strengthened by this promise, Jacob made his way to the "city of Nahor," or Haran, in northern Mesopotamia and got in touch with the family of his mother Rebekah. (Genesis 24:10-15; 27:42, 43; 28:10) Within the next thirty-one years Jacob became the father of twelve sons and a daughter, Dinah, and other unnamed daughters. (Genesis 37: 35; 46:7) The last of the twelve sons, Benjamin, was born near Bethlehem after Jacob's return to the Promised Land after God's angel had given him the surname Israel. His father Isaac died years after Jacob's twelfth son was born. (Genesis 35:16-29; 32:24-28) It was not God's will that those twelve sons of Jacob or Israel should become twelve separate nations, with only one of such nations inheriting the rights and privileges of God's covenant with Abraham. Instead, the twelve sons of Jacob or Israel clung together to form one nation, but composed of twelve related tribes. This nation did prove to be the particular "seed" that went through the affliction foretold by God when making the formal covenant with Abraham for the possessing of the Promised Land. How did that nation do so?

²⁴ Under the guiding providence of Jehovah God, Jacob and his children and their families moved down to the foreign land of Egypt during the course of a seven-year famine in that general area. That was in the year 1728 B.C.E., ten years after the death of his father Isaac. Jacob's eleventh son, Joseph, was then serving as Food Administrator of Egypt. Jacob (Israel) died down there, after prophesying over his sons. Over his fourth son, Judah, he spoke a prophecy having to do with Kingdom rule, saying: "The scepter will not turn

23. (a) Into what did the offspring of the twelve sons of Jacob or Israel develop? (b) Which nation proved to be the "seed" that underwent the affliction foretold to Abraham?
24, 25. (a) How did Jacob and his descendants come to be in Egypt? (b) When blessing his sons before his own death, what did Jacob prophesy about his son Judah?

aside from Judah, neither the commander's staff from between his feet, until Shiloh [meaning 'The One Whose It Is'] comes; and to him the obedience of the people will belong."—Genesis 49:10.

²⁵ Concerning Jacob's final words the prophet Moses wrote: "All these are the twelve tribes of Israel, and this is what their father spoke to them when he was blessing them. He blessed them each one according to his own blessing." (Genesis 49:28) Fifty-four years later on Joseph himself died, in 1657 B.C.E.

²⁶ The twelve tribes of Israel kept on growing in number in Egypt's province of Goshen. This frightened the Egyptian government. So it took measures to stop this growth, finally decreeing that all boy babies born should be thrown into the Nile River and thus all future fathers of the twelve tribes of Israel be killed off. Great was the affliction upon them, just as God foretold in Genesis 15:13. At this time Moses was born in the tribe of

Levi and was saved from death in the Nile River. He was brought up in the court of the king of Egypt, but, because of fighting for his oppressed people, he was obliged to flee for his life from Egypt. Thus while he was shepherding

26, 27. (a) What affliction came upon the Israelites in Egypt? (b) Who was Moses, and in whose name was he commissioned to lead the enslaved Israelites out of Egypt?

his father-in-law's sheep at Mount Horeb in Arabia, God chose him to lead the enslaved people of Israel out of Egypt and toward the Promised Land. If the Israelites down in Egypt asked Moses who sent him to them, what was Moses to say?

[27] "Then God said once more to Moses: 'This is what you are to say to the sons of Israel, "Jehovah the God of your forefathers, the God of Abraham, the God of Isaac and the God of Jacob, has sent me to you." This is my name to time indefinite, and this is the memorial of me to generation after generation.' "—Exodus 3:15.

[28] Ten times the Pharaoh or King of Egypt refused Jehovah's demand through Moses and his brother Aaron that he let the twelve tribes of Israel go free from slavery and leave Egypt in order to worship and serve their God Jehovah. The

tenth refusal was followed by a tenth plague on all Egypt, the death of all its firstborn of man and beast. The firstborn of the Israelites were passed over because their family heads killed the passover

lamb on the fourteenth day of the lunar month of Nisan, marked their doorways with its blood, and stayed indoors that night, eating the roast lamb with unleavened bread and bitter herbs. Now in fear and broken in spirit, Pharaoh, under pressure

28, 29. (a) Although Pharaoh repeatedly refused to free the Israelites, why did he finally tell them to go? (b) How many years was this after Abraham had first entered the Promised Land?

of the Egyptians, told the Israelites that night to leave the country. They proceeded to do so. Remarkably, that was four hundred and thirty years from when their faithful forefather Abraham obeyed Jehovah God and crossed the Euphrates River to enter the Promised Land. Thus we read:

²⁹ "And the dwelling of the sons of Israel, who had dwelt in Egypt, was four hundred and thirty years. And it came about at the end of the four hundred and thirty years, it even came about on this very day that all the armies of Jehovah went out of the land of Egypt. It is a night for observance with regard to Jehovah for bringing them out of the land of Egypt."—Exodus 12:40-42.

³⁰ However, in his prophecy to Abraham at the making of the covenant for the Promised Land, Jehovah God mentioned just four hundred years of affliction. Was there, then, a miscalculation? No; for Abraham's son Isaac was born in 1918 B.C.E., four hundred and five years before the passover night of Israel's liberation from Egypt, and so the affliction of Abraham's seed began when Isaac was weaned at five years of age and the half-Egyptian Ishmael afflicted Isaac by "poking fun" at him, mockingly playing with him. From then the affliction of Abraham's natural seed continued for four hundred years, till 1513 B.C.E. Hence God had not lied in this regard.

³¹ Moreover, the Israelites were to return to the Promised Land "in the fourth generation" from when their forefather Jacob (Israel) entered Egypt. This matter of generations can be reckoned through in two ways in but one tribe: In the tribe of Levi by (1) Levi; (2) Kohath; (3) Amram; and (4) Moses, who led the Israelites to the eastern border of the Promised Land before he died. Or,

---

30. For how many years, though, did Abraham's seed undergo affliction, as God had foretold, and how so?
31. Did the Israelites return to the Promised Land "in the fourth generation," as had been promised?

by (1) Levi; (2) Jochebed, the daughter of Levi (Numbers 26:59-63); and (3) Aaron; and (4) Eleazar, who entered the Promised Land. (Joshua 14:1) So neither in his prophecy concerning this matter was Jehovah God found to be lying.

[32] Since these two details mentioned in connection with God's covenant with Abraham were fulfilled exactly on the twelve tribes of Israel, it proves that they were the natural "seed" of Abraham whom God had in mind. They were the ones whom he chose to inherit the Promised Land from their forefather Abraham and they were the ones through whom a blessing was to come to all the families and nations of the earth. Not that all the nation of Israel would serve for a blessing to all mankind, but that the "seed" of the woman, whom God promised in the garden of Eden according to Genesis 3:15, would come through the nation of Israel. It was just as the former Jewish Pharisee, Saul of Tarsus, wrote to Christians in Rome:

[33] "Not all who spring from Israel are really 'Israel.' Neither because they are Abraham's seed are they all children, but: 'What will be called "your seed" will be through Isaac.' That is, the children in the flesh are not really the children of God, but the children by the promise are counted as the seed."—Romans 9:6-8.

[34] So a person's fleshly connection with Abraham or even with Isaac and Jacob is not wholly the determining thing in this case.

[35] From here on we can let a sabbath-day sermon given in a Jewish synagogue in Antioch of Pisidia of Asia Minor quickly summarize the history of

32-34. (a) What people, therefore, proved to be the ones through whom a blessing was to come to all the families of the earth? (b) Does this mean that all that nation would be a blessing to all mankind, and how does what a Jew from Tarsus wrote to Christians in Rome shed light on this?
35, 36. As explained in Acts 13:16-23, what was the history of the Israelites from the time of their leaving Egypt until the days of King David?

natural Israel for us. From Acts 13:16-23 we quote:

[36] "You Israelites and you others that fear God, hear. The God of this people Israel chose our forefathers, and he exalted the people during their alien residence in the land of Egypt and brought them out of it with an uplifted arm. And for a period of about forty years he put up with their manner of action in the wilderness. After destroying seven nations in the land of Canaan, he distributed the land to them by lot: all that during about four hundred and fifty years. And after these things he gave them judges until Samuel the prophet. But from then on they demanded a king, and God gave them Saul son of Kish, a man of the tribe of Benjamin, for forty years. And after removing him, he raised up for them David as king, respecting whom he bore witness and said, 'I have found David the son of Jesse, a man agreeable to my heart, who will do all the things I desire.' From the offspring of this man according to his promise God has brought to Israel a savior, Jesus."

[37] King David made grand preparations for building a most costly temple to Jehovah on Mount Moriah at Jerusalem. However, David's son and successor to the throne, Solomon, built the temple. For four hundred and twenty years it stood. On one occasion during the reign of King Jehoshaphat the city of Jerusalem came under threat of assault by the combined enemy forces of Moab, Ammon and Ammonim (Meunim) from Mount Seir. So the king gathered all his subjects to this temple of Jehovah and prayed for deliverance, saying: "Did not you yourself, O God of ours, drive away the inhabitants of this land from before your people Israel and then give it to the seed of Abraham,

---

37. At the temple built by David's son Solomon, what mention of the seed of Abraham was made in prayer in the days of King Jehoshaphat, and how did God respond?

your lover [or, friend], to time indefinite?" (2 Chronicles 20:7) God answered the prayer of King Jehoshaphat and his subjects at his temple and caused the destruction of the combined enemies before ever they got near Jerusalem. —2 Chronicles 20:1-29.

[38] Over the centuries the most of that "seed of Abraham" fell away from the pure worship of Jehovah God and defiled his holy temple. In retribution God let the Babylonian armies destroy the temple in the year 607 B.C.E., and for seventy years the land lay desolate without inhabitant. Meantime the thousands of the surviving Israelites were exiles in the distant territories of Babylon.

[39] However, more than a hundred and twenty-five years before that Jehovah God had inspired his prophet Isaiah to foretell the regathering of his people from their exile at even the extremities of the earth, to rebuild the temple of worship at Jerusalem. He reminded them of their relationship to him, saying: "But you, O Israel, are my servant, you, O Jacob, whom I have chosen, the seed of Abraham my friend; you, whom I have taken hold of from the extremities of the earth, and you, whom I have called even from the remote parts of it. And so I said to you, 'You are my servant; I have chosen you, and I have not rejected you.' "—Isaiah 41:8, 9.

[40] In the year 537 B.C.E. a faithful remnant of Israelites came back from exile in Babylon for the purpose of rebuilding the temple on its original location in Jerusalem. They began by building an altar at the location of the former one and offering sacrifices to Jehovah. But because of enemy interference it was first twenty-one years later

---

38. Did that "seed of Abraham" hold firmly to the worship of Jehovah, and so what finally occurred?
39, 40. (a) Long before this, what did Jehovah through his prophet Isaiah foretell as to the regathering of the exiled "seed of Abraham," and when did that regathering take place? (b) How long did the rebuilt temple stand, and what happened to the inhabitants of Judea after that?

that the temple was finished on Mount Moriah. (Ezra 3:1 to 6:15) This temple, which later underwent a remodeling, stood for five hundred and eighty-five years and some months. Then it was destroyed, in the year 70 of our Common Era, by the Roman armies, to fulfill the prophecies of Jesus the royal descendant of King David. (Matthew 23:37, 38; 24:1-16; Luke 19:41-45; 21:5-24) The inhabitants of Judea who survived the destruction of Jerusalem and its temple—reportedly 97,000 of them—were "led captive into all the nations."—Luke 21:24.

[41] Since that disastrous year the Israelites or Jews have been without a temple on Mount Moriah in Jerusalem, and also without a genuine priesthood in the family line of Aaron the brother of the prophet Moses. (Exodus 28:1 to 29:44) Each year they go through a form of celebrating the solemn Day of Atonement (*Yom Kippur*), but they are unable to celebrate it according to the way prescribed in the ancient Law of Moses. So it does not even typically take away their sins and bring them back into favor with the God of Abraham, Isaac and Jacob. They continue to be a scattered people.

[42] The modern Israelites had to fight with traditional enemies to reestablish themselves in a small part of the land that the ancient kingdom of Israel once ruled. They continue to be a persecuted people, upon whom have been fulfilled during the past nineteen hundred years things foretold by the prophet Moses in Leviticus 26:14-41 and Deuteronomy 28:15-68. Instead of all the nations of the earth blessing themselves by means of those natural descendants of Abraham, Isaac and Jacob, many of the nations curse the Jews and their po-

---

41. What has continued to be the situation with the Jews since then?
42. Have these scattered natural descendants of Abraham proved to be his "seed" by means of whom all nations would bless themselves?

litical Republic of Israel. The Jews support the international organization, the United Nations, of which the Republic of Israel has been a member since May 11, 1949. They have made themselves a part of the nations that are marching to Har–Magedon, to the "war of the great day of God the Almighty." (Revelation 16:13-16) From the present-day facts, not to mention statements of the inspired Holy Bible, it is very evident that those scattered natural descendants of Abraham are not the "seed of Abraham" by means of whom all the nations of the earth were to bless themselves.

[43] Take courage, however, God's promise and purpose have not failed. He will not prove to be a liar in this matter of such importance to all mankind. By a marvelous arrangement he will have his "seed of Abraham" for the blessing of all mankind regardless of race or color. Years after Jerusalem's temple was destroyed in the year 70 C.E. and the natural Israelites were scattered God gave a revelation to a Christian Jew, the apostle John, and pointed ahead to the producing of the full number of the true "seed of Abraham." In this revelation from God as given in the last book of the Holy Bible, written about 96 C.E., John writes:

[44] "And I saw another angel ascending from the sunrising, having a seal of the living God; and he cried with a loud voice to the four angels to whom it was granted to harm the earth and the sea, saying: 'Do not harm the earth or the sea or the trees, until after we have sealed the slaves of our God in their foreheads.' And I heard the number of those who were sealed, a hundred and forty-four thousand, sealed out of every tribe of the sons of Israel: Out of the tribe of Judah twelve thousand sealed; out of the tribe of Reuben twelve

---

43, 44. (a) Does this mean that God's purpose for the blessing of all mankind through the "seed of Abraham" has failed? (b) In this connection, what did God reveal to the apostle John?

thousand; out of the tribe of Gad twelve thousand; out of the tribe of Asher twelve thousand; out of the tribe of Naphtali twelve thousand; out of the tribe of Manasseh twelve thousand; out of the tribe of Simeon twelve thousand; out of the tribe of Levi twelve thousand; out of the tribe of Issachar twelve thousand; out of the tribe of Zebulun twelve thousand; out of the tribe of Joseph twelve thousand; out of the tribe of Benjamin twelve thousand sealed."—Revelation 7:2-8.

[45] Up till that revelation the exact number of the true "seed of Abraham" was unknown to mankind, like the unnumbered stars of the heavens and the sand grains on the seashore. Later in the revelation to John these 144,000 sealed "slaves" of God are seen in company with the principal member of the "seed of Abraham." John writes:

[46] "And I saw, and, look! the Lamb standing upon the Mount Zion, and with him a hundred and forty-four thousand having his name and the name of his Father written on their foreheads. And I heard a sound out of heaven as the sound of many waters and as the sound of loud thunder; and the sound that I heard was as of singers who accompany themselves on the harp playing on their harps. And they are singing as if a new song before the throne and before the four living creatures and the older persons; and no one was able to master that song but the hundred and forty-four thousand, who have been bought from the earth."—Revelation 14:1-3.

[47] The sacrifice of this one called "the Lamb" resulted in purchasing these 144,000 "sons of Israel" from the earth, and so it has more power than the sacrifice of a literal four-footed lamb.

45, 46. In Revelation 14:1-3, where and in whose company are these 144,000 "slaves" of God shown to be?
47. (a) How does "the Lamb" prove to be one through whom all mankind can obtain an everlasting blessing? (b) What is the Mount Zion where the symbolic Lamb and his 144,000 followers are shown to be, and how does it affect mankind?

(Revelation 5:9, 10) This is the kind of sacrifice that all mankind needs in order to bless itself. So through this principal one of the true "seed of Abraham" they will receive everlasting blessing from Jehovah God. This symbolic Lamb and his 144,000 "sons of Israel" stand upon the symbolic Mount Zion. This Mount Zion was foreshadowed by the earthly Mount Zion on which King David put his royal throne and set up his capital city. (2 Samuel 5:4-9) The symbolic Mount Zion is therefore the seat of government that is higher than the earth, on which the symbolic Lamb and his 144,000 followers who have been "bought from the earth" rule over all the rest of mankind after God's kingdom is established in the heavens.

[48] The symbolic Lamb and his 144,000 sealed followers are the true "seed of Abraham" by whom all the nations of the earth must bless themselves. How they become the promised seed of Abraham the friend of God, despite the failure of the larger part of the nation of natural Israel, we shall see in another chapter.

---

48. So who make up the true "seed of Abraham" by means of whom all nations must bless themselves?

CHAPTER 9

The Human Coming
of the Prophet
Like Moses

HE prophet Moses was a member of the natural seed of Abraham the friend of God. Necessarily the promised prophet who was to be like Moses must likewise be a member of the natural "seed of Abraham." Moses belonged to the tribe of Levi, who was a great-grandson of the patriarch Abraham. When we count from this Levi the son of Jacob, Moses proves to be in the fourth generation from Levi, and was born in the year 1593 B.C.E. in the land of Egypt in a northeastern section called Goshen. (Exodus 2:1-10; 6:17-20) However, to be like Moses it was not required of the promised prophet like him to be born in the tribe of Levi. His future work required him to be born in a different one of the twelve tribes of Israel, namely, in the tribe of Judah.

² In the month of Sivan of 1513 B.C.E., or in the third month after Moses led the twelve tribes of Israel out of Egypt and across the Red Sea into Arabia, God brought them to the foot of Mount

1. Of whom was Moses a descendant, and so of what people must the promised prophet like Moses be a member?
2. Through whom as mediator did God make a covenant with the nation of Israel at Mount Sinai?

Sinai. While they were encamped there, God called Moses up Mount Sinai for him to act as a go-between or mediator in making a covenant or solemn contract between God and the nation of Israel. God told Moses to tell them: "Now if you will strictly obey my voice and will indeed keep my covenant, then you will certainly become my special property out of all other peoples, because the whole earth belongs to me. And you yourselves will become to me a kingdom of priests and a holy nation." The nation of Israel agreed to enter into a covenant with God, saying: "All that Jehovah has spoken we are willing to do."—Exodus 19:1-9.

³ Several days later Moses brought the people out of their encampment to the base of Mount Sinai. God displayed his presence on top of Mount Sinai by fire, smoke, lightnings and a quaking of the whole mountain, together with trumpet sounds. Then God proclaimed the Ten Commandments, which were to become binding on the nation of Israel. (Exodus 19:16 to 20:17) At the miraculous sights and sounds the Israelites grew very frightened. In fear they said to their mediator Moses: "You speak with us, and let us listen; but let not God speak with us for fear we may die." So the people kept their distance from the mountain, but Moses went up into the cloud-mass where God's representative angel was. (Exodus 20:18-21) Later Moses himself told the Israelites what Jehovah said regarding their request:

⁴ "At that Jehovah said to me, 'They have done well in speaking what they did. A prophet I shall raise up for them from the midst of their brothers, like you; and I shall indeed put my words in his mouth, and he will certainly speak to them all that I shall command him. And it must occur that the

---

3, 4. (a) How did God manifest his presence there at Mount Sinai? (b) When Moses went up into the mountain on that occasion, what did Jehovah tell him concerning a future prophet?

man who will not listen to my words that he will speak in my name, I shall myself require an account from him.' "—Deuteronomy 18:17-19.

⁵ In the fortieth year after that, when Moses was nearing his death, he warned his people against the demonism practiced by the native inhabitants of the Promised Land. Moses said: "These nations whom you are dispossessing used to listen to those practicing magic and to those who divine; but as for you, Jehovah your God has not given you anything like this. A prophet from your own midst, from your brothers, like me, is what Jehovah your God will raise up for you —to him you people should listen—in response to all that you asked of Jehovah your God in Horeb on the day of the congregation, saying, 'Do not let me hear again the voice of Jehovah my God, and this great fire do not let me see any more, that I may not die.' " (Deuteronomy 18:14-16) Thus God promised a future Mediator, a future Prophet like Moses, for whom they should wait rather than give themselves over to demonized magicians and diviners.

⁶ More than a thousand years after Moses died the promised prophet like him had not yet come, but the last prophet of the Hebrew Scriptures, Malachi, spoke for God, saying: "Remember, you people, the law of Moses my servant with which I commanded him in Horeb concerning all Israel, even regulations and judicial decisions. Look! I am sending to you people Elijah the prophet before the coming of the great and fear-inspiring day of Jehovah." (Malachi 4:4, 5) This indicated that the prophet like Moses, as well as one like Elijah, was yet to come. But God was timing matters.

5. Rather than their listening to magicians and diviners, for whom did Moses at the end of his life urge his people to wait?
6. More than a thousand years later, what assurance did God give through his prophet Malachi?

⁷ About four and a half more centuries passed, and then in the year 3 B.C.E. God had it announced that a special prophet was to be born, in the tribe of Levi, in the family of the high priest Aaron the brother of Moses. Was this to be the promised prophet like Moses? No! For, inside the temple of Jerusalem, God's angel Gabriel told Zechariah the priest: "Your wife Elizabeth will become mother to a son to you, and you are to call his name John. . . . and many of the sons of Israel will he turn back to Jehovah their God. Also, he will go before him with Elijah's spirit and power." (Luke 1:8-17) So this John the son of priest Zechariah was to be a prophet like Elijah, in fulfillment of Malachi's prophecy.

⁸ Within six months of that announcement concerning John's coming birth the angel Gabriel announced the coming birth of an everlasting heir to King David. So this one was to be born in the tribe of Judah and in the royal family of David. In the town of Nazareth in the province of Galilee the angel Gabriel told the virgin Jewess Mary, a descendant of King David: "You will conceive in your womb and give birth to a son, and you are to call his name Jesus. This one will be great and will be called Son of the Most High; and Jehovah God will give him the throne of David his father, and he will rule as king over the house of Jacob forever, and there will be no end of his kingdom."

⁹ This Jesus was to have no human father, but, as Gabriel said to Mary, "holy spirit will come upon you, and power of the Most High will overshadow you. For that reason also what is born will be called holy, God's Son. . . . with God no declaration will be an impossibility."—Luke 1:26-37.

---

7. (a) In the year 3 B.C.E., whose birth was foretold to the priest Zechariah? (b) Like what prophet was he to be?
8. Within six months angelic announcement was made about what other birth, and in what line of descent?
9. Whose son really was this, and how so?

[10] Jesus the Son of the Most High God was to have John as his forerunner, for, when John was born in a city of Judah in the spring of 2 B.C.E., his father Zechariah prophesied over him: "As for you, young child, you will be called a prophet of the Most High, for you will go in advance before Jehovah to make his ways ready, to give knowledge of salvation to his people by forgiveness of their sins, because of the tender compassion of our God."—Luke 1:57-78.

[11] In the early autumn of that same year, in the nearby city of Bethlehem in Judah, Mary gave birth to Jesus. Thus he was born in the birthplace of King David, to whom he was to be the permanent Heir. That same night, out in the fields near the city, Jehovah's angel appeared to shepherds and announced Jesus' birth, saying: "Have no fear, for, look! I am declaring to you good news of a great joy that all the people will have, because there was born to you today a Savior, who is Christ the Lord, in David's city." Then a heavenly army of an-

gels appeared and said unitedly: "Glory in the heights above to God, and upon earth peace among men of good will." Without delay

10. For whom was John to be the forerunner, as prophesied at his birth?
11. Where was Jesus born, and what remarkable thing occurred near the city at the time of his birth?

the shepherds followed the angel's direction and found the newborn Jesus, who was to be anointed to be the everlasting Heir and Lord of King David. (Luke 2:1-20) The word "Christ" is Greek and, like the Hebrew word Messiah, means "Anointed One."

¹² Not long afterward things began happening to Jesus the Son of the Most High God like those that happened to the prophet Moses. Moses was born in Egypt at a time when Pharaoh the king had said that all newborn Hebrew boys should be killed by being thrown into the Nile River. But Moses was saved from such a death. (Exodus 1:22 to 2:10) As regards Jesus, some time after he had been circumcised as a Jew and had been presented as a firstborn son at the temple in Jerusalem, some Oriental astrologers came to aged King Herod the Great of Jerusalem and announced the birth of a boy who was to be "king of the Jews." It was no son of diseased old Herod. So, in fear for his family, he sent the astrologers to Bethlehem, the city indicated by the prophecy of Micah 5:2, to locate this babe who threatened Herod's royal line. When the astrologers did not report back to King Herod, he sent soldiers to Bethlehem to kill off all boys there two years old and younger, thus to make sure of killing the "one born king of the Jews." (Matthew 2:1-12, 16-18) But, like Moses, the boy Jesus was preserved alive. How?

¹³ After the astrologers had visited Jesus in a house in Bethlehem, an angel told his foster-father Joseph to leave at once and take the child to Egypt and stay there until Herod the king of Jerusalem died. "So he got up and took along the young child and its mother by night and withdrew into Egypt, and he stayed there until the decease of Herod, for that to be fulfilled which was spoken by Jeho-

---

12. Like Moses, how was Jesus saved from death when he was a young child?
13, 14. Like Moses, how was Jesus called out of Egypt by God?

vah through his prophet, saying: 'Out of Egypt
I called my son.'" (Matthew 2:13-15) When,
after King Herod's death, Joseph brought Jesus
out of Egypt and back to the Promised Land, it
was a further fulfillment of the prophecy of Hosea
11:1, which reads: "When Israel was a boy, then
I loved him, and out of Egypt I called my son."
The prophet Moses came out with Israel.

[14] To Pharaoh king of Egypt, Jehovah God had
spoken by Moses concerning the whole nation of
Israel as a son, as "my first-born." (Exodus 4:22)
Moses was a part of that nation, and thus when
Jehovah called the whole nation as his firstborn
son "out of Egypt," he also called Moses as national leader out of Egypt. So Hosea 11:1 pointed
both backward to Israel and Moses and forward
to Jesus.

[15] In Hebrews 11:24-26 we read: "By faith Moses, when grown up, refused to be called the son
of the daughter of Pharaoh, choosing to be ill-
treated with the people of God rather than to have
the temporary enjoyment of sin, because he es-
teemed the reproach of the Christ as riches greater than the treasures of Egypt; for he looked
intently toward the payment of the reward."

[16] After Moses took his stand as being a Hebrew
rather than an Egyptian, Jehovah God anointed,
that is to say, appointed Moses to be his prophet,
and as such Moses was "the Christ" or "the
Anointed (Appointed) One." Of course, too, Jehovah's spirit was upon Moses as a prophet. (Numbers 11:16, 17, 24, 25) In that way Moses was
"the Christ" of that time; but in order to come
into that privileged position he had to give up the
"treasures of Egypt" and let himself "be ill-treated
with the people of God" and thus suffer reproach.
But to Moses such "reproach of the Christ" was
riches greater than all of Egypt's wealth.

15, 16. Why does Hebrews, chapter 11, refer to Moses as "the
Christ," and appropriately so?

[17] As regards Jesus, according to the angel's announcement at his birth in Bethlehem he was to become a "Savior, who is Christ the Lord." When did he become Christ or "Anointed One"? After the prophet John the son of priest Zechariah baptized Jesus in the Jordan River. Then Jesus was anointed with God's holy spirit, for we read, in Luke 3:21-23: "Now when all the people were baptized, Jesus also was baptized and, as he was praying, the heaven was opened up and the holy spirit in bodily shape like a dove came down upon him, and a voice came out of heaven: 'You are my Son, the beloved; I have approved you.' Furthermore, Jesus himself, when he commenced his work, was about thirty years old."

[18] Some days after Jesus was baptized, Simon Peter of Galilee met him. (John 1:35-42) Later on Peter said to interested non-Jews: "You know the subject that was talked about throughout the whole of Judea, starting from Galilee after the baptism that John preached, namely, Jesus who was from Nazareth, how God anointed him with holy spirit and power, and he went through the land doing good and healing all those oppressed by the Devil; because God was with him." (Acts 10: 37, 38) Not at birth, but at thirty years of age Jesus became Christ or "Anointed One." He applied to himself Isaiah's prophecy concerning the anointing with Jehovah's spirit. (Isaiah 61:1-3; Luke 4:16-21) Privately, to a Samaritan woman, he admitted that he was the Christ or Messiah. "The woman said to him: 'I know that Messiah is coming, who is called Christ. Whenever that one arrives, he will declare all things to us openly.' Jesus said to her: 'I who am speaking to you am he.' "—John 4:25, 26.

17, 18. (a) When and how did Jesus actually become "Christ"? (b) How did Jesus himself acknowledge that he had been anointed by Jehovah, that he was the Christ?

FURNISHING CREDENTIALS AS GOD'S PROPHET

[19] To prove that he was sent by God, both to the Hebrews and to the Egyptians, Moses performed many remarkable miracles or powerful works. He was used to bring ten plagues upon Egypt, to lead the Israelites across the split Red Sea and bring the waters back again while Pharaoh and the Egyptian pursuit forces were trying to cross; and in the wilderness of the peninsula of Sinai he performed a number of miracles. Thus he furnished ample credentials to prove that he was Jehovah's prophet and mediator. (Psalms 78:12-54; 105:23-43; 106:7-22) No less so than Moses, Jesus Christ performed many miracles to furnish evidence of this kind that God had sent him and was with him. With a word he calmed the raging sea of Galilee that threatened to capsize the boat in which he and his apostles were crossing; he even walked on its waters to join them in their boat. (Matthew 8:23-27; 14:23-34) When John the Baptist, who had been imprisoned by King Herod Antipas, sent to Jesus to ask whether he was the Christ or a forerunner, here is what happened:

[20] "In that hour he cured many of sicknesses and grievous diseases and wicked spirits, and granted many blind persons the favor of seeing. Hence in answer he said to the two [disciples of John]: 'Go your way, report to John what you saw and heard: the blind are receiving sight, the lame are walking, the lepers are being cleansed and the deaf are hearing, the dead are being raised up, the poor are being told the good news. And happy is he who has not stumbled over me.' "—Luke 7:18-23; also Matthew 11:2-6.

[21] Moses never raised anyone from the dead, but Jesus raised a number of dead persons.—Luke 7:11-16; 8:41-56; John 11:1-46.

19-21. (a) Like Moses, what miracles did Jesus perform to prove that he had been sent by God? (b) What miraculous works did Jesus perform that far exceeded anything that Moses had done?

[22] Many persons began to believe that Jesus was the promised prophet like Moses. "When the men saw the signs he performed, they began to say: 'This is for a certainty the prophet that was to come into the world.' " When he was speaking at the temple in Jerusalem, "some of the crowd that heard these words began saying: 'This is for a certainty The Prophet.' Others were saying: 'This is the Christ.' " (John 6:14; 7:40, 41) Jesus did not publicly advertise himself as being the Christ and the promised prophet like Moses. He let his matchless works testify as to who he was. He said to doubting ones: "I have the witness greater than that of John, for the very works that my Father assigned me to accomplish, the works themselves that I am doing, bear witness about me that the Father dispatched me. In fact, if you believed Moses you would believe me, for that one wrote about me."—John 5:36, 46.

[23] When Moses came to the Hebrews to lead them out of their slavery in Egypt, he came in the name of Jehovah, the God of their forefathers. When sending Moses from Arabia back to Egypt, God told Moses: "You go, and you must gather the older men of Israel, and you must say to them, 'Jehovah the God of your forefathers has appeared to me, the God of Abraham, Isaac and Jacob, saying: "I will without fail give attention to you and to what is being done to you in Egypt." ' " Back in Egypt, Moses asked Pharaoh in the name of Jehovah to let the Israelites go free. But Pharaoh said: "Who is Jehovah, so that I should obey his voice to send Israel away? I do not know Jehovah at all and, what is more, I am

22. (a) Who did many that heard Jesus and saw the signs he performed believe him to be? (b) What did Jesus say bore witness to his identity, and who did he say had written about him?
23. In whose name did Moses speak both to the Israelites and to Egypt's Pharaoh?

not going to send Israel away." Later, before sending Moses and his brother Aaron back to Pharaoh, "God went on to speak to Moses and to say to him: 'I am Jehovah. And I used to appear to Abraham, Isaac and Jacob as God Almighty, but as respects my name Jehovah I did not make myself known to them.'" (Exodus 3:16; 5:1, 2; 6:2, 3) So Moses was now used to make God's name known in a special way.

[24] Like Moses, Jesus came in the name of God his heavenly Father. To his unbelieving countrymen he said: "I do not accept glory from men, but I well know that you do not have the love of God in you. I have come in the name of my Father, but you do not receive me; if someone else arrived in his own name, you would receive that one." (John 5:41-43) In a final prayer together with all his faithful apostles Jesus Christ said to God: "I have made your name manifest to the men you gave me out of the world. . . . Holy Father, watch over them on account of your own name which you have given me, in order that they may be one just as we are. When I was with them I used to watch over them on account of your own name which you have given me; and I have kept them."—John 17:6, 11, 12.

[25] Very plainly, then, Hebrews 2:11, 12 applies the fulfillment of Psalm 22:22 to Jesus Christ and says: "For this cause he is not ashamed to call them 'brothers,' as he says: 'I will declare your name to my brothers; in the middle of the congregation I will praise you with song.'" Yes, like Moses, Jesus published the name of Jehovah. What prophet before him or after him produced such credentials as Jesus Christ did to prove himself a true prophet sent by God?

24, 25. What did Jesus say, showing that he too came in the name of God, and so what name did he declare?

MEDIATOR

²⁶ For the freeing of the Hebrews from slavery and oppression in demon-worshiping Egypt, the prophet Moses was used by Jehovah God to intro-

duce the passover supper to the Israelites on the fourteenth day of the lunar month Nisan. (Exodus 12: 1-28, 39, 43-49) What did Jesus Christ do that corresponded with this?

²⁷ As a faithful Jew Jesus kept the passover each year down to his last one, which he celebrated with his twelve apostles in Jerusalem on the night of Nisan 14 of the year 33 C.E. After that he let himself be slaughtered by his enemies as a sacrifice, like a human passover lamb, to fulfill the prophetic meaning contained in the original passover celebrated down in Egypt in 1513 B.C.E. The prophecy of Isaiah 53:7 had said concerning him: "He was being brought just like a sheep to the slaughtering; and like a ewe that before her shearers has become mute, he also would not open his mouth." (Acts 8:30-35) After Jesus was baptized and anointed with God's spirit John the Baptist directed his own disciples to Jesus and said: "See, the Lamb of God that takes

26, 27. (a) In the year 33 C.E., what did Jesus do that corresponded with the passover sacrifice instituted through Moses in Egypt? (b) Where in the Scriptures is Jesus identified as a lamb for sacrifice?

away the sin of the world!" (John 1:29) Later, the apostle Paul plainly identified Jesus as the symbolic Lamb, saying: "Christ our passover has been sacrificed. Consequently, let us keep the festival." (1 Corinthians 5:7, 8) So Moses provided the prophetic types; Jesus provided the realities of the things typified.

[28] The yearly celebration of the typical passover was made a part of the Law covenant that Moses was used as a mediator to establish between Jehovah God and the nation of Israel. (Exodus 24:1-8; 23:14, 15; Deuteronomy 16:1-8) Jesus Christ, for his part, made any further celebrating of the passover out of date and told his disciples to celebrate, instead, each year the "Lord's evening meal" with unleavened bread and wine, to symbolize his own sacrifice as the Lamb of God. When he offered to them the common cup of wine to drink, he said: "This cup means the new covenant by virtue of my blood, which is to be poured out in your behalf." (Luke 22:14-20; Matthew 26:17-29) By those words Jesus pointed to the fact that he would be the Mediator of a new covenant between Jehovah God and his faithful disciples, by means of his own human blood.

[29] In 1513 B.C.E. the prophet Moses mediated the Law covenant between the nation of natural Israel and Jehovah God. But that covenant was not to last forever, for, in the prophecy of Jeremiah 31:31-34, God foretold the making of a different covenant, a new covenant, a better covenant that would really take away human sins.

[30] By the sacrifice of himself Jesus provided the sacrifice needed to put this new covenant into force with God. Thus Jesus became the Mediator of the promised "new covenant." With good rea-

---

28. Why is the celebrating of the passover now out of date, but what is to be commemorated by Christians?
29, 30. (a) As Moses mediated the Law covenant, what role does Jesus have in connection with the new covenant? (b) How do the Scriptures show this?

son the apostle Paul later wrote: "There is one God, and one mediator between God and men, a man Christ Jesus, who gave himself a corresponding ransom for all." (1 Timothy 2:5, 6) Because Jesus rendered a better service to God than that of Moses, Hebrews 8:6 says: "Now Jesus has obtained a more excellent public service, so that he is also the mediator of a correspondingly better covenant, which has been legally established upon better promises." There was no woman mediator, or mediatrix, of the Law covenant. Moses' older sister Mary (or Miriam) was not used as a mediatrix between God and Israel. (Numbers 12:1-15, *Douay Version*) Likewise, there is no mediatrix of the new covenant. So in this respect of being a mediator between God and man, Jesus Christ is a prophet like Moses.

[31] In the last year of his earthly life Jesus was gloriously transfigured before his apostles Peter, James and John on a lofty mountain, possibly Mount Hermon. During this transfiguration a visionary Moses and Elijah appeared to be with the glorified Jesus and talking with him "about his departure that he was destined to fulfill at Jerusalem." (Luke 9:28-36; Matthew 17:1-9) The apostle Peter understood this association of Moses with Jesus to mean that Jesus was that promised Prophet foreshadowed by Moses. Peter said that, as a result of this transfiguration miracle in the "holy mountain," we "have the prophetic word made more sure," including the prophecy about the prophet like Moses.—2 Peter 1:16-19.

[32] After the sacrificial death and resurrection of Jesus Christ and his glorification in heaven, the apostle Peter preached in the temple of Jerusalem. Peter had just performed a miracle in the "name

---

31. In the last year of Jesus' earthly life, how was the prophecy about the prophet like Moses made more sure for us?
32, 33. After Jesus' death and resurrection, how did Peter publicly identify Jesus as the prophet like Moses?

of Jesus Christ the Nazarene." A crowd gathered, and Peter told them that they had mistreated Jesus Christ because of ignorance.

[33] "But," said Peter, "in this way God has fulfilled the things he announced beforehand through the mouth of all the prophets, that his Christ would suffer. Repent, therefore, and turn around so as to get your sins blotted out, that seasons of refreshing may come from the person of Jehovah and that he may send forth the Christ appointed for you, Jesus, whom heaven, indeed, must hold within itself until the times of restoration of all things of which God spoke through the mouth of his holy prophets of old time. In fact, Moses said, 'Jehovah God will raise up for you from among your brothers a prophet like me. You must listen to him according to all the things he speaks to you. Indeed, any soul that does not listen to that Prophet will be completely destroyed from among the people.' "—Acts 3:1-23; also, see Acts 7:37.

[34] Since Jesus Christ now glorified in heaven fulfills God's prophecy concerning the Prophet like Moses, we should listen to what this Greater Moses has to say to us. It means everlasting life to us to heed the above words of the apostle Peter.

---

34. So why should we listen to what Jesus Christ says?

CHAPTER 10

How Could One Man Die for the World of Mankind?

THERE was a loving purpose behind the human coming of the Son of God nineteen centuries ago to become the Prophet like Moses. Certainly the coming of Moses as God's prophet in the sixteenth century before our Common Era was of priceless benefit to the oppressed descendants of the patriarch Abraham in the land of Egypt. In the same way the coming of the Son of God to serve as a Prophet like Moses should be of still greater benefit, not to just the nation of Moses' people only, but also to all the rest of the world of mankind. He came, not only like Moses to declare and exalt the name of Jehovah, but also to die as a human sacrifice for all mankind, that we might have life eternal. How could this be so?

[2] The resurrected Jesus Christ, now rewarded with glory in the heavens, is higher and better than the angels up there. If he were still a man, this could not be so. Regarding this fact we read,

1. What was the loving purpose behind the human coming of the Son of God nineteen centuries ago?
2, 3. (a) After his death and resurrection, to what position in the heavens was Jesus exalted? (b) But how do the Scriptures show that he was lower than the angels when he was on earth?

in Hebrews 1:3, 4: "After he had made a purification for our sins he sat down on the right hand of the majesty in lofty places. So he has become better than the angels, to the extent that he has inherited a name more excellent than theirs." For this reason the "inhabited earth to come" has been put in subjection to the glorified Jesus Christ rather than to mere angels. For a while, as a perfect man on earth, he was lower than the angels, but now by reason of his glorification in heaven he is above the angels. In explaining how so, Hebrews 2:5-9 quotes Psalm 8:4-6 and says:

³ "For it is not to angels that he has subjected the inhabited earth to come, about which we are speaking. But a certain witness [the psalmist David] has given proof somewhere, saying:

'What is man that you keep him in mind,
   or the son of man that you take care of him?
You made him a little lower than angels;
   with glory and honor you crowned him,
   and appointed him over the works of your hands.
All things you subjected under his feet.'

For in that he subjected all things to him God left nothing that is not subject to him. Now, though, we do not yet see all things [including the "inhabited earth to come"] in subjection to him; but we behold Jesus, who has been made a little lower than angels, crowned with glory and honor for having suffered death, that he by God's undeserved kindness might taste death for every man."

⁴ Thus, prophetically in the psalm quoted, Jesus is called a man and the son of man. Repeatedly, when on earth, he spoke of himself as the "Son of man." (Matthew 8:20; 9:6; John 1:51) This showed that he had not just materialized as a man as angels had previously done or that he had been

---

4. (a) What is indicated by that expression "Son of man" as applied to Jesus? (b) How do the Scriptures make clear the reason why Jesus was born as a human?

incarnated as a man, but that he had been born as a man and was a son of mankind. As it is written, in Galatians 4:4, "when the full limit of the time arrived, God sent forth his Son, who came to be out of a woman and who came to be under law." In this way he was made lower than the heavenly angels. What was the purpose of this? It was his suffering a human death, "that he by God's undeserved kindness might taste death for every man." Why did *he* have to be the one needing to die?

⁵ It must be remembered that, when the disciples of John the Baptist were directed by him to the baptized, anointed Jesus, John said to them: "See, the Lamb of God that takes away the sin of the world!" (John 1:29, 36) The whole world of mankind was under sin. In Romans 6:23 it is clearly stated that "the wages sin pays is death." For this reason all the world of mankind was dying, in order to pay the penalty of sin. Well, then, in order for the "sin of the world" to be taken away, there had to be payment of the penalty of sin, namely, death, by someone innocent who was under no condemnation of death. In other words, in order to take away the "sin of the world," the "Lamb of God" had to die for the world of mankind, shedding his lifeblood for the world.

5. Why was it necessary for Jesus to die to take away the "sin of the world"?

[6] A literal four-footed, woolly lamb could not take away the sin of the world, nor even the sin of one single human creature, by shedding its blood and being offered as a sacrifice on an altar. A lamb is an animal lower and of less value than a human creature. When the shepherd Abel, the second son of Adam and Eve, killed some firstlings of his flock and offered their fatty pieces on an altar, those sacrificed sheep could not take away his inborn sin and free him from the condemnation of death. His older brother Cain, a cultivator of the ground, offered some "fruits of the ground"; but this was not acceptable to God because it was a bloodless offering, not a living sacrifice. (Genesis 4:1-7; Hebrews 11:4) What Hebrews 9:22 says on this point is unmistakable in its meaning: "Unless blood is poured out no forgiveness takes place."

[7] This is true, because God says: "The soul [or, life] of every sort of flesh is its blood by the soul [or, life] in it. Consequently I said to the sons of Israel: 'You must not eat the blood of any sort of flesh, because the soul of every sort of flesh is its blood. Anyone eating it will be cut off.' "—Leviticus 17:14.

[8] For over fifteen hundred and eighty years the nation of Israel offered the sacrifices of bulls, goats, sheep and doves, down till the destruction of the temple of Jerusalem in 70 C.E., and yet all those millions of animal sacrifices did not take away the sin of the nation. Their animal sacrifices, repeated year after year, did not make them perfect or really cleanse them from sin and lift the condemnation to death. Those sacrifices were

---

6, 7. (a) Could a literal lamb take away the inborn sin of the world and free men from the condemnation of death? (b) Nevertheless, according to God's law, what must be poured out for forgiveness to take place, and why?
8, 9. What purpose was served by the millions of animal sacrifices offered by the nation of Israel, and how is this explained at Hebrews 10:1-4?

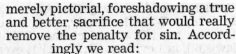

merely pictorial, foreshadowing a true and better sacrifice that would really remove the penalty for sin. Accordingly we read:

9 "Since the Law has a shadow of the good things to come, but not the very substance of the things, men can never with the same sacrifices from year to year which they offer continually make those who approach perfect. Otherwise, would the sacrifices not have stopped being offered, because those rendering sacred service who had been cleansed once for all time would have no consciousness of sins any more? To the contrary, by these sacrifices there is a reminding of sins from year to year, for it is not possible for the blood of bulls and of goats to take sins away."—Hebrews 10:1-4.

10 The reason why the blood of sacrificed animals could not take sins away is very plain to see: they are lower than man; they are not of equal value with man, and man has not descended from such lower animals. The first man, Adam, was created perfect, fully formed, and separate from the lower animals, so that God was obliged to create a wife, a perfect woman, for Adam. Each different kind of the lower animal forms of life was created by God, but not "in

10. Why could the blood of sacrificed animals not take away man's sins, but what kind of sacrifice was required to accomplish this?

God's image," in the way that Adam was. (Genesis 1:20-28; 2:7-23) Evidently, then, a human sacrifice was needed, a perfect one at that. As God's law said, in Leviticus 22:21 (*AV*), even regarding animal sacrifices, "it shall be perfect to be accepted; there shall be no blemish therein." Who could give such a human sacrifice?

¹¹ No human creature deriving his life from Adam could present himself as the necessary perfect human sacrifice to God in behalf of all his fellowmen. Why not? Because he had descended from Adam after Adam had sinned and was driven out of the garden of Eden and away from the "tree of life." All of us are dying, because we are sinners. Why we are sinners is stated in Romans 5:12-14: "Through one man sin entered into the world and death through sin, and thus death spread to all men because they had all sinned . . . death ruled as king from Adam." The wise, observing King Solomon said in prayer to God: "There is no man that does not sin." (1 Kings 8: 46) Solomon's father David said to God: "Look! With error I was brought forth with birth pains, and in sin my mother conceived me." (Psalm 51: 5) The Christian apostle Paul refers to what was written in Psalm 14:1-3 and makes the following argument by means of God's law:

¹² "Above we have made the charge that Jews as well as Greeks are all under sin; just as it is written: 'There is not a righteous man, not even one; there is no one that has any insight, there is no one that seeks for God. All men have deflected, . . . ' Now we know that all the things the Law says it addresses to those under the Law [to the Jews], so that every mouth may be stopped and all the world [Jews and Gentiles] may become liable to God for punishment. . . . For all have

11, 12. Why could no descendant of Adam qualify as the acceptable sacrifice to God in behalf of all his fellowmen, and what scriptures show this to be true?

sinned and fall short of the glory of God."
—Romans 3:9-23.

[13] So the natural Jews, who were under God's
law through the prophet Moses, could not say that
only the non-Jews or uncircumcised Gentiles were
sinners because such Gentiles were not under the
law of Jehovah God. God's law through Moses
condemned even the Jews under it as being sinners
just as much so as the Gentiles. So not even the
most God-fearing Jew under the Mosaic law could
offer himself as an acceptable sacrifice for all mankind, nor even for his own Jewish people. The
payment of even the largest sum of lifeless, bloodless money by any or all of the rich men would not
meet the needs of the situation, anymore than the
bloodless offering made by Cain, the first son of
Adam and Eve. Hence we read:

[14] "Those who are trusting in their means of
maintenance, and who keep boasting about the
abundance of their riches, not one of them can by
any means redeem even a brother, nor give to God
a ransom for him; (and the redemption price of
their soul is so precious that it has ceased to time
indefinite) that he should still live forever and
not see the pit."—Psalm 49:6-9.

THE SATISFACTORY RANSOM

[15] Notice, please, that Psalm 49 speaks of redeeming or buying back and of giving a ransom.
No money ransom by the rich people was able to
buy back a person from death for him to live forever and not go into the pit of the grave. Everlasting life was not that cheap; otherwise, the rich
people would have the advantage over the poor.
For this word "ransom" the Biblical *Cyclopædia*
by J. M'Clintock and J. Strong, in its volume 8,

13, 14. (a) Would someone under the Mosaic law have been more
acceptable as a sacrifice for sins than a Gentile? (b) Could the
payment of a large sum of money redeem mankind from death,
making it possible for them to live forever?
15. What is meant by "ransom"?

page 908, gives the following definition: "A price paid to recover a person or thing from one who detains that person or thing in captivity. Hence prisoners of war or slaves are said to be ransomed when they are liberated in exchange for a valuable consideration. (1 Corinthians 6:19, 20) Whatever is substituted or exchanged in compensation for the party is his ransom."

[16] For a modern-day illustration, the New York *Times*, under date of May 30, 1961, reported concerning the court trial of an official under the Nazi German dictator Adolf Hitler, and said: "JERUSALEM (Israeli Sector), May 29—Adolf Eichmann's proposal to ransom 1,000,000 Jews for 10,000 Western trucks was related at his trial today." Under the earlier date of May 22, 1961, the New York *Times* said the following on its editorial page under the heading "Ransoming Castro's Prisoners":

> Thus Fidel Castro was acting in a well-defined, if hardly creditable, tradition when he made his proposal to trade the 1,000 rebel prisoners he holds for 500 bulldozers. The parallel with the Hitlerian regime's offer during World War II to trade Hungarian Jews for trucks comes quickly to mind. . . . Paying ransom to a totalitarian dictator is distasteful under any circumstances.

The ransoming negotiations with the Cuban ruler broke down, for the time being, as free friends and relatives lovingly sought to provide the ransom, not by the sacrifice of other human lives, but by the payment of material goods, lifeless and bloodless.

[17] The ransoming of all mankind would open up the way for them to gain everlasting human life in perfection on the earth, to which Paradise would

---

16. Give some modern-day illustrations of the paying of ransom.
17. (a) What prospects would the ransoming of mankind open up for them? (b) As indicated by the Scriptures, what would God require in exchange for what Adam had lost for all mankind?

be restored. For this reason the God of justice refused any lifeless, bloodless ransom for the liberation of all mankind. What he would require in exchange for that which Adam had lost for all mankind, Jehovah God indicated in his law through Moses, when he said: "If a fatal accident should occur, then you must give soul for soul [or, life for life], eye for eye, tooth for tooth, hand for hand, foot for foot, branding for branding, wound for wound, blow for blow." (Exodus 21: 23-25) That is to say, like shall go for like; a human life shall go for a human life, in order that equal justice may be rendered without partiality. To this effect God says, in Numbers 35:30: "Every fatal striker of a soul should be slain as a murderer at the mouth of witnesses, and one witness may not testify against a soul for him to die."

¹⁸ To show that no money ransom may be accepted from a murderer who wants to escape with his life, Numbers 35:31 said: "And you must take no ransom for the soul [or, life] of a murderer who is deserving to die, for without fail he should be put to death." Hence the willful murderer had to be refused a place of safety inside an Israelite "city of refuge."

¹⁹ In the case of an accidental manslayer, he could flee to a city of refuge and find safety in it. However, in order to avoid being killed by the dead person's closest relative who acted as an "avenger of blood," the accidental manslayer had to remain inside the city of refuge till the then serving high priest of the nation of Israel died. The accidental manslayer could not buy his freedom and protection against being killed outside the city of refuge by paying a money ransom before the high priest died. In Numbers 35:32 God said:

18, 19. (a) How did God's law concerning the Israelite 'cities of refuge' show that human life could not be ransomed with money? (b) By what means could the accidental manslayer be set free, and why?

"And you must not take a ransom for one who has fled to his city of refuge, to resume dwelling in the land before the death of the high priest." This was as if the high priest laid down his own life as a ransom that the accidental manslayer might go free.

[20] Insisting upon absolutely exact justice, Moses said, in Deuteronomy 19:21: "Your eye should not feel sorry: soul will be for soul, eye for eye, tooth for tooth, hand for hand, foot for foot."

[21] Such a requirement on the part of divine justice created a situation impossible for imperfect, dying humans, but it was nothing unjust on God's part. It upholds the majesty of his law and also the dignity of human life. It shows that we cannot set aside God's justice or leave it out of consideration anymore than God himself can. If this made it hard for mankind to be ransomed and redeemed, it made it no less hard for Jehovah God himself. However, this strict sticking to absolute justice created no situation that God could not handle. It merely called upon God's merciful love and also his wisdom and power to provide a ransom sacrifice for all mankind without violating his own perfect justice.

[22] God's purpose to do so may be referred to in Hosea 13:14, which reads: "From the hand of Sheol I shall redeem them; from death I shall recover them. Where are your stings, O Death? Where is your destructiveness, O Sheol?" Especially so, since the Christian apostle Paul quotes from that verse, in 1 Corinthians 15:55.

[23] Jesus Christ revealed the solution to the super-

20. How does Deuteronomy 19:21 emphasize the divine requirement of absolute justice?
21. (a) What do we learn from this requirement of justice in God's law? (b) Did this make impossible the ransoming of mankind?
22. What apparent reference to God's purpose to provide a ransom is recorded in the book of Hosea?
23. As explained by Jesus Christ, what ransom provision for mankind was made?

human problem when he said to his disciples: "The Son of man came, not to be ministered to, but to minister and to give his soul a ransom in exchange for many."—Matthew 20:28; Mark 10:45.

24 History shows that Jesus Christ, "the Son of man," actually did lay down his human life as a ransom for multitudinous mankind, on Nisan 14 of the year 33 C.E. Commenting on the historicalness of this fact, the apostle Paul writes: "This is fine and acceptable in the sight of our Savior, God, whose will is that all sorts of men should be saved and come to an accurate knowledge of truth. For there is one God, and one mediator between God and men, a man Christ Jesus, who gave himself a corresponding ransom for all."—1 Timothy 2: 3-6.

25 For his part, the apostle Peter may have had in mind the words of John the Baptist when pointing to the baptized, anointed Jesus: "See, the Lamb of God that takes away the sin of the world!" (John 1:29) Using a similar symbolism, the apostle Peter wrote to fellow Christians, who were "sprinkled with the blood of Jesus Christ," and said: "You know that it was not with corruptible things, with silver or gold, that you were delivered from your fruitless form of conduct received by tradition from your forefathers. But it was with precious blood, like that of an unblemished and spotless lamb, even Christ's."—1 Peter 1:2, 18, 19.

ONE MAN FOR A WORLD

26 Nevertheless, how could Jesus Christ, one man, by his human death ransom the whole world of mankind? Why is not an individual ransom

24. Did Jesus Christ actually lay down his life as a ransom for mankind, and what does the reliable historical record of the Bible say about this?
25. With what symbolism does the apostle Peter describe the ransom?
26-28. As explained at Romans 5:12, 15-19, how was it possible for one man by his death to ransom all mankind?

sacrifice required for each member of the human family? It was all through the undeserved kindness of God, and his wisdom explains it for us briefly, in Romans 5:12, 15-19, in these words:

²⁷ "Through one man sin entered into the world and death through sin, and thus death spread to all men because they had all sinned— . . . For if by one man's trespass [Adam's trespass in the garden of Eden] many died, the undeserved kindness of God and his free gift with the undeserved kindness by the one man Jesus Christ abounded much more to many. Also, it is not with the free gift as it was with the way things worked through the one man that sinned.

²⁸ "For the judgment resulted in condemnation from one trespass [of Adam], but the gift resulted in a declaration of righteousness from many trespasses [of Adam's many descendants]. For if by the trespass of the one man [Adam] death ruled as king through that one, much more will those who receive the abundance of the undeserved kindness and of the free gift of righteousness rule as kings in life through the one person, Jesus Christ. So, then, as through one trespass [of Adam] the result to men of all sorts was condemnation, likewise also through one act of justification [by Jesus Christ] the result to men of all sorts is a declaring of them righteous for life. For just as through the disobedience of the one man [Adam] many were constituted sinners [by inheritance], likewise also through the obedience of the one person [Jesus Christ] many will be constituted righteous [free of condemnation]."

²⁹ That inspired argument balances Jesus Christ, one man, off with Adam, one man. Adam was created perfect, although he was a man "a little lower than angels." (Genesis 1:26-28; 2:7; Psalm

---

29. Explain how Jesus was born a perfect human, as Adam was perfect.

8:5; Hebrews 2:6, 7) Jesus was born a perfect human, in spite of the fact that his mother was an imperfect Jewess, Mary the daughter of "Heli, the son of Matthat." (Luke 3:23, 24) The father of Jesus was not the carpenter Joseph, who became the son-in-law of Heli, Mary's father. No, but Mary bore Jesus while she was still in a virgin state, a miracle because Jehovah God was the Father of Jesus. Her conceiving of Jesus in her womb was by means of God's holy spirit, as explained to her by the angel Gabriel. (Luke 1:26-37) Jesus had been a spirit Son of God in heaven, God's "only-begotten Son," and, in order that his only-begotten Son might be born as a perfect human creature, Almighty God divested the Son of his heavenly godlike existence and transferred his life from heaven to Mary's womb by means of God's invisible active force or spirit.

[30] Thus this heavenly Son, who was God's Spokesman or "Word," was developed as a human child for nine months in the womb of his virgin mother, but not inheriting sin, imperfection and death from Mary's original earthly father, Adam. God remained the heavenly Father of Jesus, and he had no sinful earthly father. Hence the apostle John says: "So the Word became flesh and resided among us, and we had a view of his glory, a glory such as belongs to an only-begotten son from a father; and he was full of undeserved kindness and truth." (John 1:14) The apostle John does not call Jesus a "God-man," and neither does any other Bible writer do so. Jesus in the flesh was not a mixture of earthly and spiritual, flesh and spirit. He was not a spirit person clothed with flesh, but John 1:14 says he "became flesh" or was made flesh. He was a whole man.

---

30. (a) Who was the Father of the child Jesus? (b) Was Jesus a "God-man" or was he really human?

[31] If Jesus, when he was baptized at thirty years of age, had been a so-called God-man and a combination of spirit person and fleshly person, he would have been superhuman and would have had more value than a ransom for all mankind. The perfect justice of God would not unjustly accept more value than that of the thing to be ransomed. His law as given through Moses plainly stated that like should go for like. It was the perfect man Adam that had sinned and so had lost for his offspring human perfection and its privileges. Jesus must likewise be humanly perfect, to correspond with the sinless Adam in Eden. In that way he could offer a ransom that *exactly* corresponded in value with what the sinner Adam lost for his descendants. This requirement of divine justice did not allow for Jesus to be more than a perfect man. That is why, in writing 1 Timothy 2:5, 6, the apostle Paul uses a special word in Greek, *antílytron,* to describe what Jesus offered in sacrifice to God.

[32] According to *A Greek and English Lexicon of the New Testament* (1845 edition), by John Parkhurst, M.A., as revised by J. A. Major, D.D., this Greek word *antílytron* means: *"a ransom, price of redemption,* or rather *a correspondent ransom.* 'It properly signifies a *price* by which captives are *redeemed* from the enemy; and that kind of *exchange* in which the *life of one is redeemed by the life of another.'* So Aristotle uses the verb *antilytróo* for *redeeming life by life."* (Page 47, column 2) Very properly, then, the *New World Translation of the Holy Scriptures* renders 1 Timothy 2:5, 6 as follows: "For there is one God, and one mediator between God and men, a man Christ Jesus, who gave himself a corresponding ransom

---

31, 32. (a) If Jesus had been a "God-man," what effect would this have had on his qualifications as a ransom for mankind? (b) How does the Greek word used by the apostle Paul at 1 Timothy 2:5, 6 to describe what Jesus offered in sacrifice show that Jesus did not present more than a perfect human life?

for all." Thus the perfect Jesus as a human sacrifice did not outbalance in value the human perfection and life that Adam lost.

[33] When he sinned and was sentenced to death, Adam's race or offspring were all unborn in his loins, and so they all died in him. By natural inheritance they have all been born dying. They died by the mishap of birth from sinner Adam. Jesus as a perfect man had a race or offspring unborn in his loins, when he died innocently as a perfect human sacrifice, and this possible human race died with him. He died as an unmarried man who had not raised a family of his own. Jesus' dying as a childless man, his unborn human offspring counterbalanced all the race that Adam has reproduced till now.

[34] In this way Almighty God provided in his Son Jesus Christ a "corresponding ransom for all." One perfect man, Jesus Christ, was thus able to die for all mankind. On the third day Jehovah God raised him from the dead, after which he ascended into heaven with the full value of his corresponding ransom, to present it to the God of absolute justice, in behalf of all mankind.—Hebrews 9:24.

[35] By offering a ransom for the offspring of Adam and Eve, Jesus Christ redeemed Adam's offspring as his own. He not only redeemed or repurchased his 144,000 followers who become joint heirs with him in the heavenly kingdom but also redeemed all the remainder of mankind. (Revelation 1:5, 6; 5:9, 10; 1 John 2:1, 2) Though he died childless, unmarried, he will have a heavenly Bride, namely, his congregation of 144,000 faithful disciples who are espoused to him as to one

---

33. How can it be said that what Jesus offered up in sacrifice counterbalanced all the race that Adam has produced?
34. After being raised from the dead, to whom did Jesus present the value of his corresponding ransom?
35. (a) How many did Jesus repurchase to be with him in the heavenly kingdom, and how is their relationship to him described? (b) Whom else did he redeem?

husband. (2 Corinthians 11:2; Revelation 14:1, 3; 19:7, 8; 21:2, 9-14) He will also have children on earth, not by natural procreation, but by the redemption of Adam's offspring. Foretelling that fact, the prophecy of Isaiah 9:6, 7 in the eighth century before our Common Era referred to his human birth and said:

[36] "There has been a child born to us, there has been a son given to us; and the princely rule will come to be upon his shoulder. And his name will be called Wonderful Counselor, Mighty God, Eternal Father, Prince of Peace. To the abundance of the princely rule and to peace there will be no end, upon the throne of David and upon his kingdom in order to establish it firmly and to sustain it by means of justice and by means of righteousness, from now on and to time indefinite. The very zeal of Jehovah of armies will do this."

[37] He would not be an "Eternal Father" if his earthly children died off. So for this title to be true of him, the earthly children to whom he becomes father by means of his ransom sacrifice will be given the opportunity to live forever on a peaceful earth under his princely rule. Those of ransomed mankind who have died as a result of Adam's original sin will enter into this opportunity by means of a resurrection from the dead under God's kingdom by Jesus Christ. Then by faith they will have to accept his perfect human sacrifice as a ransom to free them from condemnation due to inheriting sin and imperfection. As it is written in Isaiah 53:10-12:

[38] "If you will set his soul [or, life] as a guilt offering, he will see his offspring, he will prolong his days, and in his hand what is the delight of Jehovah will succeed. Because of the trouble of his

36, 37. For Jesus to be an "Eternal Father," as foretold of him in the prophecy of Isaiah, what opportunity must be given to his earthly children, even to those now dead?
38. As prophesied at Isaiah 53:10-12, what has Jesus done on behalf of sinful mankind?

soul he will see, he will be satisfied. By means of his knowledge the righteous one, my servant, will bring a righteous standing to many people; and their errors he himself will bear. . . . due to the fact that he poured out his soul [or, life] to the very death, and it was with the transgressors that he was counted in; and he himself carried the very sin of many people, and for the transgressors he proceeded to interpose."

³⁹ All this explains why the Son of God, who "became flesh" nineteen centuries ago, could correctly say: "I am the living bread that came down from heaven; if anyone eats of this bread he will live forever; and, for a fact, the bread that I shall give is my flesh in behalf of the life of the world." —John 1:14; 6:51.

---

39. What is the "living bread that came down from heaven," of which the Son of God spoke, and what results to the eaters of it?

CHAPTER 11

The Founding of the True Christian Congregation

HE prophet Moses was associated with the congregation of natural Israel for forty years during its march to the Promised Land. So we read in Acts 7:38: "This is he that came to be among the congregation in the wilderness with the angel that spoke to him on Mount Sinai and with our forefathers, and he received living sacred pronouncements to give you." Jesus Christ, the promised Prophet like Moses, is likewise associated with a congregation, not, however, the congregation of natural Israel. Down to this day the nation of Israel, including their Republic of Israel, have rejected him, denying that he is the Prophet like Moses. In his last year on earth as a man, he told his apostles that he would build a congregation, evidently not that of Israel.

² It was after two years of public activity that Jesus asked his apostles: "Who are men saying the Son of man is?" They said: "Some say John the Baptist, others Elijah, still others Jeremiah or one of the prophets." But what did they themselves think? "You, though, who do you say I am?" Jesus asked. "In answer Simon Peter said: 'You

---

1. Is the congregation with which Jesus Christ is associated the same as the one with which Moses was associated, and why so?
2. When Jesus asked his apostles what they believed as to his identity, what was the reply, and what did Jesus say at that time concerning a congregation?

are the Christ, the Son of the living God.' In response Jesus said to him: 'Happy you are, Simon son of Jonah, because flesh and blood did not reveal it to you, but my Father who is in the heavens did. Also, I say to you, You are Peter [*Pétros*], and on this rock-mass [*pétra*] I will build my congregation, and the gates of Ha'des will not overpower it. I will give you the keys of the kingdom of the heavens, and whatever you may bind on earth will be the thing bound in the heavens, and whatever you may loose on earth will be the thing loosed in the heavens.' "—Matthew 16:13-19.

[3] That meant that the congregation of Jesus Christ had not yet been built on the symbolic "rock-mass [*pétra*]," and the "keys of the kingdom of the heavens" had not yet been given to Simon Peter the son of Jonah. The next time that Jesus spoke of a congregation he was still up north but by the Sea of Galilee. He had not yet left for Jerusalem to attend the Atonement Day and the festival of the booths or tabernacles in October of 32 C.E. At that time he said to his disciples: "Moreover, if your brother commits a sin, go lay bare his fault between you and him alone. If he listens to you, you have gained your brother. But if he does not listen, take along with you one or two more, in order that at the mouth of two or three witnesses every matter may be established. If he does not listen to them, speak to the congregation. If he does not listen even to the congregation, let him be to you just as a man of the nations and as a tax collector."—Matthew 18:15-17.

[4] At that time the only congregation of God in existence was his congregation of Israel, the one

---

3. (a) Had the congregation of Jesus Christ been built at that time? (b) Later, when near the Sea of Galilee, what did Jesus say about a congregation?
4, 5. (a) To what congregation was he there evidently referring? (b) Of what congregation was Jesus himself a member, and how is this shown by his activities from youth on? (c) When was it that he said to the Israelites, "Look! Your house is abandoned to you"?

with which the prophet Moses had been and which detested tax collectors and had nothing to do with the Gentiles or people of the nations. As matters were then to develop, it would not be until in the month of May of the following year (33 C.E.) that another congregation would be founded. Since Jesus, by his birth in Bethlehem of Judah, "came to be out of a woman" and "came to be under law," he was naturally a member of God's congregation of Israel. (Galatians 4:4; Acts 7:38) Down to the time of his death in April of the year 33 C.E. he did not try to set up a separate congregation. He did not separate his disciples from the rest of the Israelites but let them attend religious services in their synagogues and the temple of Jerusalem.

⁵ In fact, "according to his custom on the sabbath day" he would enter into a synagogue and would preach according to the opportunity offered. (Luke 4:16-22) From boyhood onward he was regular in his attendance at the festivals in the temple of Jerusalem, and the last festival that he attended on earth was that of the passover in Jerusalem, in 33 C.E. (Luke 2:41-51; 22:7-18) It was not till near the end of March of 33 C.E. that he said to the Israelites: "Jerusalem, Jerusalem, the killer of the prophets and stoner of those sent forth to her,—how often I wanted to gather your children together, the way a hen gathers her chicks together under her wings! But you people did not want it. Look! Your house [temple] is abandoned to you." (Matthew 23:37, 38) So Jesus' words in Matthew 18:15-17 applied then to the congregation of Israel, but that principle or rule of action would carry over to the congregation that Jesus said he would build on a rock-mass.

⁶ Well, then, when did Jesus begin to build his congregation or "church" as something separate and distinct from the congregation of natural Is-

---

6-8. To what congregation were those being saved added, as reported at Acts 2:47, and how do the facts confirm this?

rael? The second chapter of the Acts of the Apostles tells us what happened to the disciples of Jesus Christ at Jerusalem on the festival day of Pentecost in May of 33 C.E. In its verse forty-seven, in the English King James Version Bible (as well as in Martin Luther's German Bible translation), we read: "And the Lord added to the church daily such as should be saved."

[7] However, the words "to the church" translate Greek words (*tei ekklesíai*) that were added later on to the original Greek text of Acts. But in Acts 5:11 the oldest Greek manuscripts now at hand do say this: "Consequently great fear came over the whole congregation and over all those hearing about these things," and this chapter shows that this "congregation" was associated with the apostles, including Simon Peter. (Acts 5:1-3) What congregation was that?

[8] Certainly it was not the congregation of natural Israel. It was the congregation that the resurrected, glorified Jesus Christ in heaven had begun to build on the "rock-mass." And when Acts 2:47 says that the Lord God "added . . . daily such as should be saved," he was not adding these saved ones to the congregation of natural Israel, for, by birth, they were members of that congregation. Rather, the Lord God was adding these who were experiencing a new salvation to the congregation that Jesus Christ had begun.

[9] Those being added to this new congregation were being taken away from the old congregation of natural Israel. Those to whom they were being added were the ones who had become believers on the festival day of Pentecost of 33 C.E., for we read: "Therefore those who embraced his [Peter's] word heartily were baptized, and on that day about three thousand souls were added. And

9. From where were these believers being taken, and of what group were they becoming a part?

they continued devoting themselves to the teaching of the apostles and to sharing with one another, to taking of meals and to prayers."—Acts 2:41, 42.

[10] With what salvation were those who "should be saved" being saved? It was a salvation through the sacrificed but now resurrected and glorified Jesus Christ. On that day of Pentecost the apostle Peter declared that the prophecy of Joel 2:28-32 was being fulfilled there at Jerusalem and he closed his quotation of it, saying: "And everyone who calls on the name of Jehovah will be saved." (Acts 2:14-21) Peter then pointed out that the Jesus whom they had killed fifty-two days earlier had been raised from the dead by Jehovah God and had ascended to heaven. Peter then closed his argument by quoting Psalm 110:1 as written by King David and said: "Actually David did not ascend to the heavens, but he himself says, 'Jehovah said to my Lord: "Sit at my right hand, until I place your enemies as a stool for your feet." ' Therefore let all the house [nation] of Israel know for a certainty that God made him both Lord and Christ, this Jesus whom you impaled." (Acts 2: 22-36) So now they must call on Jehovah's name through Jesus.

[11] Hence when the convicted Israelites asked the apostles: "Brothers, what shall we do?" Peter answered: "Repent, and let each one of you be baptized in the name of Jesus Christ for forgiveness of your sins, and you will receive the free gift of the holy spirit. For the promise [of Joel 2:28-32] is to you and to your children and to all those afar off, just as many as Jehovah our God may call to him." Peter was very urgent with those inquiring Jews, for we read: "And with many other

10. (a) What was the salvation that they were experiencing? (b) How did Peter argue that they must now call on Jehovah's name through Jesus in order to get saved?
11. What action did he urge his hearers to take?

words he bore thorough witness and kept exhorting them, saying: 'Get saved from this crooked generation.' " (Acts 2:37-40) That "crooked generation" from which to get saved was the old congregation of natural Israel, which Jesus himself had called a "wicked generation" looking for a sign. (Luke 11:29) Now they needed to be added to Jesus' congregation.

THE FOUNDATION FOR THE CONGREGATION

[12] From this it is evident that Jesus Christ began building his congregation on that day of Pentecost of 33 C.E. He did this from heaven. How? By pouring out holy spirit from heaven. Before that he was unable to do this, because, as John 7:39 says, "as yet [at the festival of tabernacles in 32 C.E.] there was no spirit, because Jesus had not yet been glorified." But by Pentecost of 33 C.E., Jesus was glorified, for Peter said on that day: "This Jesus God resurrected, of which fact we are all witnesses. Therefore because he was exalted to the right hand of God and received the promised holy spirit from the Father, he has poured out this which you see and hear." (Acts 2:32, 33) That day the holy spirit was poured out, not on all the nation of natural Israel there in Jerusalem for the festival, but only upon the 120 disciples of Jesus Christ who were meeting in an "upper chamber" in Jerusalem, separate from the Jewish celebrators at the temple. (Acts 1:12-15) To this effect we read the following, in Acts 2:1-4:

[13] "Now while the day of the festival of Pentecost was in progress they were all together at the same place, and suddenly there occurred from heaven a noise just like that of a rushing stiff breeze, and it filled the whole house in which they

---

12, 13. (a) So when did Jesus begin to build his congregation, and how? (b) What happened on that day of Pentecost in an "upper chamber" in Jerusalem?

were sitting. And tongues as if of fire became visible to them and were distributed about, and one sat upon each one of them, and they all became filled with holy spirit and started to speak with different tongues, just as the spirit was granting them to make utterance."

[14] Thus began the fulfillment of the prophecy of Joel 2:28-32, just as the apostle Peter explained it to the crowd of Jews and circumcised proselytes that gathered to witness this miraculous spectacle. This also fulfilled the promise of the resurrected Jesus Christ to his disciples before he ascended to heaven: "Look! I am sending forth upon you that which is promised by my Father. You, though, abide in the city until you become clothed with power from on high." (Luke 24:49) "You will receive power when the holy spirit arrives upon you, and you will be witnesses of me both in Jerusalem and in all Judea and Samaria and to the most distant part of the earth."—Acts 1:8.

[15] We remember that, when Jesus came up out of the Jordan River right after John the Baptist immersed him, God's holy spirit came down upon him and God's voice from heaven was heard saying: "This is my Son, the beloved, whom I have

14. What prophetic promises underwent fulfillment on this occasion?
15. How was Jesus on earth begotten as a spiritual Son of God, in line for a heavenly inheritance?

approved." (Matthew 3:13-17) In this way the perfect man Jesus was begotten by God's spirit and became a spiritual Son of God. Jehovah God, "the one that caused to be born," brought forth Jesus Christ, "him who has been born from that one," and Jesus Christ became the "One born from God." (1 John 5:1, 18) He became the Heir of a heavenly inheritance from God.

[16] In like manner, when the holy spirit was poured out upon the waiting disciples of Jesus at Jerusalem on the day of Pentecost, they were begotten by God by means of the holy spirit to be spiritual children of God. To these believers in Jesus Christ the words of John 1:12, 13 applied, namely: "As many as did receive him, to them he gave authority to become God's children, because they were exercising faith in his name; and they were born, not from blood or from a fleshly will or from man's will, but from God."

[17] These spirit-begotten disciples of Jesus Christ became heirs of a heavenly inheritance with him. In support of this fact we find written, in Romans 8:15-17, these words to the disciples: "You did not receive a spirit of slavery causing fear again, but you received a spirit of adoption as sons, by which spirit we cry out: 'Abba, Father!' The spirit itself bears witness with our spirit that we are God's children. If, then, we are children, we are also heirs: heirs indeed of God, but joint heirs with Christ, provided we suffer together that we may also be glorified together."

[18] For this reason the congregation that was established there in Jerusalem on the day of Pentecost was a congregation of spiritual children of God. The nation of natural Israel, of circumcised

16. Likewise, how did the disciples of Jesus at Jerusalem on the day of Pentecost become spiritual children of God?
17. Of what did these spirit-begotten disciples of Jesus become heirs, as shown at Romans 8:15-17?
18. What kind of congregation was it that was established in Jerusalem on the day of Pentecost, and with what terms is it referred to at Galatians 6:15, 16?

Jews, ceased to be the congregation of God, and the congregation of the spiritual sons of God became a spiritual Israel of God, a new creation. Upon this spiritual Israel comes peace and mercy from God, as it is written in Galatians 6:15, 16: "Neither is circumcision anything nor is uncircumcision, but a new creation is something. And all those who will walk orderly by this rule of conduct, upon them be peace and mercy, even upon the Israel of God."

[19] Another thing: On the day of Pentecost, when the holy spirit was poured out upon the congregation of Christ's disciples, they were anointed with the spirit of Jehovah God. That was true of Jesus when God's spirit was poured out upon him at the Jordan River, so that afterward he applied to himself the prophecy of Isaiah 61:1, concerning the anointing. (Luke 4:16-21) It is also true of Jesus' disciples upon whom God's spirit is poured out since Pentecost of 33 C.E., because to such ones are addressed the words of 2 Corinthians 1:21, 22: "He who guarantees that you and we belong to Christ and he who has anointed us is God. He has also put his seal upon us and has given us the token of what is to come, that is, the spirit, in our hearts."

[20] To that strong assurance the apostle John adds these words, in 1 John 2:20, 26, 27: "You have an anointing from the holy one; all of you have knowledge. These things I write you about those who are trying to mislead you. And as for you, the anointing that you received from him remains in you, and you do not need anyone [misleading] to be teaching you; but, as the anointing from him is teaching you about all things, and is true and is no lie, and just as it has taught you, remain in union with him."

---

19. How, like Jesus, are the members of his congregation anointed ones?
20. What does the apostle John say about this anointing?

[21] In Hebrew the word for "Anointed One" is *Mashíahh;* in Greek it is *Khristós.* Hence the expression Jesus Christ means Jesus the Anointed One, and the expression Christ Jesus means The Anointed Jesus. Jesus became Christ by being anointed with holy spirit, and thus he could rightly be called Jesus Christ, to identify him from others called by the name Jesus. He could also have the designation Christ appear as a title before his personal name Jesus and thus be spoken of as Christ Jesus, by the apostle Paul.

[22] Jesus' disciples also become anointed ones by being anointed with holy spirit. Just as Jesus, after his baptism, was anointed with holy spirit to preach God's message, so his disciples are anointed with holy spirit to preach God's Word. That is why the anointing that they have received from God is the means with which he teaches them the truth, to safeguard them from false religious leaders who would mislead them. For his anointed disciples of today Jesus foretold this worldwide work: "This good news of the kingdom will be preached in all the inhabited earth for a witness to all the nations; and then the end will come." —Matthew 24:14.

THE "ROCK-MASS"

[23] However, now we return to the question, What is the symbolic "rock-mass" on which Jesus Christ said he would build his congregation, according to his words in Matthew 16:18? Is it Simon Peter to whom Jesus said the words, or is it the confession that Peter made: "You are the Christ, the Son of the living God," or is it some-

---

21. How did Jesus become Christ, and so what is he properly called?
22. For what purpose are Jesus' disciples anointed with holy spirit, and how can it be said that the anointing teaches them?
23. What questions are now raised concerning the "rock-mass" on which Jesus Christ said he would build his congregation?

one or something else? Let us ask Simon Peter himself.

[24] In 1 Peter 2:3-9 the apostle says: "The Lord is kind. Coming to him as to a living stone, rejected, it is true, by men, but chosen, precious, with God, you yourselves also as living stones are being built up a spiritual house for the purpose of a holy priesthood, to offer up spiritual sacrifices acceptable to God through Jesus Christ. For it is contained in Scripture: 'Look! I am laying in Zion a stone, chosen, a foundation cornerstone, precious; and no one exercising faith in it will by any means come to disappointment.' It is to you, therefore, that he is precious, because you are believers; but to those not believing [the nation of natural Israel], 'the identical stone that the builders rejected has become the head of the corner,' and 'a stone of stumbling and a rock-mass [pétra] of offense.' These are stumbling because they are disobedient to the word. To this very end they were also appointed. But you are 'a chosen race, a royal priesthood, a holy nation, a people for special possession, that you should declare abroad the excellencies' of the one that called you out of darkness into his wonderful light."

[25] There the apostle Peter applies the prophecies of God's written Word (Isaiah 28:16; 8:14; Psalm 118:22; Exodus 19:5, 6), and he plainly says that the Lord Jesus Christ is the "rock-mass" foretold in Isaiah 8:14, against which the nation of Israel would strike the foot and take offense. A second witness of this fact is the apostle Paul, who, when writing to the Christians in Rome, did not once mention Peter as being the "rock-mass" but said:

[26] "Israel, although pursuing a law of righteousness, did not attain to the law. For what reason?

---

24. Whom does Peter identify as that "rock-mass," and how does he do so?
25, 26. When writing to Christians at Rome, to whom did the apostle Paul direct attention as being the "rock-mass"?

Because he pursued it, not by faith, but as by works. They stumbled on the 'stone of stumbling'; as it is written: 'Look! I am laying in Zion a stone of stumbling and a rock-mass [*pétra*] of offense, but he that rests his faith on it [masculine pronoun in Greek applying to the stone] will not come to disappointment.' . . . Christ is the end of the Law, so that everyone exercising faith may have righteousness."—Romans 9:31 to 10:4.

[27] The apostle Paul is even more definite about this in his letter to the Christians in Corinth, Greece, for he refers to his Jewish forefathers and says: "Our forefathers were all under the cloud and all passed through the [Red] sea and all got baptized into Moses by means of the cloud and of the sea; and all ate the same spiritual food and all drank the same spiritual drink. For they used to drink from the spiritual rock-mass that followed them, and that rock-mass meant the Christ." —1 Corinthians 10:1-4.

[28] Nor did the other apostles of Jesus Christ regard Simon Peter as the "rock-mass" on which Jesus Christ was to build his congregation. Even after Jesus spoke the words of Matthew 16:18 to Peter, the apostles James and John made this request of Jesus through their mother: "Grant us to sit down, one at your right hand and one at your left, in your glory." At this request Jesus disclaimed having appointed Peter to his right hand in the heavenly kingdom, for Jesus said: "This sitting down at my right or at my left is not mine to give, but it belongs to those for whom it has been prepared." Prepared by whom? "Prepared by my Father." (Mark 10:35-40; Matthew 20:20-23) The other apostles became indignant at such

---

27. What even more pointed statement on this matter did Paul make in his letter to Christians in Corinth?
28, 29. (a) How did the apostles James and John show that they did not believe Peter to be the "rock-mass" on which Jesus was to build his congregation, and what did Jesus' reply to them indicate? (b) Even at their last passover with Jesus, what were the apostles arguing about, as reported by Luke?

a request by James and John. Even on the night of their last passover with Jesus Christ they argued over positions.

[29] In Luke 22:24-26 we read: "There also arose a heated dispute among them over which one of them seemed to be greatest. But he said to them: 'The kings of the nations lord it over them, and those having authority over them are called Benefactors. You, though, are not to be that way. But let him that is the greatest among you become as the youngest, and the one acting as chief as the one ministering.' "—See also Mark 9:33-35.

[30] The apostle John outlived the apostle Peter. (John 21:20-24) Years after Peter died, it was John who wrote the last five books that were made part of the Holy Bible, namely, the Revelation or Apocalypse, three letters or epistles, and the Gospel of John. In the second-last chapter of the Revelation, John describes the glorious vision that was given to him of the "Lamb's wife," that is to say, the congregation as the spiritual Bride of Jesus Christ. She is pictured as a glorious heavenly city, the New Jerusalem, and, when describing it, John says:

[31] "It had a great and lofty wall and had twelve gates, and at the gates twelve angels, and names were inscribed which are those of the twelve tribes of the sons of Israel. On the east were three gates, and on the north three gates, and on the south three gates, and on the west three gates. The wall of the city also had twelve foundation stones, and on them the twelve names of the twelve apostles of the Lamb."—Revelation 21:2, 9-14.

[32] This vision, given to John years after Peter's death, gives no primacy to Peter, nor does it make

30, 31. Years after Peter died, what was the apostle John shown as to the foundation stones of the New Jerusalem, which is Christ's glorified congregation?
32, 33. (a) Does this vision show Peter to be the one on whom the Christian congregation is built? (b) In agreement with this, what did Paul say about the foundation?

him the "rock-mass" on which as a foundation the Lord Jesus Christ builds his congregation. All the other apostles are equally foundation stones with Peter. None of the apostles rests upon Peter, but all of them, including Peter, rest upon the real "rock-mass," which both the apostle Peter and the apostle Paul tell us is the Christ. In agreement with John's vision the apostle Paul writes, in Ephesians 2:19-22:

[33] "You are fellow citizens of the holy ones and are members of the household of God, and you have been built up upon the foundation of the apostles and prophets, while Christ Jesus himself is the foundation cornerstone. In union with him the whole building, being harmoniously joined together, is growing into a holy temple for Jehovah. In union with him [Christ Jesus] you, too, are being built up together into a place for God to inhabit by spirit."

[34] It was not the apostle Peter in whom the prophecy of Isaiah 28:16 concerning the laying of the foundation in the heavenly Zion was fulfilled. After Jesus ascended to heaven, Peter on the day of Pentecost said that Jesus Christ had gone to heaven to sit at God's right hand; and in his first letter, chapter two, Peter applies Isaiah's prophecy to Jesus Christ. Consequently, Peter agrees with the other apostles that Jesus Christ himself is the symbolic "rock-mass" on which Jesus builds his own congregation.

[35] In its foundations the Christian congregation of God corresponds with the former Israelite congregation of God. The Israelite congregation of God was made up of twelve tribes. The twelve tribes of Israel were founded upon the twelve sons of Israel; and, in turn, the twelve sons were found-

---

34. Did Peter agree with the other apostles on the identity of the foundation stone laid in heavenly Zion, and how did he show this? 35, 36. In the Christian congregation of God, who correspond with Jacob and his sons in relation to the former Israelite congregation?

ed upon their common father, Jacob, whose name was changed to Israel. In Genesis 49:28 we read: "All these are the twelve tribes of Israel, and this is what their father spoke to them when he was blessing them." The main foundation was the patriarch Jacob; the twelve sons were secondary foundations, upon which the whole nation directly rested.

[36] Corresponding to the patriarch Jacob or Israel is the Lord Jesus Christ in being the "rock-mass" or the main foundation of the spiritual "Israel of God." He laid down his human life that this congregation, the spiritual "Israel of God," might come into existence. Corresponding to the twelve sons of Jacob or Israel are the twelve apostles whom Jesus Christ personally chose. (Luke 6:12-16; Matthew 10:1-4; Acts 9:1-16) These all are secondary foundations resting upon the "rock-mass," Jesus Christ.

[37] Corresponding with the twelve tribes of Israel are the symbolic "twelve tribes of the sons of Israel," namely, the entire spirit-begotten, spirit-anointed congregation of which Jesus Christ is the Head. Not Peter, but the apostle John was given the vision of these symbolic twelve tribes of the spiritual "Israel of God."

[38] In Revelation 7:4-8 John names the twelve tribes, each tribe being composed of 12,000 members, namely, Judah, Reuben, Gad, Asher, Naphtali, Manasseh, Simeon, Levi, Issachar, Zebulun, Joseph and Benjamin. All together, they make up a congregation of 144,000 spiritual Israelites. Later, in Revelation 14:1-3, the apostle John sees these 144,000 tribesmen standing on the heavenly

---

37. Who in the Christian arrangement of things correspond with the twelve tribes of natural Israel?
38. (a) How many of these spiritual Israelites make up the Christian congregation, and where is this set out in the Bible? (b) Who is the main foundation on whom the New Jerusalem is built?

Mount Zion with the "Lamb of God that takes away the sin of the world." No doubt those twelve tribal names were the ones that John saw inscribed on the twelve gates of the heavenly New Jerusalem. (Revelation 21:12, 13; John 1:29, 36) This indicates that the New Jerusalem, "the Lamb's wife," is made up of 144,000 citizens. Agreeable with its twelve spiritual tribes, New Jerusalem's wall had twelve foundations inscribed with the names of the twelve apostles. The one main foundation is the Bridegroom, Jesus Christ. —Revelation 21:14.

"THE KEYS OF THE KINGDOM OF THE HEAVENS"

[39] In due time Jesus Christ did give to the apostle Peter the promised "keys of the kingdom of the heavens." (Matthew 16:19) These "keys" are, of course, not literal ones, as though the kingdom of the heavens had literal doors or gates. How a "key" can be used in a symbolic way Jesus demonstrated when, according to Luke 11:52, he said to those who were versed in the Law of Moses: "Woe to you who are versed in the Law, because you took away the key of knowledge; you yourselves did not go in, and those going in you hindered!" That "key of knowledge" could have helped the people into God's heavenly kingdom, for, in Matthew 23:13, Jesus said: "Woe to you, scribes and Pharisees, hypocrites! because you shut up the kingdom of the heavens before men; for you yourselves do not go in, neither do you permit those on their way in to go in."

[40] Contrary to the selfish action of such hypocritical scribes and Pharisees, Peter was assigned to use the keys of knowledge to open up the opportunity to enter the heavenly kingdom.

39. (a) In due time, to whom did Jesus Christ give the promised "keys of the kingdom of the heavens"? (b) Were they literal keys?
40. For what purpose was Peter to use the keys entrusted to him?

⁴¹ According to the part that Peter played on the day of Pentecost of 33 C.E., in acting as the leading spokesman under guidance of the out-poured spirit, Peter used the first one of the "keys of the kingdom of the heavens." His speech to the thousands of inquisitive Jews that day is reported in twenty-three consecutive verses of chapter two of the Acts of the Apostles, together with "many other words" with which he spoke and exhorted them to repent, be baptized and get saved. (Acts 2:14-41) By the knowledge that Peter thus imparted to the Jews he enabled them to take the necessary steps to become heirs of the heavenly kingdom with Jesus Christ.

⁴² Those Jews and circumcised proselytes then being saved were joined to the new congregation that Jesus Christ was building on himself, the true "rock-mass." As salvation back there was "for the Jew first," Peter used the first of the "keys of the kingdom of the heavens" in behalf of the Jews.—Romans 2:6-10.

⁴³ According to the seventy weeks of years of the prophecy of Daniel 9:24-27, God's special exclusive favor was to continue to the nation of natural Israel till autumn of the year 36 C.E., or three and a half years after Jesus Christ was killed sacrificially. At that time Peter was given the second one of the kingdom keys to use in behalf of the non-Jews, the uncircumcised Gentiles.

⁴⁴ Peter had never entered a Gentile home before, but now God sent to Peter a vision to teach him that God was at the point of beginning to cleanse the Gentiles for heavenly salvation. God

41. When did Peter use the first one of those keys, and with what benefit to those who heard him?
42. In behalf of whom did Peter use the first of the keys?
43. How long did God's special exclusive favor continue to natural Israel, and what use of the second kingdom key was made at the end of that time?
44. (a) Why did Peter go into the home of the Gentile Cornelius and even command those there to get baptized? (b) What opportunity was now open for Gentiles?

told Peter to go with three messengers from Caesarea, whom he had told the Italian centurion there to send to Peter at Joppa. Accordingly Peter went with them and entered the Gentile home and preached the Kingdom message to Cornelius and all those whom he had gathered in his home. While Peter was yet speaking to those Gentile listeners, God poured down holy spirit upon them and they began speaking with foreign languages and glorifying God. At this evidence of God's acceptance of these Gentile believers, Peter commanded them, not to get circumcised, but to get baptized in water. (Acts 10:1-48) The door was now open for Gentiles to enter the Kingdom.

[45] Years later, at a general Christian conference in Jerusalem, Peter spoke of his appointment to use this second symbolic "key," saying: "Brothers, you well know that from early days [thirteen years previously] God made the choice among you that through my mouth people of the nations [Gentiles] should hear the word of the good news and believe; and God, who knows the heart, bore witness by giving them the holy spirit, just as he did to us also. And he made no distinction at all between us [Jews] and them, but purified their hearts by faith. . . . we trust to get saved through the undeserved kindness of the Lord Jesus in the same way as those people also."—Acts 15:6-11.

[46] Up till the conversion of the Italian centurion Cornelius many miles away from Jerusalem, the world of mankind had been divided up into two general classes, the Jews and the Gentile nations. But now the doorway into God's heavenly kingdom with Jesus Christ was open to all mankind regardless of race or nationality. There was no further need for Peter to use any more "keys of the kingdom of the heavens." His work with the keys

---

45. Years later, what did Peter say about his appointment to use this second symbolic "key"?
46. Did Peter continue to have use for the keys?

was now finished. Jesus Christ was now building uncircumcised Gentiles as well as natural Jews into his congregation on the "rock-mass." The converted Gentiles were being made spiritual Israelites.—Ephesians 2:11-22.

[47] Since then the followers of Christ have been carrying out his commandment as set forth in Matthew 28:19, 20. Since then God has been taking out the 144,000 members of the twelve tribes of spiritual Israel from all peoples, nations and races. Today, after nineteen centuries, there is on earth only a remnant of the 144,000 members of the true anointed Christian congregation. (Revelation 12:17) But, particularly since the year 1935, Jehovah God has been graciously gathering to their side the "great crowd" of earthly worshipers foreseen and described in Revelation 7:9-17. These sheeplike people with earthly hopes have till now been faithfully joining with the anointed remnant in giving the final Kingdom witness before the war of Armageddon, as foretold in Matthew 24:14.

---

47. (a) Are there many members of the anointed Christian congregation still on earth? (b) What other group of persons have joined with the anointed remnant as active Kingdom witnesses?

CHAPTER 12

God a Person
—or Three Persons
in One God, Which?

THE word "mystery," meaning "sacred secret," is found twenty-eight times in the entire Holy Bible, not in its inspired Hebrew Scriptures but only in its inspired Greek Scriptures. In the popular *Authorized Version* of King James we read of the "mysteries of the kingdom of God," and of the "mystery of the gospel," of the "mystery of iniquity," of the "mystery of the faith," of the "mystery of godliness," of the "mystery of the seven stars," and of "Mystery, Babylon the Great," hence of the "mystery of the woman."* Once these "mysteries" were not understood and men could not explain them. (Romans 16:25; Colossians 1:26, 27) But in his due time God revealed the meaning of these sacred secrets to his faithful worshipers, so that they could be declared and made known.—1 Corinthians 15:51; Ephesians 1:9; 3:3; 6:19; Colossians 4:3.

---

* Luke 8:10; Ephesians 6:19; 2 Thessalonians 2:7; 1 Timothy 3:9, 16; Revelation 1:20; 17:5, 7, Authorized Version of the Bible.

---

1. What are some of the "mysteries" or "sacred secrets" of which the Bible speaks, and have they continued to be such?

255

[2] In 1 Corinthians 2:1 the apostle Paul reminds the Corinthian congregation that he did not try to becloud the mystery or sacred secret with extravagant speech or worldly wisdom, saying: "I, when I came to you, brothers, did not come with an extravagance of speech or of wisdom declaring the sacred secret of God to you."

[3] Here we note that the apostle Paul speaks of the mystery or sacred secret "of God." Elsewhere, also, he speaks of the "sacred secret of God" and of the "sacred secret of the Christ." (Ephesians 3:4; Colossians 2:2; 4:3; Revelation 10:7) Does this refer to what the religious clergymen of Christendom speak of as "the mystery of the Holy Trinity"? Does the Holy Bible teach such a "mystery" of a "God in three Persons," or, "three Persons in one God"? By such "mystery" of Christendom they understand that the Lord God is God, Jesus Christ is God and the Holy Spirit is God, and yet they are not three Gods but only one God in three Persons, "Father, Son and Holy Ghost." Their word "Trinity" does not occur in the Holy Bible.

[4] The Roman Catholic Church, the strongest one religious organization on earth, holds to the "Trinity" as the central doctrine of its religious belief. However, the religious organization ranking next in numbers (445,949,000 in the year 1965) is the Islamic or Mohammedan. They reject the "Trinity." According to their sacred book, Jesus denies that he is a member of a "Trinity" of three coequal Persons, for their Koran, Sura 5, section 16, verse 119, reads: "And behold! God will say: 'O Jesus the son of Mary! Didst thou say unto men, "Worship me and my mother as gods in derogation of God"?' He will say: 'Glory to Thee! Never

2, 3. (a) Since the Bible refers to the mystery or sacred secret "of God" and the "sacred secret of the Christ," what question is raised in connection with the Trinity? (b) What is Christendom's teaching of the Trinity?
4. Do both Catholics and Moslems accept the idea of a Trinity?

could I say what I had no right (to say). Had I said such a thing, Thou wouldst indeed have known it. Thou knowest what is in my heart, though I know not what is in Thine. For Thou knowest in full all that is hidden.' "—*Ali* translation.

[5] An older religious organization, though not so strong in numbers, is that of the natural Jews. These accept the Hebrew Scriptures from Moses to Malachi as being sacred and inspired. Concerning the "Trinity" we read the following in *The Jewish Encyclopedia,* Volume 12 (edition of 1909), page 260:

> . . . the concept of the union in one God of Father, Son, and Holy Spirit as three infinite persons. It was the Nicene Council and even more especially the Athanasian Creed that first gave the dogma its definite formulation: "And the Catholic Faith is this: That we worship one God in Trinity, and Trinity in Unity; Neither confounding the Persons; nor dividing the Substance." Equalization of the Son with the Father marks an innovation in the Pauline theology: "Yet to us there is one God, the Father, of whom are all things, and we unto him; and one Lord, Jesus Christ, through whom are all things, and we through him." (1 Corinthians 8:6, R.V.), while in another passage the Holy Ghost is added (1 Corinthians 12:3; compare Titus 2:13), thus rapidly developing the concept of the Trinity (2 Corinthians 13:14).

This encyclopedia goes on to say that the controversies between the Trinitarians of Christendom and the Jews concerning the "Trinity"

> centered for the most part about the problem whether the writers of the Old Testament bore witness to it or not, the Jews naturally rejecting every proof brought forward by their opponents. The latter [the Trinitarians] based their arguments on the Trisagion [meaning "Three Times Holy"] in Isaiah 6:3, a proof which had been frequently offered since Eusebius [of Caesarea, of the fourth

5. (a) Do the Jews believe in the Trinity? (b) Do Trinitarians claim that the Trinity finds any support in the Hebrew Scriptures?

century C.E.] and Gregory of Nazianzus [of the fourth century C.E.]. The convert Jacob Perez of Valentia (died 1491) even found an allusion to the Trinity in the word "Elohim" and [Martin] Luther saw distinct traces of the doctrine in Genesis 1:1, 20; 3:21; 11:7, 8, 9; Numbers 6:22; 2 Samuel 23:2; and Daniel 7:13. The Jewish polemics against this doctrine date almost from its very conception.

[6] Even today the Trinitarians argue that the Old Testament (or Hebrew Scriptures) supports their teaching of Three Persons in One God, or Trinity in Unity. Well, then, does their argument that the Trisagion (the mention of "Holy" three times together) in Isaiah 6:3 proves the "Trinity" hold good? Isaiah 6:3 (*AV*) says concerning the seraphim about God's throne: "And one cried unto another, and said, Holy, holy, holy, is the LORD [Jehovah, in the traditional Hebrew text] of hosts: the whole earth is full of his glory."

[7] Does that say that the LORD (*AV*), or Jehovah (*AS*), is three Persons in One? Or does it say that there are three Lords or three Jehovahs? No! For in Mark 12:28-30 Jesus Christ quoted Moses' words to the nation of Israel in Deuteronomy 6:4, 5, which read: "Listen, O Israel: Jehovah our God is one Jehovah. And you must love Jehovah your God with all your heart and all your soul and all your vital force." So Jesus himself confirmed that there is only one Jehovah.

[8] Similar to Isaiah 6:3, the account of Revelation 4:8 (*AV*) speaks about the living creatures about God's heavenly throne and says: "And they rest not day and night, saying, Holy, holy, holy, Lord God Almighty, which was, and is, and is to come." Does this saying of "holy" three times

6, 7. (a) In what way do Trinitarians claim that Isaiah 6:3 supports their teaching? (b) How does Jesus Christ, when quoting from the Hebrew Scriptures, show that these Trinitarians are wrong in their conclusions?
8. What expression found at Revelation 4:8 is like that at Isaiah 6:3, and how does the oldest Greek manuscript containing the book of Revelation affect any Trinitarian claims made concerning this scripture?

here mean that the Lord God Almighty is Three Persons, or that there are three Lords God Almighty? If there are three Almighty Ones, how could there be one most mighty? Furthermore, the Sinaitic Greek manuscript of the fourth century C.E., the oldest Greek manuscript containing the book of Revelation, repeats the word "holy" eight (8) times, not three times, in Revelation 4:8; and it would be foolish to argue that this means that there are eight Persons in the one Lord God Almighty.

⁹ That the Lord God Almighty seated on the throne is just one Person, not three, Revelation 4:9 to 5:13 proceeds to show. How? It states that the Lord God Almighty has in his hand a scroll sealed with seven seals. Then the "Lion that is of the tribe of Judah, the root of David," steps forward and takes the scroll out of the hand of the Lord God Almighty. After that a new song is sung in praise of this Lamb, saying: "You were slaughtered and with your blood you bought persons for God out of every tribe and tongue and people and nation, and you made them to be a kingdom and priests to our God, and they will rule as kings over the earth."

¹⁰ Then all creatures in heaven and on earth join in saying to the Lord God Almighty on the throne and to the Lamb, the Lion of the tribe of Judah: "To the one sitting on the throne and to the Lamb be the blessing and the honor and the glory and the might forever and ever." Everybody with clear vision can see here the distinction and separation that are made between the Lord God Almighty and the Lamb or glorified Jesus Christ in heaven. Furthermore, there is no mention or picture made here of the holy spirit and no praises

---

9, 10. (a) How does Revelation 4:9 to 5:13 show that the Lord God Almighty is just one Person, separate and distinct from "the Lamb" Jesus Christ? (b) From this and other scriptures in Revelation, what do we observe as to the holy spirit?

sung to the holy spirit. So this miraculous vision given to the apostle John takes in just two personages, not three, and one of these two personages alone is "God Almighty." All through the rest of the Revelation to John a difference is drawn between the Lord God Almighty on his throne and the Lamb, "his Christ," and leaving out the holy spirit.—Revelation 7:10; 11:15, 16.

[11] But what about the argument of the Trinitarians concerning the Hebrew "Elohim," which is translated "God" in Genesis 1:1? There we read: "In the beginning God [*Elohim*] created the heavens and the earth." The Trinitarians remind us very strongly that the word *elohim* literally means "gods," and hence that the One who created heaven and earth was "Gods." And then, following the suggestion of the German religious reformer, Martin Luther, they quote Genesis 1:26 (*AV*), which reads: "And God said, Let us make man in our image, after our likeness." Here God (*Elohim*) says: "Let *us* [plural] make man in *our* [plural] image, after *our* [plural] likeness." Here the Trinitarians say, God (*Elohim*) was talking to himself and he could thus talk to himself because He is, not one Person, but Three Persons, a Trinity. But is anything wrong here?

[12] Yes, because *Elohim* means, not "Persons," but "Gods." So by such argument the Trinitarians make themselves to be polytheists or worshipers of many Gods. Moreover, in the next verse from the beginning, in Genesis 1:2, a number of modern Bible translations do not say "the Spirit of God," but say, *The Anchor Bible* of 1964, "And only an awesome wind sweeping over the water"; *An American Translation*, edition of 1948, "And a tempestuous wind raging over the surface of the

---

11, 12. (a) What support for their teaching do Trinitarians claim to find in the Bible's use of the Hebrew word *Elohim*, but what is wrong with their argument? (b) Does the second verse of Genesis refer to the "Third Person" of the Trinity, and how do modern Bible translations help one to determine this?

waters"; *The Torah - The Five Books of Moses* of 1962, "And a wind from God sweeping over the water"; *The Holy Bible in Modern English* (Ferrar Fenton) of 1928, "But the breath of God vibrated over its fluid face"; and the *New World Translation* of 1961, "And God's active force was moving to and fro over the surface of the waters." So here no "Third Person" of a "Trinity" is referred to actually.

[13] Well, then, if God or *Elohím* was not talking to himself in Genesis 1:26 and also in 3:22; 11:7, to whom was He really talking? To the angels, say the Jews. But evidently it was to God's "master worker," who found what he was fond of in the "sons of men." (Proverbs 8:22-31) That is to say, God was talking to the one who is called "The Word of God" in Revelation 19:13. This Word of God is spoken of by the apostle John also in John 1:1-3, where, according to *An American Translation,* we read: "In the beginning the Word existed. The Word was with God, and the Word was divine. It was he that was with God in the beginning. Everything came into existence through him, and apart from him nothing came to be." Also, Colossians 1:16, 17 (*AT*): "All things were created through him and for him. He existed before all things and he sustains and embraces them all." Thus, at man's creation, *Elohím* talked to his only-begotten Son, "the Word of God."

[14] It is therefore evident that the title *Elohím,* which has the form of a plural noun, is the plural of excellence or of majesty, as grammars of the Hebrew language point out, and is not a plural form to denote a combination of several fellow members. For that reason, in the Hebrew text, *Elohím,* when applying to Jehovah as God, has a

---

13. To whom, then, was God talking at Genesis 1:26, and how do other portions of the Bible show this?
14. Why is the title *Elohím* in the plural form when referring to Jehovah, and how do the accompanying verbs corroborate this?

verb in the singular number and not in the plural number as if indicating several persons. So, in Genesis 3:5, it does not say, "God [*Elohim*] know," as of several persons knowing, but, "God [*Elohim*] knows," as of one person.

[15] The title *Elohim,* when used as a plural form of excellence or of majesty, is applied, not only to Jehovah, but also to others who are considered and worshiped each one as a God. For instance, when the Israelites brought the lone Ark of the Covenant into their war camp for help, the enemy Philistines got afraid and said: "God [*Elohim*] is come [not, are come] into the camp." (1 Samuel 4:7, *AV*) In Judges 8:33 we read concerning the unfaithful Israelites: "They appointed Baal-berith as their god [*elohim*]." Also: "They went into the house of their god [*elohim*] and ate and drank and called down evil upon Abimelech." (Judges 9:27) In Judges 11:24 Judge Jephthah asks the Ammonites: "Is it not whoever Chemosh your god [*elohim*] causes you to dispossess that you will dispossess?"

[16] Also, in Judges 16:23, 24 the Philistine god Dagon is four times called *elohim;* likewise in 1 Samuel 5:7. Concerning unfaithful King Solomon and his subjects we read, in 1 Kings 11:5, 33: "Solomon began going after Ashtoreth the goddess [*elohim*] of the Sidonians and after Milcom the disgusting thing of the Ammonites." "The reason why is that they have left me and begun to bow down to Ashtoreth the goddess [*elohim*] of the Sidonians, to Chemosh the god [*elohim*] of Moab and to Milcom the god [*elohim*] of the sons of Ammon."

[17] In 1 Kings 18:27 the prophet Elijah taunted the prophets of Baal, saying: "Call at the top of your voice, for he is a god [*elohim*]." In 2 Kings

15-17. Give other Scriptural examples of the use of the title *elohim* to convey the idea of excellence or majesty.

1:2, 3, 6, 16 Baal-zebub is called *elohim*. In 2 Kings 19:37 and Isaiah 37:38 the Assyrian Nisroch is called *elohim*.*

[18] Certainly the calling of each one of these idol gods by the title *elohim* did not mean that each such god was a "trinity." Neither does the applying of *Elohim* to Jehovah mean that He is more than one Person. For a certainty, then, the Christian Bible writers got no Trinitarian ideas from the inspired Hebrew Scriptures.

IS THERE A TRINITARIAN "SECOND PERSON"?

[19] Do not be offended at the question, but, Is Jesus Christ the "Second Person" in a "Trinity" of "God the Father, God the Son, and God the Holy Ghost"? Let the Holy Bible answer. When the angel Gabriel announced the coming birth of Jesus to Mary, he said: "This one will be great and will be called Son of the Most High; . . . Holy spirit will come upon you, and power of the Most High will overshadow you. For that reason also what is born will be called holy, God's Son." (Luke 1:32-35) Since Jesus is the "Son of the Most High" and so is "God's Son," how can Jesus be the Most High God himself? Or be 'equal in power and glory' with the heavenly Father? He could not be such, nor does the Holy Bible say this.

[20] Hence, when the Son let God his heavenly Father transfer his life from heaven to the virgin's womb, he showed that he was not even trying to

---

* See also Isaiah 44:6; 45:5, 14, 21; Daniel 1:2 (twice); Hosea 13:4; Amos 5:26; 8:14; Jonah 1:5; Micah 4:5. Compare Acts 7:43 with Amos 5:26, where the Greek word *theós* (singular) compares with *elohim*.

18. (a) Is it reasonable to conclude that each of these gods was a "trinity"? (b) So did the Christian Bible writers learn about the Trinity from the inspired Hebrew Scriptures?
19. How does an announcement by the angel Gabriel answer the question, Is Jesus Christ the "Second Person" in a "Trinity" of coequal members?
20, 21. Rather than trying to make himself resemble the Most High, how did Jesus act, as shown at Philippians 2:5-11?

be like the ancient king of Babylon, who said: "I shall go up above the high places of the clouds; I shall make myself resemble the Most High." (Isaiah 14:14) Just to the contrary of that was the way that the godlike "Son of the Most High" acted, as described by the apostle Paul in Philippians 2:5-11, which says:

[21] "Christ Jesus, who, although he was existing in God's form, gave no consideration to a seizure, namely, that he should be equal to God. No, but he emptied himself and took a slave's form and came to be in the likeness of men. More than that, when he found himself in fashion as a man, he humbled himself and became obedient as far as death, yes, death on a torture stake. For this very reason also God exalted him to a superior position and kindly gave him the name that is above every other name, so that in the name of Jesus every knee should bend of those in heaven and those on earth and those under the ground, and every tongue should openly acknowledge that Jesus Christ is [what?] Lord to the glory of God the Father."

[22] If Jesus Christ were already, from the beginning, the Most High God, how, then, could "God the Father" exalt him any farther or give him a "superior position," higher than the position he had occupied before he became a man? Impossible! When resurrecting his Son Jesus from the dead and exalting him to heaven, God the Father did not exalt the Son to be His equal, but graciously gave to him the second-highest place in all the realm of life. Hence now every creature in heaven and earth and the dead people yet to be resurrected from the ground have to confess Jesus, not as God, but as "Lord," and their doing so serves

22. (a) How does what God did for his Son Jesus after resurrecting him show that Jesus was not the Most High God? (b) What is meant by the statement that "in the name of Jesus every knee should bend . . . to the glory of God the Father"?

to the "glory of God the Father." In Jesus' name every knee will bend to God the Father, as God foretold in Isaiah 45:23, 24: "To me every knee will bend down, every tongue will swear, saying, 'Surely in Jehovah there are full righteousness and strength.' " Worship will be rendered to God through the Lord Jesus.

[23] Jesus always acknowledged himself as underneath God, subject to God. He plainly declared that the heavenly Father was his God, the God of Jesus Christ. When he came to John the Baptist to be baptized, he acknowledged the heavenly Father as his God, for then he fulfilled Psalm 40:6-8, just as Hebrews 10:5-10 says:

[24] "When he comes into the world he says: ' "Sacrifice and offering you did not want, but you prepared a body for me. You did not approve of whole burnt offerings and sin offering." Then I said, "Look! I am come (in the roll of the book it is written about me) to do your will, O God." ' After first saying: 'You did not want nor did you approve of sacrifices and offerings and whole burnt offerings and sin offering'—sacrifices that are offered according to the Law—then he actually says: 'Look! I am come to do your will.' He does away with what is first that he may establish what is second. By the said 'will' we have been sanctified through the offering of the body of Jesus Christ once for all time."

[25] There Jesus called the heavenly Father his God, whose will he came to earth to do. So he laid down a perfect human sacrifice, the "body" of flesh that God had prepared for him to this end. When he was dying on the torture stake, he acknowledged the heavenly Father as his God, as

23, 24. What did Jesus acknowledge concerning his heavenly Father, and how is this shown by the prophecy he fulfilled at the time he presented himself for baptism?
25. When dying on the torture stake, how did Jesus show that he acknowledged the heavenly Father as his God?

Matthew 27:45, 46 tells us: "From the sixth hour on a darkness fell over all the land, until the ninth hour. About the ninth hour Jesus called out with a loud voice, saying: *'Eli, Eli, lama sabachthani?'* that is, 'My God, my God, why have you forsaken me?'" He thus fulfilled Psalm 22:1. Jesus was certainly not calling out to himself or asking why he had forsaken himself. Without hypocritical show he was really calling out to his God in heaven.

[26] On the morning of his resurrection day he did not raise himself from the dead, nor did he have what some clergymen have called "a spontaneous resurrection" (something like 'spontaneous combustion'). It was not as one Roman Catholic picture book said: "Jesus is God. Only God could make himself come back to life. Jesus arose from the dead on Easter Sunday." However, on Pentecost, fifty days after Jesus' resurrection, the apostle Peter said to the Jews: "God resurrected him by loosing the pangs of death, . . . This Jesus God resurrected, of which fact we are all witnesses. Therefore because he was exalted to the right hand of God . . . God made him both Lord and Christ, this Jesus whom you impaled."—Acts 2:24, 32-36.

[27] In agreement with all this, Hebrews 5:7, 8 says: "In the days of his flesh Christ offered up supplications and also petitions to the one who was able to save him out of death, with strong outcries and tears, and he was favorably heard for his godly fear. Although he was a Son, he learned obedience from the things he suffered." When Jesus was dead for parts of three days, God was not dead, for Habakkuk 1:12 says: "Are you not from long ago, O Jehovah? O my God, my Holy One, you do not die." (*NW; AT; Mo; Ro*) So the immortal God could raise Jesus Christ from the dead.

---

26. Who raised Jesus from the dead, and how do you know?
27. (a) When Jesus was a man of flesh, to whom did he pray? (b) Was it God who was dead when Jesus died?

[28] Shortly after Jesus Christ was raised from the dead he spoke of the One who had raised him out of death as his God. He appeared to Mary Magdalene and said to her: "I have not yet ascended to the Father. But be on your way to my brothers and say to them, 'I am ascending to my Father and your Father and to my God and your God.'" (John 20:11-17) The resurrected, glorified Jesus Christ worships the heavenly Father as his God the same as Jesus' own disciples do.

[29] Because Jehovah the Most High is God to him, Jesus Christ can serve as God's High Priest. Hence, according to Psalm 110:4, "Jehovah has sworn (and he will feel no regret): 'You are a priest to time indefinite according to the manner of Melchizedek!'" And Hebrews 5:5, 6 says: "Christ did not glorify himself by becoming a high priest, but was glorified by him who spoke with reference to him: 'You are my Son; I, today, I have become your father.' Just as he says also in another place: 'You are a priest forever according to the manner of Melchizedek.'" The God worshiped is higher than his high priest. So Jehovah God is higher than his High Priest Jesus.

[30] As God's High Priest, Jesus was privileged to offer an acceptable human sacrifice, the blood of which sacrifice was applied also to God's "new covenant" for the benefit of Jesus' disciples.

[31] For this reason Jesus Christ is also privileged to serve as the "one mediator between God and men." (1 Timothy 2:5, 6; Hebrews 8:6 to 9:28) In being mediator of a covenant between God and men Jesus Christ is like the prophet Moses, who mediated the old Law covenant between Jehovah God and Israel. As to this it is written, in Gala-

---

28. After his resurrection, to whom did Jesus say he would be ascending?
29, 30. Who made Jesus Christ a high priest, and what does this indicate?
31. What is shown by the fact that Jesus is the "mediator between God and men"?

tians 3:19, 20: "It [the Law] was transmitted through angels by the hand of a mediator. Now there is no mediator where only one person is concerned, but God is only one." According to this Bible rule, Jesus Christ as Mediator was not dealing with himself as if he were two persons and mediating between himself. Jesus could not do that, for Jesus is only one person. Jesus was mediating between the anointed Christian congregation and God, who is "only one," not three persons. Jesus Christ and his Father Jehovah are not one God, but are separate and distinct persons; and Jehovah as God is higher and greater than his Mediator, Jesus Christ.

[32] True, Jesus, when discussing shepherding work, did say: "I and the Father are one." (John 10:30) They were one, not bodily, but in work, for Jesus was doing the will of his heavenly Father, who had sent Jesus and had anointed him with holy spirit. Jesus wanted his faithful disciples to come to a similar unity with him and his Father. So Jesus prayed to Him as "the only true God," saying:

[33] "This means everlasting life, their taking in knowledge of you, the only true God, and of the one whom you sent forth, Jesus Christ. Just as you sent me forth into the world, I also sent them forth into the world. And I am sanctifying myself in their behalf, that they also may be sanctified by means of truth. I make request, not concerning these only, but also concerning those putting faith in me through their word; in order that they may all be one, just as you, Father, are in union with me and I am in union with you, that they also may be in union with us, in order that the world may believe that you sent me forth. Also, I have given them the glory that you have given me, in

32, 33. (a) What did Jesus mean by his statement, "I and the Father are one"? (b) In this connection, what did he pray regarding all who would put faith in him?

order that they may be one just as we are one. I in union with them and you in union with me, in order that they may be perfected into one." —John 17:3, 18-23.

[34] Jehovah God as the Sender and Anointer is greater than the anointed Jesus, the Sent One. (John 13:16; Isaiah 61:1; Luke 4:16-21) Jesus was a servant or slave to the One whose will he obeyed. (Romans 6:16; Isaiah 42:1-5; Matthew 12:15-22) In fact, Jesus told his faithful apostles: "The Father is greater than I am." (John 14:28) The apostle Paul backed up Jesus Christ in that statement, when Paul wrote: "The head of the Christ is God." (1 Corinthians 11:3) "There is . . . one Lord [Jesus Christ], one faith, one baptism; one God and Father of all persons, who is over all and through all and in all." (Ephesians 4:4-6) There is only *one* "God and Father of all persons"; and since that exclusive one is "over all," he is over his Son Jesus Christ. This Son is next below "God the Father." As for the holy spirit with which Jesus was anointed, this spirit is not a person at all but is God's invisible active force by means of which God carries out his holy will and work.—Acts 10:38; Isaiah 61:1; Luke 4:16-21.

[35] Consequently, as regards that "mystery of the Holy Trinity," the Sacred Bible says nothing about it, for it does not exist.*

---

* The words "in heaven, the Father, the Word, and the Holy Ghost: and these three are one. And there are three that bear witness in earth," as found in 1 John 5:7, 8 of the *Authorized* (King James) *Version*, are not found in the oldest Greek manuscripts nor in modern Bible versions, such as *AS, AT, NEB, Mo, Ro, RS, NW,* and others. (See page 3 for explanation of abbreviations used here.)

34. (a) Since Jehovah God sent Jesus to the earth and anointed him, and Jesus obeyed him, what does this show as to their relative positions? (b) Who did Jesus say was greater: the Father or himself? and how did the apostle Paul back up Jesus' statement? (c) What is the position of the "one God and Father" in relation to all others, including his Son Jesus Christ?
35. Does the Bible teach the "mystery of the Holy Trinity"?

CHAPTER 13

Are You Under the Ten Commandments of Moses?

I N JOHN 1:17 it is written: "The law was given by Moses, but grace and truth came by Jesus Christ." (*AV*) Naturally the question arises: To whom was that law given, and are you and all other persons, Buddhists, Hindus, Confucianists, Shintoists, Mohammedans, Christians, Jews, and all other religious people, under that law given by means of the prophet Moses? If that law given by him came from the one true God, would it not be universal in its embrace and so would it not apply to all the inhabitants of the earth and also continue to apply to them forever? If we are seeking to do the will of our Creator, the Maker of heaven and earth, we should desire to know the answers to such questions.

[2] Nineteen hundred years ago the Christian congregation was interested in such questions. Why? Because, for the first three and a half years of its existence, the Christian congregation was made up exclusively of Jews and circumcised proselytes.

1. What questions arise concerning the law given by means of Moses, and why should we want to know the answers?
2. Why were such questions of particular interest to the Christian congregation at its beginning?

After such Jews and proselytes became Christians, were they still under the 'law given by Moses'? To the Jewish Supreme Court of Jerusalem the Jewish Christian Stephen said: "This is the Moses that said to the sons of Israel, 'God will raise up for you from among your brothers a prophet like me.' This is he that came to be among the congregation in the wilderness with the angel that spoke to him on Mount Sinai and with our forefathers, and he received living sacred pronouncements to give you."—Acts 7:37, 38.

[3] The Ten Commandments were the first of the "living sacred pronouncements" that were given at Mount Sinai, through the angel of Jehovah God. Not all persons around the earth are familiar with those Ten Commandments. So here we quote them for our readers:

(1)   I am Jehovah your God, who have brought you out of the land of Egypt, out of the house of slaves. You must not have any other gods against my face.

(2)   You must not make for yourself a carved image or a form like anything that is in the heavens above or that is on the earth underneath or that is in the waters under the earth. You must not bow down to them nor be induced to serve them, because I Jehovah your God am a God exacting exclusive devotion, bringing punishment for the error of fathers upon sons, upon the third generation and upon the fourth generation, in the case of those who hate me; but exercising lovingkindness toward the thousandth generation in the case of those who love me and keep my commandments.

(3)   You must not take up the name of Jehovah your God in a worthless way, for Jehovah will not leave the one unpunished who takes up his name in a worthless way.

(4)   Remembering the sabbath day to hold it sacred, you are to render service and you must do all your work six days. But the seventh

---

3. With whom did the Ten Commandments originate, and what requirements did they set out?

day is a sabbath to Jehovah your God. You must not do any work, you nor your son nor your daughter, your slave man nor your slave girl nor your domestic animal nor your alien resident who is inside your gates. For in six days Jehovah made the heavens and the earth, the sea and everything that is in them, and he proceeded to rest on the seventh day. That is why Jehovah blessed the sabbath day and proceeded to make it sacred.

(5)   Honor your father and your mother in order that your days may prove long upon the ground that Jehovah your God is giving you.

(6)   You must not murder.

(7)   You must not commit adultery.

(8)   You must not steal.

(9)   You must not testify falsely as a witness against your fellow man.

(10)   You must not desire your fellow man's house. You must not desire your fellow man's wife, nor his slave man nor his slave girl nor his bull nor his ass nor anything that belongs to your fellow man.—Exodus 20:2-17.

[4] Now, were you ever under those Ten Commandments? If you were, are you still under them? You may ask, How could I be under them when I was not there at Mount Sinai more than thirty-four centuries ago when they were given, before the Buddhist era, the East Indian (Saka) era, the Greek Olympiad era, the Roman era, and the Mohammedan era? Of course, you were not there personally, but were your ancestors there at the giving of the Ten Commandments in the month of May of the year 1513 B.C.E.? To this last question the natural Jews or Israelites will answer Yes. They are correct.

[5] At that time Jehovah was the God of the ancestors of those circumcised Jews. He was not the God of the Babylonians, Assyrians, Arabs, Egyptians, Hittites, Canaanites, and other ancient nations in Asia and Europe. He had not brought up

4. Whose ancestors were present when the Ten Commandments were given?
5, 6. To whom is the First Commandment addressed, and how does Exodus 19:3-6 support this?

those nations out of Egypt and out of a slavery down there. Hence they were not the ones spoken to in the first of the Ten Commandments by the words: "I am Jehovah your God, who have brought you out of the land of Egypt, out of the house of slaves." (Exodus 20:2) Rather, it was the twelve tribes of the sons of Israel. In proof of this we read:

⁶ "Moses went up to the true God, and Jehovah began to call to him out of the mountain, saying: 'This is what you are to say to the house of Jacob and to tell the sons of Israel, "You yourselves have seen what I did to the Egyptians, that I might carry you on wings of eagles and bring you to myself. And now if you will strictly obey my voice and will indeed keep my covenant, then you will certainly become my special property out of all other peoples, because the whole earth belongs to me. And you yourselves will become to me a kingdom of priests and a holy nation." These are the words that you are to say to the sons of Israel.' "—Exodus 19:3-6.

⁷ When told this, the representative older men of the Israelites said: "All that Jehovah has spoken we are willing to do." Three days later Jehovah, by means of his angel, delivered to the Israelites the Ten Commandments by word of mouth. Frightened at the awesomeness of what they saw and heard, the Israelites told Moses: "You speak with us, and let us listen; but let not God speak with us for fear we may die." (Exodus 19:7 to 20:19) Some time later, after further laws were given to them and written down, the nation of Israel entered into a formal solemn contract or covenant with Jehovah God through his mediator Moses. The account of this is found in Exodus 24: 1-8. Commenting on how this covenant of the Law was put in force between Jehovah God and the

---

7, 8. When and how did the nation of Israel enter into a formal covenant with Jehovah God?

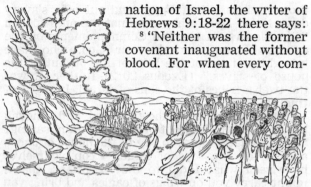

nation of Israel, the writer of Hebrews 9:18-22 there says:

⁸ "Neither was the former covenant inaugurated without blood. For when every commandment according to the Law had been spoken by Moses to all the people, he took the blood of the young bulls and of the goats with water and scarlet wool and hyssop and sprinkled the book itself and all the people, saying: 'This is the blood of the covenant that God has laid as a charge upon you.' . . . Yes, nearly all things are cleansed with blood according to the Law, and unless blood is poured out no forgiveness takes place."

⁹ The forefathers of those Israelites, namely, Abraham, Isaac, Jacob (Israel), and the twelve sons of Jacob, were not under that covenant of Law and were not under the Ten Commandments as a set, as a collected body or code of laws. It is true that, when Jehovah announced the coming birth of Abraham's son Isaac, Jehovah made this statement concerning Abraham: "All the nations of the earth must bless themselves by means of him. For I have become acquainted with him in order that he may command his sons and his household after him so that they shall keep Jehovah's way to do righteousness and judgment; in order that Jehovah may certainly bring upon Abraham what he has spoken about him." Also:

9, 10. Although Abraham kept Jehovah's commands and did what was righteous, did he have the Ten Commandments?

"Abraham listened to my voice and continued to keep his obligations to me, my commands, my statutes, and my laws." (Genesis 18:17-19; 26:5) But note this:

[10] Jehovah God is not reported as making any declaration of the Ten Commandments to Abraham, either before he brought Abraham into the covenant for the blessing of all the nations of the earth or even after that. He gave Abraham no tablets of stone on which the Ten Commandments were inscribed. (Genesis 12:1-8; 15:1-21) Nevertheless, Abraham did "righteousness and judgment" in God's sight.

[11] In the last year of his life Moses plainly stated that Abraham, Isaac, Jacob and the twelve sons of Jacob were not under the Law covenant and its Ten Commandments. In Deuteronomy 5:1-22 the prophet writes: "Moses proceeded to call all Israel and to say to them:

[12] " 'Hear, O Israel, the regulations and the judicial decisions that I am speaking in your ears today, and you must learn them and be careful to do them. Jehovah our God concluded a covenant with us in Horeb. It was not with our forefathers that Jehovah concluded this covenant, but with us, all those of us alive here today. Face to face Jehovah spoke with you in the mountain out of the middle of the fire. I was standing between Jehovah and you at that particular time to tell you the word of Jehovah, (for you were afraid because of the fire and did not go up into the mountain,) saying, "I am Jehovah your God, who brought you out of the land of Egypt, out of the house of slaves. You must never have any other gods against my face." ' "

[13] Then Moses continued on repeating the remaining ones of the Ten Commandments, after which he added: "These Words Jehovah spoke to

11-13. How did Moses make it plain that their forefathers were not under the Law covenant and its Ten Commandments?

all your congregation in the mountain out of the middle of the fire, the cloud and the thick gloom, with a loud voice, and he added nothing; after which he wrote them upon two tablets of stone and gave me them."

[14] That the Law was not prior to Moses, we read in Romans 5:13, 14, in these words: "Until the Law sin was in the world, but sin is not charged against anyone when there is no law. Nevertheless, death ruled as king from Adam down to Moses [over sinners]."

[15] The Law covenant, based on the Ten Commandments and hundreds of added commandments, statutes and ordinances, separated the nation of circumcised Israelites from all other nations. Those nations were non-Israelites or Gentiles. To people who were once uncircumcised Gentiles the apostle Paul wrote: "You were at that particular time without Christ, alienated from the state of Israel and strangers to the covenants of the promise, and you had no hope and were without God in the world." (Ephesians 2:11, 12) Those in the "state of Israel" were under covenant to keep God's law, with hope of a reward, for the covenant stated, in Leviticus 18:5: "You must keep my statutes and my judicial decisions, which if a man will do, he must also live by means of them. I am Jehovah."

[16] Sincere Israelites who tried to keep the righteous law of God found that, instead of its pronouncing them to be righteous or sinless, the Law pronounced them to be sinners who could not earn their own right to everlasting life. Hence by their works of the Law they did not gain the life held out to them but kept on dying.

---

14. According to Romans 5:13, 14, did the Law apply prior to the time of Moses?
15. (a) What did the apostle Paul mean when he said that Gentiles were "strangers to the covenants of the promise"? (b) What hope was set before those who were under covenant to keep God's law?
16. Were the Israelites able to gain life by works of the Law?

[17] Under the Law one of the worst punishments was for a violator of it, after he had been killed, to have his body hung on a tree in public disgrace. Concerning this, Deuteronomy 21:22, 23 said: "In case there comes to be in a man a sin deserving the sentence of death, and he has been put to death, and you have hung him upon a stake, his dead body should not stay all night on the stake; but you should by all means bury him on that day, because something accursed of God is the one hung up; and you must not defile your soil, which Jehovah your God is giving you as an inheritance."

[18] The Law covenant that was mediated by Moses was binding upon all the descendants of those Israelites who directly entered into the covenant with Jehovah God at Mount Sinai or Horeb. That was why Jesus, who was born of Mary a Jewish virgin, was born under the Law as a Jew, he being circumcised on the eighth day. This did not prove to be to his disadvantage, for, as a perfect man whose life was from heaven, Jesus was able to keep the Law perfectly and so the Law declared him to be righteous and deserving of everlasting life. Besides this, there was another purpose in Jesus' being born under the Law. What was that?

[19] The apostle Paul states this in Galatians 4:4, 5, saying: "When the full limit of the time arrived, God sent forth his Son, who came to be out of a

17. What was one of the worst punishments for a violator of the Law?
18. (a) Upon whom besides those who were at Mount Sinai when the Law was given was that covenant binding? (b) Did this include Jesus?
19. As pointed out at Galatians 4:4, 5, why was Jesus born under the Law?

woman and who came to be under law, that he might release by purchase those under law, that we, in turn, might receive the adoption as sons." For the Jews to be released from God's condemnation due to their sins, it was necessary for a Jew who kept God's law perfectly to die as a ransom for them.

[20] Because of entering into a covenant of Law through Moses the Jews came under a special responsibility before God that rested on no other people or nation, for none of the Gentile nations were under the obligations of a covenant solemnized with God. For that reason, although the Gentiles also were sinners and hence dying, the Jews alone came under God's curse because of being violators of God's covenant including the Ten Commandments. So, in order for Jesus' death to cover the cursed sinful case of the Jews as well as the sin of the Gentiles, it became necessary for Jesus to suffer and die in a certain way, namely, on a tree or torture stake.

[21] Galatians 3:10-14 explains such a need in this way: "All those [Jews and circumcised proselytes] who depend upon works of law are under a curse; for it is written: 'Cursed is everyone that does not continue in all the things written in the scroll of the Law in order to do them.' [Deuteronomy 27:26] Moreover, that by law no one is declared righteous with God is evident, because 'the righteous one will live by reason of faith.' [Habakkuk 2:4] Now the Law does not adhere to faith, but 'he that does them shall live by means of them.' [Leviticus 18:5; Nehemiah 9:29] Christ by purchase released us [circumcised Jews, like the apostle Paul] from the curse of the Law by be-

20, 21. (a) Who alone came under God's curse because of being violators of the Law covenant, and why? (b) As explained at Galatians 3:10-14, why was it necessary for Jesus to die in the manner that he did, that is, on a tree or torture stake?

coming a curse instead of us [Jews], because it is written: 'Accursed is every man hanged upon a stake.' The purpose was that the blessing of Abraham might come to be by means of Jesus Christ for the nations [Gentiles], that we might receive the promised spirit through our faith [not by becoming Jews under the Law]."

²² That is why the Christianized Jew Paul writes concerning his yet unbelieving Jewish brothers: "I bear them witness that they have a zeal for God; but not according to accurate knowledge; for, because of not knowing the righteousness of God but seeking to establish their own, they did not subject themselves to the righteousness of God. For Christ is the end [finish] of the Law, so that everyone exercising faith may have righteousness."—Romans 10:1-4.

²³ Jesus Christ could not destroy the Law that God had put in force upon Israel. But Jesus could fulfill it and bring its purpose to reality so that God would have no further use for it. Jesus Christ stated that this was his very purpose in coming as a Jew. He said, in his famous Sermon on the Mount: "Do not think I came to destroy the Law or the Prophets. I came, not to destroy, but to fulfill; for truly I say to you that sooner would heaven and earth pass away than for the smallest letter or one particle of a letter to pass away from the Law by any means and not all things take place." (Matthew 5:17, 18) Hence Jesus did not teach his Jewish disciples to break the Law mediated by Moses, but he himself lived and died in order to fulfill it, producing the realities of which the things of the Law were only advance shadows. —Hebrews 10:1-10.

---

22. Following the death of Christ, how was it possible for the Jews to attain to a righteous standing with God?
23. For what purpose in connection with the Law did Jesus come as a Jew, and so did Jesus teach his disciples to disregard the Law mediated by Moses?

²⁴ What, then, happened to the Law? Since Jesus died as a perfect Jew who kept the Law, the effect of his death was to abolish the Law of commandments that served as a barrier causing enmity or hatred between the two peoples, between the circumcised Jews and the uncircumcised Gentiles. That is what Paul, who was "an apostle to the nations," writes, saying to the Gentile believers:

²⁵ "Now in union with Christ Jesus you who were once far off have come to be near by the blood of the Christ. For he is our peace, he who made the two parties one and destroyed the wall in between that fenced them off. By means of his flesh he abolished the hatred [or, enmity], the Law of commandments consisting in decrees, that he might create the two peoples in union with himself into one new man and make peace; and that he might fully reconcile both peoples in one body to God through the torture stake, because he had killed off the hatred [enmity] by means of himself. And he came and declared the good news of peace to you, the ones far off, and peace to those near [the circumcised Jews], because through him we, both peoples, have the approach to the Father by one spirit. Certainly, therefore, you are no longer strangers and alien residents, but you are fellow citizens of the holy ones and are members of the household of God."—Ephesians 2:13-19.

²⁶ Jesus Christ provided the means for the abolition of the Law, but it was Jehovah God who took it out of the way, canceling it by (so to speak) nailing it to the stake on which his Son Jesus Christ died. Writing especially to uncircumcised Gentile believers, Paul says:

²⁷ "Though you were dead in your trespasses and in the uncircumcised state of your flesh, God made

---

24, 25. What effect did Jesus' death have on the Law, and what did this mean to the Gentile believers?
26, 27. Who actually took the Law out of the way, and how does the Bible show this?

you alive together with him. He [God] kindly forgave us all our trespasses and blotted out the handwritten document against us, which consisted of decrees and which was in opposition to us [because of condemning us as sinners]; and He [God] has taken it out of the way by nailing it to the torture stake. Stripping the governments and the authorities bare, he [God] exhibited them in open public as conquered, leading them in a triumphal procession by means of it. Therefore let no man judge you in eating and drinking or in respect of a festival or of an observance of the new moon or of a sabbath; for those things are a shadow of the things to come, but the reality belongs to the Christ."—Colossians 2:13-17.

[28] Jesus Christ died on Nisan 14 of the year 33 C.E., but it was first three and a half years later that the opportunity was opened for the Gentiles to become members of the anointed Christian congregation. That was when the apostle Peter was sent to preach God's kingdom to the Gentile centurion Cornelius in Caesarea. Those uncircumcised Gentiles were never under the Law mediated by Moses, for they were never in the covenant of Israel with Jehovah God. So by now becoming anointed Christians they did not come under the Law, not even under the Ten Commandments of that covenant of Law. On the other hand, the Jewish believers in Christ became free of that Law, including its Ten Commandments.—Galatians 4:31 to 5:6.

[29] The Holy Bible does not make a difference between the Ten Commandments and the rest of the covenant of the Law. It lumps the Ten Commandments and the Law covenant all in one as

28. When was the way opened for Gentiles to become members of the anointed Christian congregation, and did they thereby come under the Law with its Ten Commandments?
29, 30. According to the apostle Paul's letter to the Romans, are the Ten Commandments to be viewed as distinct from the rest of the Law?

inseparable. Showing that, when he uses the expression "the Law," he also means the Ten Commandments, the apostle Paul writes, in Romans 7:6-11:

[30] "Now we have been discharged from the Law, because we have died to that by which we were being held fast, that we might be slaves in a new sense by the spirit, and not in the old sense by the written code. What, then, shall we say? Is the Law sin? Never may that become so! Really I would not have come to know sin if it had not been for the Law; and, for example, I would not have known covetousness if the Law had not said: 'You must not covet.' [The Tenth Commandment] But sin, receiving an inducement through the commandment [the Tenth Commandment], worked out in me covetousness of every sort, for apart from law sin was dead. In fact, I was once alive apart from law; but when the commandment [the Tenth Commandment, or all Ten Commandments] arrived, sin came to life again, but I died. And the commandment which was to life, this I found to be to death. For sin, receiving an inducement through the commandment [by defining sin and condemning it], seduced me and killed me through it."—See also James 2:8-11.

[31] Even in his Sermon on the Mount, Jesus, when speaking about the Law, referred to some of the Ten Commandments. (Matthew 5:17-21, 27; 7:12) As a prophet like Moses, he has acted as Mediator for a new covenant between his disciples and God. (Jeremiah 31:31-34; Hebrews 9:11-16) Consequently Jesus' disciples are under the law of this new covenant. On the very night that Jesus announced the new covenant to his apostles, he said concerning the cup of wine: "This cup means the new covenant by virtue of my blood," and after-

---

31. Under what covenant and what commandment are Jesus' disciples?

ward* he said to them: "I am giving you a new commandment, that you love one another; just as I have loved you, that you also love one another." (Luke 22:20; John 13:34) Unlike eight of the Ten Commandments, this "new commandment" is not "Thou shalt not" or "You must not." How powerful, then, is this new commandment against sinning?

[32] In his letter to the congregation in Rome, the apostle Paul stresses the power of love against sinning. He refers to himself and his fellow missionary Timothy as being adequately qualified "ministers of a new covenant," in 2 Corinthians 1:1; 3:6; and in Romans 12:9, 10; 13:8-14 he writes: "Let your love be without hypocrisy. Abhor what is wicked, cling to what is good. In brotherly love have tender affection for one another. . . . Do not you people be owing anybody a single thing, except to love one another; for he that loves his fellow man has fulfilled the law. For the law code, 'You must not commit adultery, You must not murder, You must not steal, You must not covet,' and whatever other commandment there is, is summed up in this word, namely, 'You must love your neighbor as yourself.' Love does not work evil to one's neighbor; therefore love is the law's fulfillment. Do this, too, because you people know the season, . . . But put on the Lord Jesus Christ, and do not be planning ahead for the desires of the flesh."

[33] Thus their not being under the Ten Commandments of the old Law covenant mediated by

---

* See the book *"All Scripture Is Inspired of God and Beneficial,"* page 289, last column under "John." Also, *A Harmony of the Synoptic Gospels in Greek,* by E. D. Burton and E. J. Goodspeed, pages 280-284.

32. Does love have the power to keep one from working harm to one's neighbor? Explain.
33. (a) Does the fact that Christians are not under the Ten Commandments make them feel free to sin? (b) What does it really magnify?

Moses resulted in no lawlessness on the part of the true Christians. Why not? Because they were under the law of the new covenant mediated by Jesus Christ. God's grace or undeserved kindness to those in or under the new covenant does not make them feel free to sin. "For," says Romans 6: 14, 15, "sin must not be master over you, seeing that you are not under law but under undeserved kindness. What follows? Shall we commit a sin because we are not under law but under undeserved kindness? Never may that happen!" Accordingly it is not outrageous nor is it an incitement to sin when we say that we today are not under the Ten Commandments. Rather, it magnifies God's undeserved kindness to us through Christ. "The Law was given through Moses, the undeserved kindness and the truth came to be through Jesus Christ."—John 1:17.

CHAPTER 14

Must You Keep a Weekly Sabbath Day?

N VARIOUS lands laws have been enacted by the governments to protect the religious observance of a sabbath day or rest day each week. Fines are even laid upon persons who profane the day by doing certain types of work or by keeping open shop. At times the Sabbath law fixes a certain day that is observed by only the most powerful religious group. This creates a hardship, as, for instance, the Mohammedans celebrate their Sabbath on Friday, the natural circumcised Jews observe Saturday, the seventh day of the week, and the Catholics and Protestants of Christendom consider Sunday to be sacred as the weekly sabbath and hence a special time for going to church. Since all those sabbath days each week are observed, presumably, to the one and the same God, the question bobs up, Which one is the correct sabbath day? Or, it may even be allowable to ask the question, profane though the question may sound, Do we today have to keep a weekly sabbath day toward God?

[2] In the first century of our Common Era the Jews, who were scattered throughout the earth,

---

1. (a) Do all religious groups observe their sabbath on the same day? (b) What questions are therefore asked?
2. When did first-century Jews observe their weekly sabbath day, and in obedience to what commandment?

observed their weekly sabbath day from sundown of what is called Friday to sundown of Saturday. They would hold religious services in the Jewish synagogues during that time. They kept the weekly sabbath in obedience to the Fourth Commandment, which reads: "Remember the sabbath day and keep it holy. Six days you shall labor and do all your work; but the seventh day is a sabbath of the LORD your God: you shall not do any work—you, your son or daughter, your male or female slave, or your cattle, or the stranger who is within your settlements. For in six days the LORD made heaven and earth and sea, and all that is in them, and He rested on the seventh day; therefore the LORD blessed the sabbath day and hallowed it." —Exodus 20:8-11, *Torah*.

[3] The Lord God was very strict about the keeping of the weekly sabbath day on the part of his people in the Law covenant. He said to Moses: "You shall keep the sabbath, for it is holy for you. He who profanes it shall be cut off from among his kin. Six days may work be done, but on the seventh day there shall be a sabbath of complete rest, holy to the LORD, whoever does work on the sabbath day shall be put to death."—Exodus 31:14, 15, *Torah*.

[4] This punishment was enforced. For example, "once, when the Israelites were in the wilderness, they came upon a man gathering wood on the sabbath day." He was put in custody, and Moses inquired what to do with him. "Then the LORD said to Moses, 'The man shall be put to death: the whole community shall pelt him with stones outside the camp.' " The community did so.—Numbers 15:32-36, *Torah*.

3, 4. How serious a thing was it for those under the Law covenant to profane the sabbath day?

[5] In God's commandment there was no command for the Israelites to attend a synagogue on the weekly sabbath day, but, in process of time, the custom of doing so grew up. As a man on earth Jesus Christ observed the custom. The account in Luke 4:16 says: "He came to Nazareth, where he had been reared; and, according to his custom on the sabbath day, he entered into the synagogue, and he stood up to read." Was he thus setting an example for his congregation of disciples to follow? In considering this question, we have to bear in mind that Jesus "came to be out of a woman" and "came to be under law." (Galatians 4:4) Consequently, as a born Jew, circumcised on the eighth day, Jesus was obliged to keep the weekly sabbath in obedience to the Fourth Commandment. But as a natural Jew he was obliged also to keep the Jewish passover and Pentecost and the Festival of Booths or Tabernacles. And, according to the Bible record, he did so. Are Jesus' disciples therefore bound to keep, not only the weekly sabbath, but also all other Jewish festivals? If they must keep one observance, why not all?

[6] But, then, would not the example of the Christian apostle Paul argue that the members of Christ's congregation must keep the weekly sabbath the same as the Jews do? Note Paul's example. On his second missionary trip he entered Europe, and Acts 17:1-3 tells us: "They [Paul and his companions] now journeyed through Amphipolis and Apollonia and came to Thessalonica, where there was a synagogue of the Jews. So according to Paul's custom he went inside to them, and for three sabbaths he reasoned with them

5. (a) Why did Jesus go to the synagogue on the sabbath day? (b) In determining whether this set an example for all his disciples to follow, what should we bear in mind?
6-8. (a) Why does Paul's going into "a synagogue of the Jews" on the sabbath not argue that Christians are to keep the weekly sabbath? (b) What was Paul's reason for going to the Jewish synagogue on the sabbath?

from the Scriptures, explaining and proving by references that it was necessary for the Christ to suffer and to rise from the dead, and saying: 'This is the Christ, this Jesus whom I am publishing to you.' "

[7] However, this does not prove that Paul as a Christian continued keeping the sabbath law as he used to do as a Jewish Pharisee. If Paul was, as a Christian, celebrating the weekly sabbath there in Thessalonica, why does the record not say that Paul went to the *Christian* congregation on the Jewish sabbath day, meeting with his Christian companions? Why does it say that he entered into the *Jews'* synagogue on their sabbath day?

[8] Plainly it was because the Jews kept the sabbath day and met in their synagogues on that day, and so Paul could conveniently preach to them all by going to their synagogue on *their* meeting day, at *their* meeting time. So, in itself, Paul's course at Thessalonica does not prove that this Christian apostle was observing a *Christian* sabbath and thus setting an example for fellow Christians, to whom he wrote: "Become imitators of me, even as I am of Christ." (1 Corinthians 11:1) Otherwise, Christians would have to keep the weekly sabbath by meeting with Jews in their synagogues.

[9] Furthermore, the sabbath day on which Paul attended the Jews' synagogue was from sundown of Friday to sundown of Saturday, whereas Catholics and Protestants of Christendom observe their sabbath day on Sunday, from midnight to midnight. So, even in their weekly sabbath observance, the religious people of Christendom are not imitating either the Christian apostle Paul or Jesus Christ.

---

9. Do worshipers who observe their sabbath day on Sunday imitate the Christian apostle Paul or Jesus Christ?

[10] However, some will argue and say, The obligation to keep the sabbath day preceded even the giving of the Ten Commandments at Mount Sinai in 1513 B.C.E., and the sabbath obligation began with man's creation in the garden of Eden. Sabbatarians holding this idea point to Genesis 2:3, which reads: "And God blessed the seventh day and declared it holy, because on it God ceased from all the work of creation which He had done." (*The Torah*) The seventh day that the Lord God blessed and sanctified or declared holy is the last day of a week of creative activity toward earth.

[11] However, Genesis 2:3 is not drawn up in the form of a law. It merely states a fact and does not say that all mankind must keep the seventh day of each week (from Friday at sundown to Saturday at sundown) as a sabbath for desisting from unnecessary earthly or secular work. In the "history of the heavens and the earth" and in the "book of Adam's history," as contained in the first five chapters of Genesis, there is no record that God put the first man and woman, Adam and Eve, in the garden of Eden under a weekly sabbath law. (Genesis 2:4; 5:1) Adam and Eve were sentenced to death and driven out of the garden of Eden, not for breaking any announced sabbath-day law, but for breaking the announced law against eating the forbidden fruit. The serpent did not tempt Eve to break any sabbath law. If there was no such sabbath law applying to perfect man and woman, how could the serpent tempt Eve on such a law? He could not do so, even though Adam and Eve were created near the end of the sixth day and their next day would be the seventh day that God blessed and sanctified.—Genesis 2:15-17; 3:1-3.

10. When, according to the arguments put forth by some persons, did the obligation to keep the sabbath day begin?
11. Does Genesis 2:3 show that Adam and Eve in Eden were obliged to keep a weekly sabbath day?

[12] Certainly after God drove Adam and Eve out of the garden of Eden as lawbreakers, God did not lay upon them a sabbath law for all their sinful, imperfect offspring. True, the Lord God did say to Noah, the tenth generation in the line of descent from Adam, in the year 2370 B.C.E.: "Go, you and all your household, into the ark, because you are the one I have seen to be righteous before me among this generation. . . . For in just seven days more I am making it rain upon the earth forty days and forty nights; and I will wipe every existing thing that I have made off the surface of the ground." (Genesis 7:1-5) God here spoke of "seven days" more.

[13] True, also, that in the following year near the end of the flood, Noah "went on waiting still another seven days" before send-

ing out a dove from the ark for the second time. After the dove returned with a fresh leaf in its beak, Noah "went on waiting still another seven days" before sending out the dove again, never to return. After that God told Noah to get out of the ark with all its inmates. (Genesis 8:8-17) This indicates that away back there they broke up the calendar year into weeks of seven days. But the Bible account says nothing about Noah's keeping a holy sabbath.

12, 13. What is proved by the fact that periods of "seven days" are mentioned in the time of Noah?

[14] After Noah and his family offered up sacrifice to God outside the ark, God gave his law concerning the eating of animal flesh and the strict observing of the sacredness of the blood of animals. God also introduced his solemn covenant with all mankind against any occurring again of such an earth-wide flood. However, he said nothing to our common forefather Noah about keeping the seventh day of each week holy by desisting from all nonreligious work. But sabbatarians will argue that God said nothing to Noah about sabbath keeping because it was already in practice by Noah and his family and, if God mentioned it after the Flood, he would be repeating a law already in force and recognized. But is that so?

[15] Are laws left unmentioned and not put on the record because they are already in operation and do not need repetition in a code or list of laws? God's law for all mankind concerning the sanctity of blood was definitely stated to Noah and his three sons, our forefathers. Why, then, did God mention the law on blood and bring it in when giving the Israelites the Law through the prophet Moses? Was that not an unnecessary repetition of a universal law already in force? (Leviticus 17: 10-16) Also, if it would have been a needless repetition for God to mention a sabbath law to Noah and his sons after the flood, 1,657 years after Adam's creation, was it not also an unnecessary repetition for God to put a sabbath-day law in the Ten Commandments only 856 years after Noah came out of the ark? To be consistent regarding such matters we should have to reason so.

---

14. (a) Was any mention of the sabbath made by God to Noah after the flood? (b) But what do sabbatarians say was the reason for this?
15. Does the Bible confirm the theory that laws already in operation are thereafter left unmentioned and do not need repetition?

[16] There is no Bible record that after the flood Noah and his sons, Japheth, Shem and Ham, and Abraham and Isaac and Jacob and the twelve tribes of Jacob (Israel) down in Egypt kept a sabbath law, observing the seventh day of each week as holy. The Egyptians did not let the Jews have one day off each week from their slave work to celebrate any sabbath. The first Bible record of any sabbath observance by man is in the account of the Israelites after coming out of Egyptian slavery and being on their way to Mount Sinai to receive there the Ten Commandments from God.

[17] In order to feed the millions of Israelites and the "vast mixed company" with them in the wilderness God began causing a fall of miraculous manna morning after morning. The Israelites asked why they were commanded to pick double the amount of manna on the sixth morning. So Moses said: "It is what Jehovah has spoken. Tomorrow there will be a sabbath observance of a holy sabbath to Jehovah." When some Israelites broke this divine command, Jehovah said: "Mark the fact that Jehovah has given you the sabbath. That is why he is giving you on the sixth day the bread of two days. Keep sitting each one in his own place. Let nobody go out from his locality on the seventh day." Now why did God need to say this if all along up till then the Israelites had been

16. In the Bible is there any record that a weekly sabbath was kept before the Israelites came out of Egyptian slavery?
17. In connection with God's instructions on what provision of food for the Israelites did God institute a sabbath observance?

keeping the sabbath law? But now, for the first time in the Bible we read this account of sabbath observance. "And the people proceeded to observe the sabbath on the seventh day."—Exodus 16:13-30; 12:37, 38.

[18] Till then, in 1513 B.C.E., all mankind had been under no sabbath law since man's creation, nor have all men been under such a law since. Plainly, the Israelites were the first people, the first nation, and the only nation, to be put under a sabbath law. Not all men have been under the Fourth Commandment of the Ten Commandments as given at Mount Sinai through Moses. (Exodus 20:8-11) In proof of that fact, we read, in Exodus 31:12-18, these words:

[19] "And Jehovah said further to Moses: 'As for you, speak to the sons of Israel, saying, "Especially my sabbaths you are to keep, for it is a sign between me and you during your generations that you may know that I Jehovah am sanctifying you. And you must keep the sabbath, for it is something holy to you. A profaner of it will positively be put to death. . . . It is a covenant to time indefinite. Between me and the sons of Israel it is a sign to time indefinite, because in six days Jehovah made the heavens and the earth and on the seventh day he rested and proceeded to refresh himself." ' Now as soon as he had finished speaking with him on Mount Sinai he proceeded to give Moses two tablets of the Testimony, tablets of stone written on by God's finger."

[20] That the sabbath law was a sign (Hebrew, ōth) between God and only Israel, sanctifying only Israel, is confirmed for us nine hundred and two years later, in 611 B.C.E., when God commanded the prophet Ezekiel in Babylon to say this to the

18, 19. (a) Does the sabbath law apply to all mankind? (b) How does Exodus 31:12-18 prove this?
20. How did what God had the prophet Ezekiel say to the Israelites show that the sabbath law differentiated them from all the Gentile nations?

Israelites: "So I brought them forth from the land of Egypt and brought them into the wilderness. And I proceeded to give them my statutes; and my judicial decisions I made known to them, in order that the man who keeps doing them might also keep living by them. And my sabbaths I also gave to them, to become a sign between me and them, in order for them to know that I am Jehovah who is sanctifying them." (Ezekiel 20:10-12) He was not sanctifying all the nations by giving all nations the sabbath law, but was sanctifying only the nation of Israel by giving to it alone the sabbath law. As a sign it differentiated Israel from all the Gentile nations.—Deuteronomy 5:15.

[21] The weekly sabbath law, just like the sabbath years, was a part of the Law covenant of Jehovah with Israel through the mediator Moses. As long as that Law covenant continued in force between God and the nation of Israel the natural Israelites were bound to keep it. Consequently, when the Law covenant was abolished by means of the propitiatory sacrifice of the perfect Israelite Jesus Christ, the weekly sabbath law was also abolished as a part of that covenant. Although the natural Jews today refuse to recognize that fact, they are under no weekly sabbath requirement now; their sabbath keeping since 33 C.E. has not had God's recognition or approval. He grants no righteousness for sabbath keeping.—Ephesians 2:15.

[22] The new covenant between Jehovah God and the congregation of Jesus Christ includes no weekly sabbath law. (Jeremiah 31:31-34; 1 Corinthians 11:22-26) We read, in Hebrews 8:3 to 9:15: "In his saying 'a new covenant' he has made the former one obsolete. Now that which is made obso-

---

21. Of what was the sabbath law a part, and so are the Jews obligated before God to keep it today?
22. Is there a sabbath law included in the new covenant, and what has happened to the "former" covenant?

lete and growing old is near to vanishing away. For its part, then, the former covenant used to have ordinances of sacred service and its holy place upon this earth. . . . However, when Christ came as a high priest of the good things that have come to pass through the greater and more perfect tent not made with hands, that is, not of this creation, . . . he is a mediator of a new covenant, in order that, because a death has occurred for their release by ransom from the transgressions under the former covenant, the ones who have been called might receive the promise of the everlasting inheritance." The old Law covenant with natural Israel is the "former" covenant, now "obsolete," that has vanished away. The new covenant mediated by Christ is the one now in force.

[23] Christ's congregation does not observe the weekly sabbath any more than it observes the Jewish new moons or passover or other Jewish festivals. In Colossians 2:13-17 the apostle Paul called our attention to this, saying: "God made you alive together with him. He kindly forgave us all our trespasses and blotted out the handwritten document against us, which consisted of decrees and which was in opposition to us; and He has taken it out of the way by nailing it to the torture stake. . . . Therefore let no man judge you in eating and drinking or in respect of a festival or of an observance of the new moon or of a sabbath; for those things are a shadow of the things to come, but the reality belongs to the Christ." So we should not let sabbath-keeping religionists take us to task or pass adverse judgment upon us because we do not keep a weekly sabbath day. If Jews choose to keep on observing the shadows in the Law given through Moses, let them do so. True Christians who are in the new covenant will observe the realities with God's approval.

23. Why do true Christians not observe a weekly sabbath day?

[24] Since the end of the sixth creative day Jehovah God has been enjoying his great sabbath day, desisting from work of earthly creation. (Exodus 20:11) Christ's disciples enter into God's sabbath keeping by desisting from their own works at trying to justify themselves. Instead, they rest by faith in the righteousness and sacrifice of the Son of God. Telling us how Christians in the new covenant enter into God's rest, to enjoy it every day of the week, Hebrews 3:19 to 4:11 contrasts Jews and Christians, saying:

[25] "So we see that they [the unbelieving Jews] could not enter in because of lack of faith. Therefore, since a promise is left of entering into his rest, let us fear that sometime someone of you may seem to have fallen short of it. For we have had the good news declared to us also, even as they also had; but the word which was heard did not benefit them, because they were not united by faith with those who did hear. For we who have exercised faith do enter into the rest, just as he [God] has said: 'So I swore in my anger, "They shall not enter into my rest," ' although his works were finished from the founding of the world [in 4026 B.C.E.]. For in one place he has said of the seventh day as follows: 'And God rested on the seventh day from all his works,' and again in this place [in Psalm 95:11, in David's day in the eleventh century B.C.E.]: 'They shall not enter into my rest [God's rest].'

[26] "Since, therefore, it remains for some to enter into it, and those [Jews] to whom the good news was first declared did not enter in because of disobedience, he again marks off a certain day by saying after so long a time [after more than 2,900 years from man's creation to King David] in David's psalm 'Today'; just as it has been said

24-27. Into what sabbath do Christ's disciples enter as shown at Hebrews 3:19 to 4:11, and how?

above: 'Today if you people listen to his own voice, do not harden your hearts.' For if Joshua had led them into a place of rest [when Israel entered the Promised Land in 1473 B.C.E.], God would not afterward have spoken [in David's time] of another day. So there remains a sabbath resting for the people of God. For the man that has entered into God's rest has also himself rested from his own works, just as God did from his own [in 4026 B.C.E.].

[27] "Let us [Christians in the first century of our Common Era] therefore do our utmost to enter into that rest, for fear anyone should fall [like the Jews] in the same pattern of disobedience."

[28] So, now, back to our original question, Must you keep a weekly sabbath day? The Holy Bible answers No! Instead, the thing to do is to enter into "God's rest" by exercising faith in his life-saving provision through his Son Jesus Christ. The account in Genesis 2:1-3 does not say that God took up working creatively again with regard to our earth after the sixth creative day had ended with the creation of Adam and Eve. God has been enjoying a great rest day ever since. He invites us to enter into it with him by resting each one "from his own works" at self-justification and by believing God's Word and putting faith in his provision for salvation through Jesus Christ. So let us keep God's rest every day.

---

28. (a) Does God require you to keep a weekly sabbath day? (b) Into what rest are you invited to enter?

CHAPTER 15

God's Permission of Wickedness Soon to End

MANY heartbroken persons have cried out in anguish, 'If there is a God, why does he permit all this sorrow, suffering and wickedness?' Because of not knowing the answer to this question, they have lost faith in God. So if we too do not desire to become atheists, agnostics or infidels through lack of understanding, we must go to God's written Word, the Holy Bible, for his own explanation of why He has permitted wickedness.

[2] Naturally we ask questions such as these: Has God done an injustice to mankind by permitting wickedness to prevail over the earth for all these millenniums? Or has God shown weakness, as if he is unable to control the situation? Is it right for us to take offense at God's long permission of wickedness and stumble into disbelief because of it? Because such worldwide wickedness hurts us so much, should we disown God, yes, put him out of our lives?

---

1. (a) Faced with sorrow, suffering and wickedness, what question have many persons asked? (b) Why is it important to know the answer God gives in his written Word?
2. What straightforward questions on this subject are here asked?

³ According to the Bible, Satan the Devil said that even the most upright man would disown God if things did not go his way and if the deeds of wicked people spoiled his happy condition. At a conference of the angelic sons of God in heaven, Satan the Devil came also "from roving about in the earth and from walking about in it." So Jehovah God called Satan's attention to a man down there on earth, Job in the land of Uz, as being different from all others, "a man blameless and upright, fearing God and turning aside from bad." Satan was not impressed at this but said that Job was a God-fearing man because he was enjoying a shielded life of prosperity under God's protection.

⁴ "But," continued Satan, "for a change, thrust out your hand, please, and touch everything he has and see whether he will not curse you to your very face." God did not choose to thrust out his own personal hand against Job. Why should he? But, to put Job to the test and to silence Satan the Devil, God permitted Satan to thrust out his hand against Job: "Only against him himself do not thrust out your hand!" So Satan brought against Job wicked men, Sabeans and Chaldeans who violently took away the thousands of Job's livestock. Lightning or fire from heaven destroyed his seven thousand sheep. A windstorm struck the house where his seven sons and three daughters were feasting and caused it to collapse, killing them all. When all this calamity was reported to Job in rapid succession, did Job do as Satan said that he would do, curse God to his very face? What would you have done if you had been Job under those

---

3. (a) Who claimed that even the most upright man would disown God if the deeds of wicked people were allowed to spoil his happiness? (b) On what occasion reported in the Bible was this claim made?

4, 5. (a) Who brought calamity upon Job, and why did God permit it? (b) How did Job react in the face of all this calamity?

circumstances? Here is what Job, though grieved, said:

⁵ "Naked I came out of my mother's belly, and naked shall I return there [that is, to the ground, to which he could point]. Jehovah himself has given, and Jehovah himself has taken away. Let the name of Jehovah continue to be blessed." —Job 1:1-21.

⁶ Not silenced by this, Satan challenged God to give him further permission to afflict Job, this time touching Job's bones and flesh. Then, surely, Job would become anti-God and curse Him. So, with God's permission, Satan struck Job with a repulsive, stinking disease from head to foot. His breath became loathsome to his wife, and she said: "Are you yet holding fast your integrity? Curse God and die!" Next, three friends came, considered his situation and told him he was a hypocritical sinner, being punished openly by God for his secret sin. Job denied that he was a man of a bad private life and now undergoing the punishment that he deserved; but he ascribed to God the right to treat him nicely and also to treat him otherwise even though Job continued righteous. His accusing friends were put to silence; and a young man, listening in, spoke in defense of Jehovah God, as One who could restore people.

⁷ Finally Jehovah God himself spoke to Job and showed how weak man was in comparison with how mighty God was without needing man's help. Job admitted the truth of this, at last saying: "I do repent in dust and ashes." Then God condemned Job's accusers, told how Job would pray

---

6. (a) After this, what further affliction did Satan bring upon Job? (b) What did Job's wife urge him to do? Of what did three of his friends accuse him? But what position did Job take?
7. (a) What fact did Jehovah himself point out to Job? (b) How was Job rewarded for his endurance? (c) What was proved by this test?

for them, and restored Job to good health so that he lived for a hundred and forty years more.

His wife also bore him ten more children, seven sons and three daughters. Job became a prosperous stock raiser again, with twice as many livestock. (Job 2:1 to 42:17) In view of this we ask, Did it prove to be rewarding for Job to hold onto God in spite of wickedness that sorely tried him by God's permission? The outcome of Job's endurance answers Yes! By permitting this test God proved Satan the Devil to be a liar and vindicated himself, disproving all charges of injustice.

[8] This is no fairy tale or myth, merely a made-up story with a nice moral. It is a true-life story, an authenticated historical happening, one vouched for by God himself. (Ezekiel 14:14, 20; James 5:11) Let us learn from it and not attribute wrong to God.

[9] Of course, we can open up the question of God's rightness and discuss it. The patriarch Abraham did so, before God destroyed Sodom and Gomorrah by fire and sulphur from the skies. Thinking of his nephew, righteous Lot, and his family in Sodom, Abraham asked: "Is the Judge of all the earth not going to do what is right?" (Genesis

---

8. Did those things really happen to Job?
9. Can it rightly be said that God is unjust in his dealings with mankind?

18:25) Even though many human judges accept bribes and twist justice, we should expect the "Judge of all the earth" to do perfectly right. And he always does. The Christian apostle Paul asks questions and answers them from the Bible, saying: "What shall we say, then? Is there injustice with God? Never may that become so! For he says to Moses: 'I will have mercy upon whomever I do have mercy, and I will show compassion to whomever I do show compassion.' So, then, it depends, not upon the one wishing nor upon the one running, but upon God, who has mercy."—Romans 9:14-16.

[10] Well, then, instead of doing you an injustice, is God having mercy upon you and showing compassion to you by permitting wickedness till now, yes, more wickedness than ever in our day? Let us see.

[11] About six thousand years ago, in the garden of Eden, Adam and Eve confessed to having broken God's law, for which they deserved death. Jehovah God was then faced with the need to make a far-reaching judicial decision. He could hold to strict justice and show mercy and compassion to nobody mixed up in the case. As man's Creator and Lawgiver he had told Adam in the garden of Eden: "As for the tree of the knowledge of good and bad you must not eat from it, for in the day you eat from it you will positively die." (Genesis 2:17) God, as Judge, could have interpreted that law to specify a "day" twenty-four hours long and could then have put Adam and Eve to death that same day, in all righteousness.

[12] Had God done that, in all justice, what would have resulted? Adam and Eve would have died

---

10, 11. In determining whether God has shown mercy to you by permitting wickedness until now, what events in the garden of Eden should be considered?
12. (a) What would have happened to you if God had not allowed wickedness to continue but had put Adam and Eve to death at once? (b) So has God been merciful to you?

childless. Then what would have happened to you? You would have died in Adam's loins and never have been born! Did God do you wrong in letting you be born at all, even if it has been with your naturally inheriting sinfulness, imperfection and condemnation to death? No! He has shown mercy to you.

[13] Another thing, one of greater concern to God himself: when God created Eve and married her to Adam, he blessed them both and said: "Be fruitful and become many and fill the earth and subdue it, and have in subjection the fish of the sea and the flying creatures of the heavens and every living creature that is moving upon the earth." (Genesis 2:18-24; 1:26-28) Now, if God had put childless Adam and Eve to death on that same twenty-four-hour day in which they had sinned, what would have happened to God's purpose to have all earth filled with a righteous human race living in a Paradise? It would have had to wait till after God's long rest day ended, which day of God's resting from earthly creation has not yet ended but has at least a thousand years yet to go. How so?

[14] Because, after Jehovah God created Adam and Eve, his sixth creative day ended and his seventh day of desisting from earthly creative work began, which day he blessed and made sacred. In view of that, God was not going to profane his own sacred "day" of sabbath keeping by doing earthly creative work, by creating another perfect man and woman to take the place of Adam and Eve after their execution to death. God does not lie and deny himself. So he would have had to wait till his rest day ended and, after it ended, he could create another perfect man and woman to fill the earth

13, 14. If God had put Adam and Eve to death immediately after they sinned, what would have happened to his purpose for the earth, and how so?

with a righteous race. This, of course, would be accompanied by a test of their perfect obedience also, as in the case of Adam and Eve. But God did not choose to wait. So what did he do? He showed mercy.

¹⁵ On a Jewish sabbath day the Son of God, Jesus Christ, once asked this question: "Is it lawful on the sabbath to do good or to do injury, to save or to destroy a soul?" Then he miraculously healed a man with a withered right hand. (Luke 6:6-10; Matthew 12:9-13) When Jesus' disciples were accused as sabbathbreakers, he showed the accusers to be wrong and added: "If you had understood what this means, 'I want mercy, and not sacrifice,' you would not have condemned the guiltless ones." (Matthew 12:1-7) Accordingly, the heavenly Father of Jesus Christ was not violating his own long rest day by showing mercy back there in Eden's garden. Showing mercy to whom?

¹⁶ Of course, it was a mercy to the sinful Adam and Eve that God did not destroy them on that twenty-four-hour day, but took the judicial viewpoint of one day as meaning a thousand years. (2 Peter 3:8) Consequently we read concerning Adam: "He became father to sons and daughters. So all the days of Adam that he lived amounted to nine hundred and thirty years and he died." (Genesis 5:4, 5) Adam thus died within a thousand years of time. In view of this we can appreciate that, back there in the garden of Eden, Jehovah God showed mercy and compassion mainly to Adam's then unborn offspring, including you. God purposed to make merciful provision for Adam's offspring. God's love dominated him rather than strict justice.

---

15. (a) How did Jesus show that it was right to do a merciful deed on the Jewish sabbath day? (b) So was God violating his rest day by showing mercy in Eden?
16. To whom did God show mercy there in Eden, and how?

WHY THE WICKED ONE IS PERMITTED TO LIVE

[17] For a fact, there must have been someone behind that serpent in Eden that made it talk to Eve and deceive her with a lie and tempt her into sinning against God her Creator. That was a wicked thing to do. Who did that wicked thing? It was an angelic son of God who had rebelled against his heavenly Father and who was now tempting God's earthly children to do the same thing. It was the self-made Satan the Devil, who did the talking by means of the speechless serpent. He became doubly guilty, for not only did he himself rebel and slander God his Father but he also tempted Eve and Adam to sin rebelliously against God. Why did God not at once destroy Satan the Devil after he caused Adam and Eve to fall?

[18] Satan the Devil had to be proved a liar and a false god. He had told Eve that she and her husband would become like God for eating the forbidden fruit. It required a period of time for that to be proved a lie. (Genesis 3:1-5) Satan the Devil had made himself a god over mankind by bringing them over on his side as a rebel against God. So Satan had to be proved a false god, the worship of whom would result only in wickedness, calamity and death. Furthermore, he had corrupted the very first man and woman on earth. Well, then, could God ever put a perfect man and woman on earth for filling it with a righteous race and not have them go wrong when tempted by Satan the Devil? To determine this point would take time. Would Jehovah God have to wait till his rest day ended and then create another perfect man and woman to prove that he could produce perfect human creatures of unswerving faithfulness to Him? What guarantee was there that Satan the Devil

---

17. Who was behind the serpent that spoke to Eve, and of what wicked things was he guilty?
18. Why did God allow Satan to remain for a time instead of destroying him at once after he caused Adam and Eve to sin?

would not also succeed against another perfect human pair? Jehovah God decided to prove the matter in his own favor on his own rest day. How?

[19] Almighty God did not destroy that particular serpent there in Eden, neither did he destroy the greater Serpent, Satan the Devil, at once. Choosing a different course, one of matchless wisdom, Jehovah God said to the greater Serpent: "I shall put enmity between you and the woman and between your seed and her seed. He will bruise you in the head and you will bruise him in the heel." (Genesis 3:14, 15) It would take time for the "woman" here meant to produce her seed. It would also take time for the greater Serpent to produce his seed. It would require some time before the greater Serpent could bruise the woman's seed in the heel and also before her seed could bruise the greater Serpent in the head. Bruising the woman's seed in the heel would be a wicked act, and that meant that Almighty God would have to permit wickedness for a time. But, no matter how much time it would take, the greater Serpent and his seed were marked for everlasting destruction as objects of God's wrath. At the same time the seed of the "woman" was marked for deliverance to everlasting life as an object of God's mercy.

[20] In Romans, chapter nine, verses 14-16, of which we have already quoted (on page 302), the apostle Paul argues in the above manner, to show that God does not destroy the wicked ones immediately, in order to spare the righteously disposed ones. In Romans 9:17-26, the apostle Paul first quotes Exodus 9:16 and follows it up thus:

19. (a) Rather than destroying the Devil, what did Jehovah God say to him? (b) What would the fulfillment of this prophecy require, but for what were the Serpent and his seed marked and for what was the seed of the "woman" marked?
20-23. (a) In Romans chapter 9, who does the apostle show is spared because God does not destroy the wicked ones immediately? (b) Why was wicked Pharaoh allowed to remain for a time? (c) What fine illustration does the Scripture use to show man's position in relation to God?

²¹ "For the Scripture says to Pharaoh: 'For this very cause I have let you remain [alive, in wickedness toward the twelve tribes of Israel], that in connection with you I may show my power, and that my name may be declared in all the earth.' So, then, upon whom he [God] wishes he has mercy, but whom he wishes he lets become obstinate [as he did with Pharaoh of Egypt].

²² "You will therefore say to me: 'Why does he yet find fault? For who has withstood his express will?' O man, who, then, really are you to be answering back to God? Shall the thing molded say to him that molded it, 'Why did you make me this way?' What? Does not the potter have authority over the clay to make from the same lump one vessel for an honorable use, another for a dishonorable use?

²³ "If, now, God, although having the will to demonstrate his wrath and to make his power known, tolerated with much long-suffering vessels of wrath made fit for destruction, in order that he might make known the riches of his glory upon vessels of mercy, which he prepared beforehand for glory, namely, us, whom he called not only from among Jews but also from among nations, what of it? It is as he says also in Hosea: 'Those not my people I will call "my people," and her who was not beloved "be-

loved"; and in the place where it was said to them, "You are not my people," there they will be called "sons of the living God." ' "—Hosea 2:23; 1:10.

²⁴ God did not destroy Pharaoh of Egypt right after he refused the first request of the prophet Moses to let the Israelites go free from Egypt. Instead, God began bringing plagues on all Egypt to induce Pharaoh to let Jehovah's people go. After he, at the request of Pharaoh, lifted each plague, Pharaoh would harden his heart or make it stubborn. Of course, Jehovah God could have prevented Pharaoh from hardening his heart, by killing him off and not tolerating him any longer. Jehovah did not hurry Pharaoh's destruction but tolerated him "with much long-suffering," even though Pharaoh was getting harder, with a greater degree of obstinacy, all the time. Just why was this? Jehovah God explained it to Pharaoh.

²⁵ After the sixth plague had been lifted and Pharaoh had recovered himself and turned obstinate again, Jehovah said to him by means of Moses: "Send my people away that they may serve me. For at this time I am sending all my blows against your heart and upon your servants and your people, to the end that you may know that there is none like me in all the earth [including Egypt with all its idols]. For by now I could have thrust my hand out that I might strike you and your people with pestilence and that you might be effaced from the earth. But, in fact, for this cause I have kept you in existence, for the sake of showing you my power and in order to have my name declared in all the earth."—Exodus 9:13-16.

²⁶ If Jehovah had cut off Pharaoh right at the start, it would not have given opportunity for Je-

---

24. How did God demonstrate "much long-suffering" in dealing with Pharaoh?
25. Why did Jehovah not destroy Pharaoh at once when he refused to let the Israelites go free?
26, 27. What opportunities were there for Jehovah to show his power in Egypt and at the Red Sea when the Israelites were on their way out of Egypt?

hovah to show all his diversified power that all the magicians, sorcerers and astrologers of Egypt could not duplicate. What Jehovah was doing to Egypt became common knowledge in all the earth after each plague, and people would be talking about God's name in all the earth. Even after Jehovah had struck Egypt with the tenth and last plague, which took the life of Pharaoh's firstborn son and the lives of the firstborn of all his cattle, Jehovah God had not yet shown Pharaoh the full extent of his power to prove that there is no god like Jehovah in all the earth. Jehovah let Pharaoh harden his heart after that, so that he went in pursuit of the departing Israelites who were now seemingly trapped on the western shore of the Red Sea.

[27] When matters got extreme for the Israelites, Almighty God opened up a way for them through the Red Sea to the eastern shore. God had marked Pharaoh and his pursuit troops as "vessels of wrath made fit for destruction," and so he left the pathway through the seabed open till Pharaoh and his troops got between the walls of seawater on each side. Then as Moses, safe on the eastern shore, stretched out his hand over the sea, God let the walls of water collapse right upon the trapped Egyptians and drowned them.

[28] Not since the great flood of Noah's day had there been such a show of Jehovah's power. It caused Jehovah's name to be declared in all the earth. Forty years later the pagan inhabitants of the Promised Land were still talking about it, in great fear. (Exodus 9:17 to 15:16; Joshua 2:8-11) Up till that glorious display of divine power at the Red Sea, Jehovah God was preserving his chosen people like "vessels of mercy." Up till then the Israelites had had to suffer much oppression at the hand of the "vessels of wrath made fit for de-

---

28. (a) As a result, what was made known in all the earth? (b) Who were like "vessels of mercy" in this case, and how did God make known his glory in connection with them?

struction," but it was worth it to see this show of God's power for His glory and for the complete deliverance of his people. Then his people could appreciate why Almighty God had permitted all that wickedness on Egypt's part for so long a time.

[29] In the garden of Eden, God made the prophetic statement, as recorded in Genesis 3:14, 15, concerning the great Serpent (that is, Satan the Devil) and his seed. Ever since then these ones have been "vessels of wrath made fit for destruction." As a whole they have been permitted to exist for almost six thousand years till now. During all this long stretch of time much wickedness has been perpetrated in the earth by reason of the activity of the greater Serpent and his seed. Nineteen centuries ago God permitted them to bruise the seed of the "woman" in the heel in the outstanding case of Jesus Christ. During all these thousands of years why has God permitted all this wickedness down to its terrible state today?

[30] Just as he permitted Pharaoh of Egypt to remain in existence and carry on all his wickedness against Jehovah's people, so God has let Satan the Devil remain in existence in order to show forth His power over all of Satan's earthly evildoers, soon now, in the "war of the great day of God the Almighty" at the place called in the Hebrew tongue Har–Magedon. After that he will bind Satan the Devil and all his demons and inactivate them in the abyss during his promised kingdom. —Revelation 16:13-16; 20:1-3.

[31] In the meantime, while Almighty God has been tolerating Satan and his wicked agents in

---

29. Ever since Eden, who have been tolerated by God as "vessels of wrath made fit for destruction," and for what have they been responsible?
30. Why has God let Satan and the wickedness caused by him continue until our day, and when will this situation be brought to an end?
31. (a) While God has been tolerating Satan, for what has he been allowing himself time? (b) What was being done in connection with faithful men and women prior to the bringing forth of the "seed" of the "woman"?

heaven and earth for all these thousands of years, God has been allowing himself time for bringing forth at last the promised "seed" of the "woman." Preliminary to his beginning to bring forth this seed of the woman there has been a lot of activity on God's part. During this period of preliminary activity God has tested the faith, devotion and endurance of many faithful men and women, such as Abel, Enoch, Noah, Abraham, Sarah and Moses. Call to mind the proving of Job's endurance under terrible mistreatment by Satan the Devil. This was a small-scale illustration of why God the Almighty permits wickedness and how he rewards those persons who loyally endure in faith to the finish.

[32] Nineteen hundred years ago God brought forth the first and principal one of the woman's seed, namely, Jesus Christ. Since then he has been preparing the rest of the woman's seed, who are to be associated with Jesus Christ in the glory of his heavenly kingdom. These ones, 144,000 in number, are those "vessels of mercy" spoken of by the apostle Paul. During the time that God has been preparing all these, he has had to exercise much long-suffering and to tolerate further the wicked, the "vessels of wrath," holding off their destruction. Why? "In order that he might make known the riches of his glory upon vessels of mercy, which he prepared beforehand for glory, namely, us, whom he called not only from among Jews but also from among nations [the Gentile nations, since the year 36 C.E.]."—Romans 9:22-24; Revelation 7:4-8; 14:1, 3.

[33] God has about completed now the selecting and preparing of the predetermined number of

_____
32. (a) When did God bring forth the principal one of the woman's seed, and how many others are to be associated with that one in the heavenly kingdom? (b) Who are those "vessels of mercy" referred to by the apostle Paul, and, while preparing them, why has God continued to tolerate the "vessels of wrath"?
33. Who are now associating with the remaining ones of the 144,000 and, with them, tasting of God's mercy?

144,000. So, particularly since 1935 C.E., a "great crowd" of sheeplike persons are being gathered out from among the wicked elements of the world of mankind. They are being assembled together with the remaining ones of the 144,000, to form "one flock" under the "one shepherd." (Revelation 7: 9-17; John 10:16; Matthew 25:31-46) These "other sheep" also taste of God's mercy in these times when the long-restrained wrath of God is about to be poured out upon the workers of wickedness.

[34] All these facts are an indication that God's permission of wickedness is soon to end and that God's kingdom of righteousness is soon to take charge of all the earth for mankind's blessing.

[35] Do not be disturbed, then, at the great increase of wickedness in these latter days. This was foretold as evidence that God's permission of it is soon to end. "When the wicked ones sprout as the vegetation and all the practicers of what is hurtful blossom forth, it is that they may be annihilated forever. But you are on high to time indefinite, O Jehovah. For, look! your enemies, O Jehovah, for, look! your own enemies will perish; all the practicers of what is hurtful will be separated from one another." (Psalm 92:7-9) Speaking of the end of this wicked system of things, Jesus Christ said: "Because of the increasing of lawlessness the love of the greater number will cool off. But he that has endured to the end is the one that will be saved." (Matthew 24:12, 13) To be saved, take full advantage of God's mercy now and keep on enduring till God's wise permission of wickedness ends. In that way you will share also with Jesus Christ in proving Satan the Devil to be a liar and in vindicating Jehovah God as the truthful One.

---

34. Of what are these facts an indication?
35. Why should we not be disturbed at the great increase of wickedness, but what should we do now?

CHAPTER 16

"The Conclusion of the System of Things"

MODERN science calculates that in the distant future, because of tremendous changes in the sun of our solar system, this earth will be turned into an uninhabitable mass floating around in space, dead, with no signs of life upon it. This fanciful theory of twentieth-century scientists is not in agreement with the written Word of earth's Creator. Their theory differs from God's purpose regarding the earth. When God put man and woman on earth, he located them in the garden of Eden and told them to fill the entire earth and subdue it as a home for all their offspring. (Genesis 1:26-28) The Creator has not changed in this purpose.

2 Almost three thousand three hundred years after man's creation, Jehovah God referred to the earth and spoke of himself as "the One who firmly established it, who did not create it simply for nothing, who formed it even to be inhabited." (Isaiah 45:18) Yes, long after the first man and his wife had sinned and brought death upon the

---

1. What does modern science forecast will happen to the earth in the distant future, but does their theory agree with God's purpose?
2, 3. (a) Long after man's creation, how did Jehovah show that his purpose for the earth had not changed? (b) What do the Scriptures testify as to the permanence of the earth?

313

generations of their offspring, God inspired King Solomon to write: "A generation is going, and a generation is coming; but the earth is standing even to time indefinite." (Ecclesiastes 1:4) That the earth will remain, God further states in these words:

³ "He has founded the earth upon its established places; it will not be made to totter to time indefinite, or forever." (Psalm 104:5) "He began to build his sanctuary just like the heights, like the earth that he has founded to time indefinite." (Psalm 78:69) "The meek ones themselves will possess the earth, and they will indeed find their exquisite delight in the abundance of peace. Watch the blameless one and keep the upright one in sight, for the future of that man will be peaceful. But the transgressors themselves will certainly be annihilated together; the future of wicked people will indeed be cut off."—Psalm 37:11, 37, 38; Matthew 5:5.

⁴ What, then, does the expression "the end [or, consummation] of the world" mean, as found in certain old popular translations of the Bible?* For centuries the clergymen of Christendom have taught that this meant the destruction both of our earth and of the heavenly bodies about it; but this is wrong, unscriptural. In the original Greek text of the Bible this expression is *syntéleia tou aiónos,* and it has no reference to the end of the literal earth and the rest of our solar system. More

---

* See the German translation of Dr. Martin Luther of the sixteenth century C.E., the Roman Catholic *Douay Version* (English) and the *Authorized* (King James) *Version* of the seventeenth century, the *English Revised Version* of the nineteenth century, and the *American Standard Version* and George Lamsa's Bible Version of the twentieth century.

---

4. (a) What have many people in Christendom been taught that the "end of the world" means? (b) How do recent Bible translations help to make clear the meaning of the expression in the original Greek text?

recent Bible translations show this by rendering the Greek expression in another way, such as "the close of the age" (*AT*), "the end of the age" (*NEB*), "the conclusion of the age" (*Ro*), "the full end of the age" (*Yg*), "the consummation of this state" (*CMD*)†, and "the conclusion of the system of things." (*NW*) Thus the original Greek expression refers to the end of a state of things on the earth, the termination of a system of things, but not to the end of the earth itself in literal fire.

⁵ Since the earth itself will never be destroyed by God, how will the people then living on the earth know that the "age" or "state" or "system of things" has reached its end or is in its conclusion? Four of Jesus' apostles asked him that very question on Tuesday, Nisan 11, of the year 33 C.E., or three days before  he was put to death. Matthew 24:3 reports this, saying: "While he was sitting upon the Mount of Olives, the disciples approached him privately, saying: 'Tell us, When will these things be, and what will be the sign of your

† *Sacred Writings of the Apostles and Evangelists of Jesus Christ Commonly Styled the New Testament,* by G. Campbell, J. MacKnight and P. Doddridge, and published by Alexander Campbell in 1828 in Bethany, Virginia, U.S.A.

5. As to the "conclusion of the system of things," what did the apostles ask Jesus?

presence* and of the conclusion of the system of things?' "—See also Mark 13:3, 4; Luke 21:7.

⁶ In those words the apostolic disciples wanted to know ahead of time the "sign . . . of the conclusion of the system of things." If they lived to see the "sign," they would then know that the present "system of things" on earth was at its end or in its conclusion. If they did not live to witness the "sign," then the later disciples of Jesus Christ would know what it meant and they would know the particular message of God to preach at that time. As tradition locates the apostle John's death about the end of the first century C.E., he lived to see the destruction of the city of Jerusalem and its temple in the year 70 C.E. However, though he survived all the other apostles, he did not live to see the "sign." But are we who are living today seeing the "sign"? To make sure, we must compare Jesus' words with the facts of modern history.

⁷ Already, about two years before the apostles asked this question, Jesus had spoken to them about the "conclusion of the system of things." When speaking to the people by the Sea of Galilee, he gave an illustration (or parable) of the wheat and the weeds (or tares) and that of the dragnet that was let down into the sea. In explaining the meaning of these prophetic illustrations, he said:

⁸ "The sower of the fine seed is the Son of man; the field is the world [kósmos]; as for the fine

---

* The original Greek word *parousía* is here translated "presence" in the following translations: That by J. B. Rotherham, that by Robert Young, that by Ferrar Fenton, that by Pablo Besson in Spanish, and *The Emphatic Diaglott* by Benjamin Wilson, and the marginal readings of the *English Revised Version* and the *American Standard Version*.

---

6. What would the appearance of that "sign" indicate, and how can we know if we today are seeing that "sign"?
7-9. What had Jesus said about the "conclusion of the system of things" in two parables at an earlier time?

seed, these are the sons of the kingdom; but the weeds are the sons of the wicked one, and the enemy that sowed them is the Devil. The harvest is a conclusion [*syntéleia*] of a system of things [*aión*], and the reapers are angels. Therefore, just as the weeds are collected and burned with fire, so it will be in the conclusion [*syntéleia*] of the system of things [*aión*]. The Son of man will send forth his angels, and they will collect out from his kingdom all things that cause stumbling and persons who are doing lawlessness, and they will pitch them into the fiery furnace. There is where their weeping and the gnashing of their teeth will be. At that time the righteous ones will shine as brightly as the sun in the kingdom of their Father. . . .

⁹ "Again the kingdom of the heavens is like a dragnet let down into the sea and gathering up fish of every kind. When it got full they hauled it up onto the beach and, sitting down, they collected the fine ones into vessels, but the unsuitable they threw  away. That is how it will be in the conclusion [*syntéleia*] of the system of things [*aión*]: the angels will go out and separate the wicked from among the righteous and will cast them into the fiery furnace. There is where their weeping and the gnashing of their teeth will be."—Matthew 13: 37-43, 47-50.

¹⁰ When we keep in mind the fact that the "weeds" are poisonous and that the Jews to whom Jesus spoke were not permitted by God's law to eat all sorts of fish and sea creatures, but ate only fish with scales and fins, we can appreciate the need for separating the wheat from the weeds and the fine kind of fish from the unsuitable kind. Just like that, there would be suitable persons for the kingdom of the heavens and there would be those unsuitable for it.

¹¹ There would be those like weeds, mere imitation Christians, unfit for the kingdom of the heavens, and there would be those like real wheat, true, dedicated, baptized, faithful Christians, begotten of God's spirit, real "sons of the kingdom." The time for separating imitation Christians, "the sons of the wicked one," from genuine Christians, "the sons of the kingdom," would be during the conclusion of the system of things, "the completion of the age" or "period." (Matthew 13:39, 49, *Ferrar Fenton*) When this work of separating the false Christians from the real heirs of God's kingdom took place, it would be a proof or a "sign" that we are in the "conclusion of the system of things." Are we in it now? Yes.

¹² During the years of World War I, namely, 1914-1918, there was great persecution carried on by the fighting nations against true Christians who proclaimed the ending of this system of things and who held fast to their allegiance to God's kingdom of the heavens. After World War I ended, and particularly from the year 1919 forward, there was a great separating of all persons who

---

10. How do these parables show that there would be persons suitable for the kingdom of the heavens and others who would be unsuitable?
11. Who are the "sons of the kingdom" and who are the "sons of the wicked one," and of what is the separating of them from one another a "sign"?
12. Into what two general classes have people been separated particularly since the year 1919?

claimed to be Christians into two general classes: (1) those who stayed in the religious organizations of Christendom and who favored the League of Nations (now the United Nations) as the international agency for world peace and security, while at the same time holding fast to their nationalism; and (2) those who obeyed the divine command, "Get out of her, my people, if you do not want to share with her in her sins, and if you do not want to receive part of her plagues." (Revelation 18:4) These ones got out of Babylon the Great, that is to say, out of the world empire of false religion based on the religion of ancient Babylon, which world empire includes Christendom with its more than a thousand religious denominations.

[13] The ones that got out proved themselves to be those whom God calls "my people," making a full dedication of self to Jehovah God and being baptized in water as Jesus was, and then preaching and teaching the good news of God's Messianic kingdom as being the only hope of mankind. They could not be real "sons of the kingdom" if they had joined Christendom in giving support to the League of Nations as the world's hope for international peace and security.

[14] So they differ from the "sons of the wicked one," this one being Satan who sows symbolic "weeds." They are spiritual sons of the true God, Jehovah, for he has begotten them through his spirit and by means of his written Word. In the year 1919 this small remnant of the "sons of the kingdom" began to be organized for postwar work, and on September 1-8 they held a general convention at Cedar Point, Ohio, U.S.A., to inform themselves on the work ahead of them. Over two hundred newly dedicated Christians were baptized in

---

13. How have some proved themselves to be God's people and "sons of the kingdom"?
14. In what have the spiritual sons of God put their hope, but to what organization did others look in hope after the first world war?

water, and the president of the convention delivered a public address on "The Hope for Distressed Humanity" to thousands of listeners. He Scripturally proved God's kingdom to be that "hope" and said concerning the then proposed League of Nations:

> The Lord's displeasure is certain to be visited upon the League, however, because the clergy—Catholic and Protestant—claiming to be God's representatives, have abandoned his plan and endorsed the League of Nations, hailing it as a political expression of Christ's kingdom on earth.—*The Watch Tower*, as of October 1, 1919, page 298, column one.

[15] In 1931 the remnant of the "sons of the kingdom" embraced the name "Jehovah's witnesses," in order to distinguish themselves from the religionists of Christendom who profess to be Christian. Since that year hundreds of thousands of other God-fearing persons have 'got out of Babylon the Great' and have taken their stand alongside the spiritual remnant of the "sons of the kingdom," joining them in preaching the good news of God's kingdom world wide. They do not want to be found inside Babylon the Great when the conclusion of this system of things ends and when the symbolic "weeds" and the symbolic "unsuitable" fish are cast into the symbolic "fiery furnace" and are thus destroyed forever.—Matthew 13:41, 42, 49, 50.

"THE SIGN" OF THE CONCLUSION OF THIS SYSTEM

[16] In the year 33 C.E. the apostles asked Jesus Christ for "the sign . . . of the conclusion of the system of things." Did he then refer back to his

---

15. (a) Since 1931, by what name have these "sons of the kingdom" been distinguished? (b) Who besides the spirit-begotten "sons of the kingdom" are preachers of God's kingdom?
16. In what kind of language did Jesus set out the "sign . . . of the conclusion of the system of things"?

parabolic illustrations of the wheat and the weeds and the dragnet of fish? No. He used quite literal language in foretelling further evidences to prove that we are in the "conclusion of the system of things." After giving general information as to events that would precede the "conclusion," he said:

17 "These things must take place, but the end [*télos*] is not yet. For nation will rise against nation and kingdom against kingdom, and there will be food shortages and earthquakes in one place after another. All these things are a beginning of pangs of distress. Then people will deliver you up to tribulation and will kill you, and you will be objects of hatred by all the nations on account of my name. Then, also, many will be stumbled and will betray one another and will hate one another. And many false prophets will arise and mislead many; and because of the increasing of lawlessness the love of the greater number will cool off. But he that has endured to the end is the one that will be saved. And this good news of the kingdom will be preached in all the inhabited earth for a witness to all the nations; and then the end [*télos*] will come."—Matthew 24:6-14; see also Mark 13:7-13; Luke 21:9-19.

18 Wars there would be prior to the conclusion of the system of things, so Jesus foretold, but now here at the "beginning of pangs of distress" war of an unusual kind would break out. It would be war in which the nations and kingdoms embroiled in it would organize a total mobilization of the people of each nation and kingdom. It would be war, not just between armies in the field of battle and navies on the seas, but between whole peoples, whole nations regimented. Have we as yet had war

---

17. What are some of the features of that "sign," and where are they recorded?
18. Although there would be wars prior to the conclusion of the system of things, what would distinguish war at this time?

of this kind? History answers Yes! Since when? Since the unforgettable year of 1914. Listen:

[19] Says *The Encyclopedia Americana,* Volume 28 of the 1929 edition, page 257, column 2, under the heading "War":

> During the Great War of 1914-18 practically the entire industries of the nations involved were diverted from the usual channels to the one great task of keeping the armies in the field supplied. Great science and skill are applied to the conduct of military operations and the principles on which they ought to be conducted are carefully investigated in the light of experience.

[20] Says the book *The Shaping of the Modern World 1870-1914,* by Maurice Bruce, pages 926, 927 of the 1958 edition:

> THE UNWANTED WAR
> Lloyd George was right in thinking that no one at the head of affairs quite wanted war in 1914. Austria-Hungary, for example, after years of indecision and unable to solve her own internal troubles, desired only to raise her prestige by a victorious local war against Serbia. From that everything else followed. Germany had to pay the price of the 1879 alliance by supporting, perhaps lightheartedly, her one remaining ally. If this support led to a general war, then Germany preferred it in 1914 rather than when Russia and France had had more time to gain strength. . . . No one had realized how little room for maneuvre remained as a result of the history of the preceding decade. So, in the summer of 1914, the Great Powers entered upon the first of the total wars of the twentieth century during which four empires disappeared, millions of lives were lost, and the economic basis of the prosperity of the nineteenth century was completely undermined.

[21] No wonder that 1913 has been called "the last normal year." Since then the world of mankind has entered into an "age of violence" that has steadily grown worse till now.

19, 20. According to the records of history, what kind of war began in 1914?
21. Since 1913, in what kind of age has mankind lived?

²² If no one at the head of affairs on earth wanted war in 1914, the invisible "god of this system of things," namely, Satan the Devil, wanted war. Why? Because in that year the "times of the Gentiles," or, "the appointed times of the nations," would end, after which the birth of God's Messianic kingdom in the heavens would take place. Satan the Devil wanted to continue as "god of this system of things" and did not want the earthly nations under his control to submit peacefully to the newborn heavenly kingdom of God by Jesus the Messiah. Hence Satan the Devil fomented war in 1914 over the issue of world domination. —2 Corinthians 4:4.

²³ In the very same prophecy on the "sign" of the conclusion of the system of things, Jesus foretold the fulfillment of the "times of the Gentiles," or, "the appointed times of the nations," which Gentile nations include those of Christendom. In the prophecy as recorded by the Christian disciple Luke, Jesus foretold the destruction of Jerusalem that occurred in 70 C.E. and referred to the Gentile Times, saying: "For there will be great necessity upon the land and wrath on this people [the unbelieving Jews]; and they will fall by the edge of the sword and be led captive into all the nations [Gentiles]; and Jerusalem will be trampled on by the nations, until the appointed times of the nations [Gentiles] are fulfilled."—Luke 21:23, 24, NW; AV.

²⁴ As regards those "times of the Gentiles," even before the magazine *The Watch Tower* began to be published in July of 1879, dedicated, baptized Christians who became associated with this magazine were pointing out from the prophetic scrip-

---

22. Who was the real instigator of the war that began in 1914, and why?
23. As reported at Luke 21:24, to what "times" did Jesus refer in his prophecy on the "sign," and what did he say about them?
24. Was there any advance notice given concerning the end of those "times of the Gentiles"?

tures of the Holy Bible that those "times" would end in 1914 and that then the time would be due for God's kingdom to be fully established in heaven.

25 From the prophecy of Daniel, chapter four, they pointed out that these Gentile Times would be seven in number, each "time" period being a prophetic year of three hundred and sixty literal years and the total of "seven times" therefore amounting to 2,520 years. Those Gentile Times began in the year that Jerusalem was destroyed by the king of Babylon who had the dream that is recorded in Daniel 4:1-27, the Jewish lunar year running from the spring month of Nisan of 607 B.C.E. and running down till Nisan of 606 B.C.E. Since the Babylonian armies destroyed Jerusalem in the summer of 607 B.C.E. and the land of Judah became desolate by the beginning of autumn, those 2,520 years of the Gentile Times would end in 1914 of our Common Era, about October 1 of the year.*

26 When Jerusalem was destroyed in 607 B.C.E. and the Jewish king was taken captive to Babylon, "Jehovah's throne" on which the Jewish kings of David's line had sat in Jerusalem was overturned. (1 Chronicles 29:23; Ezekiel 21:25-27) Thus the typical or small-scale kingdom of Jehovah God over the Jews passed out of existence and the pagan Gentile nations took over the total domination of the earth without any interference of God's kingdom. From then on mankind has had Gentile world powers dominate the earth, one after the other, namely, Babylon, Medo-Persia, Greece or Macedonia, Rome, and the alliance of Great Britain and the United States of America,

---

* For further explanation, see "Babylon the Great Has Fallen!" God's Kingdom Rules!, pages 174-181.

25. How was it known when the Gentile Times would end?
26. With what event was God's typical kingdom put out of existence in 607 B.C.E., and who dominated the earth after that?

without interference of any Davidic kingdom of God.

²⁷ Consequently, when the Gentile Times were due to end in 1914 C.E., it was the time for the Gentile nations to lose their total domination of the earth that they had exercised since 607 B.C.E. without the interference of God's kingdom. It was the time for God's kingdom in the line of King David to be reestablished, not on earth in the non-christian city of Jerusalem in the Middle East, but in the heavens, in the hands of the Permanent Heir of King David, namely, the resurrected, glorified Jesus Christ at God's right hand. Accordingly God's Messianic kingdom was born in the heavens in 1914, at the end of the Gentile Times about October 1. Satan the Devil, "the god of this system of things," did not want his system of things to end, and so he was opposed to the birth of that kingdom. For that reason he started World War I in 1914 over the issue of world domination.

²⁸ By no means was the outbreak of World War I in 1914 accidental and unrelated to Bible prophecy. It came right on time—God's marked time— and it indicated that the "appointed times of the nations" were ending that year, to allow for the due birth of God's kingdom in the heavens. The birth of God's heavenly kingdom meant that the "conclusion of the system of things" had begun, with a "beginning of pangs of distress" for all the earthly nations. Since then we have been in the period that Jesus Christ called "the conclusion of the system of things." Jehovah God, by means of his Christ, has taken up his power again to dominate all the earth as its Creator. Over this fact

---

27. (a) In what way did the situation change for the Gentile nations in 1914 C.E.? (b) Where was God's kingdom in the line of King David reestablished in that year?
28, 29. (a) What time period began with the birth of God's heavenly kingdom? (b) How did the holy creatures of heaven respond to God's taking up Kingdom power by means of Christ?

the holy creatures of heaven are grateful and, according to Revelation 11:15-18, they say:

²⁹ "The kingdom of the world has become the kingdom of our Lord and of his Christ, and he will rule as king forever and ever. . . . We thank you, Jehovah God, the Almighty, the One who is and who was, because you have taken your great power and begun ruling as king. But the nations became wrathful, and your own wrath came, and the appointed time for the dead to be judged, and to give their reward to your slaves the prophets and to the holy ones and to those fearing your name, the small and the great, and to bring to ruin those ruining the earth."

³⁰ The first total war of human history, in coming exactly on time, was not all that there was to the "sign" proving that the "conclusion of the system of things" had begun in the year 1914. Jesus foretold also food shortages and famines, earthquakes, pestilences, the growing hatred of people for one another, even those in Christendom, the increasing of lawlessness and of lovelessness on mankind's part, and the persecution of his true disciples, these becoming an object of hatred by all the nations. In addition to World War I, have we had all these other things? Yes.

³¹ Not only did such things accompany and follow World War I of 1914-1918, but they continue to afflict us and grow worse. Amid all this world distress and violence, Jehovah's witnesses continue to endure as faithful followers of Jesus Christ, even though they are, as Jesus foretold, "objects of hatred by all the nations on account of my name." (Matthew 24:9) If they endure until the end of their affliction and tribulation at the hands

---

30. In addition to total war, what were some of the other features of the "sign," and have these things occurred?
31. (a) How do Jehovah's witnesses react to the foretold persecution they suffer at the hands of the nations? (b) What is their attitude toward the lawlessness and lack of love that are now so prevalent?

of the nations, it means their eternal salvation. They do not persecute people of other religions, but try to help them to get out of Babylon the Great before her destruction comes. They do not take part in the increasing of lawlessness and violence, nor do they let their love of Jehovah God and Jesus Christ and of fellowman cool off.

³² In expression of their love they obediently take part in the fulfillment of Jesus' prophecy on the "sign," when he said: "And this good news of the kingdom will be preached in all the inhabited earth for a witness to all the nations; and then the end will come." (Matthew 24:14; Mark 13:10) At the time of first printing this book, Jehovah's witnesses were preaching God's newborn kingdom in more than 190 lands and in more than 160 languages.

³³ All these fulfillments of Jesus' prophecy not only prove that he was a true prophet like Moses, but also make the foretold "sign" stand out very clearly to our eyes of understanding, proving that the "conclusion of the system of things" began at the close of the Gentile Times in 1914. So we are now nearing its end in the "war of the great day of God the Almighty" and the putting of Satan the Devil out of action for the thousand years of Christ's reign over mankind.—Revelation 16:14, 16; 20:1-3.

³⁴ However, the foretold "sign" stands out even more clearly to our view when we consider still other features of the "sign" that prove the "presence" (parousía) of Jesus Christ, showing us what he would do when present again. It will be encouraging to us to consider these other features in the next succeeding pages.

32. In expression of their love for God and for their fellowmen, in what activity are Jehovah's witnesses engaged, and to what extent is this work being done?
33. All these fulfillments of prophecy since 1914 prove that we are living in what time period, and when will it end?
34. Is there any more to this "sign" than what we have already considered?

CHAPTER 17

The Return of the Prophet Greater Than Moses

OSES, who was saved from death as a babe in the Nile River, fled from Egypt at the age of forty years in order to preserve his life. This Moses the enslaved Israelites "disowned, saying, 'Who appointed you ruler and judge?'" and he became as dead to them. Forty years later, at the command of Jehovah God, Moses returned to Egypt as God's prophet to deliver God's chosen people and lead them out of Egypt and to the Promised Land. (Acts 7:20-35) Likewise, Jesus, who, as a babe, was saved from death at the hands of King Herod, was rejected by his own people when he was thirty-three and a half years old and was put to death. Almighty God raised him from the dead and summoned him to a distant country, that is to say, to heaven itself. Before his death he told his faithful apostles that he was going away but that he would return and then receive them home to himself.—John 14:1-4.

² At the time that he ascended to heaven from the midst of his disciples on the Mount of Olives,

---

1. (a) How does Moses' being disowned by his people and then returning to them in Egypt many years later find a parallel in the case of Jesus Christ? (b) Before dying, what promise did Jesus make to his faithful apostles?
2, 3. At the time that Jesus ascended to heaven, how was his promise to return confirmed?

328

this promise of his return was made more sure, for we read, in Acts 1:9-11, the following words:

[3] "And after he had said these things, while they were looking on, he was lifted up and a cloud caught him up from their vision. And as they were gazing into the sky while he was on his way, also, look! two men in white garments stood alongside them, and they said: 'Men of Galilee, why do you stand looking into the sky? This Jesus who was received up from you into the sky will come thus in the same manner as you have beheld him going into the sky.'"

[4] More than ten days later, the apostle Peter said to a crowd of worshipers in the temple of Jerusalem: "Repent, therefore, and turn around so as to get your sins blotted out, that seasons of refreshing may come from the person of Jehovah and that he may send forth the Christ appointed for you, Jesus, whom heaven, indeed, must hold within itself until the times of restoration of all things of which God spoke through the mouth of his holy prophets of old time. In fact, Moses said, 'Jehovah God will raise up for you from among your brothers a prophet like me. You must listen to him according to all the things he speaks to you.'"—Acts 3:19-22.

[5] So, as prefigured by Moses' return to Egypt after forty years of absence, Jesus Christ must return at God's due time, "the times of restoration of all things of which God spoke through the mouth of his holy prophets." This would mean the time for restoring God's kingdom in the line of David's family, which time was at the end of the "appointed times of the nations" in 1914. Did Jesus Christ return in that year? Did his "presence" begin then?

---

4. When talking to a crowd in Jerusalem, what did the apostle Peter say about the time for the return of the Prophet greater than Moses?

5. What was to be 'restored' at this time, and in what year was this due to take place?

⁶ Most people will say, 'Our eyes did not see him return then.' Well, at the time that Jesus ascended to heaven, the two angels who appeared did not say that the onlooking apostles would see "this Jesus" come again. They merely told the apostles that Jesus would come back. How? "Thus in the same manner as you beheld him going into the sky." They saw him go away but would not see him return. The angels' words, "thus in the same manner," do not say 'thus in the same body.' As to the manner of his going away, "a cloud caught him up from their vision" so that he became invisible to them. His return would therefore be invisible. The words "thus in the same manner" call attention to the fact that the world of mankind in general did not see Jesus going into heaven; only the disciples there with him, the "men of Galilee," saw him leave.

⁷ The words "thus in the same manner" would accordingly mean that the world of mankind would not see him come again. Not even the disciples there with him would see him return, for he would have to raise them from the dead after he returned. This agrees with Jesus' promise to his apostles before his death: "A little longer and the world will behold me no more, but you will behold me, because I live and you will live." (John 14:19) Hence the natural eyes of the world of mankind will never see Jesus Christ again on earth. The impossibility of their seeing him with human eyes is stated in these words, in 1 Timothy 6:14-16: "Until the manifestation of our Lord Jesus Christ. This manifestation the happy and only Potentate will show in its own appointed times, he the King of those who rule as kings and Lord of those who

---

6. (a) In what "manner" would Jesus return, and how is this indicated by the manner in which he ascended to heaven? (b) Who were the only ones that saw Jesus going into heaven?
7. (a) Would the world in general see Jesus come again? (b) How does the Bible show that it would be impossible for one to see the glorified Jesus Christ with human vision?

rule as lords, the one alone having immortality [among such earthly kings and lords], who dwells in unapproachable light, whom not one of men has seen or can see."

[8] We must never forget how Jesus Christ was raised from the dead. The apostle Peter, to whom the resurrected Jesus appeared out of the invisible realm, says: "Christ died once for all time concerning sins, a righteous person for unrighteous ones, that he might lead you to God, he being put to death in the flesh, but being made alive in the spirit." (1 Peter 3:18; 1 Corinthians 15:5) In discussing the resurrection of the faithful disciples of Jesus Christ, the apostle Paul calls him "the last Adam" and says:

[9] "It is sown a physical body, it is raised up a spiritual body. If there is a physical body, there is also a spiritual one. It is even so written [in Genesis 2:7]: 'The first man Adam became a living soul.' The last Adam became a life-giving spirit. Nevertheless, the first is, not that which is spiritual, but that which is physical, afterward that which is spiritual. The first man is out of the earth and made of dust; the second man is out of heaven. As the one made of dust is, so those made of dust are also; and as the heavenly one is, so those who are heavenly are also. And just as we have borne the image of the one made of dust [the first man Adam], we shall bear also the image of the heavenly one. However, this I say, brothers, that flesh and blood cannot inherit God's kingdom."—1 Corinthians 15:44-50.

[10] Thus Jesus Christ was resurrected as a "spiritual body," and was "made alive in the spirit." Had he taken back the sacrifice of his "flesh and blood,"

8, 9. As explained by the apostles Peter and Paul, in what form was Jesus raised from the dead?
10. (a) Since Jesus was "made alive in the spirit," how was it possible for his disciples to see him after his resurrection? (b) Why does Jesus no longer need a fleshly body?

he could not have inherited God's heavenly kingdom. In his resurrection he "became a life-giving spirit." That was why for most of the time he was invisible to his faithful apostles. Just as spirit angels had previously done, he was obliged to materialize a body of flesh in order to make himself visible to his earthly disciples from time to time. Each time he would dematerialize the fleshly body assumed and would disappear into the spirit realm. He needs no human body any longer. "For we know that Christ, now that he has been raised up from the dead, dies no more; death is master over him no more. For the death that he died, he died with reference to sin once for all time." (Romans 6:9, 10) Accordingly he does not return in a visible body of flesh, inasmuch as he does not need to be sacrificed once again.

[11] The return of Jesus Christ from heaven is therefore as a spirit person. His second "presence" is unseen to natural human eyes.

[12] How, then, are we to understand the words of Revelation 1:7? There the apostle John writes: "Look! He is coming with the clouds, and every eye will see him, and those who pierced him; and all the tribes of the earth will beat themselves in grief because of him. Yes, Amen." The Revelation to John is a symbolic book, for Jesus "sent forth his angel and presented it in signs." The clouds and the seeing mentioned in Revelation 1:7 are therefore to be understood figuratively. The clouds are symbolic; the seeing him is by means of the eyes of discernment that behold the evidences marking his coming. Those who literally "pierced him" nineteen hundred years ago are no longer alive on earth. So they picture others on earth who imitate the conduct of "those who pierced him"

---

11. At Christ's second "presence," will he be visible to human eyes?
12. (a) Is what Revelation 1:7 says about Christ's return literal or symbolic, and how do you know? (b) In what sense, then, do people "see" him, and who are "those who pierced him"?

by piercing his followers yet on earth.—Matthew 25:40, 45; Acts 9:1-5.

[13] When Jesus ascended to heaven before his on-looking disciples, a cloud rendered him invisible to them. (Acts 1:9) Certainly if he came again, even with a literal human body, and was accompanied by clouds and had to remain at cloud level above the earth, nearsighted people on earth would not be able to see him, except with powerful binoculars or telescopes. Also, the act of uniting his still living remnant of disciples with him at his return is said to be not at the level of the earth; but, in 1 Thessalonians 4:17, we read: "Afterward we the living who are surviving will, together with them, be caught away in clouds to meet the Lord in the air; and thus we shall always be with the Lord." Hence Revelation 1:7 does not disprove that his return, arrival and presence must be invisible. Neither do Matthew 24:30; 26:64; Mark 13:26 and Luke 21:27 do so.

"THE SIGN OF YOUR PRESENCE"

[14] It was most fitting, therefore, that his apostles should ask Jesus for a future sign, saying: "Tell us, When will these things be, and what will be the sign of your presence and of the conclusion of the system of things?" (Matthew 24:3) As his return and second "presence" (*parousia*) would be in the spirit and invisible to human eyes, a "sign" would be needed to give proof that he had arrived and was present. According to the way that the apostles framed their question, the "sign" that would indicate the "conclusion of the system of things" would also indicate his invisible, spiritual "presence." In the preceding chapter we have noted a number of features of the "sign" that

13. If Jesus were to come literally "with the clouds," would it be possible for every human eye to see him?
14. Why, then, would a "sign" of Christ's second presence be needed in order to prove that he had arrived, and since what year has that "sign" been in evidence?

have been in evidence since the year 1914 C.E. and that prove that, since that date, we have been in the "conclusion of the system of things." So those very same features now in evidence prove also that the second but invisible presence or parousia of Jesus Christ is a fact today.

[15] We have still further features of the "sign" now in effect to add to the proof that the "life-giving spirit," the Lord Jesus Christ, has returned and is in his second "presence." In answer to the question of his apostles regarding a "sign" Jesus said:

[16] "Immediately after the tribulation of those days the sun will be darkened, and the moon will not give its light, and the stars will fall from heaven, and the powers of the heavens will be shaken. And then the sign [semeíon] of the Son of man will appear in heaven, and then all the tribes of the earth will beat themselves in lamentation, and they will see the Son of man coming on the clouds of heaven with power and great glory. And he will send forth his angels with a great trumpet sound, and they will gather his chosen ones together from the four winds, from one extremity of the heavens to their other extremity." —Matthew 24:29-31; Mark 13:24-27.

[17] The first part of the "tribulation of those days" upon the nations began with World War I in 1914-1918. Since then things have not looked so favorable for us with respect to the sun, moon and stars and the physical "powers of the heavens." Why not? Because of what modern science is revealing to us and what applied science is attempting to do. But, besides that, the "sign of the Son

15, 16. What further features of the "sign" did Jesus provide to help us to identify this as the time of his second "presence"?
17. (a) When did the first part of the "tribulation of those days" begin? (b) Since then, why have things not looked favorable for man with respect to the sun, moon and stars and the physical "powers of the heavens"? (c) What other "sign" has also appeared in heaven?

of man" has appeared "in heaven." It is the "sign" of the presence of Jesus Christ in the heavenly kingdom, inasmuch as he was installed and enthroned as Messianic King in 1914. Since then God has sent forth the "rod" of Christ's strength out of the heavenly Zion, in fulfillment of Psalm 110: 1, 2 and Hebrews 10:11-13.

[18] It is true that the apostles asked Jesus for a "sign," but it was a future sign as regards his second presence, not his first presence of nineteen centuries ago. Those apostles were not part of the faithless generation concerning which Jesus said: "A wicked and adulterous generation keeps on seeking for a sign." (Matthew 16:1-4) They did not join the Pharisees and Sadducees in demanding of Jesus a "sign from heaven" to prove that he was the promised Messiah or Christ. By what they then observed about Jesus and what they heard from him, they were convinced that he was the Messiah.

[19] Back there, when Jesus asked them: "You, though, who do you say I am?" Peter answered: "You are the Christ, the Son of the living God." Even years before that, the apostle Nathanael had said: "Rabbi, you are the Son of God, you are King of Israel." (Matthew 16:15, 16; John 1:49) So at that time they did not need any "sign from heaven" to believe in the "presence" of the Messiah or Christ in their midst. The Pharisees and Sadducees and other unconvinced Jews saw the man Jesus present among them, but they did not see in him the Messiah or Christ. Thus they did not discern the first "presence" of the Messiah or Christ among them.

18. Why did the Pharisees and Sadducees ask Jesus to show them a "sign from heaven," but did Jesus' apostles join them in this?
19. (a) Who did the apostles say that they believed Jesus to be? (b) Although many Jews saw Jesus with their physical eyes, what did they fail to discern concerning him?

²⁰ The "sign from heaven" for which those unbelievers were asking was, in effect, the event foretold in Daniel 7:9-14, where the prophet says: "I kept on beholding [in my visions during the night] until there were thrones placed and the Ancient of Days sat down. . . . The Court took its seat, and there were books that were opened. . . . I kept on beholding in the visions of the night, and, see there! with the clouds of the heavens someone like a son of man happened to be coming; and to the Ancient of Days he gained access, and they brought him up close even before that One. And to him there were given rulership and dignity and kingdom, that the peoples, national groups and languages should all serve even him. His rulership is an indefinitely lasting rulership that will not pass away, and his kingdom one that will not be brought to ruin."

²¹ Nineteen centuries ago during the bodily "presence" of the Messiah or Christ on our earth it was not the time for this prophetic vision to be fulfilled. But at the end of the Gentile Times in 1914 C.E. the time did arrive for Daniel's vision to be fulfilled; and it was, according to the many features of the "sign" of Christ's second "presence" or *parousía* that have come true.

²² From the heavenly throne, in which Jehovah God seated him, God sent forth the "rod" of Christ's strength from the heavenly Zion and toward the earth where the enemy nations are. In this way the Messiah or Christ has come to earth to begin his second "presence" here. It did not require his direct personal coming as a spirit person. Since he has all the needed power in heaven and on earth, it required only his turning of his attention to the earth and the extending of his

20, 21. What was the "sign from heaven" for which those unbelievers were asking Jesus, but when did it undergo fulfillment?
22. In what way has Christ come to earth to begin his second "presence"?

royal power to the earth for him to be present again. Hence his "presence" now is invisible.

23 The many features of the "sign" are plainly evident for all persons on earth today to see. With their eyes of discernment they can "see the Son of man coming on the clouds of heaven with power and great glory." He is no longer a lowly man on earth, "a man of sorrows, and acquainted with grief." (Isaiah 53:3, *AV*) He is now a heavenly King, enthroned, crowned. He now possesses glory and power that are superhuman, although he is rendered invisible to human eyes by the "clouds of heaven" that attend his coming and presence. However, the work that he is having done in the earth is not invisible to our eyes. What work? Matthew 24:31 tells us:

24 "And he will send forth his angels with a great trumpet sound, and they will gather his chosen ones [his elect] together from the four winds, from one extremity of the heavens to their other extremity." The angels that he has sent forth to this work are not visible to our eyes anymore than he himself is; but their work of gathering together Christ's followers who are the ones chosen for the heavenly kingdom goes on. These are the elect or chosen ones on whose account the days of the "great tribulation" are cut short that some "flesh" may be "saved" at the final climax of the "conclusion of the system of things." (Matthew 24:21, 22) On earth today only a remnant survives of the 144,000 "chosen ones," who are dedicated, baptized Christians, begotten by the spirit of Jehovah God to be the joint heirs with his Son Jesus Christ in the heavenly kingdom. (Romans 8:14-17) Reports show less than 12,000 now surviving.

---

23. How is it possible for all persons on earth today to "see the Son of man coming on the clouds of heaven with power and great glory"?
24. (a) As foretold at Matthew 24:31, what work is Christ having done that is visible to our eyes? (b) Who are the "chosen ones" that are gathered, and how many of them remain on earth today?

[25] Note now this feature of the "sign." After the "beginning of the pangs of distress" during 1914-1918 and from the first postwar year of 1919 forward these anointed, spirit-begotten "chosen ones" in all parts of the earth have been gathered together as a Christian organizational unity. From where? "From the four winds [north, south, east and west], from one extremity of the heavens to their other extremity." You will now find them in Australia, New Zealand, Japan and other parts of the Eastern Hemisphere as well as in the Americas of the Western Hemisphere. Attend, if you please, any one of their yearly celebrations of the Lord's supper or evening meal on its anniversary date, the night of the fourteenth day of the lunar month of Nisan, and you will observe these "chosen ones" partaking of the emblematic bread and wine, as commanded by Jesus Christ. (1 Corinthians 11:20-29; Matthew 26:26-30) In the year 1931 the remnant of "chosen ones" all around the globe embraced the designation "Jehovah's witnesses," to show that they had been "gathered together" out of all the religious systems of Babylon the Great, including Christendom.—*The Watch Tower,* September 15, 1931.

[26] How has the gathering of them together been accomplished? Surely under the guidance of angels whom the glorified "Son of man" has sent forth. (Matthew 13:39-42; 18:10; Psalm 91:11, 12) It has taken place at the sounding, as it were, of a great trumpet, that is to say, the proclamation worldwide of "this good news" of the birth of God's heavenly kingdom in 1914, the kingdom of the enthroned "Son of man." (Matthew 24:14) With spiritually enlightened eyes these "chosen

---

25. (a) From where are these "chosen ones" gathered, and so where are they found on the earth? (b) By what name are they known?
26. (a) Under whose guidance have the "chosen ones" been gathered? (b) How has the gathering been done "with a great trumpet sound," and to what have the "chosen ones" been gathered?

ones" have discerned the "sign of the Son of man" and they have unitedly gathered to it as to a standard or beacon or signal.* They have gathered to it in full allegiance to God's heavenly kingdom, in response to the symbolic "great trumpet sound." (Isaiah 27:13) The cutting short of the days of the "great tribulation such as has not occurred since the world's beginning until now" has allowed the angels the time and the conditions for gathering together these "chosen ones."

[27] Another feature of the "sign" now in evidence is the activity on earth of the "faithful and discreet slave." In his prophecy on the "sign" Jesus further said: "Who really is the faithful and discreet slave whom his master appointed over his domestics, to give them their food at the proper time? Happy is that slave if his master on arriving finds him doing so. Truly I say to you, He will appoint him over all his belongings."—Matthew 24:45-47.

[28] Is this "faithful and discreet slave" an individual man? No; he must be a class of true Christians who feed their fellow Christians, the Master's "domestics," with spiritual food from the Holy Bible. Since Jesus Christ as the Master "appointed" this "slave" nineteen centuries ago in the days of the twelve apostles, and since that slave is

---

* In Matthew 24:30 the Greek word for "sign" is *semeíon*. In the ancient Greek *Septuagint* translation of the inspired Hebrew Scriptures this Greek word *semeíon* is given the meaning of "standard, signal, ensign." See Isaiah 11:12; 18:3; Jeremiah 6:1; 51:27; Numbers 21:8, 9, for instances.—See *The Journal of Theological Studies*, as of October, 1964, pages 299, 300, under the heading "The Ensign of the Son of Man (Matthew 24:30)," by T. Francis Glasson.

The Bible translation by Dr. Ferrar Fenton uses the word "signal" in Matthew 24:3, 30.

27. As another feature of the "sign," what did Jesus say about a "faithful and discreet slave"?
28. (a) Why is it said that this "slave" must be a composite one, and of whom is it composed? (b) What legal agency have they used to accomplish their work?

now on earth after the arrival and second "presence" of the Master Jesus Christ, he must be a composite slave, a class of faithful anointed followers of Him. This class must be composed of all those "chosen ones" whom the angels under Christ's command have gathered together into a united theocratic organization since 1919. History proves that they have used the corporation Watch Tower Bible & Tract Society of Pennsylvania as their agency for doing the spiritual feeding work and general management of Christian activities worldwide of the Master's "domestics."

[29] Since the issue of October 15, 1931, the front page of their official magazine *The Watchtower* has displayed the legend " 'You are my witnesses,' says Jehovah."—Isaiah 43:12.

[30] In 1965 this magazine *The Watchtower* was being printed in 68 languages, with a printing of 4,550,000 copies of each issue. As for all the publications of the Watch Tower Society, these are printed in more than 160 languages and are being distributed in more than 190 lands around the globe. This feeding program is carried on under now more than ninety Branch offices of the Watch Tower Society. This gives us some idea of the enlargement of the scope of the work of the "faithful and discreet slave" class since the angelic gathering of them began in 1919. It proves undisputably that then the newly arrived Master appointed this "slave" class to be "over all his belongings" on earth. The activity of this appointed "slave" class in such an enlarged way from 1919 till now is another outstanding feature of the "sign of your presence," Christ's second parousia.

[31] Jesus' prophecy concerning the "sign" included the parabolic illustrations of the "ten

29, 30. What is their official magazine, and why is the extent of the distribution of the publications of this Society significant?
31. (a) Who have entered into the joys foretold in the parables of the "ten virgins" and of the talents, and since what year? (b) Of what are these parables, too, a part?

virgins," five wise and five foolish, and of the talents. These also have been undergoing fulfillment since the year 1914; and the faithful "chosen ones" have, since the year 1919, entered into the  joys foretold in those parables. (Matthew 25:1-30) Their fulfillment adds further modern-day features to the sign to prove the "presence" of Christ in Kingdom power.

[32] As a grand climax to his prophecy on the "sign" of his presence and of the conclusion of the system of things Jesus gave the parable of the sheep and the goats, the separating of them and the giving to each class its just deserts. Showing that the fulfillment of the parable belongs to the time of his second "presence" at the conclusion of this system of things, Jesus began the parable by saying: "When the Son of man arrives in his glory, and all the angels with him, then he will sit down on his glorious throne. And all the nations will be gathered before him, and he will separate people one from another, just as a shepherd separates the sheep from the goats. And he will put the sheep on his right hand, but the goats on his left." —Matthew 25:31-33.

[33] Other scriptures show that, at the end of the Gentile Times in 1914, the glorified Son of man sits down on a throne, but not on a material one

---

32. With what parable did Jesus climax his prophecy on the "sign" of his presence, and how does his introduction to this parable show when it applies?
33. (a) Where does Christ sit down on his throne? (b) What work must be accomplished now, before the complete end of this system of things?

at Jerusalem or any other place on earth. His "presence" in royal glory does not require him as a spirit person to be directly at the earth. From his heavenly throne he can give his attention to the earth and extend his power there, directing his angels in the work of separating people among all nations to whom he gives his attention. This he does before the "conclusion of the system of things" ends in the "war of the great day of God the Almighty" at Armageddon. Before the end of the opposed nations at Armageddon takes place, "this good news of the kingdom" has to be preached to all the nations for a witness, after which the complete end comes to this system of things. (Revelation 16:14, 16; Matthew 24:14; Mark 13:10) So now is the time for the separating work.

³⁴ Those gathered to the King's right hand of favor as "sheep" include people of all nationalities. They do good to the "chosen ones," Christ's spiritual brothers who are joint heirs of his kingdom. Those gathered to the King's left hand of disfavor as "goats" are the people of all nationalities that refuse to do good to even "one of these least ones," one of Christ's spiritual brothers, the remnant of the "chosen ones" yet on earth.—Matthew 25: 34-45.

³⁵ Such a separation of all the peoples in general has been going on particularly since the year 1935, as statistics show. Symbolic sheep are taking their stand as dedicated, baptized witnesses of Jehovah in full support of God's kingdom as being the rightful government over all the earth. The symbolic goats persist in rejecting God's kingdom, as they prefer this "system of things," which is under the control of the "Devil and his angels." (Matthew

---

34. What distinguishes the symbolic sheep from the goats?
35. How are the symbolic sheep taking their stand in support of God's kingdom, and in what work do they join the remnant of the "chosen ones"?

25:41) Whereas the dwindling remnant of the elect or "chosen ones" are "objects of hatred by all the nations," just as Jesus foretold (Matthew 24: 9), yet hundreds of thousands of sheeplike people are dedicating themselves to God and getting baptized as in symbol of this dedication. They are joining with the remnant of anointed "chosen ones," Christ's spiritual brothers, in preaching "this good news of the kingdom" and announcing the "presence" of Jesus Christ in the heavenly kingdom. They act as Jehovah's witnesses.

[36] The separating work of this kind now going on is part of the "sign" proving Christ's invisible "presence." It adds to the proof that the Prophet greater than Moses has returned. The separating work will be completed by the time that the destruction of Babylon the Great, the world empire of false religion, takes place, to be followed immediately by the war of Almighty God's great day.

[37] It is highly important for us to recognize what the "sign" means—Christ's invisible presence in his capacity of King. It is vitally important for people to submit to him as King and let him put them with the "sheep on his right hand." Shortly the King will destroy Babylon the Great and will fight against all her political paramours in the "war of the great day of God the Almighty." Thus all the symbolic "goats" will be destroyed everlastingly as if by a consuming fire that reduces its victims to smoke and ashes.—Matthew 25:41.

[38] The Lord Jesus Christ warned of this by closing his prophecy on the "sign" of his presence and of the conclusion of the system of things by saying: "And these [the goats just spoken of] will depart into everlasting cutting-off [as their pun-

36. Of what is this separating work a part, and by when will it be completed?
37, 38. (a) What does fulfillment of the "sign" mean? (b) Why is it vital for people to submit to Christ as king now, and how did Jesus show this in the concluding words of his prophecy on the "sign" of his presence?

ishment], but the righteous ones [the sheep] into everlasting life." (Matthew 25:46) When the goat-like persons are punished with everlasting destruction, the sheeplike righteous people will joyfully respond to the King's invitation: "Come, you who have my Father's blessing, inherit the kingdom prepared for you from the founding of the world. For I became hungry and you gave me something to eat; I got thirsty and you gave me something to drink. I was a stranger and you received me hospitably; naked, and you clothed me. I fell sick and you looked after me. I was in prison and you came to me. . . . Truly I say to you, To the extent that you did it to one of the least of these my brothers, you did it to me." (Matthew 25:34-40) This will mean that the King, Jesus Christ, the Prophet greater than Moses, will reign over these sheeplike ones who inhabit the earthly realm or territory of his kingdom, forever, because they have discerned, understood and obeyed the "sign of [his] presence."

Freeing the Dead People
from Ha'des

THE freeing of dead people from what the Holy Bible calls "Ha'des" means their being resurrected from the dead. From the time that Adam's firstborn son Cain killed his godly brother Abel, billions of humankind have died and gone to Ha'des. The freeing of all these from Ha'des under God's kingdom in the hands of Christ is a heart-cheering truth that Jehovah God teaches us in his written Word. Impossible though such a truth may seem, Jehovah God will not be found lying in this remarkable thing, for he has given a guarantee of it. How? By freeing his beloved only-begotten Son from Ha'des nineteen centuries ago.—Acts 17:31.

[2] Just before Jesus Christ told his apostles that "he must go to Jerusalem and suffer many things from the older men and chief priests and scribes, and be killed, and on the third day be raised up," he said to the apostle Peter: "On this rock-mass I will build my congregation, and the gates of Ha'des will not overpower it." (Matthew 16:18, 21) This did not mean that the congregation of his

---

1. What does the freeing of dead people from Hades mean for them, and what guarantee has Jehovah God given as to its certainty?
2. When Jesus said that "the gates of Hades" would not overpower his congregation, what did he mean?

spiritual brothers would be spared from entering in through the "gates of Ha'des" and going into Ha'des. Rather, it meant that they would die and go to Ha'des but with hope of a resurrection from Ha'des, its "gates" not being able to hold them prisoner forever.

[3] Even Jesus Christ spent part of three days in Ha'des, that is, Nisan 14-16 of the year 33 C.E. He was buried in a "new memorial tomb" quarried in a rock-mass, belonging to a rich Jew of Arimathea. But on the third day an angel from God rolled the sealed stone away from the entrance, and later the disciples, on arriving, found the tomb to be empty. (Matthew 27:57 to 28:10) Fifty days later the apostle Peter, who had visited the empty tomb, told how the "gates of Ha'des" were unable to hold Jesus prisoner, saying:

[4] "God resurrected him by loosing the pangs of death, because it was not possible for him to continue to be held fast by it. For David says respecting him, 'I had Jehovah constantly before my eyes; because he is at my right hand that I may never be shaken. On this account my heart became cheerful and my tongue rejoiced greatly. Moreover, even my flesh [while still alive] will reside in hope; because you will not leave my soul in Ha'des, neither will you allow your loyal one to see corruption. You have made life's ways known to me, you will fill me with good cheer with your face.' [Psalm 16:8-11] Brothers, it is allowable to speak with freeness of speech to you concerning the family head David, that he both deceased and was buried and his tomb is among us to this day. Therefore, because he was a prophet and knew that God had sworn to him with an oath that he would seat one from the fruitage of his loins upon

---

3, 4. (a) Did Jesus Christ go to Hades? (b) How did the apostle Peter show that the "gates of Hades" were not able to hold Jesus prisoner?

his throne, he saw beforehand and spoke concerning the resurrection of the Christ, that neither was he forsaken in Ha'des nor did his flesh see corruption. This Jesus God resurrected, of which fact we are all witnesses."—Acts 2:23-32.

⁵ Years afterward, when sending a message to congregations in Asia Minor, Jesus said: "Do not be fearful. I am the First and the Last, and the living one; and I became dead, but, look! I am living forever and ever, and I have the keys of death and of Ha'des." (Revelation 1:17, 18) Being in possession of those keys, the resurrected, glorified Jesus is able to unlock those "gates of Ha'des" and let his faithful congregation out by raising them from the dead. Even before his own death and resurrection Jesus said: "The hour is coming in which all those in the memorial tombs will hear his voice and come out." (John 5:28, 29) So now his own resurrection from the dead and his being given the "keys of death and of Ha'des" made more certain their hearing the voice of the Son of man and coming out of the memorial tombs, out of Ha'des.

⁶ When Jesus Christ was freed from Ha'des, he was "made alive in the spirit," not in the flesh. So says 1 Peter 3:18. In what way, then, is his congregation of Kingdom joint heirs made alive in the resurrection? Necessarily in the spirit, since they are to inherit the heavenly kingdom with him. This is exactly what the congregation is told in Romans 6:3-6, in which the apostle Paul says: "Do you not know that all of us who were baptized into Christ Jesus were baptized into his death? Therefore we were buried with him through our baptism into his death, in order that, just as Christ

---

5. Who now has the 'key of Hades,' and what does that mean for Christ's congregation?

6, 7. In what way will the congregation of Kingdom joint heirs be made alive in the resurrection, and how is this indicated in the apostle Paul's letter to the Romans?

was raised up from the dead through the glory of the Father, we also should likewise walk in a newness of life. For if we have become united with him in the likeness of his death, we shall certainly also be united with him in the likeness of his resurrection; because we know that our old personality was impaled with him, that our sinful body might be made inactive, that we should no longer go on being slaves to sin."

[7] Though dying with sinful flesh, they will not be raised in sinful flesh. They will be "made alive in the spirit," like him.

[8] The apostle Paul makes this even more certain when, writing to the Christian congregation, he describes the resurrection of the congregation from Ha'des, saying: "It is sown in corruption, it is raised up in incorruption. It is sown in dishonor, it is raised up in glory. It is sown in weakness, it is raised up in power. It is sown a physical body, it is raised up a spiritual body." In proof of this, the apostle Paul goes on to say:

[9] "If there is a physical body, there is also a spiritual one. It is even so written [in Genesis 2:7]: 'The first man Adam became a living soul.' The last Adam [Jesus] became a life-giving spirit. Nevertheless, the first is, not that which is spiritual, but that which is physical, afterward that which is spiritual. The first man is out of the earth and made of dust; the second man [Jesus, the Son of man] is out of heaven. As the one made of dust [Adam] is, so those made of dust are also; and as the heavenly one [Jesus Christ] is, so those who are heavenly are also. And just as we have borne the image of the one made of dust [Adam], we shall bear also the image of the heavenly one [the resurrected Jesus Christ]."

8, 9. (a) When the apostle Paul wrote to the Christian congregation, with what kind of body did he say they would be raised from Hades? (b) What argument did he present in support of this?

¹⁰ The apostle Paul now shows why the congregation must be "made alive in the spirit" in their resurrection, saying: "However, this I say, brothers, that flesh and blood cannot inherit God's kingdom, neither does corruption inherit incorruption. Look! I tell you a sacred secret: We shall not all fall asleep in death, but we shall all be changed, in a moment, in the twinkling of an eye, during the last trumpet. For the trumpet will sound, and the dead [of the congregation] will be raised up incorruptible, and we [the congregation] shall be changed. For this which is corruptible must put on incorruption [to inherit God's kingdom], and this which is mortal must put on immortality. But when this which is corruptible puts on incorruption and this which is mortal puts on immortality, then the saying will take place that is written [in Isaiah 25:8]: 'Death is swallowed up forever.' "—1 Corinthians 15:42-54.

¹¹ What about those of the congregation who are still alive on earth after Christ's second presence begins and who die after the symbolic "last trumpet" sounds for gathering the remnant of the "chosen ones"? Such ones will not need to sleep on in death in Ha'des to await the return of the Lord Jesus Christ. Hence, as soon as they die in the sinful, corruptible flesh, they will be "made alive in the spirit," being "changed, in a moment, in the twinkling of an eye, during the last trumpet." (Revelation 14:13) Of course, their dead bodies of flesh will not be "spiritualized," as certain false religious teachers argue; but their resurrected personalities will be given spiritual, heavenly bodies. In that way they will "bear also the image of the heavenly one" and be invisible, heavenly spirit

10. Why is it necessary for Christ's congregation to be "made alive in the spirit"?
11. At the time of death, what happens in the case of those of Christ's congregation who have survived into this time of Christ's second presence when the "chosen ones" are already being gathered?

creatures, sharers in the "likeness of his resurrection."

¹² In view of this, indeed, "the gates of Ha'des
will not overpower" Christ's congregation. But
how about the billions who died before Jesus
Christ began building his congregation on the
"rock-mass" in the year 33 C.E.? And how about
the other billions who died since and who have
gone to Ha'des without being members of his
congregation? When and how will they be delivered from death?

¹³ These earthly dead ones will not begin to be
raised from Ha'des before the members of Christ's
congregation have begun to be raised. That is why
the resurrection of Christ's congregation is called
"the first resurrection," it being first in time as
well as in importance and quality. That is also
why the congregation is called a "certain first
fruits of his creatures," Jesus Christ himself being
called "the first fruits of those who have fallen
asleep in death." (James 1:18; 1 Corinthians 15:
20) The expression "the first resurrection" is used
in connection with the resurrection of the congregation, in Revelation 20:4-6, which says:

¹⁴ "And I saw thrones [in heaven], and there
were those who sat down on them, and power of
judging was given them. Yes, I saw the souls of
those executed with the ax for the witness they
bore to Jesus and for speaking about God, and
those who had worshiped neither the wild beast
nor its image and who had not received the mark
upon their forehead and upon their hand. And
they came to life and ruled as kings with the
Christ for a thousand years. (The rest of the dead
did not come to life until the thousand years were
ended.) This is the first resurrection. Happy and

---

12. What other dead ones also need to be considered?
13, 14. Why is the raising from the dead of Christ's congregation
called "the first resurrection," and where does the Bible use this
expression?

holy is anyone having part in the first resurrection; over these the second death has no authority, but they will be priests of God and of the Christ, and will rule as kings with him for the thousand years."

[15] The "second death" has no authority over these happy, holy ones who are rewarded with the "first resurrection" because they are clothed upon with immortality and incorruption on being raised to life as spirit creatures in heaven. Their resurrection to life in heaven is invisible to human eyes. (1 Corinthians 15:50-54; Revelation 2:10, 11) Because of their immortal life they will have no successors in the throne, and, during the thousand years that Satan the Devil and his demons are bound and imprisoned in the abyss, they can rule as kings with the immortal Jesus Christ, at the same time rendering a priestly service to all mankind.

[16] Thus both Jesus Christ and his congregation have an experience with the place that the Bible calls Ha'des. But just what does the Bible mean by Ha'des? All those who go there get out eventually, never to return there. In the Christian Greek Scriptures, according to the earliest handwritten copies available today, the word Ha'des occurs only ten times.* The word Ha'des is Greek, whereas Jesus Christ and the first members of his congregation were Jews and spoke the Jews' language of that day. What was the word that they used instead of Ha'des? It was the word found in the Hebrew Bible, namely, Sheol. In the third

---

* The ten places of the occurrence of the word Ha'des in the Greek text of the Christian Scriptures are Matthew 11:23; 16:18; Luke 10:15; 16:23; Acts 2:27, 31; Revelation 1:18; 6:8; 20:13, 14.

---

15. Why does the "second death" have no authority over those sharing in the "first resurrection"?
16, 17. What is the Hebrew equivalent of the Greek word Ha'des, and how is this shown by the oldest Greek version of the Hebrew Scriptures?

century of our Common Era the Holy Bible was translated into Syriac and it was called the *Peshitta* (meaning "Simple") version; and the word that it uses for Ha'des is *shiúl*, corresponding to the related word *Sheol*.

[17] So the Hebrew word Sheol is the same in meaning as the Greek word Ha'des. In fact, when the Jews of Alexandria, Egypt, translated the Hebrew Scriptures into Greek for their use, they translated the Hebrew word Sheol as Ha'des. This oldest Greek version was called the Septuagint, this word meaning "Seventy" and being commonly designated *LXX*. It began to be translated about 280 B.C.E. Says *Harper's Bible Dictionary* (1952 edition), pages 745, 746:

> This unique achievement outgrew its original purpose of providing a Bible for the Jews of Alexandria, and was used by Jews throughout the eastern Mediterranean. It was the Bible of Paul, the Apostles, and the early Church. The LXX was quoted in the New Testament and used in the arguments of the Church fathers, and for this reason ceased from about A.D. 100 to be an authority to the Jews. From its text other important translations were made. It has been the Bible of the Greek Church to the present day.

[18] In the inspired Hebrew Scriptures the word Sheol (Ha'des, *LXX; Syriac,* Shiúl) occurs sixty-five (65) times.* By looking up in your own personal Bible the places where Sheol occurs in the

---

* In the Hebrew text the 65 occurrences of Sheol are: Genesis 37:35; 42:38; 44:29, 31; Numbers 16:30, 33; Deuteronomy 32:22; 1 Samuel 2:6; 2 Samuel 22:6; 1 Kings 2:6, 9; Job 7:9; 11:8; 14:13; 17:13, 16; 21:13; 24:19; 26:6; Psalms 6:5; 9:17; 16:10; 18:5; 30:3; 31:17; 49:14 (twice), 15; 55:15; 86:13; 88:3; 89:48; 116:3; 139: 8; 141:7; Proverbs 1:12; 5:5; 7:27; 9:18; 15:11, 24; 23:14; 27:20; 30:16; Ecclesiastes 9:10; Song of Solomon 8:6; Isaiah 5:14; 14:9, 11, 15; 28:15, 18; 38:10, 18; 57:9;

---

18. How many times is the word Sheol used in the inspired Hebrew Scriptures, and, as shown by its use in the Bible, what does it mean?

Hebrew text, as given in the footnote below, you can see for yourself how Sheol has been translated into the Bible of your language. In the *American Standard Version* it is always translated as Sheol. But in the popular *Authorized Version* of King James I of England, published back in 1611 C.E., it is translated as "the grave" 31 times and as "the pit" 3 times, in the main text, and 2 times as "the grave" in the marginal reading (in Isaiah 14:9; Jonah 2:2), where the main text reads "hell."* Translating the Hebrew word as "the grave" agrees with the Bible usage of the word Sheol, namely, to mean the common grave of dead mankind in the bosom of the earth, the sea furnishing, however, a watery burial place for countless many.

[19] For example, in Isaiah 38:10 King Hezekiah speaks of the "gates of Sheol." But Jesus Christ, when referring to the resurrection of his congregation, speaks of the "gates of Ha'des." (Matthew 16:18) Also, according to the Hebrew text, Psalm 16:10 reads: "For thou wilt not leave my soul to Sheol; neither wilt thou suffer thy holy one to see corruption." (*AS*) But when the apostle Peter quotes this verse on the day of Pentecost of the year 33 C.E., he says, according to the Christian Greek Scriptures: "Because thou wilt not leave my soul unto Ha'des, neither wilt thou give thy Holy One to see corruption." (Acts 2:27, *AS*) Peter's usage of the word Ha'des thus gives full approval to the Greek *Septuagint* in translating

Ezekiel 31:15, 16, 17; 32:21, 27; Hosea 13:14 (twice); Amos 9:2; Jonah 2:2; Habakkuk 2:5.

Sheol (with an adverbial ending) occurs another time, a sixty-sixth time, in Isaiah 7:11, according to *RS, AT, Mo, NW, Vg, Dy,* French *Jerusalem* edition, and R. Kittell's *Biblia Hebraica*.

* All together, the *King James Version* translates Sheol 31 times as "hell."

19. What scriptures show that Sheol and Hades mean the same thing?

the Hebrew word Sheol by the Greek word Ha'des. The two words, Sheol and Ha'des, are thereby seen to mean the same thing, namely, the common grave of dead mankind in the ground.

[20] The cases of Jesus Christ and his congregation are actual illustrations of the fact that it is not the physical body with which a person dies that is raised from the dead or freed from Ha'des. What is raised is the personality that the person has developed by the time of his death and that identifies him and that helps us to remember his personal history. It is this personality that is brought back into existence by being clothed upon with a suitable live body at the resurrection time. In this way the soul that once died because of sin or as a sacrifice is re-created. As it is stated, in Psalm 104:29, 30, in an address to God: "If you take away their spirit, they expire, and back to their dust they go. If you send forth your spirit, they are created; and you make the face of the ground new."

[21] Correctly, then, the apostle Peter applied to Jesus Christ the words of Psalm 16:10: "You will not leave my soul [not, my human body] in Ha'des." (Acts 2:27-31) The human body of flesh, which Jesus Christ laid down forever as a ransom sacrifice, was disposed of by God's power, but not by fire on the altar of the temple in Jerusalem. The flesh of a sacrifice is always disposed of and put out of existence, so not corrupting. But the value of the fleshly sacrifice remains and counts in behalf of the one offering the sacrifice.

[22] So, if the patriarch Abraham had been allowed to go through with the actual sacrifice of

---

20. How do the cases of Jesus and his congregation help us to understand just what is resurrected?
21. (a) As shown by Peter's quotation from Psalm 16:10, what was raised from Hades in the case of Jesus? (b) What happened to the human body that Jesus had laid down in sacrifice?
22. Who was pictured by both Isaac and the ram that Abraham offered on Mount Moriah, and what was done with the body of the ram?

his son Isaac on Mount Moriah, he would have bled Isaac's killed body first and then would have burned the body to smoke and ashes. God did not let the matter go that far, but provided a ram to be substituted for Isaac, and this ram was burned on the altar that Abraham had built. (Genesis 22: 1-14) On this occasion Isaac pictured God's only-begotten Son Jesus Christ, and the ram whose body was bled and then burned on the altar as a sacrifice pictured Jesus Christ.—John 1:29, 36.

[23] Hence Jesus Christ was not resurrected with the sacrificed human body, but, as 1 Peter 3:18, 19 truthfully tells us, "Christ died once for all time concerning sins, a righteous person for unrighteous ones, that he might lead you to God, he being put to death in the flesh, but being made alive [not in the flesh, but] in the spirit. In this state also he went his way and preached to the spirits in prison." As a spirit the resurrected Jesus could preach to other spirits in the invisible realm. Consequently, when he ascended to heaven, he did not, even as he could not, take the sacrificed human body with him. He took up with him the value of his sacrificed human life, this being pictured by his blood.

[24] In proof of this we read, in Hebrews 9:11, 12, 24: "When Christ came as a high priest of the good things that have come to pass . . . he entered, no, not with the blood of goats and of young bulls, but with his own blood, once for all time into the holy place and obtained an everlasting deliverance for us. Christ entered, not into a holy place made with hands, which is a copy of the reality, but into heaven itself, now to appear before the person of God for us." Thus the fleshly body of Jesus Christ was disposed of on earth by Almighty God and not taken to heaven by Jesus.

23, 24. After his resurrection, what did Jesus take with him to heaven, and how is this explained at Hebrews chapter 9?

[25] This is further made clear for us in Hebrews 13:11, 12, which reads: "The bodies of those animals whose blood is taken into the holy place by the high priest for sin are burned up outside the camp. Hence Jesus also, that he might sanctify the people with his own blood, suffered outside the gate [after which his fleshly body was disposed of by Almighty God]." Eight verses later we read, in Hebrews 13:20: "The God of peace, who brought up from the dead the great shepherd of the sheep with the blood [not the body] of an everlasting covenant, our Lord Jesus." Accordingly, Jesus Christ was raised from the dead as a spirit person, and not in the fleshly body in which he died as a human sacrifice.

[26] The so-called Apostles' Creed is not found in the Holy Bible and is really not "apostolic." Its statement, "I believe in . . . the resurrection of the body," is not based on the Bible and is not taught by the Bible. Rather, in the resurrection, Almighty God re-creates the soul with the same personality, not with the same physical body. That is why each one will be able to recognize himself and to be identified by those who formerly knew him. In the resurrection Christ's congregation will,

25. In what way does Hebrews 13:11, 12, 20 add to the evidence that Jesus was not raised in the fleshly body in which he had died as a human sacrifice?
26. (a) Does the Bible teach that one will be resurrected with identically the same physical body one had at death? (b) How will it be determined what kind of body each one will have?

each, "be raised up a spiritual body," just as Jesus Christ himself was. The rest of the human dead who will be freed from Ha'des or Sheol will be raised up with suitable human bodies, according to the rule: "As for what you sow, you sow, not the body that will develop, but a bare grain, it may be, of wheat or any one of the rest; but God gives it a body just as it has pleased him." —1 Corinthians 15:37, 38.

[27] When testifying before a pagan Roman governor who believed, not in the resurrection, but in the immortality of the human soul, the apostle Paul said in refutation of the Jewish high priest and elders: "I believe all the things set forth in the Law and written in the Prophets; and I have hope toward God, which hope these men themselves also entertain, that there is going to be a resurrection of both the righteous and the unrighteous." (Acts 24:14, 15) In his letters to the Corinthian congregation the apostle Paul spoke much of the resurrection. In all the inspired Christian Greek Scriptures ("New Testament") the word "resurrection" (*anástasis*) occurs forty-one (41) times, besides the expression "earlier resurrection" (*exanástasis*) once.* The faithful men and women of ancient times before Christ's death and resurrection also believed in the resurrection of the dead by God's power.—Hebrews 11:17-19, 35.

[28] With all fitness the last book of the Holy Bible gives us a picture of the resurrection of the "rest of the dead" (those not included in Christ's congregation of 144,000 members) after the wick-

---

* In Luke 2:34 the Greek word *anástasis* is rendered "rising again" (*AV; NW*) or "rising" (*RS*).

27. (a) When testifying before a Roman governor, what did the apostle Paul say as to the kind of people who would be resurrected? (b) Is the resurrection a subject about which the Bible has much to say?
28, 29. What picture of the resurrection of those not included in Christ's congregation of 144,000 members does the last book of the Bible present?

ed organization of Satan the Devil is done away with in heaven and on earth. In Revelation 20:11-14 we read these words of John:

[29] "And I saw a great white throne and the one seated on it. From before him the earth and the heaven fled away, and no place was found for them. And I saw the dead, the great and the small, standing before the throne, and scrolls were opened. But another scroll was opened; it is the scroll of life. And the dead were judged out of those things written in the scrolls according to their deeds. And the sea gave up those dead in it, and death and Ha'des gave up those dead in them, and they were judged individually according to their deeds. And death and Ha'des were hurled into the lake of fire. This means the second death, the lake of fire."

[30] The death that is traceable back to the sinner Adam will be destroyed, just as we read in the next chapter, in Revelation 21:4: "And death will be no more, neither will mourning nor outcry nor pain be any more. The former things have passed away."

[31] The Adamic death that we inherited will thus be "hurled into the lake of fire" and itself die in "second death." For that reason the literal sea will give up those drowned in it who inherited Adamic death, and Ha'des

30, 31. (a) What will become of Adamic death, and how is this shown in the Scriptures? (b) How many of those in Hades or Sheol will come back?

or Sheol will give up all those dead in it. Ha'des, the common grave of dead mankind, will be emptied of all its dead and will cease to be. It will die out forever. Graveyards will then not ruin the beauty of our earth. Funeral parlors and tombstones will be removed. Thus by means of Jesus Christ, who has the "keys of death and of Ha'des," Jehovah God will hurl Ha'des into the "lake of fire" that symbolizes the "second death." Ha'des will then be one of those "former things" that will have "passed away." But what will be the outcome to all those on earth who then stand before the One seated on the "great white throne"? Let us examine the Bible and see.

CHAPTER 19

Judgment Day—When for All Mankind? How Long?

THE apostle Peter was one of those inspired men who foretold the destruction of the wicked organization of Satan the Devil in heaven and earth in a fiery time of trouble. This trouble will result in destruction to that world empire of false religion, "Babylon the Great," and to the imperfect political governments of this earth; it will also result in the binding of Satan the Devil and his demon angels and the hurling of them into the abyss, to be shut up there under seal for a thousand years. (Revelation 18:1-24; 19:11 to 20:3) This will occur according to God's unbreakable word; and concerning this the apostle Peter writes: "By the same word the heavens and the earth that are now are stored up for fire and are being reserved to the day of judgment and of destruction of the ungodly men. However, let this one fact not be escaping your notice, beloved ones, that one day is with Jehovah as a thousand years and a thousand years as one day."

1. What will the destruction of Satan's wicked organization include, and how does the apostle Peter describe this?

360

[2] Those words, in 2 Peter 3:7, 8, do not say that the "day of judgment and of destruction of the ungodly men" will be a thousand years long. No; that "day of judgment and of destruction of the ungodly men" will occupy a comparatively short period of time at the end of this system of things. That is to say, it will occupy enough time to bring about (1) the destruction of Babylon the Great, the final plagues upon whom come "in one day" and whose judgment arrives "in one hour," figuratively speaking; also (2) the destruction of the visible political organization of Satan's rulership; and (3) the binding and hurling of Satan and his demons into the abyss. For this "day of judgment and of destruction of the ungodly men" the "heavens and the earth that are now" are being "reserved." So that "day" comes and passes before the thousand years of Christ's reign begins. (Revelation 18:8-10; 19:1, 2, 19-21; 20:1-3) So that "day" does not correspond with the first thousand years of the "new heavens and a new earth." —2 Peter 3:13.

[3] Why, then, after he mentions "the day of judgment and of destruction of the ungodly men," does Peter say: "However, let this one fact not be escaping your notice, beloved ones, that one day is with Jehovah as a thousand years and a thousand years as one day"? Peter says those words to show that God will not be slow or late about bringing that "day of judgment and of destruction" upon the ungodly men. These men are saying, 'Where is that promised day of Jehovah? It will not come in our day, for "all things are continuing exactly as from creation's beginning."' —2 Peter 3:3, 4.

---

2. How long is the "day of judgment" to which the apostle Peter here refers, and when will it come?
3. Then why does Peter go on to say that "one day is with Jehovah as a thousand years"?

⁴ By the apostle Peter's time more than two thousand four hundred years had passed since the global flood of Noah's day, in which flood "the world of that time suffered destruction when it was deluged with water." But now in our day it is more than four thousand three hundred years since Jehovah God punished that "ancient world" by the Flood. (2 Peter 3:6; 2:5) To ungodly men now living "in the last days," that seems like a very long time; but to Jehovah God that is less than five days of time, seeing that he measures a "thousand years as one day." That is not very long for God to wait. He is timeless, and in comparison with eternity or everlastingness a thousand years is as nothing. Psalm 90:2, 4, addressed to Jehovah God, says: "Even from time indefinite to time indefinite you are God. For a thousand years are in your eyes but as yesterday when it is past, and as a watch during the night."

⁵ Consequently, men who today ridicule the warning of the coming of the "day of [condemnatory] judgment and of destruction of the ungodly men" and the destruction of the "heavens and the earth that are now" are throwing themselves off guard and are due to be overtaken by sudden destruction. That is why the apostle Peter, after pointing out that God does not measure time as we humans do, says:

⁶ "Jehovah is not slow respecting his promise, as some people consider slowness, but he is patient with you because he does not desire any to be destroyed but desires all to attain to repentance. Yet Jehovah's day ["the day of judgment and of destruction of the ungodly men"] will come as a thief, in which the heavens will pass away with a

---

4. According to Jehovah's calculation of time, how long has it been since the global flood of Noah's day destroyed the wicked? 5, 6. (a) Why is it dangerous to ridicule warning of the coming of this "day of judgment"? (b) Rather than ridiculing, what should we wisely do before that destruction comes?

hissing noise, but the elements being intensely hot will be dissolved, and earth and the works in it will be discovered. Since all these things are thus to be dissolved, what sort of persons ought you to be in holy acts of conduct and deeds of godly devotion, awaiting and keeping close in mind the presence of the day of Jehovah, through which the heavens being on fire will be dissolved and the elements being intensely hot will melt!"—2 Peter 3:9-12.

⁷ It is after that removal of the earthly and heavenly parts of the organization of Satan the Devil that "new heavens and a new earth" will take complete charge of man's affairs on this planet earth. Hence, in the next verse, the apostle Peter adds: "But there are new heavens and a new earth that we are awaiting according to his promise, and in these righteousness is to dwell." —2 Peter 3:13.

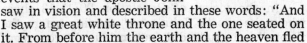

⁸ Under these "new heavens" and in the "new earth" the judgment of mankind, the living and the dead, will proceed. This is the order of events that the apostle John saw in vision and described in these words: "And I saw a great white throne and the one seated on it. From before him the earth and the heaven fled

7. After Satan's organization is destroyed, what will take complete charge of human affairs?
8. When will the judging, not only of the living but also of the dead among mankind, take place, and how is this order of events shown in the vision recorded by the apostle John?

away, and no place was found for them. And I saw the dead, the great and the small, standing before the throne, and scrolls were opened. But another scroll was opened; it is the scroll of life. And the dead were judged out of those things written in the scrolls according to their deeds. And the sea gave up those dead in it, and death and Ha′des gave up those dead in them, and they were judged individually according to their deeds."—Revelation 20:11-13.

⁹ The Judge seated on the "great white throne" is Jehovah God. However, he does not judge mankind directly during the thousand years of Christ's reign but uses his only-begotten Son Jesus Christ as his Deputy. The procedure will be just as Jesus said: "The Father judges no one at all, but he has committed all the judging to the Son, . . . he has given him authority to do judging, because Son of man he is. Do not marvel at this, because the hour is coming in which all those in the memorial tombs will hear his voice and come out, those who did good things to a resurrection of life, those who practiced vile things to a resurrection of judgment."

¹⁰ In harmony with those words in John 5:22, 27-29 the apostle Paul, when speaking to the highest judicial court in Athens, Greece, said to those judges: "God . . . has set a day in which he purposes to judge the inhabited earth in righteousness by a man whom he has appointed, and he has furnished a guarantee to all men in that he has resurrected him from the dead."—Acts 17:30, 31.

¹¹ In the vision of Revelation 20:11-13 those whom the apostle John saw "standing before the throne" to be judged do not include the congrega-

---

9, 10. Who will do the judging, and how do the Scriptures show this?
11. What group is not included among those whom John saw "standing before the throne," and why so?

tion of Christ's 144,000 faithful followers. This congregation takes part in the "first resurrection," and concerning them Revelation 20:4-6 says: "I saw thrones, and there were those who sat down on them, and power of judging was given them. . . . they will be priests of God and of the Christ, and will rule as kings with him for the thousand years." Through the "first resurrection" they come to life in heaven as spirit persons and so do not stand with mankind on earth before God's judgment throne.

[12] Instead of coming under judgment with mankind, they are given "power of judging," and for this reason they sit down on heavenly thrones. So they serve, not only as heavenly kings and priests with Jesus Christ, but also as associate judges with him over mankind. Their term of office as judges with Jesus Christ is the same as their reign, namely, a thousand years long. Hence the judgment day of mankind under the "new heavens" will be a thousand years long.

[13] In view of this fact the apostle Paul wrote the congregation of holy ones in ancient Corinth, Greece, and asked: "Do you not know that the holy ones will judge the world? And if the world is to be judged by you, are you unfit to try very trivial matters? Do you not know that we shall judge angels? Why, then, not matters of this life?" (1 Corinthians 1:1, 2; 6:2, 3) This includes what Jesus promised to his faithful apostles for leaving all earthly things and following him, saying: "In the re-creation [or, regeneration; rebirth], when the Son of man sits down upon his glorious throne,

---

12. (a) What power is given to those who share in the "first resurrection"? (b) How is the length of this judgment day of mankind therefore revealed to us?
13, 14. (a) In his letter to Christians at Corinth, who did the apostle Paul show would share in judging the world? (b) In this connection, what promise did Jesus make to his faithful apostles, and to what does the expression "twelve tribes of Israel" here refer?

you who have followed me will also yourselves sit upon twelve thrones, judging the twelve tribes of Israel."—Matthew 19:27, 28.

[14] Here the expression "twelve tribes of Israel" appears to take in the whole race of mankind, for whom Jesus Christ serves as High Priest and for whom he offered himself as a sacrifice of atonement, like those sacrificial victims on the Jewish Atonement Day.—Leviticus 16:1-31; Hebrews 9: 11-16, 24-28; 1 John 2:1, 2.

[15] These 144,000 associate judges with Jesus Christ had to qualify first for their heavenly position of judgeship. Hence they are all on trial since Pentecost of 33 C.E. as members of Christ's congregation, and at their death in the flesh final judgment is rendered respecting them and is held on record until the time for the "first resurrection" to begin toward them. That these 144,000 Christians having the "new birth" faced judgment while on earth to determine their everlasting future, the apostle Peter plainly stated, when he wrote:

[16] "You yourselves also as living stones are being built up a spiritual house for the purpose of a holy priesthood, to offer up spiritual sacrifices acceptable to God through Jesus Christ. . . . let none of you suffer as a murderer or a thief or an evildoer or as a busybody in other people's matters. But if he suffers as a Christian, let him not feel shame, but let him keep on glorifying God in this name. For it is the appointed time for the judgment to start with the house of God. Now if it starts first with us, what will the end be of those [in the 'house of God'] who are not obedient to the good news of God?"—1 Peter 1:1-3; 2:5; 4:15-17.

15, 16. When do the 144,000 members of Christ's congregation themselves face judgment, and how does the apostle Peter plainly state this?

[17] Thus the judgment is pronounced and executed upon Christ's congregation of 144,000 "holy ones" before the judgment begins upon the world of mankind in general. This is why the apostle Paul wrote to the congregation of "holy ones" and said: "We shall all stand before the judgment seat of God; for it is written [in Isaiah 45:23]: ' "As I live," says Jehovah, "to me every knee will bend down, and every tongue will make open acknowledgment to God." ' So, then, each of us will render an account for himself to God." (Romans 1:1-7; 14:10-12) Also, since Jesus Christ serves as Deputy Judge for Jehovah, the apostle Paul writes to the congregation:

[18] "Therefore we are also making it our aim that . . . we may be acceptable to him. For we must all be made manifest before the judgment seat of the Christ, that each one may get his award for the things done through the body, according to the things he has practiced, whether it is good or vile." —2 Corinthians 5:9, 10.

[19] By practicing what is good in this earthly life as imitators of Jesus Christ, and by proving faithful to the death, the 144,000 are judged worthy of the "first resurrection" to heavenly life as immortal, incorruptible spirit sons of God. When they experience their resurrection from the dead, they come forth from the sleep of death to what Jesus called a "resurrection of life." (John 5:28, 29) They instantaneously enter into the fullness and perfection of life. They are thus found qualified to sit down on heavenly thrones with Christ and have the "power of judging" given to them.

17, 18. (a) To whom was the apostle Paul writing when he said, "We shall all stand before the judgment seat of God"? (b) Why did he also say, "We must all be made manifest before the judgment seat of the Christ"?
19. At the time they are raised from the dead, what reward is given to those sharing in the "first resurrection"?

JUDGING THE "LIVING AND THE DEAD"

[20] To a Christian superintendent who was in line to be one of the heavenly judges of mankind, the apostle Paul wrote: "I solemnly charge you before God and Christ Jesus, who is destined to judge the living and the dead, and by his manifestation and his kingdom." (2 Timothy 4:1) In the apostle John's vision, in Revelation 20:11-13, we see the human "dead" coming forth from the sea and from Ha'des or Sheol to stand before the "great white throne" to be judged. Who, then, are the "living" who are also to be judged on earth? In Jesus' parable of the sheep and the goats, which he gave as a climax to his prophecy regarding the "sign of [his] presence and of the conclusion of the system of things," he indicates who those "living" ones are. They are the sheeplike persons who survive the "conclusion of the system of things" and who enter, without dying as human creatures, into the new system of things under God's Messianic kingdom.—Matthew 25:31-46.

[21] The fact that there will be human survivors of the "conclusion of the system of things" is allowed for by Jesus' words in his prophecy on the "sign" thereof. He gave no exact time for the passing away of the "heavens and the earth that are now," but he urged those who desired to survive to be on the watch, saying:

[22] "Heaven and earth will pass away, but my words will by no means pass away. Concerning that day and hour nobody knows, neither the angels of the heavens nor the Son, but only the Father. For just as the days of Noah were, so the presence [*parousía*] of the Son of man will be. For as they were in those days before the flood, eating and drinking, men marrying and women

---

20. (a) At 2 Timothy 4:1, whom does it say that Christ Jesus is to judge? (b) Who are the "living" that are to be judged on earth?
21, 22. When speaking of the "conclusion of the system of things," how did Jesus indicate that there would be survivors?

being given in marriage, until the day that Noah entered into the ark; and they took no note until the flood came and swept them all away, so the presence of the Son of man will be. . . . Keep on the watch, therefore, because you do not know on what day your Lord is coming."—Matthew 24: 35-42; Luke 17:26, 27.

[23] In 2370-2369 B.C.E. eight human souls survived the Flood, namely, Noah and his sons Japheth, Shem and Ham and their four wives. (1 Peter 3:20) Apart from these survivors, "the world of that time suffered destruction when it was deluged with water." (2 Peter 3:6; 2:5) The system of things of before the Flood ended, but Noah and his family survived its end and afterward resumed their godly living on the same earth free from ungodly people. That historic fact is used as a prophetic picture that there will be human survivors of the end of this present system of things.

[24] These survivors are the "sheep" class who do good to Christ's spiritual brothers on the earth and whom he therefore places on his right hand of favor and protection. After they survive the "conclusion of the system of things," they have set before them an opportunity to gain "ever-

23. How many survived the Flood, and of what is the fact that there were survivors a prophetic picture?
24. (a) Who will survive the "conclusion of the system of things"? (b) Does their survival mean that they have gained "everlasting life"?

lasting life" in the "new earth" under the heavenly kingdom. (Matthew 25:46) After their survival they are still imperfect, sinful and dying; but if they continue obedient to God and his Messianic kingdom, they will in time be fully recovered from this condition that they inherited from sinner Adam.

[25] With that blessed goal in view they need to pass the test that will be applied during the thousand-year reign of Jesus Christ. They must always have in mind that they yet need to have a favorable judgment passed upon them at the end of the thousand years. By that time "death," that is, Adamic death, will have completely given them up. They will be alive in human perfection and will be able to pass the final, decisive test in perfect obedience to God. Having never died in the flesh, they need no resurrection. They are the ones "living" whom Jesus Christ must judge at his kingdom.—2 Timothy 4:1.

[26] However, the human "dead" are also to be judged. To this end they must have a resurrection. Giving assurance of this, the apostle John describes the prophetic vision of this, saying: "I saw the dead, the great and the small, standing before the throne, and scrolls were opened. But another scroll was opened; it is the scroll of life. And the dead were judged out of those things written in the scrolls according to their deeds. And the sea gave up those dead in it, and death and Ha'des gave up those dead in them, and they were judged individually according to their deeds." (Revelation 20:12, 13) Will the resurrection of these individuals prove to be one "of life" or one "of judgment"?—John 5:28, 29.

---

25. When do they still need to have a favorable judgment passed upon them, but to what condition will those "living" ones have attained by that time?
26. For the human "dead" to be judged, what must take place, and from where do they come?

²⁷ According to the vision given to John, dead humans, all the way back to Adam's martyred son Abel, will come back from death in Ha'des or in the sea. They will not come back all at one time, that is, on one twenty-four-hour day. The return of the dead will provide problems and obligations for those alive on earth; due preparation will have to be made by the living. This will call for order to be observed in the resurrection, and the Messianic King and Judge, Jesus Christ, will have consideration for the living ones. Those resurrected in due order will be absorbed into the living arrangements of the "new earth." Those coming back to life on earth will need and will be given help to adjust themselves to the righteous new order of things. Finally the last dead one in the sea or in Ha'des will come forth. Resurrection will then be complete.

²⁸ A "scroll of life" will be in process of being written up, to contain the names of those judged deserving of everlasting perfect human life on earth under God's eternal kingdom. They will have to make a favorable record for themselves in the "new earth." Why?

²⁹ Because they will be judged, not according to their deeds during this present system of things before the destruction of Babylon the Great and the "war of the great day of God the Almighty" at Armageddon, but according to their deeds in the new system of things, that is to say, after Satan and his demons are bound and imprisoned in the abyss. Of course, the personality that people built before the flood of Noah's day or during this present system of things will affect them. It will at

---

27. (a) Who will be raised from the dead? (b) Will they come back all at once?
28. Whose names will be written on the "scroll of life"?
29. (a) According to what deeds will the resurrected ones be judged? (b) Will their past course of life in any way affect them then? (c) What help will be given to all willing ones?

first help them or hinder them during the thousand years of Christ's reign. For that reason, things will then be either more endurable or less endurable for individuals. (Matthew 11:20-24) But the purpose of Christ's millennial government will be to help all the willing ones on earth to cultivate righteousness to the degree of perfection.—Isaiah 26:9.

[30] There will be no need to go over the record of their past life in the flesh, because the judges in heaven well know that people's past life of sin and imperfection already condemns them. But Christ died as a ransom sacrifice to relieve mankind of sin and imperfection and the penalty thereof. Hence earth's inhabitants will then be "judged out of those things written in the scrolls according to their deeds." These "scrolls" will first be opened up after the present wicked "heavens" and "earth" of Satan's organization have fled away from before the face of the Judge on the "great white throne." What do those scrolls contain? Not the record of the past life of all men who then come up for judgment. The scrolls are something in addition to our present Holy Bible. As the book *"Babylon the Great Has Fallen!" God's Kingdom Rules!* says, they

> are the law books of Jehovah. That is, they are the publications setting forth his will for all people on earth during Christ's millennial reign. After what is written in these law "scrolls" has been published and made known, the people will be judged by what laws and instructions are found written in those scrolls "according to their deeds," not their deeds committed in this life or before the scrolls were published, but their deeds afterward as long as they are on judgment.—Page 646, paragraph 1.

---

30. (a) Why will the ones resurrected not then be judged on the basis of what they did in their past life in the flesh? (b) What does the scripture mean when it says that they will be "judged out of those things written in the scrolls according to their deeds"?

[31] If some persons willfully refuse to learn righteousness and holiness or willfully fall away from such required qualities, they may be executed sooner or later before the thousand years of the judgment day are ended. They will then not be returned to Adamic death or to Ha'des but will be destroyed eternally. As Revelation 20:15 states, "Whoever was not found written in the book of life was hurled into the lake of fire." As regards such persons who were resurrected from the dead, their coming back to life from Ha'des or the sea turns out to be "a resurrection of judgment," a resurrection that led at last to condemnation to extinction.—John 5:28, 29.

[32] However, what about those persons who make the proper progress during Christ's thousand-year reign and who attain to human perfection and personal righteousness by the end of those thousand years? They will then be subjected to a final test that will determine their eternal future. This supreme test will come when Satan the Devil and his demons are let loose from the abyss. "Now as soon as the thousand years have been ended, Satan will be let loose out of his prison, and he will go out to mislead those nations in the four corners of the earth, Gog and Magog, to gather them together for the war. The number of these is as the sand of the sea. And they advanced over the breadth of the earth and encircled the camp of the holy ones and the beloved city. But fire came down out of heaven and devoured them. And the Devil who was misleading them was hurled into the lake of fire and sulphur, where both the wild beast and the false prophet already were; and they will be tormented day and night forever and ever. . . .

---

31. What will happen to any persons who willfully refuse to conform to the righteous ways of that new system of things?
32. When the thousand years are ended, to what will perfected mankind be subjected, and why?

This means the second death, the lake of fire."
—Revelation 20:7-10, 14.

[33] At the end of the thousand years of reigning
Jesus Christ will turn over the kingdom and its
earthly subjects to Jehovah God the Final and
Supreme Judge. (1 Corinthians 15:24-28) Satan
the Devil and his demons will be let loose upon
earth's inhabitants, who are fully recovered from
all the bad effects of Adam's fall into sin. The
ones who let themselves be misled, the number of
whom is just as indefinite to our knowledge now
as the "sand of the sea," will rebel against the
"beloved city," God's capital organization, and the
"holy ones" occupying it. They will estrange themselves from Jehovah God and his universal organization, like distant "nations in the four corners
of the earth, Gog and Magog." Their "nations"
will not be "written in the book of life." So God
will execute his condemnatory judgment upon
them as if by raining down a devouring fire from
heaven upon them. They will go into the "second
death" of endless annihilation. The past resurrection of any such will turn out to be "a resurrection
of judgment."

[34] What, though, about those perfected humans
who faithfully pass this final test of their exclusive
devotion to God and his Christ and who get their
names "written in the book of life"? Will they be
taken from earth to heaven, or where will they
enjoy God's award to them of everlasting life? The
past resurrection of any of these will prove to be
"a resurrection of life." (John 5:28, 29) But where
will they forever spend that life after the Millen-
nium? (Revelation 20:5) Let the Bible tell us.

---

33. (a) Who will sit as the Final Judge of mankind? (b) How
many will be misled at that time, and against what does the
Bible show that they will rebel? (c) In the case of such ones, of
what kind does their past resurrection prove to be?
34. (a) Of what kind does the past resurrection of those proving
faithful under test prove to be? (b) What question arises as to
where they will enjoy the award of everlasting life?

CHAPTER 20

Earth's Future
as a Paradise
in God's Purpose

IMMEDIATELY after the apostle John writes, "Whoever was not found written in the book of life was hurled into the lake of fire," he continues on to say:

2 "And I saw a new heaven and a new earth; for the former heaven and the former earth had passed away, and the sea is no more. I saw also the holy city, New Jerusalem, coming down out of heaven from God and prepared as a bride adorned for her husband. With that I heard a loud voice from the throne say: 'Look! The tent of God is with mankind, and he will reside with them, and they will be his peoples. And God himself will be with them. And he will wipe out every tear from their eyes, and death will be no more, neither will mourning nor outcry nor pain be any more. The former things have passed away.' "—Revelation 20:15 to 21:4.

3 Does this mean that, after the thousand years of Christ's reign with his 144,000 associated

1, 2. In Revelation, following what does the apostle John tell about New Jerusalem coming down out of heaven?
3, 4. (a) Does this mean that, following Christ's thousand-year reign, New Jerusalem will leave heaven and come down to occupy the earth? (b) Why would it be foolish to think so?

375

judges, kings and priests in heaven and after the everlasting destruction of all the wicked ones whose names were "not found written in the book of life," then the "holy city, New Jerusalem," will leave the "new heaven" and literally come down to our earth and occupy it forever? For one thing, it would be foolish to think so, because New Jerusalem's measurements are so enormous. Revelation 21:16 tells us what an angel of God found its measurements to be: "And the city lies four-square, and its length is as great as its breadth. And he measured the city with the reed, twelve thousand furlongs; its length and breadth and height are equal."

⁴ As a furlong or *stádion* was at least an eighth of a mile long, this would mean that the New Jerusalem was fifteen hundred miles in circumference at the base, or 375 miles to each of its four sides. It would therefore be 375 miles high, thus towering up into what is today "outer space" for man. A city like that, if centered on the site of ancient Jerusalem, which is only about thirty-five miles from the Mediterranean Sea, would spread out into Lebanon, Syria, Jordan and Egypt and into the Mediterranean Sea. And how about eleva-tor (or lift) service to the top, 375 miles up? There will be no such city in or on the "new earth," for the New Jerusalem is symbolical.

⁵ In Revelation 21:9-14 God's angel shows the apostle John that "the holy city Jerusalem coming down out of heaven from God" is a symbol of "the bride, the Lamb's wife." It is accordingly a sym-bol of Christ's congregation of 144,000 disciples who have part in "the first resurrection" to im-mortal life in heaven. That is why it is written of these 144,000: "These are the ones that keep fol-lowing the Lamb no matter where he goes. These

5. What is this "holy city Jerusalem" that comes "down out of heaven from God"?

were bought from among mankind as a first fruits to God and to the Lamb." —Revelation 14:4.

[6] Never will they return to our literal earth and become persons of flesh and blood again. Neither will their Bridegroom Jesus Christ do so. That would be an eternal humiliation of them, inasmuch as earthly man is made "a little lower than angels." (Hebrews 2:7; Psalm 8:5) Rather, the bride of 144,000 members will never cease to be part of the "new heaven," high above the "new earth." The only way in which they will, as the "Lamb's wife," come down to the earth is by directing their attention to earth's inhabitants and joining with their heavenly Bridegroom in blessing all mankind. The New Jerusalem comes down from heaven in this way at the beginning of the thousand-year reign of Christ, when the "new heaven" and "new earth" are established.

[7] In Revelation 21:23, 24 we read concerning the bridal New Jerusalem: "And the city has no need of the sun nor of the moon to shine upon it, for the glory of God lighted it up, and its lamp

6. (a) Will Jesus Christ and his bride ever return to earth in flesh and blood? (b) In what way, then, does the "New Jerusalem" come "down out of heaven from God," and when does this occur?
7, 8. How will it be true that "the nations will walk by means of" the light from New Jerusalem?

was the Lamb. And the nations will walk by means of its light."

[8] Thus all the peoples who have made up the nations of human history prior to the "war of the great day of God the Almighty" at Armageddon will receive enlightenment from the heavenly New Jerusalem and conduct themselves aright by means of that light, whereas the 144,000 associate rulers of Christ as "kings of the earth" will "bring their glory into it." In consequence of this, the mental, religious and social darkness due to Satan the Devil, "the god of this system of things," will be completely dispersed. With that Blinder of men's minds out of the way, Jehovah God, the One who at earth's creation said: "Let the light shine out of darkness," will shine on the hearts of men "to illuminate them with the glorious knowledge of God by the face of Christ."—2 Corinthians 4:4-6.

[9] The "new earth" will be indeed an enlightened place. This expression "new earth" does not refer to a new earthly globe upon which mankind will live forever, anymore than the expression "new heaven" refers to a sky different from the one we earthlings now have above us bedecked with the sun, moon, planets, comets, galaxies and other heavenly bodies that are made known to us by naked eye, visual telescopes and radio telescopes. The "new heavens," of which God directly made a promise long ago in Isaiah 65:17; 66:22, will be the new heavenly ruling powers, namely, the glorified Lord Jesus Christ and his Bride, his 144,000 faithful disciples, all these replacing Satan the Devil and his demon angels, who are "the world rulers of this darkness," "the wicked spirit forces in the heavenly places" of this present time. (Ephesians 6:11, 12) Correspondingly, the "new earth" will not mean a new earthly globe on which to live forever. It will mean all saved mankind

9. To what does the expression "new heavens" refer, and what is the "new earth"?

living as a righteous society in a new system of things under the "new heavens" and yet living on this same terrestrial globe.

¹⁰ Concerning the enlightenment that will fill the literal earth and the effect of this on earth's inhabitants, Isaiah 11:9 says: "They will not do any harm or cause any ruin in all my holy mountain; because the earth will certainly be filled with the knowledge of Jehovah as the waters are covering the very sea."

¹¹ Not only will the wild beasts of the forest and field again become friends of mankind, but the beastly qualities that men have developed through millenniums of human degradation will be stripped away in favor of new, humane, godly personalities. The prophecy of Isaiah 65:17-25 supplements that of Isaiah 11:1-9 by saying: " 'Here I am creating new heavens and a new earth; and the former things will not be called to mind, neither will they come up into the heart. . . . The wolf and the lamb themselves will feed as one, and the lion will eat straw just like the bull; and as for the serpent, his food will be dust. They will do no harm nor cause any ruin in all my holy mountain,' Jehovah has said."

¹² No longer will the earth be plowed up by all the violent instruments of mortal warfare. Depending upon no international organization such as the League of Nations, the United Nations and the International Court of Justice for world peace and security, the people are prophetically invited in Psalm 46:8-11 to come to God for security: "Come, you people, behold the activities of Jehovah, how he has set astonishing events on the earth. He is making wars to cease to the extremity

10. What does Isaiah 11:9 say concerning the enlightenment that will then fill the earth?
11. What will be true of the wild beasts then, and what change will take place in the personalities of men themselves?
12. To whom will mankind look for security, and with what result?

of the earth. The bow he breaks apart and does cut the spear in pieces; the wagons he burns in the fire. 'Give in, you people, and know that I am God. I will be exalted among the nations, I will be exalted in the earth,' Jehovah of armies is with us; the God of Jacob is a secure height for us."

[13] Already, since the year 1919, the year in which the victorious nations of World War I adopted the League of Nations, Jehovah's witnesses have exalted the worship of the one living and true God above all lofty things of this system of things. They have stuck to the rule of life laid down by God's prophet in Isaiah 2:2-5:

[14] "And he will certainly render judgment among the nations and set matters straight respecting many peoples. And they will have to beat their swords into plowshares and their spears into pruning shears. Nation will not lift up sword against nation, neither will they learn war any more. O men of the house of Jacob, come and let us walk in the light of Jehovah."

[15] The prophet Micah, who lived at the same time as Isaiah, expressed a similar prophecy but added the words: "And they will actually sit, each one under his vine and under his fig tree, and there will be no one making them tremble; for the very mouth of Jehovah of armies has spoken it. For all the peoples, for their part, will walk each one in the name of its god; but we, for our part, shall walk in the name of Jehovah our God to time indefinite, even forever." (Micah 4:1-5) In this way the prophet Micah calls attention to the effect on the earth that this turning of implements to peaceful, constructive uses will have. Under the blessing of the "God of peace" all earth will be cultivated into a Paradise.

13, 14. To what rule of life set out in Isaiah 2:2-5 do Jehovah's witnesses adhere even now?
15. What good results of turning implements to peaceful uses does the prophet Micah mention?

[16] In the "war of the great day of God the Almighty" the time will have come for Jehovah of armies to "bring to ruin those ruining the earth." (Revelation 11:13-18; 16:14, 16) The sheeplike people who survive that war at Armageddon will believe in fulfilling the purpose concerning the earth that Jehovah God stated to the first man and woman in the garden of Eden: "Subdue it, and have in subjection the fish of the sea and the flying creatures of the heavens and every living creature that is moving upon the earth." Man in that garden of Eden or "Paradise of Pleasure" was assigned "to cultivate it and to take care of it" and to extend it all around the globe. (Genesis 1: 28; 2:8-15) To this day man has not carried out God's purpose regarding man's earthly home.

[17] However, Jesus Christ is the great Son of man, and to him, rather than to inferior angels, Jehovah God "has subjected the inhabited earth to come, about which we are speaking. But a certain witness has given proof somewhere [in Psalm 8: 4-6], saying: 'What is man that you keep him in mind, or the son of man that you take care of him? . . . All things you subjected under his feet.' " This Son of man, Jesus Christ, is "crowned with glory and honor for having suffered death" as a perfect man. He will see to it that God's purpose concerning the earth, as stated to the perfect man in the Paradise of Pleasure, is completely carried out and the whole earth is transformed into a Paradise in obedience to God's will.—Hebrews 2:5-9.

---

16. What purpose for the earth did God state to the first man and woman in Eden, and has that purpose yet been carried out by man?
17. Who is the Son of man to whom "the inhabited earth to come" has been subjected, and what does this mean for the earth?

[18] Jesus Christ had this in mind nineteen hundred years ago, on the day of Nisan 14 of the year 33 C.E. An evildoer, hanging on a torture stake alongside the dying Jesus, said to this man over whose head was posted the inscription, "This is the king of the Jews," these words of faith: "Jesus,  remember me when you get into your kingdom." What did Jesus say in answer on that day when everything seemed contrary to his getting into a kingdom? The account tells us: "And he said to him: 'Truly I tell you today, You will be with me in Paradise.'" (Luke 23:38-43) On that very day both Jesus and that sympathetic evildoer went to Ha'des. On the third day Jesus was brought out from behind the "gates of Ha'des" and thereafter was exalted to heaven, to await the time for his kingdom at the end of the Gentile Times in 1914 C.E. In his kingdom, after the "war of the great day of God the Almighty" at Armageddon, the King Jesus Christ will make good his word to that dying evildoer. How? Not only by resurrecting him to renewed life on earth, but also by having  the whole earth cultivated into a Paradise. The evil-

18. (a) Nineteen hundred years ago, what promise did Jesus make to an evildoer who was put to death alongside him? (b) How will that promise be fulfilled?

doer resurrected on earth will thus be in Paradise with the King who has turned his attention and energies to the earth.

[19] By means of the heavenly Mount Zion, the heavenly Jerusalem, Jehovah God will make the earth a most productive place. In it there will be an abundance of food for all, both for those who survive the "war of the great day of God the Almighty" and for all the billions of dead whom the sea and Ha'des will give up at God's command through Christ. The prophecy will go into fulfillment:

[20] "Jehovah of armies will certainly make for all the peoples, in this mountain, a banquet of well-oiled dishes, a banquet of wine kept on the dregs, of well-oiled dishes filled with marrow, of wine kept on the dregs, filtered. And in this mountain he will certainly swallow up the face of the envelopment that is enveloping over all the peoples, and the woven work that is interwoven upon all the nations. He will actually swallow up death forever, and the Lord Jehovah will certainly wipe the tears from all faces. And the reproach of his people he will take away from all the earth, for Jehovah himself has spoken it. And in that day one will certainly say: 'Look! This is our God. We have hoped in him, and he will save us. This is Jehovah. We have hoped in him. Let us be joyful and rejoice in the salvation by him.' "—Isaiah 25:6-9.

[21] There will be a stop to the present process with mankind, that "a generation is going, and a generation is coming" on the same old earth. Instead, all human creatures whose names are "found written in the book of life" after the final test will remain for all time on the Paradise earth

---

19, 20. Will there be ample food for earth's inhabitants, and what does Isaiah 25:6-9 say about this?

21, 22. (a) Will people continue to die then? (b) Where will those who pass the final test successfully continue to live for all time, as the psalmist shows?

to praise and serve Jehovah God through Jesus Christ, for "the earth is standing even to time indefinite." (Ecclesiastes 1:4; Revelation 20:13-15) The words of Psalm 115:15-18 will be true of these dwellers in the earthly Paradise:

²² "You are the ones blessed by Jehovah, the Maker of heaven and earth. As regards the heavens, to Jehovah the heavens belong, but the earth he has given to the sons of men. The dead themselves do not praise Jah, nor do any going down into silence. But we ourselves will bless Jah from now on and to time indefinite. Praise Jah, you people [*Hebrew*, Hallelujah]!"

²³ Thus it will not be in vain that Jehovah God blessed the seventh day of his creative week, making it sacred. His resting or desisting from earthly creative work for the seven thousand years of this "seventh day" will not have let things go to wreck and ruin, even though Satan's rule and sin and death did enter into man's experience and prevail for six thousand years. By the end of God's great rest day or sabbath his glorious purpose regarding our earth and mankind will come to blessed reality. The sacred purpose of his rest day will be grandly realized through his beloved Son Jesus Christ, who is called "the Son of man." God's own sabbath day will have served for the eternal benefit of obedient mankind.—Genesis 2:2, 3.

²⁴ To all eternity our earth will bear a distinction such as no other planet throughout endless space will enjoy. To all eternity, throughout all creation, it will be a glorious showpiece to Jehovah's praise. Not that it will be the only planet that will ever be inhabited, but that it will be the only planet to which the Creator of all good things sent his

23. What will therefore be the result of this seventh day of God's creative week?
24, 25. (a) In what ways will our earth forever bear a distinction that no other planet will enjoy? (b) By redeeming from the earth 144,000 to be "joint heirs with Christ" in heaven, what has Jehovah caused to be made known?

only-begotten Son to become a man and die sacrificially to recover the planet's inhabitants from sin and its penalty death. It will be the only planet on which Jehovah, by means of his Son Jesus Christ, will have fought the "war of the great day of God the Almighty" to show his power over all his enemies in heaven and on earth and to vindicate himself as the Universal Sovereign.—Jeremiah 50: 25; Psalm 140:7; Acts 4:24.

[25] Earth will be the only planet from which Jehovah God will redeem 144,000 faithful members of its human inhabitants to be the wifelike associates of his heavenly Son Jesus Christ, to be "heirs indeed of God, but joint heirs with Christ." (Romans 8:16, 17) The purpose of showing such marvelous undeserved kindness to these 144,000 who are redeemed from among men was that "there might be made known through the congregation the greatly diversified wisdom of God, according to the eternal purpose that he formed in connection with the Christ, Jesus our Lord." —Ephesians 3:10, 11.

CHAPTER 21

God Vindicated
as Being No Liar

OD is not a man that he should tell lies, neither a son of mankind that he should feel regret. Has he himself said it and will he not do it, and has he spoken and will he not carry it out?" (Numbers 23:19) The answer to this compound question as raised by the prophet Balaam in about the year 1473 B.C.E. is Yes!

² In all the more than thirty-four centuries since those words were spoken God has done as he has said and he has carried out what he has spoken. He has not proved to be a liar, but he has proved to be the very opposite of the great "liar and the father of the lie," Satan the Devil. (John 8:44) God, the only one whose name is Jehovah, has lived up to the statement made by the prophet Samuel of the ancient nation of Israel: "The Excellency of Israel will not prove false, and He will not feel regrets, for He is not an earthling man so as to feel regrets." (1 Samuel 15:29) He does not prove false to us in not carrying out his recorded purpose and promises, neither does he prove to be like an imperfect earthling man in having to feel regrets over what he has stated his purpose to be.

1, 2. How has Jehovah God proved that he is no liar and that he is not like men who may feel regrets over promises they make?

He has not left his trusting people of today disappointed, but down to this year he has irresistibly carried out his Word.

[3] In comparison with the numberless gods and goddesses of the worldly nations, how unusual a God Jehovah the Creator is! Having formed and declared his purpose as to how things shall work out to his praise and credit and for the blessing of righteously disposed mankind, and having the unlimited power to carry out his purpose to the finish, He truly knows the end of his works from the beginning of them. When he foretold the fall of ancient Babylon and the fall of her modern counterpart Babylon the Great and the deliverance of his people therefrom, Jehovah God truthfully said:

[4] "Remember this, that you people may muster up courage. Lay it to heart, you transgressors. Remember the first things of a long time ago, that I am the Divine One and there is no other God, nor anyone like me; the One telling from the beginning the finale, and from long ago the things that have not been done; the One saying, 'My own counsel will stand, and everything that is my delight I shall do'; the One calling from the sunrising a bird of prey [a symbolic bird], from a distant land the man [Cyrus the Great] to execute my counsel. I have even spoken it; I shall also bring it in. I have formed it, I shall also do it."—Isaiah 46:8-11.

[5] Those recorded words are not just the writing of an ancient Hebrew prophet as if he were bragging about a national God, a God who is peculiar to only the ancient Hebrews, Jews or Israelites.

3, 4. (a) Why can it truthfully be said that, from the very beginning of his works, God knows what the outcome will be? (b) What did Jehovah say in this connection when foretelling the fall of Babylon and the deliverance of his people?
5. (a) Is Jehovah, whom Isaiah served as a prophet, merely a national God of the Jews? (b) Did the Christian apostles also look to His sayings for information concerning events in their time?

The words are the writing of a prophet of the One who is God over all, the "King of the nations," as the Hebrew prophet Jeremiah calls him. (Jeremiah 10:7) Yes, Isaiah was a prophet of the "King of the nations," and not of a mere tribal God. (Romans 3:29, 30) The Christian apostles of our first century agreed with the sayings of Jehovah God as written down by his prophet Isaiah. Those Christian apostles quoted those prophetic sayings and spoke of the fulfillment of them. They agreed that Jehovah God is the One and only One who knows the end of his works from the beginning. An example of where the apostles took note of prophecy occurred about 49 C.E.

⁶ At that time the apostles were faced with the question of whether non-Jewish (Gentile) believers would have to make Jews of themselves by getting circumcised and thus obliging themselves to keep the whole Law of the prophet Moses. The question was submitted to a gathering of apostles and older men of the congregation in Jerusalem. There the missionaries Symeon Peter, Paul and Barnabas produced factual evidence to show that for more than ten years God had been accepting non-Jewish believers into the Christian congregation without requiring them to get circumcised in the flesh.

⁷ Thereupon the disciple James, a half brother of Jesus, rose up and referred to the fulfillment of Hebrew prophecy in which God foretold how he foreknew that he would accept uncircumcised believers from the non-Jewish nations into the congregation of Jesus Christ. James pointed out that since the year 607 B.C.E. the royal booth of King David had fallen down and lain in ruins, for, since

6. When the question of circumcision for non-Jewish believers arose in the early Christian congregation, what evidence was produced for consideration?
7. (a) Was this acceptance of non-Jewish believers into the Christian congregation something that God had foretold? (b) As shown by James, what foretold action was Jehovah God also taking as to the royal "booth of David"?

that year, King David had had no active successor sitting on "Jehovah's throne" in Jerusalem. But now Jehovah God had anointed Jesus the descendant of David with holy spirit as the Permanent Heir of King David and had raised up this anointed Jesus from the dead and had made him sit down at the right hand of Jehovah God in the heavens. In this way God had now rebuilt the ruins of the royal booth of King David that had fallen down.

[8] Moreover, God was now joining to Jesus Christ as his joint heirs not only the remnant of Jews who remained faithful but also the believing people from the Gentile nations, God putting his name Jehovah upon these Gentile believers also without requiring them to be circumcised in the flesh. God foretold this at least over 800 years in advance and he foretold it over his own name.

[9] The disciple James commented on this fact of God's foreknowledge, saying: "Brothers, hear me. Symeon has related thoroughly how God for the first time [in 36 C.E.] turned his attention to the nations to take out of them a people for his name. And with this the words of the Prophets agree, just as it is written [in Amos 9:11, 12, *LXX*], 'After these things I shall return and rebuild the booth of David that is fallen down; and I shall rebuild its ruins and erect it again, in order that those who remain of the men may earnestly seek Jehovah, together with people of all the nations, people who are called by my name, says Jehovah, who is doing these things, known from of old.'" —Acts 15:1-18; Galatians 5:3, 4; 2:1-3.

[10] That was undeniable proof in those days of the Christian apostles that the same God, Jehovah, was then still alive and at work. He had then be-

---

8. What privileges was God extending even to believing Gentiles at this time, and how long in advance had he foretold this?
9. Where in the Bible are these things recorded?
10. Who is the God of the Christian congregation, and how could the early Christians know that?

come the God of the Christian congregation made up not only of previously circumcised Jews but also of uncircumcised Italians, Greeks, and other non-Jewish nationalities. Long in advance Jehovah God had "known from of old" the things that He was then doing with the Christian congregation. This proved that Jehovah was now the God of the Christian congregation, whereas he had abandoned the unbelieving circumcised Jews, no longer favoring them above the Gentile nations. By definitely foreknowing and then foretelling what he would do at a certain time, he made it possible for his faithful worshipers to identify him as being the One who was irresistibly doing the things that were taking place.

[11] This illustrates the kind consideration and loving provision of Jehovah God for his faithful worshipers. He has not kept secret from his people his movements and his contemplated works. He forewarned Noah and his family in order that they might prepare for their survival through the Flood. He forewarned his people concerning the destruction of Jerusalem by the Babylonians in 607 B.C.E. He forewarned his Jewish Christian worshipers by his Son Jesus Christ concerning the destruction of Jerusalem by the Romans in the year 70 C.E. He is now forewarning his Christian worshipers and witnesses concerning the oncoming destruction of this present system of things in the "war of the great day of God the Almighty." The world in general does not take heed to the warning and get saved. So his own works that he has foreknown as due to be performed down at the end of the system of things he has foretold for the benefit of his worshipers today and has revealed them in his due time.

---

11. Cite examples to show that God has shown loving consideration for his worshipers by telling them, in advance, of his works.

¹² It is just as the prophet Amos was inspired to say to Jehovah's people in the ninth century B.C.E.: "If a horn is blown in a city [to warn of an attack], do not also the people themselves tremble? If a calamity occurs in the city [notably Jerusalem], is it not also Jehovah who has acted? For the Lord Jehovah will not do a thing unless he has revealed his confidential matter to his servants the prophets." (Amos 3:6, 7) Such revelation places upon the prophets the responsibility to tell to the people the secret or confidential matter of Jehovah, that the people may be informed in advance and thus be able to take the right action. Jehovah has confidence in himself to foretell things because he knows that he will not prove to be a liar in respect to these things. He reveals his deeds that he has foreknown that, when he does them, it may be correctly understood and appreciated that He is the One that did them and unfailingly carried out his word and will.

¹³ Many centuries ago Jehovah God foreknew his own works for these days in the "conclusion of the system of things." When the writing of all sixty-six books of the Holy Bible was finished by the end of the first century of our Common Era, He finished declaring in advance his own works for the present day. (Revelation 1:1-3; 22:18, 19) From the written record we can see with eyes of discernment that He is at work, doing these final things that he has declared from the beginning. The kingdom of his Christ has been born in the heavens. The "war of the great day of God the Almighty" at Armageddon is unavertibly approaching. (Revelation 12:1-10; 16:13-16) Also,

---

12. (a) When Jehovah informs his prophets in advance of the things that he will do, what responsibility does it place on those prophets? (b) Because Jehovah has revealed his deeds in advance, what is it possible for us to appreciate when they are fulfilled?
13. (a) Where do we find God's advance declaration of works that he would do in these days? (b) Is God doing those things that he foretold? (c) What events that he has foretold are now drawing near?

the thousand-year reign of his Son Jesus Christ in the rebuilt "booth of David" is getting nearer for the everlasting deliverance and blessing of distressed mankind.

[14] Unbelieving, skeptical men will no longer be permitted to scoff at the existence, the name, the Word and the universal sovereignty of Jehovah God. By doing the works that he has foreknown and foretold, he will make their scoffing die upon their lips. As he has repeatedly said, from the days of ancient Egypt onward, "the nations [the Egyptians and all others, including those of today] will have to know that I am Jehovah."*

[15] In these days of increasing violence and turbulence among peoples and nations Jehovah's words in Psalm 46:10 deserve our attention: "Give in, you people, and know that I am God. I will be exalted among the nations, I will be exalted in the earth." Now is the time for enlightened intelligent action. It behooves us to know that there is one living, true God and that this God is Jehovah. It is urgent upon us to know him now and acquaint ourselves with him now before he executes his vengeance upon men and nations who refuse to know him and come to peaceful relations with him.

[16] In dealing with Him we are not fooling with an unreality. He is not like the gods of the ancient nations, who have proved to be no gods and whose worship must perish from the earth. His words and manifestations, his prophecies and his historic

---

* See Exodus 6:7; 7:5, 17; 8:22; 10:2; 29:46; 31:13; Deuteronomy 29:6; 1 Kings 20:13, 28; Isaiah 49:23; Ezekiel 6:7, 10, 13; 36:23; 39:6, 28; Joel 2:27; 3:17. In Ezekiel's prophecy alone God declares more than sixty times his purpose to have individuals and nations "know that I am Jehovah."

---

14. How will God put to silence the scoffing of unbelievers, and what will they have to know?
15. What is it urgent for all of us to do now?
16. What kind of God is Jehovah, and as what has he already been vindicated?

deeds down till the present time, prove that he is a living personal Reality. He alone is the most high and all-powerful God, and the worship of Him must at last pervade all the realm of living creation in heaven and on earth. He has already vindicated himself as being no liar but as being "the God of truth." (Psalm 31:5) We do ourselves an everlasting benefit to seek his goodwill now. "Everyone who calls on the name of Jehovah will be saved."—Acts 2:21; Joel 2:32; Romans 10:13.

CHAPTER **22**

How to Become One of God's "Men of Good Will"

EVER, since first the words were spoken nearly two thousand years ago, have they lost their heartwarming appeal: "Glory to God in the highest: and on earth peace to men of good will." These were the words, not of men on earth, but of heavenly creatures, God-fearing angels. In glory they appeared to shepherds who were watching their sheep by night in the fields outside Bethlehem at the time that the virgin Jewess Mary gave birth to Jesus, the Son of God. (Luke 2:4-14, *Dy*) The words then spoken showed how angels felt about the birth of the Son of God as a human babe.

² Aside from being charmed by the angels' beautiful words, how do we feel about that act of God in sending his only-begotten Son to be born on earth as an infant? Do we, with the angels, feel that 'glory in the highest' should be given to God? Those angels were higher than men, and they felt that such glory should be given to God in the highest. We are men, but are we "men of good"

---

1. What words spoken to shepherds near Bethlehem show how angels felt about the human birth of the Son of God?
2. What questions should we ask ourselves about this matter?

will" to whom peace from God belongs? In our hearts we want to be such.

³ How can we make sure that we are the "men of good will" to whom the "peace" is assured? Can we do so by having goodwill toward God and his Son? Can we do so by having merely kindly religious sentiments toward God, that is to say, to the heavenly Father of the Son who on earth took the name of Jesus? Hardly that! Why so? Because the very people among whom the Son of God was born as one of their own race and nation had kindly religious sentiments toward his heavenly Father, Jehovah God. But has that people, the natural descendants of the patriarch Abraham, had the peace that is promised to "men of good will"? Human history from the destruction of Jerusalem by the Romans in the year 70 C.E. down to the present day shouts back *No!* Why has that been so with that nation, favored as it was with being entrusted with all thirty-nine books of the inspired Hebrew Scriptures? To help us to understand why, a circumcised man of their own race, a one-time Pharisee among them, said:

⁴ "What, then, is the superiority of the Jew, or what is the benefit of the circumcision? A great deal in every way. First of all, because they were entrusted with the sacred pronouncements of God. What, then, is the case? If some did not express faith, will their lack of faith perhaps make the faithfulness of God without effect? Never may that happen! But let God be found true, though every man be found a liar, even as it is written: 'That you might be proved righteous [or, justified] in your words and might win when you are being judged.' " "The good will of my heart and my sup-

---

3. (a) Does being one of the "men of good will" mean that we merely have kindly religious sentiments toward God? (b) How does the situation with the natural descendants of Abraham show this?

4. Although being entrusted with the "sacred pronouncements of God" and having a "zeal for God," in what did the Jews in general fail to exercise faith?

plication to God for them are, indeed, for their salvation. For I bear them witness that they have a zeal for God, but not according to accurate knowledge; for, because of not knowing the righteousness of God but seeking to establish their own, they did not subject themselves to the righteousness of God. For Christ is the end of the Law, so that everyone exercising faith may have righteousness."—Romans 3:1-4, *NW; NEB; AV;* 10:1-4; Psalm 51:4.

⁵ Those zealous stickers to the Law given through Moses had kindly religious sentiments toward God. However, because of lack of faith they did not have goodwill toward his Son. Now, if they did not have goodwill toward His only-begotten Son, how could they really have goodwill toward Jehovah God? They could not do so, in spite of all that they might say. They had a zeal toward God, but it was not according to accurate knowledge. They refused to take in the additional knowledge concerning the "righteousness of God" that is gained, not through self-justifying works of the Mosaic Law, but through faith in the atonement sacrifice of Jesus Christ. For that reason God could not keep up his goodwill toward them. Because of their conduct in not subjecting themselves to the "righteousness of God," his goodwill toward them as a chosen nation ceased. They did not become men of God's goodwill.—Amos 3:1, 2.

⁶ From this Bible illustration it becomes clear to us that the important thing to have is God's goodwill toward us, not what we imagine to be our goodwill toward God. We must become men having God's goodwill. The greatest man of God's goodwill, or God's greatest 'man of goodwill,' was

---

5. Why did those people who continued to stick to the Law given through Moses lose God's goodwill?
6, 7. (a) Which is more important: our feeling that we have goodwill toward God or our having God's goodwill toward us? (b) As recorded by Isaiah, what did Jehovah prophetically say about his goodwill for Jesus Christ and his disciples?

Jesus Christ when on earth. In the Hebrew Scriptures, in Isaiah 49:8, 9, God spoke prophetically of his goodwill toward Jesus Christ and his disciples, saying:

[7] "This is what Jehovah has said: 'In a time of good will I have answered you, and in a day of salvation I have helped you; and I kept safeguarding you that I might give you as a covenant for the people, to rehabilitate the land, to bring about the repossessing of the desolated hereditary possessions, to say to the prisoners, "Come out!" to those who are in the darkness, "Reveal yourselves!"' "—*NW*, edition of 1958, marginal reading.

[8] The application of those prophetic words was widened out to refer also to Christ's footstep followers, when the Christian apostle Paul wrote under inspiration, as follows: "Sharing in God's work, we urge this appeal upon you: you have received the grace of God; do not let it go for nothing. God's own words are: 'In the hour of my favour I gave heed to you; on the day of deliverance I came to your aid.' The hour of favour has now come; now, I say, has the day of deliverance dawned."—2 Corinthians 6:1, 2, *NEB*.

[9] There is a very strong reason why the apostle Paul reminds Christians to take advantage of Jehovah's "time of good will" and Jehovah's "day of salvation," and not misuse the opportunity. This favorable time stands in contrast with Jehovah's "day of vengeance." One sabbath day, when preaching to the synagogue in Nazareth, Jesus Christ put these two periods in contrast with each other when he read from Isaiah 61:1, 2, which says: "The spirit of the Lord Jehovah is upon me, for the reason that Jehovah has anointed me to

---

8. On the basis of that prophecy, what did the apostle Paul urge Christ's followers to do?
9. With what did Jesus show that Jehovah's "year of good will" is contrasted, and how?

tell good news to the meek ones. He has sent me to bind up the brokenhearted, to proclaim liberty to those taken captive and the wide opening of the eyes even to the prisoners; to proclaim the year of good will on the part of Jehovah and the day of vengeance on the part of our God."—Luke 4:16-19; 21:20-22.

¹⁰ The "day of vengeance on the part of our God" is rapidly getting closer with respect to Babylon the Great and her political paramours. (Revelation 17:1 to 18:20; 19:1, 2) Now, already so late in the day, it is urgent for us to take to heart the words of Paul in 2 Corinthians 6:1, 2 and seek God's favor or goodwill.

¹¹ In this brief "hour of favour," this "day of deliverance," this "year of good will on the part of Jehovah," he is offering to mankind "grace" or undeserved kindness. This is something too precious for us to spurn, refusing it. How can we avail ourselves of it and gain God's goodwill? The apostle Paul tells us how to do so in the preceding lines of his same letter, writing:

¹² "But all things are from God, who reconciled us to himself through Christ and gave us the ministry of the reconciliation, namely, that God was by means of Christ reconciling a world to himself, not reckoning to them their trespasses, and he committed the word of the reconciliation to us. We are therefore ambassadors substituting for Christ, as though God were making entreaty through us. As substitutes for Christ we beg: 'Become reconciled to God.' The one [Jesus Christ] who did not know sin he [Jehovah God] made to be sin [or, a sin offering] for us, that we might become God's righteousness by means of him." —2 Corinthians 5:18-21.

10. Why is it urgent for us to seek God's goodwill now?
11, 12. As explained by the apostle Paul, how can we avail ourselves of God's undeserved kindness and gain his goodwill?

[13] In ancient times "ambassadors" were sent to a nation that was at war or that threatened war, in order to bring about peaceful relations between those who were at enmity with each other. (Isaiah 33:7; Luke 14:31, 32; 19:14) All mankind, inheritors of sin and imperfection from the sinner Adam, are naturally at enmity with Jehovah God. We could not meet God's perfect requirements, and so God lovingly, mercifully, took steps to make it possible for us to meet his requirements for gaining everlasting life in happiness.

[14] God took the first steps to reconcile us to himself, to win us over to friendliness to him, to render us no more opposed to him, to bring us into agreement and harmony with him. For this reason he sent his Son, who "did not know sin," to become a perfect man and to "be sin for us," to die as a human sin offering, in order to relieve us of the charge and penalty of sin. Being relieved of the charge of sin in this way, we could appear righteous in God's eyes, "become God's righteousness by means of him."

[15] In Colossians 1:21, 22 the apostle Paul says: "Indeed, you who were once alienated and enemies because your minds were on the works that were wicked, he now has again reconciled by means of that one's fleshly body through his death, in order to present you holy and unblemished and open to no accusation before him."

[16] In Romans 5:6-11 the apostle Paul remarks on how God took the first steps to show us favor, when he writes: "Christ, while we were yet weak, died for ungodly men at the appointed time. For hardly will anyone die for a righteous man; indeed, for the good man, perhaps, someone even

---

13, 14. (a) The reference here to "ambassadors" implies what as to man's position in relation to God? (b) Who took the first steps to effect our reconciliation to God, and how?
15. What does Colossians 1:21, 22 say about this provision for reconciliation and its effect?
16. How does Romans 5:6-11 emphasize the love shown by God in taking the first steps to show us favor?

dares to die. But God recommends his own love to us in that, while we were yet sinners, Christ died for us. Much more, therefore, since we have been declared righteous now by his blood, shall we be saved through him from wrath. For if, when we were enemies, we became reconciled to God through the death of his Son, much more, now that we have become reconciled, we shall be saved by his life. And not only that, but we are also exulting in God through our Lord Jesus Christ, through whom we have now received the reconciliation."

[17] So, then, to come under Jehovah's goodwill, what must we do? We have to recognize that we are sinners unacceptable to God and that we need to be reconciled to God. Certainly if God has no pleasure in sin, we need to feel sorrow because of our sins, repent of our sins. This will lead us to convert, turn around and go in the direction opposite from that of the sinful way of this world. That was what the apostle Peter told the Jews shortly after Jesus died and was resurrected and returned to God in heaven: "In this way God has fulfilled the things he announced beforehand through the mouth of all the prophets, that his Christ would suffer. Repent, therefore, and turn around so as to get your sins blotted out, that seasons of refreshing may come from the person of Jehovah."—Acts 3:18, 19.

[18] Since Jesus Christ is God's High Priest and he offered himself as a sin offering to God for us, we can experience the lifting of the condemnation and charge of sin through his sacrifice. This obliges us to accept his sacrifice for us, exercising faith in it and its power to cleanse us from sin. So we must confess our sins to God and beg him to relieve us

---

17. What must we do if we are to come under Jehovah's goodwill, and how is this made clear by what the apostle Peter said?
18, 19. (a) How can we avail ourselves of God's provision to relieve us of the condemnation of sin? (b) What did the apostle Paul say to the Jews, emphasizing that men cannot make themselves righteous?

of the charge of sin through the ransom sacrifice of his Son Jesus Christ. The apostle Peter pointed out this fact to the first uncircumcised Gentile believer, the Italian Cornelius: "This is the One decreed by God to be judge of the living and the dead. To him all the prophets bear witness, that everyone putting faith in him gets forgiveness of sins through his name." (Acts 10:42, 43) We cannot make ourselves righteous. The apostle Paul emphasized that fact to the Jews, who were trying to render themselves righteous by works of the Law, saying:

[19] "Let it therefore be known to you, brothers, that through this One a forgiveness of sins is being published to you; and that from all the things from which you could not be declared guiltless by means of the law of Moses, everyone who believes is declared guiltless by means of this One [that is, Jesus Christ]."—Acts 13:38, 39.

[20] Thus our reconciliation to God is through Jesus Christ. So, after we repent of our sins and convert to righteousness, what do we need to do in order to continue righteous in God's sight? We need to become followers of his Son Jesus Christ. This means that we must imitate him. How? Well, although he "came to be under law" by being born of a Jewish virgin and although he was dedicated to God as Mary's firstborn son on the fortieth day at Jehovah's temple in Jerusalem, yet at the age of thirty years he dedicated his earthly life fully to God. Why? In order to serve the interests of God's kingdom that John the Baptist was then preaching and also to reconcile mankind to God. Hence he went to John the Baptist to get baptized and thus give an outward symbol of this dedication to God to do God's special will. (Galatians 4:

20, 21. (a) Whose followers must we become if we are to continue righteous in God's sight? (b) Why was Jesus baptized by John the Baptist? (c) At that time what expression made long before in the Psalms applied to Jesus?

4; Luke 2:22-27; Leviticus 12:1-4; Luke 3:21-23) What was recorded long previous in Psalm 40:6-8 then applied to Jesus, and that this is the correct application Hebrews 10:5-9 assures us, saying:

[21] "When he comes into the world he says: ' "Sacrifice and offering [of animals] you [God] did not want, but you prepared a body for me. You did not approve of whole burnt offerings and sin offering [by means of animals]." Then I said, "Look! I am come (in the roll of the book it is written about me) to do your will, O God." ' After first saying: 'You did not want nor did you approve of sacrifices and offerings and whole burnt

offerings and sin offering'—sacrifices that are offered according to the Law—then he actually says: 'Look! I am come to do your will.' "

[22] Jesus as a sinless, perfect man needed no repentance and conversion. But we as born sinners do need to repent and convert. Then, after we do repent and convert from sin, we must imitate Jesus as our "Leader" by making a dedication of ourselves to God and symbolizing this dedication by baptism in water. We must be completely submerged as Jesus was at his baptism. (Matthew 23:10; 3:13-16) This is the very thing that the resurrected Jesus Christ commanded before he left his apostles and ascended to

---

22. Why should we, too, be baptized?

heaven. He said: "All authority has been given me in heaven and on the earth. Go therefore and make disciples of people of all the nations, baptizing them in the name of the Father and of the Son and of the holy spirit, teaching them to observe all the things I have commanded you."—Matthew 28:18-20.

²³ Therefore, after we are baptized in water, we must hold fast to our dedication and be careful to do as Jesus Christ said, "observe all the things I have commanded you." We learn what all these commanded things are by making a personal study of the Holy Bible. It will be most helpful to us to have a personal copy of the Bible for our own use. Besides that, we must associate with other dedicated, baptized disciples of Jesus Christ and become part of the congregation of believers and attend its regular meetings. If we desire to hold firmly to our faith and our dedication, we will earnestly do what is commanded in Hebrews 10: 24, 25:

²⁴ "Let us consider one another to incite to love and fine works, not forsaking the gathering of ourselves together, as some have the custom, but encouraging one another, and all the more so as you behold the day drawing near."

²⁵ This explains why the dedicated, baptized witnesses of Jehovah of today have their gathering places known as Kingdom Halls, all around our earthly globe, and regularly meet in them, with brotherly Christian love. More than 23,000 congregations do so, in more than 190 lands.

23, 24. (a) What must we be careful to do after our baptism? (b) How can we learn all these things that Jesus has commanded? (c) With whom should we associate, and how can we heed the command recorded at Hebrews 10:24, 25?
25. Where do Jehovah's witnesses hold their meetings?

HELPING OTHERS TO GAIN GOODWILL

[26] However, there is a great work for the Christian congregation world wide to do. Happily, by our repentance, conversion, dedication and baptism and becoming Christ's disciples, we have become God's "men of good will," and we enjoy peace with God through Christ. What, though, about the rest of mankind? They continue at enmity toward God. Meanwhile the "year of good will on the part of Jehovah" is fast ending and the "day of vengeance on the part of our God" is getting closer. People in the midst of the world who may want to escape destruction in God's "day of vengeance" need to "become reconciled to God." Just as God did in the case of the apostle Paul and his companion Timothy, so he has "committed the word of the reconciliation to us," because we are his "men of good will."

[27] That precious word is meant to be delivered to others, and we who are dedicated to do God's will must therefore use that "word of the reconciliation" by delivering it to those needing reconciliation. With this word we must go to them as "substitutes for Christ" and beg them: "Become reconciled to God." This will lead to their deliverance and salvation.—2 Corinthians 5:18-20; 1:1.

[28] Jehovah God has in reservation immense goodness and joy for his faithful people. As his dedicated people who follow Jesus Christ we have the heartfelt longing like that expressed by the psalmist: "Remember me, O Jehovah, with the good will toward your people. Take care of me with your salvation, that I may see the goodness to your chosen ones, that I may rejoice with the rejoicing of your nation, that I may make my boast

26, 27. Why is it urgent for us to help others to become reconciled to God, and, to that end, what has God committed to his "men of good will"?
28. What longing expressed by the psalmist do dedicated Christians have, but how can they show that they are not selfish about it?

with your inheritance [the people whom you inherit]." (Psalm 106:4, 5) We should not be selfish, but we should feel urged to help others to share in such joy and goodness from Jehovah God through his Son Jesus Christ. We can do so.

²⁹ By what we see in fulfillment of Bible prophecy we know that we are in the "conclusion of the system of things" and that the full end of it is nearing. In connection with our work of reconciliation Jesus' prophecy in Matthew 24: 14 is now due for realization: "This good news of the kingdom will be preached in all the inhabited earth for a witness to all the nations; and then the end will come." Jesus' dedicated followers, God's "men of good will," are the ones appointed to do this Kingdom preaching. They are doing it, for Jehovah's dedicated, baptized Christian witnesses are preaching the good news of God's established kingdom of the heavens in more than 160 languages, in more than 190 lands. In apostolic fashion they are doing this, that is to say, "publicly and from

house to house." (Acts 20:20; 5: 40-42) The persecution as foretold in Matthew 24:9-13 does not stop them. They do not fear men who can kill only the body but not the soul; rather, they fear God, who can resurrect them from the dead. —Matthew 10:26-28.

³⁰ As a result of the preaching till now, particularly from the

29. (a) What message did Jesus say would be preached in all the inhabited earth at this time, and who are the ones that do this preaching? (b) In what way is this work done? (c) Why does persecution not stop those carrying this good news?
30. (a) Who are responding to the preaching, and under whose care do they come? (b) When God's vengeance is executed on the wicked, what will his appointed King say to these "men of good will"?

year 1935, a "great crowd" of symbolic sheep are being gathered during what time yet remains of God's "year of good will." The Lamb of God, as the "Fine Shepherd," is leading them toward their attainment of everlasting life in perfection on the Paradise earth. (Revelation 7:9-17; John 10:14-16) Because they are numbered among God's "men of good will," the King-Shepherd puts them on the right side of his royal throne. When the "day of vengeance on the part of our God" arrives at God's appointed time, what will the King say to them? "Come, you who have my Father's blessing, inherit the kingdom prepared for you from the founding of the world."—Matthew 25:31-34.

³¹ Such "men of good will" thus living will survive the "day of vengeance on the part of our God." They will inherit the earthly realm of the heavenly kingdom that God purposed from the founding of the world of mankind. Any "men of good will" who may have died before the "day of vengeance of our God" destroys the goatish, unreconciled enemies of God will enter into this earthly inheritance by means of the resurrection of the dead.—Matthew 25:41-46; 22:31, 32.

³² Toward the end of the Holy Bible the apostle John wrote these words: "And the one seated on the throne said: 'Look! I am making all things new.' Also, he says: 'Write, because these words are faithful and true.' And he said to me: 'They have come to pass!'" (Revelation 21:5, 6) Jehovah God, seated on his heavenly throne, is certain that all the things in his Holy Word for the future will come to pass. To him they are as already having come to pass. These are the "things in which it

---

31. (a) What is the inheritance that awaits them beyond God's "day of vengeance"? (b) Will those "men of good will" who may have died before then share in that inheritance?
32. (a) At Revelation 21:5, 6, how does God express confidence in the fulfillment of these promises, and why can we share that confidence? (b) How does Psalm 30 express the joyful lot that can be ours as God's "men of good will"?

is impossible for God to lie." (Hebrews 6:18) It is the highest wisdom on our part to take God at his word and live in harmony with his Word of truth as his blessed "men of good will."

"Being under his anger is for a moment, being under his good will is for a lifetime. In the evening weeping may take up lodging, but in the morning there is a joyful cry. O Jehovah, in your good will you have made my mountain to stand in strength. . . . You have changed my mourning into dancing for me; you have loosened my sackcloth, and you keep me girded with rejoicing, in order that my glory may make melody to you and not keep silent. O Jehovah my God, to time indefinite I will laud you."
—Psalm 30:5, 7, 11, 12.

INDEX TO SCRIPTURES CITED

One's joy over finding something good is doubled by sharing it with others. Doubtless, after reading this book, "Things in Which It Is Impossible for God to Lie," you feel a great and deep joy. You are eager to share with other deserving ones your joy at finding the heart-satisfying things of God's "word of truth." Feeling the same desire to share, we are happy to advise that you may have additional copies of this book at 50c a copy, these to be sent, postpaid, to any address that you designate around the globe.

—THE PUBLISHERS

HOW CAN YOU GAIN ADDED BENEFIT FROM GOD'S WORD?

By obtaining the outstanding 352-page book *"All Scripture Is Inspired of God and Beneficial."* In this volume the sixty-six books of the Bible are epitomized, one at a time. Main ideas are highlighted and particular attention is directed to the practical value of these inspired Scriptures. Part Two of this volume contains ten special studies on the inspired Scriptures and their background, such as "A Visit to the Promised Land," "Measuring Events in the Stream of Time," and "Archaeology Supports the Inspired Record." Included are maps, illustrations and many informative charts such as "Main Events of Jesus' Earthly Sojourn" and "Outstanding Prophecies Concerning Jesus and Their Fulfillment." Dark-blue hardbound cover. *"All Scripture Is Inspired of God and Beneficial"* will be sent anywhere, postpaid, for $1 a copy.

------•◆•------

BIBLE TRUTHS AT YOUR FINGERTIPS

Would you like to find pointed scriptures quickly on almost any subject embraced by the Bible? Do you have questions or personal problems that Bible counsel could help to solve if you had self-evident scriptures grouped by subject? Scriptures on 123 principal subjects are at your fingertips for instant use in the book *"Make Sure of All Things; Hold Fast to What Is Fine."* The subject coverage of this handbook ranges from "Angels" to "Work" and in between you will find scriptures that set out clearly all the main Bible doctrines plus scriptures on such subjects as "Decisions," "Encouragement," "Evolution," "Holidays," "Marriage," "Prophecy" and "Settling Personal Differences." The book is designed for speedy reference. It will be sent to you for 75 cents. To order it, see the addresses on page 416.

GOD'S WORD LIVES WHEN YOU READ

the *New World Translation of the Holy Scriptures,* **a complete Bible in modern speech for only $1.**

Clear, understandable language brings the intended meaning plainly to the reader's mind. The *New World Translation of the Holy Scriptures* brings to life the force, beauty and sense of the original writings.

Faithfulness to original-language texts and its consistency of rendering make its use satisfying.

The *New World Translation* does not obscure the name of the Most High God, Jehovah. It dignifies it by restoring it to its rightful place in the text.

Paragraph divisions aid you in reading, and descriptive page headings quickly inform you as to the subject contents on each page.

REGULAR EDITION: With Concordance, Appendix, maps, illustrations. Bound in green vinyl, measures 7¼" x 5" x 1⅛". Special Bible paper, 1,472 pages. Originally published in six volumes, now appears in a revised edition in this one volume, for $1.

DELUXE EDITION: Same features, but black or maroon flexible cover, gold-edged pages. $2.50 each.

POCKET EDITION: Only 6½" x 4½" x 1", red edging on pages. $1.50 per copy.

LARGE-PRINT EDITION: Large type, excellent for careful study, copious marginal references and helpful footnotes. Contains original edition of the *New World Translation,* now in one volume. Measures 7¼" x 5" x 2¼", 3,648 pages. $4.50 a copy.

CHIEF OFFICE AND OFFICIAL ADDRESS OF
Watch Tower Bible & Tract Society of Pennsylvania
Watchtower Bible and Tract Society of New York, Inc.
International Bible Students Association
124 Columbia Heights, Brooklyn, New York 11201, U.S.A.

ADDRESSES OF BRANCH OFFICES:

ALASKA 99501: 1438 Medfra Street, Anchorage. **ARGENTINA:** Calle Honduras 5646-48, Buenos Aires 14. **AUSTRALIA:** 11 Beresford Road, Strathfield, N.S.W. **AUSTRIA:** Gallgasse 44, Vienna XIII. **BAHAMAS:** Box 1247, Nassau, N.P. **BELGIUM:** 28 Ave. Gen. Eisenhower, Schaerbeek-Brussels. **BERLIN, WESTERN GERMANY:** 49-50 Bayernallee, Charlottenburg 9. **BOLIVIA:** Casilla No. 1440, La Paz. **BRAZIL:** Rua Licínio Cardoso, 330, Rio de Janeiro, GB, ZC-15. **BRITISH GUIANA:** 50 Brickdam, Georgetown 11. **BRITISH HONDURAS:** Box 257, Belize. **BURMA:** P.O. Box 62, Rangoon. **CAMEROUN, REP. FED. DU:** B.P. 5428, Douala Akwa. **CANADA:** 150 Bridgeland Ave., Toronto 19, Ontario. **CENTRAL AFRICAN REPUBLIC:** B.P. 662, Bangui. **CEYLON:** 11 Sakvithi Lane, Colombo 5. **CHILE:** Correo 15, Casilla 261-V, Santiago. **COLOMBIA:** Apartado Aéreo 2587, Barranquilla. **CONGO, REPUBLIC OF THE:** B.P. 7409, Leopoldville 1. **CONGO REPUBLIC:** B.P. 2.114, Brazzaville. **COSTA RICA:** Apartado 2043, San José. **CUBA:** Avenida 15 Núm. 4608, Almendares, Marianao, Havana. **CYPRUS:** P.O. Box 1800, Nicosia. **DENMARK:** Kongevejen 207, Virum Copenhagen. **DOMINICAN REPUBLIC:** Avenida Francia 33, Santo Domingo. **ECUADOR:** Casilla 4512, Guayaquil. **EIRE:** 86 Lindsay Rd., Dublin 9. **EL SALVADOR:** Apartado 401, San Salvador. **ENGLAND:** Watch Tower House, The Ridgeway, London N.W. 7. **FIJI:** Box 23, Suva. **FINLAND:** Puutarhatie 58, Tikkurila. **FRANCE:** 81, rue du Point-du-Jour, Boulogne-Billancourt (Seine). **GERMANY (WESTERN):** Am Kohlheck, Postfach 13025, (62) Wiesbaden-Dotzheim. **GHANA, WEST AFRICA:** Box 760, Accra. **GREECE:** No. 4 Kartali St., Athens 611. **GUADELOUPE:** B.P. 239, Pointe-à-Pitre. **GUATEMALA:** 11 Avenida 5-67, Guatemala 1. **HAITI:** Post Box 185, Port-au-Prince. **HAWAII 96814:** 1228 Pensacola St., Honolulu. **HONDURAS:** Apartado 147, Tegucigalpa. **HONG KONG:** 312 Prince Edward Rd., Second Floor, Kowloon. **ICELAND:** P.O. Box 251, Reykjavik. **INDIA:** South Avenue, Santa Cruz, Bombay 54. **INDONESIA:** Kotakpos 2105, Djakarta. **ITALY:** Via Monte Maloia 32 (Monte Sacro), Rome. **JAMAICA, W.I.:** 41 Trafalgar Rd., Kingston 10. **JAPAN:** 1 Toyooka-Cho, Shibamita, Minato-Ku, Takanawa P.O., Tokyo. **JORDAN:** Box 1638, Amman. **KENYA:** Box 7788, Nairobi. **KOREA:** P.O. Box 7, Sodaemun-ku P.O., Seoul. **LEBANON:** P.O. Box 1122, Beirut. **LEEWARD ISLANDS, W.I.:** Box 119, St. Johns, Antigua. **LIBERIA:** P.O. Box 171, Monrovia. **LUXEMBOURG:** 105, rue Adolphe Fischer, Luxembourg G.D. **MALAGASY REPUBLIC:** 21, avenue Dalmond, Andravoahangy-Haut, Tananarive. **MALAWI:** Box 83, Blantyre. **MALAYSIA:** 33 Poole Road, Singapore 15. **MAURITIUS:** 12, rue Lebrun, Rose Hill. **MEXICO:** Calzada Melchor Ocampo 71, Mexico 4, D.F. **MOROCCO:** D. Piccone, B.P. 1028 Principal, Tangier. **NETHERLANDS:** Voorburgstraat 10, Amsterdam 17. **NETHERLANDS ANTILLES:** Oosterbeekstraat 11, Willemstad, Curaçao. **NEWFOUNDLAND, CANADA:** 239 Pennywell Rd., St. John's. **NEW ZEALAND:** 621 New North Rd., Auckland S.W. 1. **NICARAGUA:** Apartado 183, Managua, D.N. **NIGERIA, WEST AFRICA:** P.O. Box 194, Yaba, Colony. **NORWAY:** Inkognitogaten 28 B., Oslo. **PAKISTAN:** 8-E Habibullah Rd., Lahore. **PANAMA:** Apartado 1386, Panama. **PAPUA:** Box 113, Port Moresby. **PARAGUAY:** Casilla de Correo 482, Asunción. **PERU:** Casilla No. 5178, Miraflores, Lima. **PHILIPPINE REPUBLIC:** 186 Roosevelt Ave., San Francisco del Monte, Quezon City. **PUERTO RICO 00909:** 704 Calle Lafayette, Pda. 21, Santurce. **RHODESIA:** P.O. Box 1462, Salisbury. **SIERRA LEONE:** Box 136, Freetown. **SOUTH AFRICA:** Private Bag 2, P.O. Elandsfontein, Transvaal. **SURINAM:** Box 49, Wicherstr. 8, Paramaribo. **SWEDEN:** Jakobsberg. **SWITZERLAND:** Allmendstrasse 39, 3000 Berne 22. **TAIWAN (REPUBLIC OF CHINA):** No. 5 Lane 99, Yun-Ho St., Taipei. **THAILAND:** Box 67, Bangkok. **TRINIDAD, W.I.:** 21 Taylor St., Woodbrook, Port of Spain. **UNITED STATES OF AMERICA:** 117 Adams St., Brooklyn, N.Y. 11201. **URUGUAY:** Francisco Bauza 3372, Montevideo. **VENEZUELA:** Avda. Honduras, Quinta Luz, Urb. Las Acacias, Caracas, D.F. **ZAMBIA:** Box 1598, Kitwe.

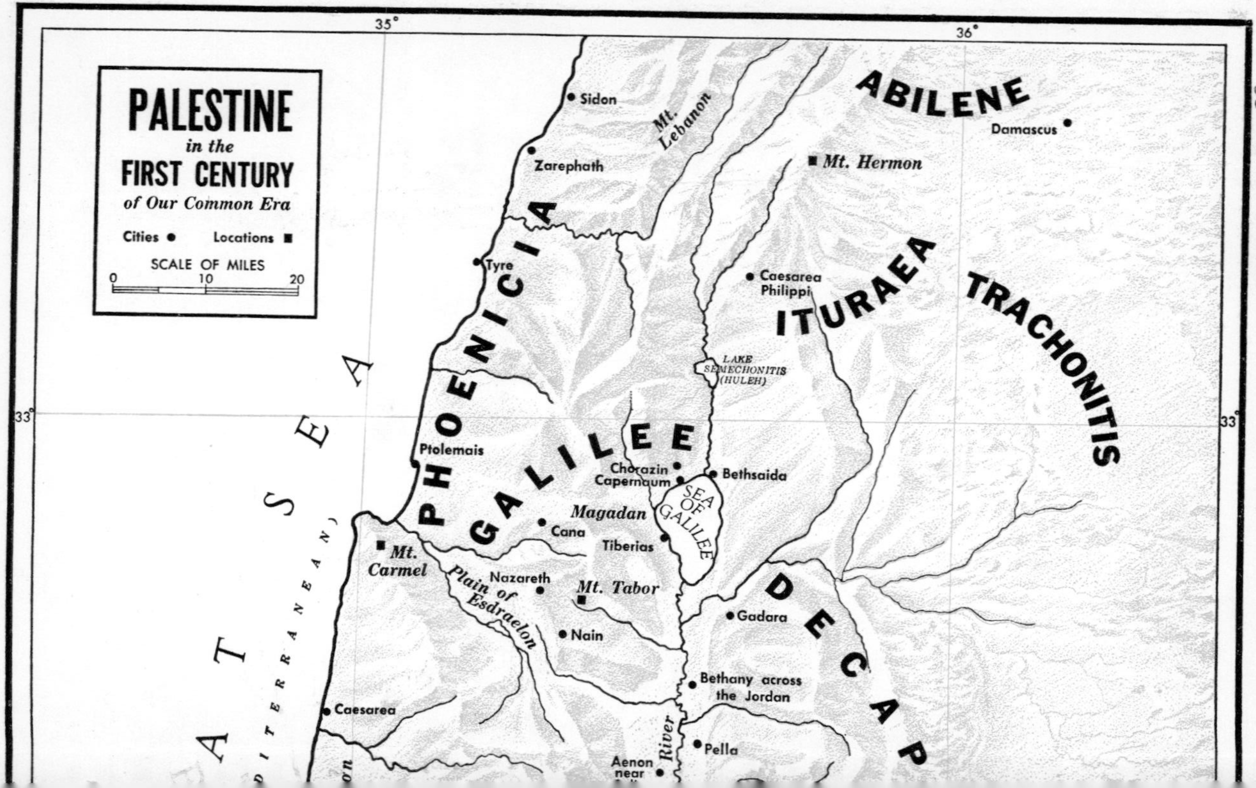

PALESTINE
in the
FIRST CENTURY
of Our Common Era

Cities ● Locations ■

SCALE OF MILES

0   10   20

ABILENE

Damascus ●

■ Mt. Hermon

Caesarea ●
Philippi

ITURAEA

TRACHONITIS

DECAP

Gadara ●

Bethany across ●
the Jordan

Pella ●

LAKE
SEMECHONITIS
(HULEH)

Bethsaida ●

SEA
OF
GALILEE

GALILEE

Chorazin ●
Capernaum ●

Magadan ●

Cana ● Tiberias ●

Mt. Tabor ■

Nain ●

Aenon
near

River

Mt. Lebanon

Sidon ●

Zarephath ●

PHOENICIA

Tyre ●

Ptolemais ●

Nazareth ●

Plain of
Esdraelon

■ Mt.
Carmel

SEA

MEDITERRANEAN

Caesarea ●

on

A T

WHAT IS "BABYLON THE GREAT"?

The mystical "Babylon the Great" is mentioned in the last book of the Bible, Revelation. There it is commanded: "Get out of her, my people, if you do not want to share with her in her sins, and if you do not want to receive part of her plagues." (Revelation 18: 4) But how can you "get out of her" if you cannot identify "Babylon the Great"? To get a complete understanding of what "Babylon the Great" is, do not fail to obtain and read the revealing book